The Hereafter Trilogy

Other Books by Miles Edward Allen

The Realities of Heaven:
Fifty Spirits Describe Your Future Home

Sex After Death:
The Spirits Speak About Love and Lust in the Astral Realms

Defending Bridey's Honor:
The Reality of Reincarnation

Games People Actually Play

Christmas Lore and Legend: The Game

The Hereafter Trilogy

The Book That Removes All Doubt

Vol. I: The Survival Files
Vol. II: The Afterlife Confirmed
Vol. III: Top-40 Remains

The Hereafter Trilogy

Copyright 2015 Miles Edward Allen

Published by Momentpoint Media

All Rights Reserved

No part of this book may be reproduced, for any reason, by any means, without written permission from the author, except for brief, clearly attributed quotations.

Cover photograph,
Aurora Borealis over Denali, Alaska, USA,
Courtesy National Park Service.
Design by Miles Edward Allen.

Ignorance is king.
Many would not profit by his abdication.
Many enrich themselves
by means of his dark monarchy.
They are his Court, and in his name
they defraud and govern,
enrich themselves
and perpetuate their power.

— Walter M. Miller, Jr.,
A Canticle for Leibowitz

Contents

Volume I: The Survival Files

Friday Evenng: Appalachian Arrival 2
Saturday Morning: Other-BodyExperiences 5
    Case 1: Seattle Shoe 12
    Case 2: Dutch Dentures 17
    Case 3: The Cavalier Nurse 20
    Case 4: The Plaids and the Pallbearer 21
    Case 5: Room Reconnoiter 24
    Case 6: From the Mouths of Babes 25
    Case 7: Seeing Is Believing 29
    Case 8: An Out-of-Bed Experience 35
Saturday Lunch: Morality and the NDA 38
Saturday Afternoon: The Spirits Speak 47
    Case 9: Good Ships and Witches 47
    Case 10: From Boys to Woman 52
    Case 11: Evidence by the Book 63
    Case 12: Jung's Dream Library 65
    Case 13: Where's the Smoke? 66
    Case 14: The R101 Disaster 68
    Case 15: Relics Revealed 72
    Case 16: Relics Revealed Revisited 79
    Case 17: The Ghosts in the Machines 85
Saturday Supper: InhumanPerfection 91
Saturday Night: How This Could Be 98
Sunday Morning I: Time for Breakfast 108
Sunday Morning II: Other Lives 115
    Case 18: Hypnotist's Heaven 120
    Case 19: The Policeman and the Painter 123
    Case 20: Death in the Garment District 127
    Case 21: The Numbers of the Beast 128
    Case 22. The Apprentice Murderer 130
    Case 23: A Town Reborn 133
Top Ten Reasons for Reincarnation 135
Sunday Morning III: Celestial Q & A 139
Sunday Lunch: Why This Could Be 146
Sunday Afternoon: Goodbye and Best Evidence 150

Volume II: The Afterlife Confirmed

Chapter 1. A Gettysburg Gathering 158
    TheTwoField-Mice 161
Chapter 2: Knock, Knock 165
    An Excitement at Epworth 165
    The Troublesome Tenant 171
Chapter 3: Who's There? 173
    Testing the Spirit 182
    Neighborly Ingenuity 176

Supporting Testimony	179
Bones Revealed	182
Word Spreads	183
Chapter 4. ... The Alien Rapper	185
Chapter 5. Visions and Dreams	194
The Wealthy Wall	194
The Ramhurst Revenants	195
Cloak & Danger	203
The Reticence of Scientists	207
Conversion Phobia I – Robert Hare	209
Chapter 6. Spontaneous Spirits	211
The Farmer's Daughter	214
Grave Mistakes	216
Grandma's Gift	219
Jumping to Confusion	219
Resisting Review	221
Conversion Phobia II – Alfred Russel Wallace	224
Chapter 7. Invited Spirit Conversations	226
Friends and Strangers	226
A Mysterious Death	230
New Meaning for "Soul Mate"	238
Conversion Phobia III – Sir William Crookes	246
Chapter 8. Qualities of Evidence	247
The Case of the Missing Information	254
A Different Kind of "Cold" Case	257
Touched By The Past	259
Chapter 9. Talking To Strangers	262
The Rationalist Spirit	262
The Murder of Jacqueline Poole	270
Fire and Iceland	274
Conversion Phobia IV – Cesare Lombroso	277
Chapter 10. The Darkness Dialogue	278
Not Seeing Is Believing	281
Conversion Phobia V – Horace Westwood	285
Chapter 11. Spirit Possessions	286
The "Deadicated" Reporter	286
The Return of Mary Roff	290
A Country Revival	294
Conversion Phobia VI – Sir William Barrett	299
Chapter 12. Angels or Aliens?	301
Common Factors	303
Reciprocal Recognition	308
Rational Witnesses	311
Conversion Phobia VII – Charles Richet	315
Chapter 13. Memories of Home	316
Family Lost & Found	316
The Rebirth of Bridey Murphy	319
The Strangers Were Lovers	322
Chapter 14. An "Eary" Dinner	329
Conversion Phobia VIII – Julian Ochorowicz	333

Chapter 15. Memories of War 334
    Round Trip to Allentown 334
    A Submariner Resurfaces 336
    One More Mission 340
Epilogue – Moving On 347

Volume III: Top 40 Remains

Introduction 350
Chapter 1: An Untimely Valentine 353
Chapter 2: Keeping Them In the Family 357
Chapter 3: Anna's Amazing Abilities 362
Chapter 4: The Spirits Seller's Spirit 371
Chapter 5: The Unforgotten Coin 376
Chapter 6: Coming Back Down Under 378
Chapter 7: Soule Proves the Soul 384
Chapter 8: Having a Friend 387
Chapter 9: The A.B.C. Séances 392
Chapter 10: Guns and Rebirth 397
Chapter 11: The Picture of Raymond Lodge 402
Chapter 12: My Mother's Brother Is My Father's Son 406
Chapter 13: A Tale of Two Tattoos 409
Chapter 14: Scotland Redux 414
Chapter 15: A Cameo Reappearance 418
Chapter 16: Ex-Actor Makes Comeback 423
Conclusion 427

Appendix: References 431

The Hereafter Trilogy, Vol. I:
The Survival Files

*In our moments of exaltation,
swept by the sublimity of music or of a sunrise,
we feel that there must be joy at the heart of the universe,
and deep intention;
yet turning again to the harsh realities of life,
with its cruelties and its crushing frustrations,
we cannot but ask,
if we have any perception, any compassion,
any philosophic wonder at all,
the ultimate questions:
What, in the name of sanity,
is the meaning and purpose of life?*

— Gina Cerminara, *Many Mansions*, p. 11.

Originally published as a separate book in 2007.

The old man is fanciful,
the meals are opinion,
the rest is research.

Friday Evening
Appalachian Arrival

Seems it strange that thou shouldst live forever?
Is it less strange that thou shouldst live at all?
This is a miracle; and that no more.

— from *Night Thoughts*, by Edward Young

He offered me a drink, but I declined, having been sipping on a Coke for the past two hours as I wound my way to the cabin. I stowed my overnight bag in the loft and followed him out to the screened porch. A gleaming sliver of sun was just vanishing behind the western hills leaving the sky streaked with golden peach and purple.

"So, you want to know about heaven," the old man said, easing down into a well-worn wicker chair "Just why is that?"

"Doesn't everyone wonder what's going to happen next?" I asked, as I pulled my recorder from my pocket, laid it on the slatted top of a small wooden table, and sat down in the rocker beside it.

"Oh, I reckon they do, but not enough to drag their butts all the way out here.

"You were a bit later then I was expecting. Were the directions okay?"

"The directions were fine. No, it's just typical for a Friday before a vacation; everything seems to come to a head an hour before you're due to leave."

"I suppose that's unavoidable," he said. "Trouble is, that feeling tends to stay with us and color our attitude toward life in general; the closer we get to the end, the more pressure we feel to get everything done, wrap it all up in a neat package and, at the same time, we keep thinking of more and more things we really ought to do before we go."

"Yeah, it can get pretty stressful," I said as I stretched my legs out and took a deep breath of forest freshened air. "But you seem to have overcome that problem."

"Being retired and living in beauty certainly helps. But, for me, much of the stress of living disappeared when I became convinced that life never truly ends."

I caught his eye. "You are absolutely certain?"

He turned to look through the screen and, his voice suddenly softer, replied, "I'm as certain that an afterlife exists as I am that there are deer in these hills."

My gaze followed his to the two does stepping carefully between the saplings along the ravine. Dasher, the old man's Chocolate Lab, raised his head from his paws and eyed the deer attentively, but made no sound. We sat still for a while, watching the deer nibbling their way through the misty dusk. A breeze momentarily stirred the leaves, the muffled rustling somehow leaving the woods quieter than silence itself.

I had met him only a few months before during a casino-night charity affair at the New Zealand embassy. My wife and I had volunteered to deal Blackjack. I was taking a break when a fellow I had known well in college waved me over to his group and ordered me a beer and the next thing I knew I was listening to this elderly gentleman speculating as to whether charity was unique to Earth or not.

He spoke with such sincerity and authority that the subject didn't seem so strange. His wavy white hair and gunmetal-framed spectacles made him look like Santa Claus in a tux, except his beard was closely trimmed and his round face well-tanned. His name was proffered when he was introduced to me but, since then, I have never heard anyone address him as anything but "sir" or refer to him except as "the old man," so I'll continue that tradition.

After he had strolled off to join another cluster — he seemed to know half of the Washington power brokers in attendance — my friend explained that the man was retired from some arcane but influential post with the State Department and now was preparing to devote his time to lecturing on Survival.[1] My friend suggested that I might want to volunteer as a test case (as he already had). Now, I had long been fascinated with the topic and had been toying with book ideas for years, so I did contact the old man and he graciously agreed to share his knowledge. And so I found myself thinking how different he looked tonight, having replaced the tuxedo with a plaid cotton shirt and well-worn jeans.

Impossible to tell how much time passed as thinking gave way to just being there, sitting on an old but comfy rocker in the deepening darkness of the West Virginia hills. Almost heaven? Close enough for me. For the moment.

Finally, I roused myself enough to say, "It's really nice up here. I bet the woods are beautiful in the snow."

> "Yep. So long as I have good neighbors with snow plows, it can be real nice here in the winter. You know, the thought of snow makes me realize I'm a bit chilly. How about bringing in a few hunks of wood and we'll have ourselves a fire?"

Indeed, goose bumps on my arms bore witness to the rapid drop in temperature. So I stood and turned off my recorder — just as well, as the only sounds it would have caught for the rest of the night were a few pleasantries amidst the crackle of the fire and then a whole lot of snoring.

---

[1] With a capital 'S' it indicates the survival of the human spirit or soul after the death of the body.

Saturday Morning
Other-Body Experiences

If a man can leave his physical body temporarily and continue to exist as a self-conscious being, the fact would prove a strong presumption that eventually when he comes to leave his physical body, i.e., to die, he will then also continue to exist as a self-conscious being in that second body.

— Robert Crookall[2]

"To begin with," he said, after I switched on my recorder, "your readers should know that I am not a medium or a mystic. In fact, I have never had a notable paranormal experience — not in this life anyway. I have simply been an ardent student of psychic phenomena since I was first drawn to it while in college. Over the ensuing decades, I have studied hundreds of books and papers dealing with the evidence for life continuing after death. There is always more to learn, but I feel that my grasp of the subject is sufficient to be of use in teaching others. Also, be aware that I am not associated with any religion. The views I express come only from evidence gathered and facts verified, not from the teachings of any church or organization."

"Duly noted," I said.

"Let's start this morning by focusing on the question: Can mind function independently of matter?

"Ever since the invention of the 'wireless' radio we have thought of long-distance communications in terms of energy travel-

---

[2] Ebon, p. 116.

ing between antennae. Television signals, for instance, are electromagnetic pulses that are created by antennae (either on broadcast towers or satellites) and travel outward until they are absorbed by something. When the pulses happen to run into another antenna (such as a satellite dish on the roof of a home) they are converted by a receiver into other signals that, ultimately, create a picture on the TV. All of which is to emphasize the point that communication always involves something being sent from one place, traveling across an intervening space, and then being received at another place."

"Seems sensible enough to me," I said.

"Such is certainly the scientific point of view. Or at least it was until a few decades ago, when physicists studying interactions at the sub-atomic level began to see evidence that information could be exchanged without traversing any intervening distance."

He pulled a book from a high shelf and showed me the cover. "Have you read this?"

I could easily read the large white type atop a photo taken from outer space of the sun peeking over the earth's curved horizon: "Arthur C. Clarke" it read, "The Light of Other Days."[3]

"Clarke is one of my favorite science-fiction authors," I replied, "but I didn't know he wrote a book about near-death experiences."

"Yes, the cover does suggest that, doesn't it. So many NDE books use 'the light' in their titles. But, no, this book is an examination of what might happen if scientists actually managed to establish and control wormholes."

"Wormholes are sort of tunnels through space-time, right? They're what fictional space ships use to get from one galaxy to another without

---

[3] Co-authored by Stephen Baxter, published by Tom Doherty Associates, 2000.

having to spend a gazillion years crossing the intervening distance. You just sort of pop into one end and promptly pop out the other."

"Only Clarke doesn't push the science hard enough to have people and ships traveling through the wormholes — just light and sound. Of course, the equipment needed to observe other places and times is huge and superbly expensive … at first. As with the development of most technologies, however, it gets smaller and cheaper and, in a remarkably short time, as the story is told, every kid on the block has a 'worm cam' on his or her wrist with which to view any action that is occurring or has occurred at any place in the universe at any time throughout history."

"That would mean an absolute end to privacy," I mused.

"As well as an end to crime, not to mention a lot of revising of history," he added, "and the book does a respectable job of exploring what all that means for society. But I didn't bring it up so we could fantasize about being the ultimate voyeurs, rather because it provides a good way to introduce the subject of viewpoints.

"The trans-dimensional tunnel known as a wormhole has, like any other tunnel, two ends. One end is where the tunnel is created, at the worm cam. The other end, known as the 'mouth' is at the point in space/time that the operator desires to observe. According to the book, this mouth can be opened anywhere, from the inside of a closet, to the inside of a person, to the inside of a star. But — now pay close attention because this is the point that I went through all this to make — but, the mouth must be opened *somewhere*."

"That," I observed, feeling a bit unsure of the route we seemed to be taking, "seems fairly obvious."

"Obvious, yes, but also very easy to forget.

"Now, pretend for a moment that you own one of these nifty devices and you decide to check up on a friend of yours who is undergoing surgery at a local hospital. You find yourself a quiet, comfortable place where you won't be interrupted for a while, slip on the headset (which gives you a three-dimensional, totally realistic image) and dial in the coordinates of the operating theater. You click the 'go' button and with only a split-second of disorientation, you seem to be above the operating table. From here you can see a film of dust on the top of the floodlights. You can see the tops of the heads of the doctors and nurses. You can see, and hear, everything within the room exactly as if you were actually hovering near the ceiling.

"You aren't familiar with the surgical procedures, but you note that everyone is calm so you assume that all is going well. Then, suddenly, there is a power failure and all the lights go out. Being in a windowless room, you can see nothing, although you can hear the surgeon curse. It only takes a moment, though, for the emergency power to kick in and order is restored. After a while, you begin to wonder what else might be happening at the hospital. Back in the room where your body reposes, your fingers tweak the worm-cam controls and the mouth of the tunnel shifts out into an adjoining corridor. To your eyes it seems that you have floated effortlessly through a wall and are now watching people moving along the hallway."

Turning to replace the book on the shelf, he asked, "What if you wanted to read the model number printed on a sticker underneath the table?"

"Well, I suppose I would use my worm-cam controls to move back through the wall and position the tunnel's mouth beneath the table so that I could look up at the sticker."

"And what if you wanted to read the numbers stamped on the electrical box holding the light switches inside the wall?"

"I don't know," I replied. "If I couldn't see the room in the darkness of the power outage, how could I see inside a wall where there would be no light? Unless this worm-cam has infra-red capabilities. That might enable viewing of the number."

> "An excellent point," he offered an approving smile. "Now go back down the hall to a small waiting area. On the table is a stack of magazines. Read me what is written on page seven of the third magazine from the top."

"Whoa! Unless someone picks up the magazine and opens it to pages six and seven, I don't think I can do that. Even if I could precisely position the mouth of the tunnel between pages six and seven, I not only would have no light to see by, but I wouldn't have the necessary perspective. I mean, in real life I can't read with my eyeball pressed up against the page. If I back away from the page to get sufficient perspective, then the other pages would be in my way."

> "Precisely."

"And, now that I think of it," I continued, "it's also a question of focus. If I get too close to something in real life my eyes can't focus on it. Just how do you focus one of these worm cams anyway?"

> "I'm afraid the authors forgot to explain that little trick," he lamented.

"Well, I'm no optician, but I know a little something about photography and I know that if you try to take a picture with no lens on the camera the result will be an indecipherable blob. Without a lens at the opening of the wormhole, all the light rays coming from all directions in the room will enter in a totally incoherent jumble and there would be no way to clarify the picture at the other end of the tunnel."

> "So, we have deduced several requirements for viewing at a distance with a worm-cam. First, you need to have light, then you need to have a lens to focus the light rays, and finally, you need to be able to position the lens so as to provide the proper angle of view and perspective of the subject. Furthermore — and this may seem

obvious, but it is an important distinction — if you want to change views you must move the lens."

"Hey," I quipped, "it's good to know that if such a thing as a worm cam is ever invented we'll be ready."

The old man grinned and went on, "Let's see if our newly considered knowledge is of any use as we take up the subject of clairvoyance, out-of-body experiences, astral travel, remote viewing, and near-death experiences."

"I never thought of all those as being the same subject."

"Well, let's find out. What is clairvoyance?"

"Literally, it means clear seeing," I replied. "The term indicates the ability to view objects and events that are beyond the normal range of sight."

"And how would this differ from remote viewing?"

"When various federal offices began experimenting with psychic spying, I guess they felt that 'clairvoyance' sounded too flaky for government work, so some bureaucrat came up with the term 'remote viewing'. A few ex-agents like to think of remote viewing as being a structured and systematic process as compared to the more casual clairvoyance, but it seems to me that they're just different names for the same thing."

"Okay. How about OBEs and astral travel?" he asked.

"'OBE,' or 'OOBE,' is an acronym for Out-Of-Body Experience. 'Astral' is an older term that refers to an alternate reality that supposedly exists in the same space as our physical world but at a different vibratory level. 'Astral travel' means pretty much the same thing as 'OBE' except that it implies the existence of an astral body in which one can traverse the astral world."

"So, one doesn't require any sort of ethereal body to have an OBE?"

I thought for a while and replied: "During an OBE, people report the sensation of leaving their physical body, but they seem to exist as a localized energy body of some sort. If this were not true, then it wouldn't be an OBE, it would simply be clairvoyance. It would probably be more accurate to have 'OBE' stand for <u>Other</u>-Body Experience."

> "You know, it probably would," he agreed. "Let's use that term from now on and see how it works out.
>
> "So, if I'm sitting in a room and a vision comes to mind of something happening at a distant place, that would be clairvoyance. But if I have the feeling of traveling in my 'other body' to that distant place and witnessing that event and then returning to my physical body, that would be an OBE?"

"I guess so."

> "The difference, then, between an OBE and clairvoyance is really a matter of the psychological perspective of the percipient — whether or not one has the sensation of leaving their physical body."

"Are you saying that one doesn't actually leave their body during an OBE?" I asked.

> "On the contrary," he said, and said no more.

After a moment, I got his point. "We're back to the worm cam, aren't we?"

He only raised an eyebrow, so I continued. "And back to the TV antennae.

"In order to perceive something, there has to be a signal sent and received. Even if the distance between sender and receiver can be eliminated via an extra-dimensional jump, the reception of a picture still requires the existence, at the observed site, of a lens of some sort located at such a point as to have the necessary viewing angle and focus to capture the scene in perspective. This is just as true in cases of so-called 'clairvoyance' as in out-of … I mean *other*-body experiences.

"Which suggests, I suppose, that clairvoyance, remote viewing, and astral travel are all actually cases of other-body experiences — sometimes with a sense of 'being there' and sometimes without."

"Okay," he agreed, "let's go on that assumption, at least for the moment."

"But NDEs are a different thing all together. Aren't they?"

"In total, they are," he said. "The near-death experience typically has several stages — the dark tunnel, the life review, the brilliant light, the overwhelming love, and the decision to return, being common ones. But virtually all NDEs begin with an OBE. The 'dying' person experiences the world as if he or she were hovering above their physical body. This stage of the NDE seems no different than the other-body experiences of healthy folks.

"Most of the OBEs that I think are particularly convincing were reported as part of NDEs. This is because NDEs are more likely to be witnessed and be better documented than other OBEs, which are typically spontaneous and generally lack supporting testimony.

"This is a copy of my current collection of best evidence for the continuation of personal identity after physical death," he said, taking down a sky-blue, wire-bound manual and handing it to me.

I opened it. The title page said: An Afterlife Casebook: Extraordinary Evidence for Extraordinary Claims.

"Go ahead," he urged, "read the first case. I'll make us some tea."

"Make mine iced if you would," I said and began to read.

Case 1— Seattle Shoe

When Maria had her first heart attack she was visiting friends in Seattle, not gathering crops in some field far removed from quality medical assistance. Even migrant workers get lucky now and then. Perhaps just as fortunate as the high-caliber cardiac care afforded Maria at Harborview Medical Center was the compassionate attention she received from the social worker in the coronary care unit. Kimberly Clark, M.S.W., was exceptionally empathic, with a knack for calming and reassuring folks who had every reason to be upset. She soon put Maria's mind at ease about family and finances and Maria came to see her as a trusted friend in a strange place.

This became evident on the fourth day, after Maria went into cardiac arrest for a second time. She was resuscitated by the medical team and seemed to be okay, but upon regaining consciousness later in the day, she became so agitated that the nurse on duty was afraid she would give herself another heart attack. Clark was called and, with considerable effort, managed to calm Maria down sufficiently to hear her story.

Maria said that after her attack that morning she had found herself floating near the ceiling of her room, watching the resuscitation procedures. She described those in the room, the things they did, and the equipment they used. After a while, she claimed, she found herself outside of the hospital building, where she noted the location and design of the emergency entrance.

Even though everything Maria said was accurate, Clark admits that she refused to believe her. "I knew the essential facts Maria was relating — the setting, the sequence of events — were true. But my professional, rational mind told me that Maria was 'confabulating,' that she was unconsciously filling in the blanks of her memory"[4] Clark felt that Maria must have gotten the details right "due to information she had somehow been privy to," although she had no idea how.

Then Maria dropped the bombshell that would reverberate throughout the NDE community for decades to come. She claimed that something on a ledge outside the building had drawn her attention and that then she found herself about three stories above the ground staring at a single shoe.

---

[4] Sharp, pp. 3 - 16.

It was a man's dark-blue tennis shoe, well-worn, one lace caught under the heel. The shoe was scuffed, Maria said, on the left side, where the little toe would be. Then Maria looked expectantly at Clark.

"It was clearly up to me," Clark reports, "to look for the shoe." Thinking that it might make Maria feel better to know that someone trusted her, Clark set off on what she was sure would be a "futile search." First she went outside and walked around the entire building. All she gained was an appreciation for the enormity of the Harborview complex. Nothing could be seen on any window ledge. Then, despite it being past quitting time, she felt impelled to do a room-to-room inspection on the third floor. "From the rooms on the east side, I saw nothing," she recalls. "On the north side — nothing. I was four rooms into the west side of the building when I pressed my face against a window pane, peered down on yet another ledge, and felt my heart go *thunk*. There it was."

Clark couldn't see if there was a worn area on the little toe because that side was away from her, but all the other details coincided perfectly with Maria's description. She opened the window and picked up the shoe. Yes, the scuff mark was also as described.

Maria was so excited when she saw the shoe that the monitoring nurse came in to see why her heart rate had jumped so high. Clark and Maria told the nurse what had happened. "By the next morning," Clark relates, "every nurse in the CCU knew Maria's story, and by afternoon, a parade of doctors and nurses and other staff members had dropped in to pay their respects to the humble shoe."

End Case 1

When I finished reading, I thanked him for the tea and said: "Some of this story seems familiar. I think I've read about it before, but I didn't realize it was so convincing."

> "It has been quoted — and misquoted — in many publications, so your sense of familiarity is understandable. What do you find so convincing about it?"

"Well, I guess it isn't really proof of Survival, since Maria didn't have much time to 'live' after she 'died.' And she really only 'died' in a technical sense, if at all, since she lived to tell the tale. But this is very strong evidence that some kind of 'astral body' (for want of a better term) exists and can operate at least semi-independently of the physical body.

"Would I be safe to assume that the report of this incident has drawn considerable fire from the skeptics?"

> "A true Skeptic (in the philosophical sense) doesn't have a position and won't take a position," he pointed out.

"You know who I mean," I contended, "those debunkers and fanatical critics who have made a career out of denying psychic phenomena."

> "Yes, I know." he admitted. "Perhaps we should call them 'super skeptics' or maybe 'überskeptics' would be more appropriate."

"This world does host some perplexing people."

> "Well, it's understandable. We all want the security of being part of the pack, but we also want to stand out from it and feel special in some way. Perhaps this is why some people seem driven to denigrate any commonly held belief. As far back in history as we can discern, most people have believed in the continuation of personality beyond the death of the body. Even though believing in something doesn't make it so, the near universality of belief in an afterlife should at least confer a predisposition to seriously evaluate evidence, even what may, at first, seem incredible.
>
> "Those who refuse to be objective tend to stay away from the truly evidential cases. I guess they just don't want to draw any more attention to incidents that undermine their position. For the most part, überskeptics prefer to make general statements dismissing all such cases as the result of either prior knowledge or lucky guesses.

> "Those few who do mention Maria's case act as if it has been discredited by an article that was once published in the *Skeptical Inquirer*."⁵

"Where else?" I muttered, rather sarcastically.

> "If you think of that magazine as biased against psi, this article, written by a few students from Simon Fraser University, isn't likely to change your opinion. In it, the students claim that they visited Harborview and managed to place a shoe on the ledge so that it could be seen easily from inside the room. This, they state, indicates that someone saw the shoe and then proceeded to discuss it within earshot of Maria. The students conclude that Maria must have overheard these comments about the shoe and incorporated them into her dying dream."

"But all that really proves," I noted, "is that it was *possible* for the students to place the shoe in a visible spot. Clearly, this was *not* the spot where Clark says she could see the shoe only by pressing her face against the window. So, by making this argument, the students have managed to challenge Clark's credibility without explicitly claiming that she made up the entire story."

> "You might say that.
>
> "You might also take note of the fact that (according to their story) even for the shoe that the students placed in such a visible spot, the details of the worn toe and lace placement would not have been visible unless the observer 'pressed against the glass.' In summary then, we are being asked by the students to believe that someone noticed a tennis shoe on the widow ledge, pressed his or her face against the glass to see that the far side of the shoe had a worn spot on the little-toe area and that a lace was tucked up under the heel.

---

⁵ Ebbern, Hayden, Sean Mulligan, and Barry Beyerstein, "Maria's Near-Death Experience: Waiting for the Other Shoe to Drop," *Skeptical Inquirer*, July/August 1996, pp. 27-33.

> This person, we are asked to believe, was so impressed by these wondrous details that he later related all of them to another person while in the presence of a deathly ill woman in a different area of the hospital. But, at the same time, this person *was not* sufficiently impressed to bother to open the window and retrieve the proof of this strange occurrence, and so left the shoe for someone else to discover.
>
> Furthermore, when Maria's experience became the talk of the hospital, neither the shoe's discoverer nor the person to whom he told the tale, nor any of the many people who must have seen this 'obvious' shoe on the ledge prior to Clark retrieving it, ever came forward to claim his or her due notoriety."

"I can see why most skepti … überskeptics are reluctant to cite that article," I said. "Nevertheless, if this was the only case with hard evidence of the existence of a conscious 'other body,' I might be tempted to accept their explanation, no matter how preposterous. After all, unlikely events do sometimes happen.

"But I suspect your interest in OBEs isn't built on a single case."

> He nodded toward the blue manual beside me. "Take a look."

Case 2 — Dutch Dentures

On 15 December 2001, the international medical journal, *The Lancet*, published a report titled "Near-death experience in survivors of cardiac arrest: a prospective study in the Netherlands."[6] This study included 344 patients who were successfully resuscitated after cardiac arrest. Of the 62 patients who reported some sort of an experience, 15 claimed that they had left their body. This is 24 percent of those who had an experience of some sort, and 4.4 percent of the total patients resuscitated.

---

[6] van Lommel, pp. 2039-42. A good overview of the study in layman's terms is available at www.iands.org/dutch_study.html.

Those who claimed some sort of an NDE were interviewed soon after their experience and again 2 years and 8 years later. Of special interest is what the report terms "a surprising and unexpected finding" that the positive, life-changing effects of the NDEs, rather than fading with time, became more and more apparent as the years passed.

This is by far the largest study of its kind and it sheds a great deal of light on the NDE process. All those critics who have managed to ignore such veridical evidence as "Maria's shoe" and have assumed that NDEs are hallucinations caused by a lack of oxygen or the administration of drugs need to take note of the chief investigator's conclusion: "Our results show that medical factors cannot account for the occurrence of NDEs."

Part of the *Lancet* report is the testimony of a coronary-care-unit nurse telling of a night when a comatose man was brought in by ambulance. During treatment, his mouth is opened to insert a breathing tube and it is discovered that he is wearing dentures. These are removed by the nurse reporting the incident and placed in a drawer of a crash cart. After about an hour of treatment the patient is transferred to the intensive care unit, still in the comatose condition in which he arrived.

The nurse does not see this patient for more than a week, then she meets him in the cardiac ward. In her own words (translated, of course, from the Dutch): "The moment he sees me, he says: 'Oh, that nurse knows where my dentures are.' I am very surprised. Then he elucidates: 'Yes, you were there when I was brought into the hospital and you took my dentures out of my mouth and put them into that cart, it had all those bottles on it and there was this sliding drawer underneath and there you put my teeth.' I was especially amazed because I remember this happening when the man was in deep coma and in the process of CPR."

The nurse inquired further and the man told her that he had seen himself lying on the bed while the staff had performed CPR. He correctly described the room he had been in and the appearance of the staff members present. She concludes: "He is deeply impressed with his experience and says he is no longer afraid of death."

End Case 2

> He saw me look up from the book and spoke: "Let me tell you why I think that is a very impressive case."

"Okay," I said, keeping my finger at my place and resting the book in my lap.

> "One of the favorite tactics of the NDE debunker is to point out that hearing is the last sense to fail as a dying brain's activity declines. And, it is true that people under anaesthesia have sometimes reported hearing conversations among surgical staff during operations. So, it is claimed that many, if not all, NDE/OBEs are hallucinations based upon sounds made by people and equipment as consciousness shuts down. Indeed, this might explain some OBEs and some part of many NDEs, but it certainly does not account for most NDEs. And this is an excellent example of one that is unaccounted for.
>
> "There is no mention of any sound accompanying the placing of the dentures in the drawer, but let's assume that the nurse actually announced 'I'll put his dentures in this drawer.'"

"Not very likely," I interjected. "Especially in the emergency room frenzy."

> "Yes, but even if she described her actions over the public-address system, the man had no way of knowing *who* was taking his teeth. In the unlikely event that his coma allowed for some hearing, his eyes — at least his *physical* eyes — certainly were not functioning. Yet he knew that the drawer was 'underneath' the cart, and, most importantly, he recognized this nurse as the teeth taker 'the moment' he saw her again, before she had a chance to speak."

"I see your point," I said, "and I certainly feel more comfortable accepting the shoe story now that I know it doesn't stand alone."

> "Oh, there are many such veridical stories. Curiously, at least two other good cases involve shoes![7] But, I'm particularly fond of the next one, which also involves hospital procedures and a nurse."

"Maybe you just have a thing for nurses," I joked. But he barely smiled and so I flipped the book open.

Case 3 – The Cavalier Nurse

Dr. Raymond Moody, philosopher, psychiatrist, and author of the best-selling *Life After Life,* relates an incident[8] in which he was attempting to resuscitate an elderly woman. While he was giving her closed-heart massage, a nurse on duty in the emergency room hurried into an adjoining storage area to get some medication he needed. This was packaged in a glass vial that was intended to be opened by snapping the thin neck with one's fingers. Protocol called for protecting the fingers by wrapping the vial in a paper towel. Upon her return, the nurse handed Moody the vial open and ready for use.

When the woman regained consciousness, she looked directly at the nurse and admonished: "Honey, I saw what you did, and you're going to cut yourself doing that."

The astonished nurse confessed that she didn't want to take the time to find a paper towel, so she had broken the vial with her bare fingers.

End Case 3

"I was wondering when we were going to get to Moody," I said, "after all he is the father of the near-death experience."

> "Well, Moody coined the term, but he would be the first to point out that the experiences have been reported at least as far back as Plato. Moody does deserve our respect and admiration for risking his career by publishing the book that triggered most of the research

---

[7] Ring/Valarino, pp. 67-69.
[8] Moody, *Light Beyond,* pp. 19-20.

into NDEs. It's hard to imagine now, but prior to 1975, unless you had undergone the experience yourself, you probably hadn't heard of it.

"What do you think of his story?"

"It's short but neat," I said. "And it beautifully counters the idea that patients extrapolate their OBEs from sounds they overhear while comatose. It is extremely unlikely that anyone, even if they were awake and possessed exceptionally sharp hearing, could detect the snapping of a glass vial in a room adjoining a noisy emergency room. It is even less likely that a comatose person, whose chest was being urgently pounded, could properly interpret the meaning of such a minute click. The idea that someone could do all that *and* discern whether the vial was held by bare or paper-towel-covered fingers is so preposterous … well, I'd sooner believe that all toys are made at the North Pole by tiny elves."

"I take it, then, that you are convinced of the reality of the NDE/OBE?"

"I'm convinced that something is happening that is unexplainable in terms of materialism or scientism. But I'm not ready to commit to any new theory."

"Let's give Dr. Moody another opportunity then, shall we? The next case is what he calls his "most dramatic story." He related it to me in recent conversations.[9] The subject was his neighbor and friend whom he considered "the salt of the earth."

Case 4 — The Plaids and the Pallbearer

June[10] was in her mid-30s when she elected to undergo what was supposed to be routine gall-bladder surgery. The routine was shattered when her heart stopped beating. As the doctors were attempting to resuscitate

---

[9] In March and April of 2005.
[10] Parts of June's story were related (as two separate incidents) in *The Light Beyond*. Her name has been changed in deference to her family's privacy.

her, June sensed herself rising from her physical body and moving out into a hospital corridor where she encountered a few of her friends and family members who had gathered quickly. (The hospital was within a short walk of their home in northeastern Alabama.) She attempted to attract their attention but failed. Her strongest memory of the group is that her daughter was dressed in mismatched plaids.

Moving on down the corridor, June came upon her brother-in-law. As she was attempting to communicate with him, a friend of his happened along and asked him why he was there. In answer, she heard her brother-in-law say that he had intended to visit an uncle who lived out-of-town, but now he thought he should stick around because June was going to "kick the bucket" and he might be needed as a pallbearer.

Next, June found herself having a typical NDE-tunnel experience at the end of which she encountered two translucent beings, one of whom was an infant. To her inquiry as to their identity, the infant peeled back his outer covering as one might take off a bathrobe and transformed into an adult male. "I am your brother," he stated. As far as June knew, she only had sisters.

Upon regaining consciousness, June discussed these events with her family and discovered that they all checked out. Her father confessed that his first child was a boy who died within a few days of birth and was never mentioned within the family. Her brother-in-law confirmed that he had been standing apart from the others when his friend came along and he sheepishly admitted to making the remark about being a pallbearer. And, when questioned about the mismatched plaids, June's maid said that in her rush to get the family to the hospital, she had grabbed the top two items in the daughter's laundry basket (not heeding their patterns) and told her to get dressed.

June's testimony was confirmed independently in interviews Dr. Moody held with June's surgeon, her father, her brother-in-law, and her maid.

End Case 4

"Most dramatic indeed! This case would be very tough to explain by any means other than actual travel in the other body."

"Give it a try," he prompted.

"Well, I suppose she could have learned that she had a brother without being conscious of the fact, but goodness knows that would be a strange way to reveal it to herself. And why bother at such a critical time in her life? Having a male sibling could hardly have an impact on whether she lived or died."

"But, however improbable, you are right to point out that unconscious knowledge is a possible explanation for the brother incident."

"Then," I continued, "I guess June could have read the mind of her brother-in-law to learn of his remarks about being a pallbearer."

"An excellent point," he said, "although überskeptics deny the possibility of mind reading. Also, that doesn't explain how June knew he was down the hall from the rest of the family when his friend approached him."

"No, nothing does, except clairvoyance, and we agreed that's just another kind of OBE. The same thing goes for her daughter's clothes. You know," I mused, "I'm sure that I'll forget many of the particulars I learn this weekend, but I'll never shake the image of that little girl in those mismatched plaids."

"Then I bet you'll appreciate the story about the woman who didn't believe there was a heaven. When she had an NDE, she was very upset to discover the reality of an afterlife, for she never liked

> to be proven wrong. Furthermore, during her OBE she noticed that she had been dressed in a nightgown that didn't match her robe and she was furious to think that she would have to spend eternity in mismatched clothing!"

"That's a good one," I chuckled. "I didn't know you had comedic aspirations."

> "Oh, that's not a joke," he replied. "It's from a collection of actual cases about the impact of NDEs on those who don't believe in heaven.[11]
>
> "Anyway, if there's a more evidential OBE story than June's, I haven't heard it. At least as far as adults are concerned. Now let's look at what the younger ones have to say about OBEs."

I took my cue to resume reading.

Case 5 — Room Reconnoiter

Rick was an adult when he related his story to Dr. Melvin Morse,[12] but it began when he fell deathly ill at the age of 5. He remembers leaving his body and watching the medics carrying him out of his house, loading his body into the ambulance and driving away. But, atypically, he didn't follow his body in the ambulance. Instead, he stuck around long enough to see his father weeping as his family got into their car to go to the hospital. Then, he claims: "I went ahead to the hospital to see what kind of room I was going to get. I saw a girl who was about 12 years old in the room that I was supposed to go into. Since I was so sick, they decided to move her and give me the room alone."

Following this observation, Rick continued with a more typical experience involving a tunnel and a bright light. The light was all knowing and

---

[11] Cox-Chapman, pp. 134-135.
[12] Morse, pp. 177-179.

all loving, but he knew that if he entered it he could not return to his family.

When Rick came out of his coma several days later, his family was astounded to hear that he knew about his father's tears and about the girl being moved from his room prior to his (body's) arrival at the hospital.

End Case 5

"The bit about the girl being transferred to another room makes for an interesting twist to the story," I said. "But that is the kind of thing that might have been mentioned in the presence of the comatose boy."

"True enough," he replied, "and the father's tears?"

"Probably not mentioned, but easy enough to guess. Although I hesitate to impugn the testimony of a young child with no apparent motive to make up a story. It's also tough to imagine that a 5-year-old was so culturally indoctrinated as to fabricate the tunnel and the loving light. No, all together, the story adds to the evidence of Survival. Nevertheless, I'd much prefer to hear such testimony sooner than two decades after the event occurred."

"Your wish is my command."

Case 6 – From the Mouths of Babes

There are many hundreds of accounts, such as the one cited in Case 5, in which adults recall having NDEs as children; the following are highlights from some of the rarer instances in which children have provided evidence of NDEs while they are still children, thus minimizing any possible distortion over time.

The first is from a study published by pediatrician Melvin Morse in 1986, the rest from other sources as cited.

June, at the age of 8 — gets her hair caught in a swimming pool drain and her heart stops for 45 minutes. A few months later, during a medical interview, June tells of floating above her body, going up a tunnel, and visiting a bright and cheerful place where "a nice man asked me if I wanted to stay."[13]

Sam, at the age of 8 — suffers cardiac arrest as a result of an adrenal gland disease. As a 9-year-old undergoing a routine medical exam, he suddenly, and somewhat shyly, tells the doctor: "About a year ago, I died." Encouraged to elaborate, he tells of floating above his body and trying unsuccessfully to stop a doctor from hitting him on the chest. Then he flew quickly into the sky and through a tunnel to a place where he met glowing angels (without wings). There he saw a fence and knew that if he crossed it he could not return to his life. He wanted to stay there, he claimed, but God made him go back.[14]

Mike, at the age of 4 — falls from a high dive and lands on his head. His mother finds him and thinks he is dead. When he regains consciousness he tells her that he was floating out of his body and then a shaft of yellow light surrounded him. Then he heard a voice asking him if he wanted to live or die and, thinking of his mother, he decided to live.[15]

José, at the age of 3 years, 8 months — almost drowns and spends the next 2 weeks in a coma. At the age of eleven, without any prompting, he tells his mother that he remembers having risen into the air and seeing her and his father crying. Then he met people he liked who shone very brightly. He felt good and wanted to stay with these people but they told him he could not.[16]

Todd at the age of 2 years, 8 months — is asked by his mother if he remembers what happened 4 months earlier when he was almost electrocuted by biting into an electrical cord. (Todd had no heartbeat or respiration for at least 25 minutes.) He replies that he went into a room that had

---

[13] Morse, p. 37.
[14] Moody, *Light Beyond*, pp. 58-59.
[15] Serdahely, pp. 33-41.
[16] Ring, *Lessons*, pp. 105-6.

"a very bright light in the ceiling" and that "a very nice man ... asked me if I wanted to stay there or come back to you."[17]

Nathan, at the age of 7 months — is operated on for a collapsed intestine. The surgeons report that they "almost lost him." When Nathan is 2 years old, he starts drawing pictures of a person in a beam of yellow light beneath a rainbow. In answer to his mother's query as to why he keeps drawing the same picture, Nathan replies that he is drawing himself so he can remember the time he went up in the sky. Then he says, "Remember when I was a baby and I hurt so bad? I went up in the yellow light and through a rainbow and I didn't hurt any more. There were people there that told me I had to go back because you and dad still needed me."[18]

Charlotte, at the age of 6 months — was hospitalized for severe renal and circulatory failure. Against the expectations of the doctors, she survived. At the age of 3½, as her mother was speaking of the impending death of her grandmother, Charlotte asked: "Will Grandma have to go through the tunnel to get to see God?"[19]

End Case 6

"Whew! This is some very touching stuff." I paused a while to figure out my feelings.

"The stories are both heartwarming and heartrending. I mean, I have friends who have lost young children. I'm sure they'd appreciate any evidence that those children's souls survived death ..."

"But?"

"But ... Well, these stories do support the idea of Survival, but they're actually about children who were saved. The heartrending questions are 'Why aren't they all saved?' and 'Did my child make the choice to leave?'"

---

[17] Gabbard, p. 156
[18] Nathan's story was reported by his mother at http://members.tripod.com/celestialtravelers/nat.html.
[19] Herzog, p. 1074. I assigned the pseudonym "Charlotte."

"Certainly, many children are so badly injured or dissipated that their physical bodies cannot be repaired," he said sadly. "As for making choices, well I don't have good statistics, but I have read a whole lot of these cases and my impression is that the question about staying or returning is more of a survey than a decision point. As with the case of 'Sam', it often doesn't seem to be up to the children, even when they are asked. So, no matter how lovely heaven seems or how pleasant it feels, I doubt that any child stays there if it is physically possible to return to a loving family.

"Any other observations?"

"These accounts are pretty strong evidence that NDEs are not the result of cultural indoctrination. Last I heard anyway, Fisher-Price hadn't created a line of crib toys with tunnels leading to heaven. And, in the accounts given, its clear that the kids weren't trying to satisfy an authority figure who was asking leading questions. What was this Morse study you mentioned?"

"Dr. Morse compared 121 children who had serious diseases (but were never in danger of dying) with 12 children who had clinically died or had been very close to dying. All of the very sick group had been bedridden for extensive periods, and most had been heavily medicated, yet, in intensive interviews, not a single one of them reported experiencing anything like an NDE during their hospital stay. Of the twelve who had knocked on death's door, however, ten reported experiencing at least two elements common to NDEs and seven (58 percent) remembered having an OBE while the doctors were trying to resuscitate them.

"Dr. Morse was careful not to ask directly about OBEs or tunnels or any such common NDE element. His questions were phrased in general terms such as 'Did you have any dreams or do you remember being unconscious?' Also, he did not solicit experiencers nor did he accept volunteers; instead, he methodically went through

10 years of hospital records and interviewed every child who survived a near-fatal illness.[20] So his data isn't distorted by folks anxious to tell — and possibly exaggerate — their tales.

"In that case," I concluded, "the argument for the authenticity of OBEs is further strengthened. Do you have more on the subject?"

"I think we've looked at a pretty representative sampling of the OBEs that provide the best evidence for the existence of a non-physical body. Of course, for every case with verifiable observations there are at least a thousand cases that lack such details."

"Which means," I interjected, "that they could be hallucinations of a dying brain, as critics are wont to claim."

"If you can figure out how a brain with no detectable electrical activity manages to have complex hallucinations and then manages to store the memories thereof, you could be right.

"Unless, of course, you count the OBEs reported by people who are blind," he said, motioning once more to the book in my lap.

Case 7 – Seeing Is Believing

In the early 1990s, Kenneth Ring, Professor Emeritus of Psychology at the University of Connecticut, partnered with Sharon Cooper (then a Ph.D. candidate at New York University) to undertake the first systematic study of NDEs and OBEs in blind persons.[21] Ultimately they found and interviewed 31 persons who reported either an NDE or an OBE or both. Of these, 14 had been blind since birth, 11 lost their sight after the age of 5, and 6 suffered from severe vision impairment.

Analyzing the elements of reported NDEs, the researchers conclude that no matter the cause, degree, or length of the visual impairment "the type of NDE reported appears to be much the same and is not structurally different from those described by sighted persons."

---

[20] Morse, pp. 21-22.
[21] Ring/Cooper.

Most intriguing is the fact that of the congenitally blind (that is, those blind since birth), almost two-thirds reported <u>being able to see during their experience</u>. Here's how a few of them described their experience:

Helen, re two OBEs — reports that in both cases she was able to see her body below. She tells of being excited to see trees and people walking around outside. She also recognized certain friends and various shops in the neighborhood.

Brad, re an NDE as an 8-year-old who stopped breathing and almost died from pneumonia — says he found himself floating near the ceiling of his room at the Boston Center for Blind Children. He saw his roommate get up from his bed and go to get help and he noticed his roommate's "sheets piled partly on the floor and partly on the foot of the bed." Then he went up through the ceiling and the roof of the building and discovered that he could see his surroundings quite clearly. He remembers it being a dark and cloudy day with snow covering everything except, he says, where "the streets themselves had been plowed and you could see the banks on both sides of the streets." He saw the playgrounds beside his building and a trolley passing by.

Cheryl, re an OBE she experienced while lying on her back one summer night — says she had "a tumbling sensation" and found herself looking down at her body from a height of "10 or 12 feet in the air." Then, suddenly, she found herself transported to the house of her girlfriend, Irene. From a vantage point in the doorway of the bathroom, Cheryl observed someone kneeling in front of the toilet. It was another friend, Pat, who was holding her hair back with her left hand as she vomited into the toilet bowl. Cheryl noted the placement of all the ususal fixtures around the bathroom. Later, Pat confirmed (to the researchers) that she and Irene had been partying and "had a few too many to drink, and I ended up getting sick." Pat also confirmed Cheryl's observations that she had been holding her long hair back with her left hand "and everything like that."

Joyce, re one of her OBEs in which she found herself in a flower garden — claims she "saw the colors" of the flowers. She could tell that the air was very warm in the garden and she could hear birds singing, but "the flowers were the most vivid thing." "I can remember all these flowers," she says, even though she admits that she has never seen colors in her physical life.

Vicki, re an NDE after receiving life-threatening injuries in an automobile accident — says she found herself in a non-physical body that was "like it was made of light" viewing the accident scene from above. Then she remembers seeing herself on a table at the hospital and wondering if she was dead. Next, according to the researchers' report of her interview, "she found herself going up through the ceilings of the hospital until she was above the roof," whereupon she saw "a panoramic view of her surroundings" that included "lights and the streets down below." Then she undergoes the tunnel experience and ends up in a place with trees and flowers and people who, in her words "were made of light, and I was made of light." Prior to this Vicki says, she could detect neither light nor shadow and had "never been able to understand even the concept of light."

When an interviewer asked Vicki how she felt about suddenly being able to see, she exclaimed: "I was shocked. I was totally in awe. I mean, I can't even describe it because I thought, 'So that's what it's like!' But then I thought, 'Well, its even better than I could have imagined.'"

End Case 7

Apparently I had a frown on my face when I closed the book.

"Is something wrong?"

"No, nothing's wrong. These are astounding cases. I'm duly impressed. ... I just can't quite wrap my mind around *why* they are so impressive. I mean," I paused and thought harder, "I mean, why should it be a big deal that the blind can see during OBEs?

"Being blind," I continued, "is a condition of a person's physical body — their eyes and their nervous system — and no one takes their physical eyes along when they're having an other-body experience. The Seattle

Shoe case, for example, would be no more evidential or convincing if Maria had been blind."

"You are exceptionally perceptive and logical," he said.

I beamed.

"Actually, it would have been *less* convincing if Maria had been blind, and thus unable to identify the shoe after Clark retrieved it.

"The cases of blind persons seeing during OBEs and NDEs do not, in fact, add much to the already strong cases, but they greatly strengthen the otherwise contestable ones. Would you care to expand on that?" He looked at me questioningly.

I said nothing, and I stopped beaming.

He said: "I'll give you a hint. Think about dreams."

After a moment, I asked: "Do the blind see in their dreams?"

"As far as I have been able to determine, those persons who have been blind since birth report no sensations in their dreams that they do not have in daily life."

"So, if they don't see in their dreams, but they do see in their OBEs, then there must be something that occurs in an OBE that gives them information that they do not otherwise have.

"When I look at a chair," I continued, motioning toward the recliner he occupied, "I see a chair only because I have learned what sort of visual information can be translated as 'chair.' And I only learned that by having seen lots of chairs from various angles and perspectives."

"That," he said, "is called an experiential referent."

"But, according to these stories, people are seeing flowers and streetlights and toilets and such without any referents possibly existing in their brains."

"Perhaps it's not really 'seeing'," he suggested. "Could it be more of a mental 'knowing' or transcendental awareness?"

I thought long and hard before replying: "Well, it isn't *physical* seeing, but it is perception of light from a distance. I mean, they don't have to touch something to see it and they can't see in the dark, right?"

"Apparently. Very much like our worm cam. But, some OBErs do report being able to see in all directions at once."

"Okay, but that's just a question of seeing at a wider angle than the physical eye is capable of. The 'astral eye,' like the mouth of the wormhole, is localized in time and space; this is not my sense of transcendental awareness.

"For example, when Brad was floating above his roommate's bed in the dorm room, he may have been able to see in all directions at once, but his vision was limited by physical objects and structures, just as physical vision is limited. He saw the sheets piled half on the bed precisely because his view was from that side and because the sheets partially masked his view of the bed and the floor. Again, he did not see the building's surroundings while he was still in the room; he had to travel through the ceilings and reach the outdoors first.

"Or, consider Cheryl in the bathroom doorway or Helen exploring her neighborhood," I continued, warming to my subject, "they don't *just know* what is happening, they observe their surroundings from a particular viewpoint, and if they want a change of scene, they have to move that viewpoint.

"Then there is the matter of scale. Those who report other-body experiences may speak of tiny things such as dust particles on the top of light fixtures, but they see those particles from the same distance as a physical human would. They do not observe the dust particles on the same scale as a dust mite would. Likewise, they observe buildings as large things far away, not as doll houses. If there is no actual astral body, then how are size and scale comparisons made?

"Also, to get back to the light (no pun intended), could one be transcendentally aware of a winter's day being 'dark'? Since darkness is the absence of the sensation of light, would this require being transcendentally aware of a non-awareness?"

> "I'm sure I don't know," he said. "A lot of terms have been thrown around in an attempt to explain or rationalize these phenomena, but calling the unknown 'transcendental awareness' or 'extrasomatic vision' tells us no more than it does to claim that we are all part of the Mind of God."

"So, we're stuck with these facts," I summarized. "Blind people observe their OBE environments from the same perspective, viewpoints, scale, and sensitivities as normal vision yet their brains have not been programmed with experiential referents that could help them decipher what they are looking at. These referents must exist in a non-physical mind that is accessible by the non-physical or astral body. And the referents must have been acquired by the mind *prior* to the blind person's physical birth. At least that is the only explanation I can think of at the moment. If I'm right, then OBEs in the blind indicate the existence of a soul prior to birth, and are thus strong evidence for the survival of that soul after death.

"Whatever the case may be, we know that the blind are not dreaming or imagining these visual experiences, and, therefore, we can conclude with some confidence that sighted people are not dreaming or imagining their OBEs either."

> "I couldn't put it much better than that," he said with a grin. "Although I might add that the ability of the congenitally blind to see during OBEs might be dependent not just on the preexistence of the soul but on how many physical bodies the soul has lived in prior to this incarnation."

"You mean that the more times a soul had lived, the more experiential referents it might carry with it. That would mean that those souls that don't have visual sensations during OBEs are likely newly born souls."

> "Or at least new to Earth," he said, standing up. Why don't you read the next case while I fix us some lunch."

Case 8 – An Out-of-Bed Experience

One sunny afternoon in September, 1958, Robert Monroe tried again to prove that he wasn't crazy. For several months, he had been having what most psychiatrists would call hallucinations or, at least, very weird dreams, in which he seemed to be traveling about the countryside while his body lay inert on his couch at home.

It had all started that Spring. First, without any discernable cause, came hard cramps across his abdomen. Then the shaking started. Or, at least, he felt as if his body was shaking all over, but there was no visible movement. Fearing every nasty affliction from epilepsy to a brain tumor, Monroe fled to his family doctor, but extensive tests revealed nothing out of the ordinary. Soon, a pattern of symptoms developed: several times a week, just as he was nearing sleep, waves of vibrations would sweep over Monroe's body. Then, one night, it happened — he found himself bumping gently along his bedroom ceiling.

Fearing now for his sanity, Monroe sought the advice of a psychologist friend, Dr. Bradshaw. Fortunately for us, instead of sending him off to enjoy a padded cell (where, no doubt, many of his fellow astral travelers are ensconced) Dr. Bradshaw suggested that Monroe ought to stop fighting the sensations and see where they took him.

Where they took him is the subject of three books and the instigation for the founding of the Monroe Institute.[22] Within a few years, Robert Monroe, once a practical and successful broadcasting executive, became the West's most well-known and influential guru of out-of-body travel.

On the September afternoon in question, Monroe was still trying to confirm that he wasn't simply dreaming his ethereal jaunts. He decided that he would try to leave his body and visit Dr. Bradshaw, whom he knew to be sick in bed. Monroe figured that if he could describe Bradshaw's bedroom, which he had never visited, it would be solid evidence that he was

---

[22] The Monroe Institute of Applied Sciences is located in Faber, Virginia, USA. Its website is http://www.monroeinstitute.org.

actually out of his body — rather than out of his mind. So, after he achieved lift-out, he focused on Dr. Bradshaw and soon found himself approaching two persons who were walking towards a small out-building of some sort. He was surprised to see that one of the persons was Dr. Bradshaw, dressed not in pajamas, as expected, but in a light-colored overcoat and hat. The other person was Mrs. Bradshaw, dressed in a dark coat and hat. Confused to be observing a scene contrary to the 'reality' he anticipated, Monroe retreated the five miles to his body.

Monroe reported the incident to his wife, who insisted that his observations must be wrong, as she knew that Dr. Bradshaw was ill and in bed that day. That evening, Monroe and his wife telephoned Dr. and Mrs. Bradshaw and asked them where they were between four and five that afternoon. Mrs. Bradshaw stated "that roughly at 4:25 they were walking out of the house toward the garage. She was going to the post office, and Dr. Bradshaw had decided that some fresh air might help him, and he had dressed and gone along."[23] Further questioning revealed that the outer clothing they were wearing precisely matched what Monroe had observed.

End Case 8

I put down the book and carried my iced tea to the table. "One thing that surprises me about these stories is their lack of religious overtones. Don't many folks claim to talk with Jesus during their OBEs, at least the Christians?"

> "Many NDErs recall encountering an intelligent and compassionate being. A few take this being to be Jesus or Buddha or whatever figure is consistent with their religious upbringing," he replied. "Sometimes their descriptions change along with those beliefs. I recall one case in which a woman referred to the beings she met as 'spirit people' when she first recounted her experience; but six

---

[23] Monroe, *Journeys Out of the Body*, pp.46-47.

months later, after she had joined a church, she started referring to them as 'Jesus and the angels.'"[24]

"Most do not make any such identification," he continued, placing a bowl of green grapes on the table. "I think it interesting that NDEs are just as likely to happen to those with little or no religious orientation as to those who claim to be very religious.[25]

"Let's eat."

---

[24] Cox-Chapman, p. 17.
[25] Gallup, p. 8.

Saturday Lunch
Morality and the NDA

I wish I did not have to be so grumpy and hard to deal with when I am sick. I positively, almost angrily, dislike being sick. Dying? Dying is another matter. I almost did it once before and found it one of the great, memorable, ecstatic experiences of my life. I can see no reason why the real thing should be less joyous than the trial run.

—Arthur Ford, *The Life Beyond Death*, p. 158.

Breakfast had been a most informal affair of standing around the kitchen sipping coffee and munching on bagels, so lunch was our first meal together. He bowed his head, I followed his lead, and he prayed:

> "As we relax our bodies and prepare them to receive this nourishing meal, we are thankful for our many blessings in this wonderful world. Amen."

"I see you're not a vegetarian," I commented, as I picked up the BLT from my plate and started eating.

> "I trust you're not either," he said. "You didn't mention anything about that."

"No. I've never found the discipline to decline a good steak, I'm afraid."

> "I don't think that's anything to be afraid of," he responded. "Of course, we all feel better when we eat foods that are good for us, but to avoid certain foods on religious or moral grounds strikes me as rather insulting to the One who created them."

"How so?" I asked, "And, by the way, the sandwich is excellent!"

"That's because the tomatoes are really good this time of year. Now," he looked up and pointed a pickle spear at me, "if *I* were mandating the world's dietary regulations, beef and pork would be fine, but terrible punishments would be inflicted on anyone with taste so poor as to serve those pinkish plastic-like things that pass for tomatoes so much of the year.

"As for the morality of diets," he continued, nibbling on his pointer, "the process of living always involves destruction and rebuilding. That's true of everything from bacteria to beets to Bengal tigers; it's simply the way the physical universe was designed. Perhaps it could have been designed better, but I don't feel qualified to make a judgement on that. Besides, the main point of our discussions this weekend is, in fact, that death is a wondrous transition to a new life."

"For cows and pigs?" I mumbled through a mouthful of bacon.

"To the extent that they possess self-consciousness, I would say so, although I can't say for sure. What I do know is that most of the reports we have from the other side seem to agree with Jesus' statement that the important thing is what comes out of your mouth, not what goes in."[26]

"Perhaps you're right about that," I said, "but didn't God specifically command 'Thou shalt not kill'?"

"Ah! But exactly *who* should not be killed? If you look closely at the history of the Hebrews, as they wrote it themselves in the Torah,[27] you will find that their God clearly had no problem with killing animals — He loved those burnt offerings — or humans. Not only did Jehovah repeatedly encourage the slaughter of various

---

[26] See Matthew 15:11 and Romans 14:14.
[27] The first five books of the Old Testament.

> non-Hebrew tribes,[28] but on the first Passover, He took it upon Himself to kill the eldest child in every Egyptian family.[29] Also, other laws of the Hebrew people mandated the death penalty for an amazing number of misdemeanors, including refusing to obey one's parents, picking up twigs on the Sabbath, and using withdrawal as a form of birth control.[30] Altogether, then, I don't think one can grant much moral authority to the writings of the ancient Hebrews. But, even if you do, there is nothing in the Bible that encourages vegetarianism."

"Yes, I know those gruesome facts well" I said, "You might have added that talking to dead people was likewise a capital crime.[31] But Biblical issues aside, what are your views on the morality of killing?"

> "One needs to remember that dying is a necessary part of life; without it our planet would have been overrun with creatures long ago. Have you seen the number of deer in these hills?"

"Driving up here I almost hit several," I answered. "The ones we saw last evening and then there were more walking by when I stepped outside this morning — seems like quite a few; but I'm just a city boy."

> "Well, I don't happen to be a hunter," he said, "but it's clear to me that if deer-hunting season weren't so popular up here, the deer population would get out of hand quickly, bringing starvation, pestilence, and more death for all creatures.
>
> "That, of course, is our biggest problem as humans."

"No hunting season on us?" I asked, not certain if he was jesting or not.

---

[28] Numbers 31 gives one of many gruesome accounts.
[29] Exodus 11:4. For other tales of this death-dealing god, see 2 Kings 19:32-35 and 2 Chronicles 20:14-24
[30] See Deuteronomy 21:18-21, Numbers 15:32-36, Genesis 38:9.
[31] See Lev 20:27 and Deuteronomy 18:10.

"All our predators have been neutralized except for disease and disasters. We're overrunning the world, yet we're still shocked when epidemics and tsunamis wipe out thousands."

No reply came to me, so I continued munching on lunch.

"Anyway," he resumed after awhile, "something so ubiquitous and necessary as killing could hardly be sinful or immoral in and of itself. In my view — and it's a view endorsed by many revealed teachings — it is not so much the act that counts as the motive.

"An edifying story,[32] if you'll allow one more reference to the Bible, takes place when David was encamped at Ziklag with his exiled band of outlaws and misfits. A man in filthy, torn clothing staggers in to camp, falls to his knees in deference to David, and says that he (the messenger is never named) had been fighting alongside the Israelites when he came upon their king, Saul, wounded and in peril of being captured by the Philistines. Saul calls out to the man in his pain and says 'slay me, for anguish has seized me, and yet my life still lingers.' Seeing that Saul will not live much longer anyway, the man complies with the king's orders, thus saving Saul from a more painful and shameful death at the hands of his enemies. The man then escapes through enemy lines to bring the news of Israel's defeat. He also brings the king's crown, which he believes should now belong to David.

"Personally, I believe the man did the right thing in assisting his king to die. David apparently felt differently, he had the messenger executed ... although he did keep the crown."

"Wow, I think I need a little time to digest all this," I said, "both the meal and our conversation."

"Then let's take a leisurely stroll in the woods," he suggested and I readily agreed.

---

[32] As told in 2 Samuel 1:9. See also 2 Samuel 4:10.

The air was warm and fresh and the sunlight dappled the ground as we stepped off the wooden porch and commenced our walk with Dasher prancing at our heels. For awhile, we walked in silence enjoying the sights and sounds of nature. Then he turned towards me and spoke:

> "An area the casebook doesn't cover but we ought to at least mention is the NDA."

"Ahh, the NDA," I echoed, as I followed him down a narrow path between tall trees, "standing, I suppose, for Near Death Activities? No, I know, Non-Denominational Allegories?"

> "Perhaps you should reconsider vegetarianism," he retorted, using his walking stick to clear away a strand of spider's silk from the path, "the bacon seems to have affected your mind.
>
> "Actually, you're not far off. NDA stands for Nearing Death Awareness. It seems to have been coined to replace the term 'death-bed vision,' probably to encompass other sense impressions such as hearing and smell, and because 'visions' are too closely associated with hallucinations."

"And NDAs are not?"

> "As with NDEs, many could be, but the fact that some have imparted information otherwise unavailable leaves us with little choice than to accept them at face value. The literature is full of cases wherein a dying person claims that several deceased friends and relatives are gathering round to aid in their transition to the other side. Any nurse who has worked for long in an intensive-care unit can tell you similar stories. Occasionally, the dying person learns of the death of a loved one by seeing that person among the group."[33]

---

[33] For a thorough treatment of this topic, read *What They Saw — At the Hour of Death,*, by Karlis Osis and Erlendur Haraldsson, Hastings House, 1997.

"Let me get this straight," I said, as we stepped over a leaf-filled culvert and up onto a gravel roadway. "Someone is nearing death, and over a period of ... what, hours, days, weeks?"

> "Usually several days."

"Okay, over a period of several days, this dying person reports seeing dead people whom he has known. Are these vivid, realistic images or the more wispy, translucent type of spirits?"

> "Real enough so that the dying person often expresses surprise that others cannot see them," he said, picking up a stick from the road and throwing it for Dasher to fetch.

"But how could one set of eyes perceive what another set of eyes cannot?" I wondered.

> "Perhaps," he said, "the dying person is beginning to use the same visual apparatus that NDErs use."

"His astral eyes?"

> "Good a name as any. Sounds like a song title, doesn't it?" And then he broke into the ardent and rhapsodic palaver of a 1930's radio announcer: "And now, direct from the grand ballroom high atop the NDA building in beautiful downtown Nirvana, Wisconsin, radio KPSI is proud to bring you the otherworldly sounds of Bony Goodman and his spectral orchestra playing that perennial favorite *Astral Eyes*." And, with only the hint of a smile, he turned down another path away from the road.

"You're right," I called to his receding back. "No more bacon for either of us!"

Catching up, I tried to get back on track: "So then, sometimes the dying person sees someone among their ghostly visitors who, as far as the perceiver is concerned, shouldn't be there because that person isn't dead. And they wonder aloud about this in the presence of a nurse or one of their 'real' visitors. And when the matter is investigated, it is discovered that the questionable visitor really has died."

> "Or, that the living relatives have known of the death all along but refrained from informing the dying person for fear of unnecessarily upsetting him or her," he added.

"So who coined the term 'NDA'?"

> "I believe it was devised by a couple of hospice nurses who wrote a book called *Final Gifts*.[34] I haven't read it myself, but I looked it up a few months ago on the Internet and was astounded to see that 61 out of 62 reviewers gave it 5 stars, the highest possible rating. This is unheard of."

The question hung in the summer air for at least a minute before I broke down. "Okay, I give up, how many stars did the 62nd reviewer give the book?"

> "One."

"One," I echoed. "Isn't it wonderful how people can hold such divergent opinions."

> "Oh, that reviewer agreed that the book was superb," he said. "He just couldn't accept NDAs because they conflicted with his belief that his church, and his church alone, held the key to heaven's gate."

"Well," I said, ducking under a low branch while stooping to sarcasm, "we certainly can't have those nasty old facts interfering with our beliefs, can we?" But he said nothing and neither did the dog, so I continued: "Are NDAs common?"

> "Probably more common than NDEs," he replied, "but it's tough to say. The advent of modern medical care has had a big impact on the reports of NDAs."

---

[34] Callanan.

"Positive or negative?"

> "Both, actually. Positive, because hospitals allow researchers to locate and interview witnesses now far easier than when most people died at home. Negative, because so many people now die in a drugged stupor and are in no condition to report anything happening to them."

"You mean they die of drug overdoses," I asked.

> "Oh no! I mean that so many doctors today seem to think that their job is to prevent death, and, since that is impossible, they settle on preventing their patients from *experiencing* death by filling their bodies with pain killers. The so-called 'comfortable' death thus becomes death in a chemical haze. Morphine and other such drugs inhibit memory. This is very likely why only a minority of patients remember NDEs and is almost certainly why many do not report NDAs."

I thought this over as we walked in a silence broken only by an occasional bird call and the rustling of squirrels and chipmunks among the groundcover. I watched several squirrels scrambling to hide behind tree trunks as we approached. The smaller, quicker chipmunks were mostly brown blurs as they zipped between rocks and logs. The deer, I assumed, had heard us coming a mile away for I glimpsed no white tails bobbing over the hills.

The sight of the cabin at the end of our path broke my reverie and refocused me on the topic at hand. "It's interesting," I mused as we climbed the front stairs, "that the NDA is so much simpler than the typical NDE, yet it can be even more evidential of Survival."

> "Because the spirits involved are truly dead?"

"Yes," I agreed. "Of course it would be even better if more than one dying soul could get the message."

"Then it must be time to continue our studies," he said, as he opened the cabin door and ushered me inside. "The manual is where you left it."

Saturday Afternoon
The Spirits Speak

Sit down before fact like a little child, and be prepared to give up every preconceived notion, follow humbly wherever and to whatever abysses Nature leads or you shall learn nothing.

— T.H. Huxley[35]

Case 9 – Good Ships and Witches

Gary E. Schwartz, Ph.D., has had an undeniably distinguished career. After being graduated from Cornell as a Phi Beta Kappa, he earned his master's degree in clinical psychology and his Ph.D. in personality psychology from Harvard University. He taught at Harvard and at Yale University, where he became professor of psychology and psychiatry, director of the Yale Psychophysiology Center, and co-director of the Yale Behavioral Medicine Clinic. He has published more than 400 articles in peer-reviewed journals and presented over 600 scientific papers, and is currently professor of psychology, medicine, neurology, and psychiatry at the University of Arizona.

In the fall of 1997, during a business trip to Irvine, California, Schwartz was introduced by a colleague to Laurie Campbell, who quickly began offering messages from Schwartz' deceased mother, father, father-in-law, and others. Schwartz was impressed with the accuracy and insight of Campbell's "reading." Especially impressive were Campbell's first words to Schwartz' partner, Linda Russek, when, during this initial meeting, he called to share the experience with her. Upon being handed the telephone receiver, Campbell gave Russek a message from her father: "Thank you for the music." Only upon returning home did Schwartz find

---

[35] Huxley, p. 330.

out that, years before, his partner had set up a pillow speaker and played cassette tapes for her father as he lay dying in a hospital bed.

Schwartz was by no means ready to believe, but he could not imagine any realistic scenario for Campbell obtaining the information she offered or so accurately mimicking people she had never met. The incident inspired him to set up an experiment testing not only Campbell but also Susy Smith, a medium he had met when he moved to Tucson. The results of this experiment were impressive enough to prompt the development of a university-sanctioned research project that is described in Schwartz' book *The Afterlife Experiments*. Five psychic mediums (George Anderson, John Edward, Anne Gehman, Suzane Northrop, and Laurie Campbell) participated in one or more experiments, beginning in February of 1999 and still going on as I write this. The results of the experiments to date have been most impressive and the book is well worth reading. The following incident is especially evidential.

What the book calls "The Canyon Ranch Experiment"[36] involved three mediums doing readings for each of five sitters. The mediums worked simultaneously in different rooms. The sitters moved from one medium to another and were sequestered in a separate room while waiting for their turns to come up. The mediums were not told who the sitters were and had no way of telling what order they were being presented. During each session, the medium was prevented from seeing the sitter by two sets of doubled sheets suspended "wall-to-wall and floor-to-ceiling." The medium was prevented from obtaining clues from the sitter's voice by the simple expedient of having the sitter remain silent throughout the experiment. In short, there was no opportunity for the medium to identify the sitter or to base any guesses on the sitters age, gender, health, emotional state, or reaction to a question. During the first ten minutes of each sitting, the sitter did not respond to the medium in any way. After this time period, questions would be answered by an experimenter in the room with

---

[36] Schwartz, pp. 183-89.

the sitter calling out to the medium "yes" or "no" according to a nod or head shake by the sitter.

During the totally silent period in which a woman named Sabrina Geoffrion was the sitter, John Edward made two references to an elderly woman that the sitter believes was her grandmother. During the yes/no period (hearing only the experimenter's voice, not the sitter's) Edward said he was being shown daisies at a wedding. The sitter later explained that when her mother married, her grandmother had sewn a ring of daisies into her mother's hair. But it was after the session that the really evidential incident happened.

When Sabrina's session was concluded and she had been escorted to the holding room, Edward's next sitter was brought in. This time, however, the "silent" period was far more silent than usual. Several minutes passed, then Edward claimed that the previous sitter's grandmother had not left when her sitting was concluded. Edward could get nothing about the current sitter, but two impressions came through about the previous sitter: One was the title of the TV show *Sabrina, the Teenage Witch*. The second was *On the Good Ship Lollipop*. the signature song of Shirley Temple.[37]

Later Sabrina explained to Schwartz that it wasn't simply a matter of identifying her name. When she was in school and her classmates taunted her by calling her "Sabrina the witch," her grandmother was the one she would run to for comfort. When Schwartz asked if "on the good ship lollipop" meant anything to her, Sabrina broke out in tears. Although popular long before her time, the song was very meaningful to her because, as a young girl, she had curly hair and, when she sang and danced, her grandmother would tell her she looked like Shirley Temple. She had actually sung Shirley Temple songs for her grandmother.

End Case 9

"So, what can we glean from this case?" he asked when I looked up. But the question was apparently rhetorical, for he continued:

---

[37] First sung in the 1934 movie, *Bright Eyes*.

> "First, the possibility of fraud is virtually inconceivable. Schwartz' reputation is impeccable and his honesty unchallenged. Each session was videotaped. John Edward was not told the identity of the sitters and, even if he had somehow discovered the names of one or more, he had no way of knowing their order of presentation."

"So he could not have benefitted from any prior research."

> "Right. Also, he never saw or heard the sitter."

"So he had no opportunity to obtain the clues required to do a cold reading."

> "And, of special note in this case," he added, "the sitter who was actually in the room with Edward during his most evidential output was not the one for whom he was receiving the information."

"Which argues strongly against mind reading as an explanation."

> "Yes. Edward actually asked if the scientists were playing a trick on him by having the same person return for another session.[38] Then, in the face of assurances that it was a new sitter, Edward stuck to his claim that the messages were for the previous sitter, knowing that to do so would cause his accuracy for the current sitting to be rated as zero!"

"Do you think his hits could just be a series of lucky guesses or coincidences?" I asked. "To bring up a wedding is not a big risk for a medium, as most everybody has attended one. On the other hand, to mention such an uncommon flower as a daisy (and not roses or some flower more commonly associated with a wedding) is a bit more daring."

> "Even less common than daisies at a wedding," he pointed out, "is 'Sabrina.' Most people would be guessing a long time before they thought of that name. But, it's the song that clinches the matter.

---

[38] This lingering of spirits after the sitter leaves has been reported before. See, *Forty Years of Psychic Research*, by Hamlin Garland, p. 210.

"Consider it this way. Imagine that you are serving on a jury in a murder trial. The victim was found slumped beside a piano with a knife wound in his back. On the piano was a vase of daisies with one plucked stem. On the floor, written in the victim's blood and in his handwriting, was the word 'Sabrina.' Lying open atop the piano was the sheet music for *On the Good Ship Lollipop*."

"Okay," I said, "I can see it all now."

"Shortly after the crime, the police apprehended an ex-lover of the victim named Sabrina. When spotted, she was wearing a plucked daisy in her hair."

"It looks pretty bad for Sabrina."

"And as she was being arrested she kept whistling the tune *On the Good Ship Lollipop*.

"What say you, oh wise and fair juror? Could it all be just coincidental?"

"Guilty, beyond any reasonable doubt." I declared.

"Then," he asked, "can we affirm with equal vigor that John Edward was in actual communication with Sabrina's grandmother?"

"Oh, I suppose the source of the information could be her grand*father* impersonating her grandmother, and I cannot prove that it's not a demon from hell trying to lead us astray or an alien from Ork playing cosmic tricks. But, all things considered, I've got to go with the reality of the spirit of the grandmother as the most likely explanation.

"Once again though, I hate to make a judgement on just one case."

"You know what I think? I think you're already convinced, you're just enjoying yourself too much to quit reading the cases."

"Maybe, maybe not," I said as I picked up the manual again.

Case 10 – From Boys To Woman

In the year 1873, a few of the Fellows of Trinity College, Cambridge, in England, became convinced that neither religion nor philosophy nor history nor science were properly addressing the question of Survival. One of the group later wrote that if anything useful could be learned, it would be learned "simply by experiment and observation ... by the application to phenomena within us and around us of precisely the same methods of deliberate, dispassionate, exact inquiry which have built up our actual knowledge of the world which we can touch and see."[39] In hopes of carrying out such research, the group formed the Society for Psychical Research (SPR), an organization that remains active to this day.

From its beginnings, the SPR attracted a remarkably distinguished membership of scientists, psychologists, philosophers, and politicians who, contrary to what you might think, were generally skeptical of psychic phenomena. Many, in fact, joined with the intention of proving that there was no such thing as the paranormal, and their standards were so strict that some called the SPR "a society for the suppression of evidence."[40]

An early member of the SPR, and a founder of it's American equivalent (the ASPR), was Professor William James of Harvard University. Generally considered one of the greatest psychologists of all time, Dr. James also taught physiology and philosophy and is known as the father of American pragmatism. In the autumn of 1885, James' mother-in-law and sister-in-law attended what may have been the first sitting that Mrs. Leonora Piper ever gave to someone outside of her circle of family and friends. Rumors had been circulating around Boston ever since Piper had discovered her mediumistic talents a few years before, but she had been uncomfortable with the notoriety and had spurned outside sitters. Why his in-laws were granted an exception we do not know, but we do know that they were extremely impressed. Dr. James tried to persuade his in-laws

---

[39] Myers, p. 5.
[40] Ford, *Life Beyond Death*, p. 97.

that most marvels had earthly explanations, but he finally gave in to their insistence that he go and see for himself.

A few days later, James and his wife attended a sitting with Piper. So impressed was James that he personally took control of séance arrangements for the ensuing year and a half. Thus began the greatest — longest, best researched, most evidential — chapter in the history of Survival research. First Dr. James, then Professor Richard Hodgson, then Professor James Hyslop investigated and tested Piper over a period of almost 30 years. They brought hundreds of sitters to her under false names. They hired detectives to follow her. They even monitored her mail. They took her to England where she knew no one, kept her in the homes of SPR members, and watched her as closely as any zealous skeptic could wish. In fact, Hodgson, Professor of Legal Studies at Cambridge University, was known world-wide for his skepticism; he came to America with the announced intention of proving Piper a fraud, as he had done for other supposed mediums. And what, after nearly 16 years of research, did Hodgson conclude? In his own words: "I cannot profess to have any doubt but that the 'chief communicators' to whom I have referred in the foregoing pages, are veritably the personalities that they claim to be; that <u>they have survived the change we call death</u>, and that they have directly communicated with us whom we call living through Mrs. Piper's entranced organism."[41]

To eliminate the possibility of a medium gaining evidential material via telepathy, researchers have often tried asking for facts that are not known to anyone present at the reading. A good example of this, and of Piper's work in general, is the case of Uncle Jerry's Watch.

When Piper was first brought to England she stayed with various members of the SPR. One of her hosts (and investigators) was Sir Oliver Lodge, a professor of physics and mathematics in England and a Fellow of the Royal Society. (Like many others, Lodge was quite skeptical of an afterlife until he had studied Piper. Unlike some others, when faced with the

---

[41] Hodgson, Emphasis added.

overwhelming evidence Piper and others provided, Lodge possessed the strength of character to admit that he had been wrong and to publicly endorse personal immortality.)

According to Lodge, in late 1889, he devised an experiment to see if Piper could obtain "facts which were not only out of my knowledge but which never could have been in it."[42]

Lodge had several uncles, at least two of whom were still living, although very elderly, at the time of this test. One of these uncles, whose name was Robert, had been very close to his twin brother, Jerry, who had died some 20 years earlier. Oliver wrote to Robert asking for some object that had belonged to his twin, and Robert responded by sending a gold watch that Jerry had been fond of. Lodge told no one of the watch and, within a few hours of its receipt, he handed it to the entranced Piper.

"I was told almost immediately," Lodge reports, "that it had belonged to one of my uncles … one that had been very fond of Uncle Robert … [and] that the watch was now in possession of this same Uncle Robert, with whom its late owner was anxious to communicate. After some difficulty and many wrong attempts, *Phinuit* [Piper's control; the name is pronounced fin-WEE] caught the name, Jerry, short for Jeremiah." Then Lodge heard "This is my watch, and Robert is my brother, and I am here. Uncle Jerry. My watch."

Lodge then asked if Jerry could recall trivial details of his boyhood life with Robert. Uncle Jerry "recalled episodes such as swimming the creek when they were boys together, and running some risk of getting drowned; killing a cat in Smith's field; the possession of a small rifle, and of a long peculiar skin, like a snake-skin, which he thought was now in the possession of Uncle Robert." Lodge states that, "these details of boyhood, two-thirds of a century ago, were utterly and entirely out of my ken. My father himself had only known these brothers as men."

And how many of these details could Uncle Robert confirm? According to Lodge: "He recollected something about swimming the creek,

---

[42] Myers, "Record of Observations" pp. 436-659.

though he himself had merely looked on. He had a distinct recollection of having had the snake skin, and of the box in which it was kept, though he did not know where it was then. But he altogether denied killing the cat, and could not recall Smith's field."

Skeptics might well point out that swimming in a creek and playing with a snake skin were hardly unusual activities for boys of that place and age. But in this case, it's the miss that makes the case. For Robert had another brother, name of Frank, an old sea captain living in Cornwall. And Robert, who realized that his memory was failing him, wrote to Frank. And Frank wrote back to say that, indeed, Smith's field was a place where they used to play near their home, in Barking, Essex; and that another of their brothers did kill a cat there. Moreover, Frank clearly recalled a "foolhardy episode" involving Jerry and him swimming in the creek, near a mill-race.

It should also be noted that, even though Lodge was keeping a close eye on Piper and was confident that she had not hired anyone to snoop out any of the information, he went the extra mile in this case, sending an agent to his uncles' boyhood home to see if the facts given were known by any of the village elders, but the agent could learn nothing.

End Case 10

"This case hardly conforms to my image of a 19th century séance." I said. "You know, a half-dozen gullible folks grasping hands around a table in a darkened parlor while misty ectoplasm swirls among them and whispers issue from a trumpet floating over their heads."

> "Yes, such scenes were common at one time, and still occur today at some of the spiritualist enclaves. But Piper, and many other reputable mediums, did not require darkness and did not produce physical effects."

"Did she utilize a trumpet? What the heck is a 'trumpet' anyway?"

"Simply a cone of metal or paper similar to the megaphones used by cheerleaders to amplify their voices. Researchers are justifiably suspicious of those that float around darkened rooms, as many have been proven fraudulent. On the other hand, some mediums — I believe case 16 gives an example — have made honorable use of them under well-lighted test conditions.

"Leonora Piper simply sat down in a chair wherever she was taken and went into a trance. There can be no doubt that her trances were genuine, as she never reacted when she was tested by pricking, cutting, and blistering her skin or by having an open bottle of ammonia held beneath her nose.[43] She spoke in the normal human way. The tone, depth, and inflection of her voice varied with the personalties of those she was channeling, but the only thing spooky about the sittings were the spooks themselves."

"I didn't realize that trances could be so perilous."

"Mediums risk more than you might think. I am reminded of a story Ruth Montgomery tells of a session with the entranced Arthur Ford.[44] At one point, Ford's control, Fletcher, informed Montgomery that the medium was in great pain. Ford 'looked as peaceful as a slumbering child' to Montgomery, but she asked Fletcher to wake him. Immediately upon coming to consciousness, she reports, Ford 'clutched at his heart and groaned in agony.' She knew that he couldn't be faking, Montgomery says, 'for beads of perspiration popped out on his forehead and his suppressed moans tore at my heart.'"

"I'm surprised that Ford's control didn't wake him straightaway the moment the angina began."

---

[43] Gauld, *Mediumship*, p. 33.
[44] Montgomery, pp. 102-103.

"Not only did Fletcher fail to do so; but, after announcing the problem, he actually started to introduce one of Montgomery's deceased relatives! She had to interrupt Fletcher to get him to awaken Ford.

"Such nonchalance is not uncommon for spirit controls. As for Mrs. Piper, I can't say what Phinuit thought of being cut and burned."

"Was Piper able to recall what happened while she was in trance?" I wondered.

"No."

"That must be pretty tough. I mean, we all lose about a third of our lives to sleep, but to give, what?, several hours a day for 30 years just so other people could use you as a telephone. That's a sacrifice few would be willing to make."

"We do owe quite a debt to Piper and those like her," he agreed.

"Were there many others?"

"Piper was special, but she wasn't unique," he said. "It seems that every generation produces a handful of exceptionally talented psychics."

"I wonder why they aren't better known."

"With the possible exception of a few doddering professors of history, we all are inclined to think of the past as impoverished," he said. "A lack of televisions and computers is assumed to mean a corresponding lack of sophistication, knowledge, and even intelligence. Now that the 21st century has dawned, it is even easier to look back with disdain upon those simple bumpkins of the 19th century who actually survived without corn flakes and instant coffee.

"This is a shame," he continued, "because the era that gave us Sherlock Holmes also produced some of the sharpest minds ever to devote themselves to psychical research. The fact that events occurred before we were born, in no way reduces their evidential quality."

"Speaking of the evidence," I said, "the case of Uncle Jerry's Watch is pretty powerful stuff."

"Yes, I believe that the medium and her attending spirit made numerous evidential statements that were later verified." [Together we worked up the following list.]

1. That the watch originally belonged to one of Oliver Lodge's uncles, now deceased.

2. That this deceased uncle's name was Jerry (short for Jeremiah).

3. That the watch was currently owned by another uncle.

4. That the watch owner's name was Robert.

5. That Jerry was very fond of Robert.

6. That when the brothers were young, someone almost drowned while swimming in a creek.

7. That one of the brothers had a snake skin that was kept in a box.

8. That the brothers played in a place called "Smith's field."

9. That one of the brothers killed a cat in that field.

"Now let's see," I said, "Oliver Lodge did not know or have any way of guessing facts 6 through 9, and Uncle Robert could not recall facts 8 and 9 and only vaguely recollected number 6."

"And Uncle Frank," he added, "knew nothing of Jerry's watch and could not remember fact number 7."

"The only one who knew all of the details, then, was the person who provided them in the first place," I pointed out. "And he was dead."

"Therefore," he concluded, "those who believe that all mediumship boils down to mind reading and play acting are left with affirming that Piper somehow read the minds of, and selected specific memories from, not one, not two, but three different people, following some astral trail across England from Oliver's mind to Robert's and thence to Frank's."

"Surely not even our überskeptics would go that far," I avowed.

"Of course not. They deny that minds can be read at all, and for good reason. I think a fellow named Whately Carington said it most succinctly: 'Survival is a spectacular issue, but not a crucial issue; it is telepathy that is crucial though it may not be spectacular.'[45]"

"Meaning, I suppose, that the existence of telepathy proves that a nonphysical reality exists, thus establishing an environment for the continuance of the discarnate soul."

"Yes, but it's more than that. You know, it isn't so difficult to accept that we can mentally send and receive thoughts; the tough part is figuring out how a mind could sort through all the billions of thoughts that are being sent out at any given moment and read only the sought for message."

"Yes, I can see that the problem is not in the transmission or the reception but in the tuning."

"Without some structure, all any mind could ever receive is the 'white noise' created by the intermingling of the thoughts of every being in the universe. And this argues strongly for the existence of some sort of universal mind or discarnate communications system that routes and delivers mental images according to our intention or desire. Such a system couldn't be limited to our own minds; it would have to exist in a mental plane independent of the physical."

"I'm not sure I follow," I said. "The TV tuner that separates the signals is a part of the television set. Why couldn't our brains contain the 'telepathy tuner' necessary to sort through the waves of thoughts?"

---

[45] Carington, p. 3.

> "The television tuner works because it was calibrated at the factory to match up with signals of specific wavelength agreed upon by the broadcasters and the manufacturers. This system of agreements is not designed and maintained within the television set. Likewise, the system that allows one person to receive the thoughts of another person cannot be sustained by either party alone or together. It must have an independent, non-physical superstructure."

"Okay, I got that. Wouldn't the same argument apply to instances of clairvoyance or OBEs. I can conceive of an astral body as simply an appurtenance of the physical one, but to travel to a specific place would require an astral map of some sort, a map that could only exist in that same autonomous spiritual plane."

> "Precisely. In fact, as Carington concludes: 'The phenomena of telepathy, etc., are therefore not an alternative to survival, but a virtual guarantee of it.' Which is why the überskeptics refuse to admit to ESP despite decades of solid proof of its existence.
>
> "No, the only people who would even suggest mental telepathy as an explanation for Mrs. Piper's success are those parapsychologists who postulate the existence of super-psi."

"And what, pray tell, is super-psi?"

> "Super-psi, or super-ESP, is the nebulous notion that anything a discarnate spirit might do could also be accomplished by some extreme (and usually speculative) power of a living mind. That is, that some combination of telepathy, clairvoyance, precognition, and/or mind-control is in play rather than actual communication with the dead."[46]

"Where does mind-control come into it," I wondered.

---

[46] See, for example, Braude.

"Many places, but the most salient would be the Cross-Correspondences."

"I've heard something of those, but I'm not real clear on how they worked," I admitted.

"At one time, a few discarnate spirits had the idea that they could provide unchallengeable proof of the continued survival of their personalities by sending different parts of a message to different sitters via different mediums," he explained. "Each piece of this puzzle was designed by the spirits to make little or no sense by itself, but when the various pieces were read within the context of the others, a clear message would be seen."

"And these spirits actually accomplished this?"

"Beginning in 1901, several mediums associated with the SPR (Piper among them) who were spread across England, the United States, and India, began producing such messages. These cross-correspondences flowed freely for over three decades, ultimately comprising more than 3,000 scripts taking up some 12,000 typewritten sheets. The results were very impressive."

"Then why aren't they better known?"

"Two reasons, I think," he replied. "For one, they are too complex for their own good. The very aspects that make them so evidential also make them difficult to comprehend. Of course, it doesn't help that the spirit who initiated the whole program was a classical scholar; many of the references are obscure passages in Latin and Greek."[47]

"Ouch! I can see the first problem. Does the second involve super-psi?"

---

[47] Those interested in delving deeper should consult some of the many analytical pieces available. (More than 50 papers, many of them book-length, have been written by SPR members alone.)

"How did you guess?"

"Must be psychic," I shrugged. "So, despite the spirits' long and convoluted efforts, some folks still insist that they don't exist and that these correspondences were caused by mental powers of the living?"

"Correct. For some reason, they evidently feel an overwhelming urge to deny the possibility of an afterlife, and when the evidence is objectively evaluated, super-psi is the only alternative they have.

"To get back to our point, do you see the problem with several mediums who are spread across the globe simultaneously constructing a puzzle of Latin and Greek phrases that none of them understand?"

"Well," I pondered a moment. "I reckon there has to be some central cause of it all."

"Exactly. The only explanation for this, besides Survival, is that one of the sitters must be using his super powers to broadcast the messages into the mediums' subconscious minds while causing them to hallucinate their contacts on the other side."

"But that's ridiculous!" I exclaimed.

"More than ridiculous," he replied, "absolutely scary! I wonder sometimes if those who support the super-psi notion have considered the implications of someone actually having these awesome powers. If such a one could read one mind, he could read everyone's mind. If such a one could influence one mind, he might, even now, be influencing all of our minds. The existence of super-psi would be the paranoiacs worst nightmare."

I slowly scanned the cabin ceiling and said under my breath: "You wouldn't happen to have any kryptonite around here, would you?"

> "I don't believe you have any need to worry," he assured me, "there are a lot of cases that are very difficult if not impossible to explain via super-psi." And he nodded to me to continue reading.

Case 11 — Evidence By The Book

"Book Tests" are a category of evidence in which a discarnate entity directs an incarnate person to words or phrases written in a place never previously accessed by that person, thereby communicating a message that could not be a product of mind reading or unconscious creation by the living. The first book tests on record were initiated in 1917 during sessions held by Gladys Osborne Leonard, one of the most renowned mediums in England.

Once, when the Reverend Drayton Thomas was having a sitting with Leonard, the spirit of his father came through and told him that he had tried to communicate in the past by knocks and raps but had failed to make sufficiently distinctive and noticeable sounds.[48] A few nights later, Thomas was at home when he heard a systematic rapping punctuated three times by a loud double knock.

When next he attended a session with Leonard, the Reverend was told by *Feda* (Leonard's control) that his father had asked her to make the knocks, so she had gone to his house and attempted to spell her name using Morse code. Then *Feda* announced that the elder Thomas had devised a test. The son was to go to the bookshelf behind the door of his study, and from the second shelf up, withdraw the fifth book from the left. Near the top of page 17, he would find words describing what had occurred.

When Thomas did as instructed, he discovered that the fifth book from the left on the second shelf was a volume of Shakespeare, and in the third line from the top of page 17 (Act I, Scene 3 of King Henry VI) was the phrase: "I will not answer thee with words, but blows."

End Case 11

---

[48] Smith, A., pp. 75-76.

"I've seen stage magicians that could tell what was written on a particular page and line of a book."

> "Yes, and you can buy the trick books they use in most magic shops or online. You may also have seen or read magicians telling how to perform such feats with a person's own books," he continued, "but this always requires a minute or so of private access to the library to set up the trick. Our dear Mrs. Leonard, on the other hand, was not a professional magician and had never set foot in the Thomas home.

"So, Leonard would have had to conceive of the play-on-words that linked the raps with the Shakespeare quote, then mentally searched the son's library for a book containing *Henry VI Part I*, and then somehow read pages without opening the book."

> "The very task we agreed was impossible with neither light, nor lens, nor perspective."

"Yes."

"But," I wondered, "how is that evidence for Survival? I mean, what advantage would a discarnate spirit have that would allow *it* to accomplish such a feat?"

> "I don't know," he admitted. "But it was the father's library, so it is more probable that the information came from his memory than from the medium's conjectured (and incomprehensible) ability to read closed books at a distance. And, of course, we have *Feda's* testimony, which we have no ground to discount.
>
> "On the other hand, perhaps the plane that supports astral bodies also has astral books that can be read with astral eyes even when their physical counterparts remain closed and on the shelf.
>
> "Now consider a similar case sans the involvement of a medium.

Case 12 – Jung's Dream Library

The famous psychoanalyst, C.G. (Carl Gustave) Jung tells of a sort of uninvited book test in the form of a vision.[49] One night, as he lay in bed feeling deeply concerned about the recent death of a friend, Dr. Jung sensed that friend's presence in the room. At first, Jung doubted his feelings, but then he decided that proof was irrelevant and that he might as well give his spectral visitor the benefit of the doubt. "The moment I had that thought," Jung relates, "he went to the door and beckoned me to follow him."

And so, Dr. Jung followed (in his vision) his friend "out of the house, into the garden, out to the road, and finally to his house. ... I went in and he conducted me to his study. He climbed on a stool and showed me the second of five books with red bindings which stood on the second shelf from the top."

Jung was unacquainted with the man's study and did not know what books he owned. Curious, he went the next morning to his friend's widow and obtained permission to "look up something" in the man's library. "Sure enough," he reports, "there was a stool standing under the bookcase I had seen in my vision, and even before I came closer I could see the five books with red bindings. I stepped up on the stool so as to be able to read the titles. ... The title of the second volume read: 'The Legacy of the Dead.'"

End Case 12

> "The argument for the Survival explanation is even stronger in this example because there is no third party involved and because the beckoning friend clearly implies a planned destination. On his own, Dr. Jung could have had an OBE and might have envisioned his recently departed friend, but he had no reason to travel to his friend's library. The impetus for that trip could only have come from his friend's spirit."

---

[49] Jung, pp. 312-313.

"And, even if he had dreamed up the library visit," I added, "why would he envision the book but not the book's title?"

"Why, indeed?"

"Was Jung a believer in Survival?"

"Although he never confirmed such a belief in his books, Jung once wrote in a letter that 'In each individual case I must of necessity be sceptical, but in the long run I have to admit that the spirit hypothesis yields better results in practice than any other.'"[50]

Case 13 – Where's the Smoke?

Sometimes, the writing to be discovered is neither in a book nor on its cover. One of the better known examples of this type of phenomena was reported by Thomas Sugrue in his book on the famous psychic, Edgar Cayce.[51]

According to Wesley Ketchum, M.D., who worked with Cayce early on, one of the ingredients in a recommended preparation was specified by the entranced Cayce as "Oil of Smoke." Dr. Ketchum had never heard of Oil of Smoke and the local druggists could find no such item in their catalogs. Ketchum had no alternative but to have another reading in hopes of determining where this arcane substance could be found.

Cayce directed them to a drugstore in Louisville, KY (about 150 miles away), but the manager of that drugstore responded to their telegram by saying that he had never heard of Oil of Smoke. Again, a reading was held, and this time very detailed directions were given. A bottle of the substance would be found on a specified shelf in the back of the store, behind a bottle of another preparation (which was named).

This time, the Louisville store manager wired back: "Found it." As Ketchum reported: "The bottle arrived in a few days. It was old. The label

---

[50] Wilson, p. 131.
[51] Sugrue, p. 25.

was faded. The company which put it up had gone out of business. But it was just what he said it was, 'Oil of Smoke.'"

End Case 13

"I'm surprised Cayce hasn't come up earlier," I said.

"As impressive as some of his work is, little of it makes a strong case for Survival," he replied. "Cayce definitely did some efficacious diagnostic work and many of his prescribed treatments bordered on the miraculous. But then, he was also mistaken on many occasions when he wandered from the medical arena."

"Some writers claim he was wrong all the times that he wasn't just lucky."

"You've been reading the überskeptic's websites, haven't you? They love to talk in generalities and innuendos. I've even seen a couple that mention the Oil-of-Smoke case, but only to point out that this is just an old name for Beechwood Creosote, as if Cayce was trying to mislead folks. As far as I know, the critics have never bothered to mention the astounding way the bottle was located.

"As for being lucky, well, consider one of his first patients, a 5-year-old girl who was diagnosed by medical doctors in Cincinnati as having a rare brain affliction that was invariably fatal.[52] She was having convulsions up to twenty times a day and her mind would appear totally blank. Her parents had brought her home to die, when a family friend suggested that Edgar Cayce might be able to help. And so, for the price of the railroad ticket, Cayce left his job as a bookstore clerk in Bowling Green and came back to Hopkinsville. (At the time, he thought he needed to be near the patient to do a reading.)

"In trance, Cayce said that when the girl was two years of age she had influenza (a fact he had no way of knowing) and that the flu

---
[52] Sugrue, pp. 19-22.

> germs had settled in her spine due to an injury she had sustained immediately before. (The girl's mother later testified that no one but herself knew that the girl had slipped getting out of a carriage the day before contracting the flu and had hit the end of her spine on the carriage step.) After undergoing the treatments Cayce recommended, the girl returned to normal, completely healed of her 'fatal' disease.
>
> "I don't think either the girl or her mother would admit to any "luck" being involved in that case, and there are scores of others like it in the Cayce files."

"I second your endorsement," I said, "I've always felt that Cayce provided an excellent example of one's beliefs *not* influencing trance pronouncements. In trance, he often spoke of a patient's past lives, although the conscious Cayce resisted the idea of reincarnation as contrary to his Christian faith.

"Nevertheless, I wonder if the detection of the bottle is such good evidence for Survival."

> "Do you find it easier to accept the existence of a discarnate intelligence being in contact with a retired pharmacist or that a living person could clairvoyantly search the shelves of every drugstore in Kentucky for a single small bottle."

"That does seem to stretch the concept of super-psi about as much as the case of Uncle Jerry's Watch."

> "I think you'll find that the next two cases stretch it beyond the breaking point," he said, motioning once again towards the *Casebook*.

Case 14 – The R101 Disaster

On Saturday the 4th of October 1930, at 6:24 in the evening, the airship R101 slipped its moorings in Cardington, England, and began its maiden voyage to India. Under the command of Flight-Lieutenant H. C. Irwin, the

R101 was the largest airship (otherwise known as a dirigible, zeppelin, or blimp) in the world. Its departure had been hurried to avoid stormy weather threatening along its route through France. The R101 was a new design and, like many new designs before and after it, had been pressed into service for political reasons without all the tests and trials that prudent policies might have dictated.

Less than 8 hours later, 46 of the 54 passengers and crew of the R101 were dead[53] and its fire-blackened skeleton loomed over a soggy meadow near the town of Beauvais, just north of Paris. Early on Sunday morning, heavy rains and gusting winds had brought the nose of the behemoth almost gently down to earth, but a rotating propeller on a starboard engine dug into the dirt, causing the engine to twist and ignite the hydrogen gas flowing from rents in the forward gas bags. It only took a moment for the entire ship to be engulfed in flames.

The R101 disaster shocked the British nation. It shook the government's confidence in dirigibles, and ended British efforts to develop lighter-then-air craft for commercial use. Several months were required for investigators to determine all the factors that contributed to the disaster, but a small gathering of private citizens in London knew, only two days after the crash, what the findings would be.

On Tuesday, the 7th of October, 1930, at 3 p.m., a séance was held at number 13 Roland Gardens in London, home of the National Laboratory of Psychical Research. The laboratory had been founded 5 years before by Harry Price. A keen investigator and talented magician, Price had a reputation for exposing fraudulent mediums. Joining Price for the afternoon séance were Ethel Beenbarn, Price's secretary and stenographer; journalist Ian D. Coster, who had requested the session in the hope of contacting the spirit of Sir Arthur Conan Doyle; and Eileen Garrett, a medium of growing renown in England. This was Garrett's first visit to Price's laboratory; she did not know Coster nor had she been told the purpose of the session.

---

[53] Two other crew members later died of injuries sustained in the crash, bringing the total dead to 48.

Garrett went immediately into trance and her control, *Uvani*, began to speak. He spoke not of the recently passed-on Doyle, however, but of a man named "Irwin" who was apologizing for interfering but who insisted on speaking. Then, as Price reports[54] "the voice of the medium again changed and an entity announced that he was Flight-Lieutenant H. Carmichael Irwin, captain of the R101. He was very agitated, and in a long series of spasmodic sentences gave the listeners a detailed and apparently highly technical account of how the R101 crashed."

The reporter, Coster, was at first miffed that he wasn't getting an interview with Doyle, but he quickly realized he was witnessing a historic event. He put the story out at once, and newspapers across England and around the world carried it, often with banner headlines. Transcriptions of the session were requested and carefully studied by experts investigating the crash, one of whom asked for and received an additional séance to further interview the R101's deceased crew. The government never officially endorsed Garrett's work, of course, but an official named Charlton, who examined the transcription in great detail claimed that the idea that anyone at the seance could have obtained such technical information beforehand was "grotesquely absurd."

Several of Irwin's statements — such as the ship being too heavy for its engines — were public assumptions or could be reasonably guessed. But many were technical, confidential, or simply unknown to anyone at the time. Here are three examples of such.

Irwin said: "Load too great for long flight. Same with SL-8. Tell Eckener."

No one at the seance knew the meaning of "SL-8" or recognized the name "Eckener." The British experts who reviewed transcripts of the session knew that Dr. Eckener was the designer of the *Graf Zeppelin*, but even they had to search through their records of German airships to discover

---

[54] Price, *Leaves*, chapter 6.

that "SL-8" was the identifier for a dirigible built by the Schütte-Lanz company of Mannheim, Germany.

Irwin said: "Starboard strakes started."

"Strakes," a term foreign to all at the session, was originally a naval expression that was adopted by airship designers. Strakes are parallel layers of longitudinal plates that form the sides of a ship. Irwin was formerly a navy man, so it is a term that he would be likely to use.

Irwin said: "Impossible to rise. Cannot trim. Almost scraped the roofs of Achy. Kept to railway."

Achy, a French village 12½ miles north of Beauvais, was on the R101's route. Achy was shown on the type of large-scale air-ordnance map carried by the R101, but the village was so small that it did not appear on any normal ordnance or road map. Neither did it rate mentioning in Baedeker's or Michelin's guidebooks. It does lie on the main rail line between Amiens and Beauvais. Witnesses near the town testified that the airship had passed over extremely low.

Harry Price concluded: "It is inconceivable that Mrs. Garrett could have acquired the R101 information through normal channels and the case strongly supports the hypothesis of survival."[55]

End Case 13

"Where were the survivors of the crash when the séance was held?"

"They were still in a French hospital."

"Could Garrett have been reading one or more of their minds?"

"Of the eight crew who survived, five maintained the engines, one operated the radio (wireless), and two were riggers. It is unlikely that they would have had lengthy commentary on the faults in the ship's design, and extremely unlikely that they would have been thinking of Eckener and the SL-8."

---

[55] Price, *Fifty Years*, p. 153.

"Was the radio operator who survived on duty when the ship crashed?"

"As a matter of fact, he wasn't. He was asleep in his bunk and only awakened when the ship went into a steep dive. Why do you ask?"

"Well, I thought that if the radio operator had been in the control car he might have seen the map and been aware of the name of the village they nearly scraped the roofs from."

"I hadn't thought of that; but, you're right. The most unlikely thing of all is that any of the survivors would have been aware that the ship had just passed over a village named Achy.

"But, of course, nothing can be ruled out 100 percent."

"Well, this case comes very close to being 100 percent convincing."

"The next one comes even closer."

Case 15 – Relics Revealed

In 1914, as Violet Parent was recovering from a severe illness, her deceased mother appeared to her and told her she would find a gold coin above one of the doorways in her apartment. Her husband, Gregory, later reported: "We both considered this merely a dream, for our apartment had just been thoroughly cleaned. Nevertheless, we looked, and sure enough, over a door leading to the porch we found a ten-dollar gold piece."[56]

Now, the Parents were of very modest means. He was a grocery clerk and she a housewife. They lived in a "two-room apartment of threadbare aspect." Thus they were most impressed by such a find, and so, understandably, they paid close attention to Violet's ensuing visions.

---

[56] This coin was just under ¾-inch (1.75 cm.) in diameter. Ten dollars then would equate to about $187 now. (The coin itself would actually be worth several thousand today). How it got above the Parent's door was never discovered.

Shortly, she began to fall into trances in which other spirits spoke to her. Some of these spirits claimed to be missionaries who had spent much of their earthly lives trying to convert the natives of Mexico, Southern California, and Arizona to Christianity. Other spirits said they had been Indians who were the subjects of these conversion attempts. Mrs. Parent, an illiterate woman who had grown up in St. Louis, had no idea what they were talking about. But, she understood quite well when the spirits directed her to other caches of money buried or hidden here and there around their hometown of Redlands, California. Within 6 years, the Parents had found sufficient funds to purchase their first house and automobile.

The locations of the loot were only revealed to give the Parents the means to pursue the agenda of the missionaries. They told Violet that the natives had buried numerous crosses and other religious artifacts throughout the Southwest. The padres had decided to try and prove their continuing existence in the spirit world by directing people to the location of these crosses. This would be exactly what skeptics had been asking for since the first claim of Survival was made: <u>the spirits would reveal information that no one living knew or could have known</u>.

And reveal it they did, and not just once, or twice, or thrice, which ought to have been proof enough. Over a period of 10 years, the Parents were directed to more than 50 widely separated locations across a region 600-miles long by 300-miles wide. Once they arrived at the location specified they were directed to a particular hillside or streambed or other landmark and told what they should find buried there. Sometimes the search was fruitless; perhaps because someone had already discovered the treasures, perhaps due to heavy rains or earthquakes, or it could be that the Indians simply mis-remembered the location of a ceremony. But the quests were successful often enough to net more than 1,500 crosses and other sacred objects!

Yes, you read that right. Information that only people long dead could possibly know enabled living people to find real, solid, manmade items

FIFTEEN HUNDRED times! All this in addition to hundreds of finds of gold, silver, and paper money crammed into tins and bottles, or wrapped in oilskins or decaying leather pouches that had been carefully buried by the denizens of the desert and never retrieved.

At first, the Parents did not own a car, so they had to rely on neighbors and friends to chauffeur their excursions. Typically, Violet would direct the group to the designated site (often hundreds of miles from their home) and then the others would dig in the ground, chop at cactus, or pry up boulders as necessary to reveal and retrieve the crosses. Violet, being somewhat delicate and very fearful of rattlesnakes, did little digging herself. Numerous affidavits exist, signed by people who assisted on one or more of these expeditions, testifying that they found crosses precisely where the spirits predicted.

We know all of this because Gregory Parent kept detailed notes that ultimately filled 22 journals. He gave the dates and times of every excursion and he listed every item in every find. Most importantly for posterity, 5 years after his wife died, he wrote a letter to a man named Hamlin Garland.

Garland was a Pulitzer-prize winning author of over 50 books, mostly novels and biographies. Mr. Parent was likely attracted to him because his most recent book[57] was an account of his personal experiences as an investigator for the American Society for Psychical Research. Garland was intrigued enough by what he read in the letter to visit Parent at his apartment and view his journals and several pictures of the crosses. Parent wanted Garland to write a book about the discovery of the crosses. Garland liked the idea, but being busy with other matters, he did not attempt to contact Parent again for almost 2 years, by which time Parent had died.

It took several months, but Garland managed to track down and obtain the entire collection of crosses along with Gregory Parent's journals and papers. The names of many people who had assisted the Parents in

---

[57] Garland, *Forty Years*.

their searches were listed in the papers and Garland was able to locate fifteen of them — all of whom confirmed Parent's reports. As an example, in one interview a woman told Garland: "I myself picked up two containers for her — one from the sand on the seashore and one from the bed of a stream. To say that Violet had 'planted' these gold pieces and these wads of bills is absurd. She never had coins to plant, and furthermore, the rusted and rotted condition of these containers proved their long situation in the ground."

From these interviews and papers, Garland learned enough of the Parent's story to begin work on a book. From that book, appropriately titled *The Mystery of the Buried Crosses* and published in 1939, the facts and quotes given here are derived.

As for the artifacts themselves, Garland notes that they were stored in "seventeen flat, glass-covered boxes, each case numbered and the places of discovery carefully recorded." No other classification had been done, so Garland sorted them into three groups as follows.

▸ The first grouping contained 70 figures of Christ about 3 inches long with uplifted arms [presumably from, or intended for, crucifixes]. These were probably made some 200 years earlier in the area of New Spain that would become Mexico and given out to the Indians by the Spanish padres. Garland classified them as "missionary period" along with numerous crosses and small tablets stamped with dates (from 1769 to 1800) and the names of celebrated padres. These vary from 5 to 18 inches in length. According to the spirits, they were fashioned by artisans at the Mission of San Juan Capistrano.

▸ The second, and far larger, class contained crosses that impressed Garland as "wholly barbaric in character and immensely older" than the first group. The crosses (most single-barred but some double-barred) bore representations of various animals (such as wolves, apes, and birds), fruits, shells, etc. molded upon them. The figures were tribal totems and the crosses were paraphernalia for sun-worship ceremonies imported from Central America, according to the spirits.

> Garland's third category consisted of crosses and plaques that bore human faces. The character of these faces seemed distinctly Oriental rather than Aztec or Spanish. Some of the heads were crowned with turbans and others wore tall headdresses. Perhaps the most amazing aspect was that no two of these artifacts were alike. In fact, Garland noted, this collection "appeared to be the work of many hands and many minds, not to say generations."

Most of the crosses were of varying alloys of lead, tin, copper, antimony, iron, and aluminum. Some were of silver and a few were gold.

End Case 15

"This is huge," I asserted.

> "Yes."

"I mean really HUGE!

"Like, why haven't I heard of this before? Why hasn't everybody heard of this?"

> "So," he said, "you still have questions."

"Yeah, I've got questions. Where are the crosses now? What motivated the Parents to do all that work? Have others authenticated the crosses? Has anyone else ever found such crosses? Are there any left? There must be some still out there. Do you know any good mediums? I'll bring a metal detector. How soon can we go?

> "Whoa back!" he said. "I appreciate your enthusiasm and I'll answer your questions, but first I have a question for you: What difference would it make?"

"What difference would what make?"

> "The answers to any of the questions you just asked, or any questions that might be asked. What possible impact could they have on the level of proof for Survival provided by this case?"

> I was still pondering this when he spoke up and said: "Let's break down exactly why this case is so evidential. The claim is that something was found that could not possibly have been found without information held only by dead folk. This breaks down into two separate claims. The first is that something was found. How certain can we be of that?"

"Well, if the crosses were not discovered by the Parents, then they were already available to them. Is there any evidence of that?" I asked.

> "Not that I've been able to find."

"Then, are there any records of such crosses existing previously?"

> "Garland could find only two references to the native crosses — a single footnote in an obscure padre's journal quoting an explorer as saying that in 1604 (150 years before the establishment of the first mission) he had come upon a tribe that wore crosses in their hair,[58] and a picture in the *Handbook of the American Indian,* of a similar cross dug from a mound in Wisconsin.[59] Unknown to Garland, two similar crosses had been found in 1832 at an Indian grave-mound in Georgia and an additional eight crosses were unearthed in 1924 near Tucson Arizona."[60]

"So there is evidence that this kind of thing existed, but no one is known to have possessed a large collection of them."

> "That is correct. And," he continued, "that is why the crosses are so much more evidential than the money. As silly as it is to think that Violet Parent went all over Southern California planting gold and silver coins just so she could dig them up again, it is *possible* for her to have done so, because such coins were theoretically within her reach. This remote possibility would weaken the case slightly."

---

[58] Garland, *Buried Crosses*, p. 165.
[59] *Ibid*, p.36
[60] Steiger, pp. 41-47.

"I see your point," I said. "Violet could not have begged, borrowed, or stolen the crosses because the crosses simply were not available. And, if she didn't have them, she could not have planted them."

> "Which is why the large number of artifacts is important to the case. If only three crosses had been recovered, the charge that they had been planted by the Parents might carry some weight, even if all three had been found buried beneath a couple of feet of undisturbed ground (as many were). But 1,500 items negate any such possibility. One might just as well believe that they were all planted by Paul Bunyan with the magical assistance of Babe the Blue Ox."

"So the first claim has been satisfied," I said, "we are certain that something was found."

> "Now we consider if there is or was any way that the crosses could have been found other than by direction of the dearly departed."

I shook my head slowly, "The only half-way reasonable alternative I can think of is maybe God told her."

> "I'm generally reticent to guess God's reasons for anything," he said, "but I can't imagine why He would need to pose as dead padres and spread lies about the afterlife."

"Good point. — Well, there's always the worm cam."

> "Or Violet was adept at traveling the desert in her astral body. Only one problem with either of those conjectures: How did she know where to look? Maybe, just maybe, I could accept that Violet's wandering soul somehow happened to stumble upon one of the crosses …"

"I like the image of a stumbling soul," I grinned.

"But to find them over and over again throughout an area of some 200,000 square miles? Never. ... The most super super-psi imaginable couldn't account for that. No. The only conceivable way anyone could consistently locate all those crosses is to be given directions by the persons who hid them."

"It all adds up to an extraordinarily solid proof of Survival," I said. "The only thing it lacks is replicability. Someone needs to repeat what the Parents did and find more crosses. I suggest we do that now." I stood up and stretched.

"I suggest you keep reading," he said.

I sat down, turned the page, and read.

Case 16 – Relics Revealed Revisited

When Hamlin Garland received the letter from Gregory Parent, he had just published *Forty Years of Psychic Research*, a book he felt was the final summation of his work as an investigator of the paranormal. But the letter, and the journals, papers, and artifacts he subsequently discovered, brought an unexpected and astounding capstone to his avocation. Indeed, what Garland titled "The Mystery of the Buried Crosses" would prove to be one of the most convincing, if not *the* most convincing, arguments for the survival of human consciousness after physical death.

Once he had read Parent's journals and gazed upon the 1,500 crosses with his own eyes, Garland knew that he had been handed a case of supreme importance. He also knew that the case needed to be verified by an independent researcher duplicating the feat of finding such items buried in the California desert. Despite being 76 years old, Garland realized that this task had fallen on his shoulders.

His first step was to find a medium who could contact the spirits of Gregory or Violet Parent or of the missionaries themselves. As he was considering who might be best suited for the job, Garland received a letter from a Dr. Nora Rager in Chicago who had read *Forty Years of Psychical*

Research and wished to introduce him to a medium named Sophia Williams, who had recently moved to Los Angeles. Garland interviewed Williams and found her perfect for the job. She was friendly, could work anywhere (indoors or out), anytime (day or night), was anxious to help, and made no charge for her services. As Garland writes: "It was in this providential way that I found myself in possession of a most intelligent co-investigator."[61]

In her very first session, Williams immediately became a conduit for several of Garland's deceased friends. One of whom, Henry Fuller, often acted as a control in the coming sessions. But it wasn't just the obvious acquaintances of Garland who spoke through Williams in that first session; spirits that he hardly remembered showed up, and at least one fellow that he didn't know at all. The latter identified himself as Harry Friedlander, a recently deceased friend of the stenographer whom Garland had hired to take notes of the session. Williams had never met the stenographer nor did she know he would attend the session. Friedlander accurately described his recent death in an airplane accident. Garland refers to this performance by Williams as "our first evidence of her power." There would be a lot more.

At their third sitting, on March 17, 1937, the spirit of Violet Parent spoke through the medium. She affirmed that there were more crosses to be found and she promised the aid of the padres in finding them. As the sessions continued, many of the missionaries did come through, plus several early explorers of the American Southwest.

Besides the veridical material received through Sophia Williams, there came some interesting, and reassuring, insights into the afterlife. One of the padres noted: "We have all changed our opinions about many things — not only about the Indians, but about religion. We learn the truth on this side. ... We have found now that there is no difference in creed."

---

[61] Garland, *Buried Crosses*, p. 49.

All that Garland and company managed to get from their first few expeditions were good lessons in how hot the desert could get, how steep the hills, how hard the ground, and how prickly the cactus that seemed to grow everywhere. Then on the 15th of May, 1937, while digging as instructed near the roots of an ancient oak tree some 75 miles northeast of Los Angeles, Garland's daughter, Constance, struck a cross.

Greatly inspired by this first find, Garland *et al* took every opportunity to make the lengthy excursions prescribed by the spirits. The story of the successes and failures of these trips is well told in Garland's book. Suffice it to say here that a total of 16 crosses were discovered in widely scattered and generally difficult-to-reach locations.

And so, the "research" of the Parents was duplicated and authenticated. People with no connection to the Parents, once again, have been able to find something that could not have been consistently found without information held only by the supposedly dead.

End Case 16

> "Do you still want to go searching for crosses?"

"It sounds like it would be fun," I replied. "Although, by now, most of the remaining ones are probably entombed in the foundations of condominiums and strip malls."

> "So, did your questions get answered?"

"The more I learn, the more I want to know. I intend to read that book and get the full story. But I still want to know where the crosses are now."

> "Garland's granddaughter inherited[62] those that he and Williams found and she donated them to the West Salem Historical Society. This organization is housed in the Garland homestead in the

---

[62] Garland died within a year after he completed his book on the crosses; he was 79.

town of West Salem in the county of, believe it or not, *La Crosse*, Wisconsin.[63]

"As for the original 1,500 unearthed by the Parents, Garland donated them to a California museum, but no one seems to be sure what happened to them after that."

"So we've got the 16 crosses Garland found, but we have only his word that the 1,500 others ever existed?

"The word of a highly respected man with an impeccable reputation. It is simply inconceivable that he would choose to crown his career with a fraud. And then, of course, there are the photographs."

"There are pictures?"

"Oh yes. among the numerous illustrations in Garland's book are 10 photographs of crosses and other items from the Parent's original collection."[64]

Note added for 2015 revision of this book: Up until 2011, all we have had of the relics are the few photographs published in his book and those kept by the West Salem Historical Society in Wisconsin. In December 2011, Michael E. Tymn informed Bill Stoney that their mutual friend, Lisette Coly — head of the Parapsychology Foundation and granddaughter of its founder, Eileen Garrett — had told him of a new find. While going through some boxes long stored in her basement, she had discovered a box that contained 23 of the missing artifacts (21 cross-shaped and 2 lettered plates). The box also contained a letter of transmittal from the son of Garland's publisher, that establishes that these were from Garland. Handwritten notes and tags on several of the artifacts give the date when they were

---

[63] So named by French explorers when they saw Winnebago Indians on the prairie playing a game similar to the French game of lacrosse.
[64] Keith Newlin displays a couple of these photos at: http://www.uncw.edu/garland/gallery/garframe.htm

found, showing that they were some of the originals collected by the Parents. Pictures taken by Stoney of these artifacts may be seen at www.survivaltop40.com.

"Didn't you say something about the medium in this case using a trumpet or megaphone?"

> "The way in which spirits spoke through Sophia Williams is a fascinating and evidential story unto itself," he replied. "So fascinating that I didn't mention it in the cases of the crosses because I thought it would distract from the key point that information known only to the dead was being revealed."

"Now that I have found the evidence truly convincing, can you tell me the rest of the story?"

> "Sure can. Voices from the other side could be heard in Sophia Williams' presence as high-pitched, but clear, whispers. Sometimes they seemed to emanate from her chest, sometimes from nearby objects, and sometimes from the empty air above her head, but the spirits did not use her vocal chords or tongue. This was well demonstrated on numerous occasions when researchers held their hands over her mouth or taped it shut while the voices continued unabated."

"Do you mean that Garland and his stenographer and whomever had to sit very close to Williams to hear these voices?"

> "At first they did. This is where the trumpet was utilized. They found that they could hear best when Williams held the large end to her chest and Garland listened at the small end, as if using a stethoscope to hear the voices. Then Garland got the idea that he might be able to use a microphone and amplifier to better hear the voices. He shopped around and found an early version of an intercom that consisted of two boxes connected with 60 feet of wire. This mechanism allowed him to sit in his study and listen to the voices emanating from the medium sitting several rooms away. Thus amplified, the

spirits could be heard clearly by anyone in the room. What made this set-up so convincing was that the conversations flowed smoothly between the spirits and Garland even though the transmission was one way. Williams could not hear Garland unless he depressed a button on his end of the intercom."

"Let me get this picture perfectly clear," I said. "Garland and, I would assume, one or two of his friends and family, are sitting in a room in his house listening to voices coming from this newfangled gizmo. The voices answer some question of Garland's and then he presses a button on the ..."

"Nope," he interrupted, "he never pressed the button unless he wanted to talk with the medium herself. Williams could not hear Garland's questions or commentary to the spirits."

"So, in order to carry on an intelligible conversation, the spirits of the padres and whomever must have been able to hear Garland directly. They then replied via the medium in another room. That is most unusual, indeed, and most impressive! Was she alone?" I asked.

"Most of the time, Garland's wife or some other person sat with Williams. None of them ever heard the voices while the spirits spoke to Garland through the intercom."

"What was Williams doing while all this communicating was going on?"

"Often she would sit and read a book or magazine."

I wondered: "Did she have to hold the transmitter to her chest?"

"No. Sometimes she held it in her lap, but it seemed to work just as well sitting on a table beside her."

"Could she hear the voices then?"

"At times she heard a few voices, but she believed that the spirits were teaching themselves to use the transmitter directly."

"I can see why you didn't include this information in your cases," I said. "A unique ability such as that would indeed have been a distraction from the already amazing proof of the crosses."

"Unusual, yes, but not unique," he said, and gestured once again towards the manual.

Case 17 – The Ghosts in the Machines

The interaction of departed spirits with electronic equipment was first suspected almost immediately after the invention of electronic equipment. Thomas Edison revealed in 1920 that he was developing equipment to communicate with the spirit world.[65]

If Edison ever accomplished that trick, he chose not to share his contraption with the world at large. Nevertheless, there have been a few successful attempts to augment man's natural ability with electronic devices. One of these was Hamlin Garland's success in using an intercom-like device to amplify the direct voices of medium Sophia Williams. Most of the attempts have involved trying to capture voices of the deceased on magnetic audio tape. More recently, some experimenters have tried for voices and/or pictures using videotape and TVs — as sensationaized in the 2005 movie *White Noise*.

The field has long been referred to as "EVP" (standing for Electronic Voice Phenomena) although recently the acronym ITC (for Instrumental TransCommunication) is often preferred. In 1956, the first voices from unknown sources were recorded by Attila von Szalay. Psychical investigators D. Scott Rogo and Raymond Bayless, among others, worked with Szalay and agreed that the voices seem to have a paranormal source. It must be noted that Szalay previously had exhibited mediumistic talents.[66] Soon thereafter, a filmmaker named Friedrich Jügenson heard human voices while playing back some bird songs he had recorded. He ultimately wrote

---

[65] See the October 1920 issue of *Scientific American* magazine.
[66] Estep, p. 14.

two books on the subject, one of which was read by Konstantin Raudive, a Latvian psychologist. Raudive went on to tape over 70,000 voices he considered to be of paranormal origin and wrote his own book, *Breakthrough*, which was translated into English in 1971. Since then, tens of thousands of people have taken up the pursuit of spirit voices. One of many organizations for practitioners and interested parties, the American Association - Electronic Voice Phenomena, was established in 1982 by Sarah Estep, author of the book *Voices of Eternity*.

The process of taping these other-worldly comments consists of turning on a tape recorder, asking a question, allowing the tape to run for a few moments and then rewinding the tape and playing it to see if any voices have been recorded other than your own.

Most of the communications recorded on tape are notable for their brevity, as if each word spoken required a great expenditure of energy. Aside from their presumed origin, they tend to be rather trivial. In the opinion of several critics who have looked into the matter, most of the messages are more the product of a mind that strongly desires to hear voices amongst a background of static than they are of discarnate personalities. This is probably an accurate appraisal. But then there are those pesky exceptions.

The most impressive contemporary example of communications with the other side that are enabled/facilitated by electronic instrumentation is the Spiricom.[67] This box of transistors, resistors, and other-istors was developed by George Meek, William O'Neill, George Mueller, and "Doc Nick." Meek was an engineer whose many patents, mostly in the field of air treatment, generated sufficient income for him to retire at the age of 60 and devote his life and fortune to psychical research. O'Neill was an electronic technician who seemed able to see and hear dead people. Mueller held a Ph.D. in experimental physics from Cornell University. Doc Nick

---

[67] Meek, "Spiricom"; Fuller, *Ghost*.

was a medical doctor and ham-radio operator. At the time they participated in the development of the Spiricom, both Mueller and Nick had been dead for several years.

Rather than rely on deciphering static or "white noise," the Spiricom generates 13 tones that the spirits can manipulate to create the sounds of human language. After much tinkering and many false starts, the team achieved the first real-time, recordable dialog between living and deceased on the 27th of October, 1977. In this breakthrough exchange, the spirit calling himself Doc Nick makes about 15 statements, a couple of which are unintelligible and all of which sound as if he is talking from the bottom of a copper cavern. By the time Meek made his public announcement in 1982, the quality of the voices had been improved significantly; they still sounded metallic and the hum of the overtones was still bothersome, but most everyone could understand the voices upon hearing the tapes but once.

As for verifiable material, the spirit of Mueller provided specifics about his background and education, even his social security number! Furthermore, he gave Meek two unlisted telephone numbers that proved to be for the persons he identified — persons who were exceedingly interested to know how Meek had obtained their "classified" numbers. Here's an excerpt from a tape of a Spiricom-enabled conversation in which the spirit of Mueller asks about a book that he had written in 1947 entitled *Introduction to Electronics*. Earlier, Mueller had suggested that the team refer to a copy of this book.

Mueller: Did you obtain that book of mine yet?

O'Neil: Oh, that book of yours. No sir. By the way, our friend Mr. Meek is really going all out to find that because I want to read those two pages you mentioned.

Mueller: Very well. And I want you to read that, William. There must be copies available somewhere.

O'Neil: Well, I think George, that's Mr. Meek, our friend.

Mueller: *Your* friend.

O'Neil: Yes. Even if he has to go to the Library of Congress. He'll probably do that.

Mueller: Oh, I see. Oh, all right.

Meek later reported: "No, even the Library of Congress does not have a copy. However, I eventually located the book in the archives of the State Historical Society of Wisconsin, Dr. Mueller's native state."

Several voice analyses were done on the tapes. They all showed that the voices of O'Neil and Mueller were of quite different origin.

Doc Nick stopped speaking to O'Neil soon after his voice was caught on tape. After participating in over 30 hours of taped conversations George Mueller ceased to come through. (He had warned the researchers a couple of times that he would not be able to stay with them forever.) O'Neil passed on in 1995, Meek in the winter of '99.

Although Meek had made his fortune with patents, he refused to apply for one on the Spiricom, choosing instead to offer the plans to anyone who wished to replicate his work. It became clear, however, that the Spiricom was an instrument attuned to the unique energies of O'Neil, Nick, and Mueller; it never worked for anyone else on either side of the great divide. Nevertheless, others have had moderate success with different instrumentation and many continue to labor in the ITC field.[68]

End Case 17

This is the cherry atop the whipped cream on top of the icing on the cake," I commented. "Hardly necessary, but always nice to have more proof of Survival."

"You don't think it could be a hoax?" he asked.

"Well, fraud is theoretically possible, but I can't imagine a motive. Certainly it wasn't for the money. On the other hand, I can't entirely rule

---

[68] See Mark Macy's website: http://www.world itc.org/

out the idea that someone on the outside was playing tricks on the researchers."

"There's a motive problem with that, too," he pointed out. "Why would someone spend months collecting personal data about this Mueller fellow, including his Social Security number, two unlisted telephone numbers he knew, and the fact that he was the author of a most obscure training manual, and then spend more months staying up until the wee hours of the morning carefully doling out bits and pieces of information via super ESP?"

"I can't imagine a motive for such an effort, but why are we talking ESP?" I asked. "Wouldn't some sort of radio transmission have done the job?"

"No. Most of the verifiable information on Mueller was given directly, during the development stage of the Spiricom. At that time, O'Neil could 'hear' Mueller's voice only in his mind; it was not coming through on speakers and did not register on tape. Most of the post-Spiricom, taped conversations — although astounding — are rather tedious, consisting of about what you'd expect from two engineers fine-tuning a piece of equipment.

"All of which strengthens the case, for it would have been sensible — and, no doubt, irresistible — for a charlatan to have put the telephone numbers and such on the tapes."

"Do you think anyone will ever invent an inter-dimensional communicator that works without the need for a human medium?"

"Let's hope not."

I gave him a questioning look.

"Would you really want a spirit telephone sitting beside your living-room couch?" he asked. "Sure it would be cool to call up Helen of Troy and ask if she really loved Paris in the springtime. Or, you could give Professor Einstein a ring when you're having relative trouble. And, wouldn't it be nice to ask Mr. Capone where he stashed his loot?

"But most of us felt guilty that we didn't call mom or grandma often enough when they just lived across town; imagine the burden of knowing that every long-dead great uncle and great-great-grandfather is hoping you'll take a moment to talk!"

"I hadn't really thought of it quite … "

"And don't forget," he went on, "telephones work both ways. Tired of getting calls from living people who want your money or your patronage? Just wait until every spirit with a debt to settle or an axe to grind starts ringing you up a 3 a.m."

Well, I … "

"Have you ever told an obnoxious caller to go to hell? That won't help anymore — they'll just call from there!"

Somewhat overwhelmed by such an idea, I managed to say only: "It's going to take a while for me to absorb all this."

"While your mind is doing its thing, let's go get something for our tummies to absorb," he suggested. "I thought we'd take a ride up to the Panorama, its not too far and the food is almost as good as the view."

I quickly agreed and closed the manual for the day.

As we drove, we got onto the subject of mistakes — why mediums or spirits make mistakes and what that means for the evidential value of their testimony. I didn't record that conversation, but later I wrote a brief paper on the subject that includes much of what we discussed plus a couple of points I thought of later. It seems appropriate to insert that document next in place of our rather mundane dinner conversation.

Saturday Supper Substitute
Inhuman Perfection?

Oh, if I could only leave you the proof that I continue. ... I am trying, amid unspeakable difficulties. ... The nearest simile I can find to express the difficulty of sending a message is that I appear to be standing behind a sheet of frosted glass, which blurs sight and deadens sound, dictating feebly to a reluctant and somewhat obtuse secretary.
— The spirit of F.W.H. Myers[69]

When a medium gets no message, or when a message seems inaccurate, in whole or in part, critics often claim that these "failures" taint all the evidence and, therefore, nothing has been proven. Such a view is both unfair and unreasonable.

There are at least four and often five or more parties involved in a mediumistic communication. Let's consider them one at a time, beginning with the "control."

The Control

Not all mediums (and I include channelers in this term) have an obvious control and some controls claim to be extensions of the medium's subconscious, but most mediums who go into a trance during a sitting seem to be taken over by a discarnate entity who claims to be an independent person — a human much like you and I, who just happens to be dead. The truth probably lies somewhere in between; one possibility being that the control personality is an *ad hoc* amalgam of the medium's brain and one or more spirit minds.

Now, the process of dying may be somewhat enlightening, but it can also be frightening and confusing. We have no evidence that dying

---

[69] *Proceedings of the Society of Psychical Research*, vol. xxi. p. 230.

changes one's personality or intellect. It doesn't make you nicer and it doesn't make you smarter. It doesn't make you more honest, or less prone to exaggeration, or less hungry for adulation. And it most certainly doesn't make you omnipotent or incapable of making mistakes.

All human beings make mistakes, including me. I've been known to say 'west' when I meant 'east,' thus causing folks to waste a lot of time driving in the wrong direction. I've even been known to call my good friend "Dave" when his name is "Joe." I've written the wrong total on a deposit slip, purchased the wrong brand of soap, and sometimes I have no idea where I parked my car. Chances are that you, being human, have made similar mistakes. All people do. And being dead doesn't change that.

Likewise, dying doesn't expunge the natural human tendencies to exaggerate a little to make a better impression and to fill in story gaps with a bit of fabrication. Much fuss has been made over one of Piper's controls providing messages from a persona named "Bessie Beals" — a name invented by the sitter as a test. Even though the control admitted making a mistake, some critics act as if this one incident somehow negates the three decades of solid proof provided by Piper's various controls. To me, such a display of "human" frailty only adds to the authenticity of the process.

Thus, it is neither surprising nor calamitous to occasionally catch a control being less than honest or less than perfect.

The Contacts

What is characteristic of a control is even more true of the contacts (the souls that are being contacted during the sitting). In most cases, these people are fairly new to the spirit condition. Often, they were not expecting to die and many are surprised to find themselves still aware. They will likely be more enthusiastic than the control about the prospect of speaking to a loved one who is still "in body." All this leads to uncertainty, confusion, and agitation, a sure recipe for blunders in communication.

For both controls and contacts, the way in which they gather information must also be taken into account, particularly when asked to monitor someone who is living (as in "What is so-and-so doing now?"). One of the more common mistakes spirits make is the mis-identification of country or other geographic demarcation — confusing America with Australia, for instance. But how does one identify a country? As I sit writing this, I look out my office window and see no indication of what country or state I am in. The clouds do not spell out "U.S.A.," the street below is not stamped boldly with "Pennsylvania." To a spirit drawn to a person by name, and looking around in that person's vicinity, parts of America look very like parts of Australia. Given time to search about, a higher accuracy might be attainable, but in the rapid fire Q-and-A characteristic of many sittings, a few geographical mix-ups are to be expected.

Another troublesome area for spirits seems to be time frame. On numerous occasions, spirits asked to report on an earthbound person's activities will provide a lengthy and detailed report that is absolutely wrong for the time specified but absolutely correct for another time (such as an hour earlier or the day before). On the one hand, I don't suppose we should be surprised if time doesn't run quite the same way in the next world as it does in this one. On the other hand, the problem could well lie, once again, in the way in which information is obtained. If a spirit knows what we are doing by tapping into our mental pictures of the action, this sort of chronological displacement would be expected. After all, we don't time-stamp our memories.

Historical time can also be problematic. Sometimes the only way to tell what year it is, or even what century, is by asking about historical events. But occasionally even this approach fails. Marge Rieder reports that once, when she instructed a patient "to go back in time to the Civil War, the patient immediately began describing a lifetime during the French Revolution."[70]

---

[70] Rieder, *Mission*, p. xvii.

A third type of information that spirits often have trouble communicating is persons' names. Often mediums receive a name in bits and pieces, perhaps an initial and then some symbol. The process reminds me very much of a game of charades. The name "Rose" is fairly easy to symbolize, but "Robert" or "Jerry" is a much greater challenge. For those mediums who receive much of their information via pictures, symbols, gestures, and other such impressions, some difficulty with names is to be expected.

Also, spirits sometimes confuse the living and the dead, an error likewise made by some during NDEs. Critics often reject cases solely because a claim is made that the spirit of a living person was seen along with the spirits of those who have crossed over. What these critics seem to forget is that the differences we so easily note between the corporeal and the astral may not be nearly so apparent when viewed from the other side. To a spirit, all people may appear as light forms, with only minor details to distinguish whether they still reside in the flesh or not. NDErs and others who are new to the game should be excused if they sometimes miss those details.

Difficulties are not limited to knowledge of other people and foreign places. It is perfectly natural for all people, living and dead, to forget even those personal things that others remember well. Sir Oliver Lodge recounts a most revealing incident along these lines. He once asked his children to play a game in which they were to pretend that he had died and that a medium claimed to be in touch with his spirit. The children were to test the spirit by asking questions that their father should be able to answer. But when the children asked their questions, Lodge found that he and they had totally different ideas of what incidents were significant in his life. He could not answer a single one of their questions. Finally he exclaimed in mock despair: "That settles it. I am not your father!"[71]

---

[71] Spraggett, *Arthur Ford*, p. 94.

The Medium

Now we consider the person whose body is clearly essential to the process. But the mind of the medium also seems to play a role. Even when in trance, some sort of translation process is occurring that is more or less dependent upon the medium's vocabulary and memories. This allows some room for error. Those mediums who remain awake and aware throughout the process are even more subject to making natural human mistakes in translating the symbols and feelings they receive into understandable sentences. They also must ignore the biases and assumptions of their conscious mind and are more subject to distractions and false feedback from others in the room, both in body and in spirit.

The Recorder

These days, the more scientific and evidential attempts at spirit communication are video-recorded, but many of the greatest mediums of the past were recorded only when someone in attendance was handed a pad and pencil and asked to take notes. We are safe in assuming that such folks were rarely perfect in their transcriptions. Being like the rest of us, a recorder would tend to hear what he or she expected. Some of their mistakes must have resulted in hits being counted as misses; although, to be fair, some misses were likely counted as hits.

The Sitter

And finally, we consider the person who has come for a reading by the medium. They too are subject, of course, to all the human frailties mentioned above. In addition to such, there is the problem of non-correction. Over and over, the scholar comes across cases wherein a sitter claims some information to be wrong and then later recants because they remember a forgotten person or are corrected as to a falsely held belief (*i.e.* grandma says that the house actually *was* blue, or Jim really did go to Michigan not Michigan State, or there *was* a sister who died at birth, or some such thing). Often, these corrections are not made until days or months after the reading took place. Knowing the human disposition toward laziness and forgetfulness, one can safely assume that many corrections that ought to be made never happen; thus, leaving false "mistakes" on the record.

Some skeptics might claim that this distortion of results is counterbalanced by the sitter's natural inclination to accept statements that are ambiguous. No doubt it is true that, in general commerce, sitters tend to be gullible, that they provide too much information to the medium and are too ready to count vague responses as solid hits. But in the cases that qualify for our consideration, the opposite is true. Researchers and sitters today and their fellows who investigated the great mediums of prior centuries were and are, on the whole, extremely suspicious and dubious. Today's scoring methods are clearly unfavorable to the mediums, yet the results still indicate communication from the deceased.

Thus, we must realize that all humans make mistakes and that the process of dying does not involve being sprayed with perfect juice. Errors in readings can hardly be avoided. In fact, too many mistake-free readings would be good cause for suspicion of fakery.

Faking It

Speaking of fakery, it should be pointed out that an occasional deceit is just as human as an occasional mistake. It is hardly surprising, then, to discover that mediums are not necessarily always perfectly honest.

A medium with a reputation to uphold is under a lot of pressure to perform consistently. Yet the mechanisms of their performance are just as mysterious to them as to their audience. Mediums are totally dependent on forces and spirits beyond their control. What job could be more stressful? The temptation is strong to do a bit of research so that a few facts will be available in case the spirits fail to deliver. Some mediums, being human, have succumbed to this temptation.

The famous medium Arthur Ford, for example, was discovered to possess a suitcase of news clippings that may have helped him in his "readings" of well-known people. But this discovery does not reduce the evidential value of Ford's many impressive performances under conditions that obviated the possibility of prior research.[72]

For this reason, any evidence of research should remove from consideration whatever could conceivably be obtained from research, but should not affect the evidentiary value of information impossible to obtain via research.

Non-Contact

Even getting some misinformation is preferable to getting no information at all. Sometimes a medium is criticized, even castigated, for being unable to contact the sought after spirit. Often the medium is not to blame. There are several possible reasons, quite beyond human control, for a failure to reach the other side. A spirit may have already returned to a physical body or may have advanced to levels beyond the reach of the medium. A spirit may not want to spoil your fun, relieve the suspense, or whatever. And, just because one is a spirit, doesn't necessarily mean one has an interest in talking to the living. As the psychoanalyst Nandor Fodor has opined: "Frankly, I don't think the dead care too much about us, for the simple reason that we are not too upset about the troubles of kindergarten children. ... It would be much more important and interesting, surely, to explore the possibilities of the after-death state than to worry about the possibilities of the life left behind."[73]

---

[72] See, for example, the sitting in Upton Sinclair's home (Spraggett, *Arthur Ford*, pp. 227-230).
[73] Spraggett, *Unexplained*, p.199

Saturday Night
How This Could Be

This room and all the atmosphere around you right now is full of people and full of voices — but until you turn on the TV you can't see and hear them, can you? Well, that's the way we are. It's just another dimension, another wavelength, so to speak.

— Fletcher[74]

The night was clear but warmer when we got back to the cabin so, after letting Dasher out for a twilight run, we forswore the fireplace for the fireflies and went back to our chairs on the long, narrow screened porch.

"I was thinking last evening that this really is almost heaven," I said, as I settled back and patted my too full belly.

"I reckon you mean West Virginia," he smiled, "but you'd be correct no matter where you were on earth."

"Say again?"

"It's like surfing the Web," he continued, "no matter where you are you're only one screen away from where you want to be. You just have to know what keys to punch."

"So, heaven is just a click away?"

"Different picture, same monitor.

"In Garland's last book, there is a succinct statement by the discarnate Father Espejo: 'I am not from afar, I am *here*. I am not of the sixteenth century, I am *now*.'[75]

---

[74] Spraggett, *Arthur Ford*, p. 59.
[75] Garland, *Buried Crosses*, p. 193.

"Heaven, it would seem, is the same place everything is."

"How can that be? Does this have something to do with quantum physics?"

"'Quantum' is a term used — much as 'magnetic' and 'electric' were used a century or so ago — by writers who'd like to believe that the science of the day supports their metaphysical doctrines; but, I wouldn't put much stock in such claims. In the entire world, there might be a score of folks who have a real grasp of quantum physics — and they rarely agree with one another."

"That reminds me of something I once read by the guy who headed the Fermi accelerator," I said. It went something like: 'We are drowning in theoretical possibilities not based on a single solitary fact.'"[76]

"Yes, and there is an unfortunate tendency for advocates to adopt the latest theoretical possibility as an 'explanation' of their pet concept, while ignoring the lack of factual evidence. If some fellow tells you that ghosts or some such phenomena can be explained by 11-dimensional-string theory, you'd best assume that fellow hasn't the slightest idea what he's talking about."

"So what's your explanation?" I asked.

"I don't pretend to explain anything. I rather doubt that anyone is capable of understanding the real truth. Although we hate to admit it, all the mechanisms of the universe are not necessarily amenable to human language, or even to human thought.

"Did you know that belief in psychic phenomena is greater among the better educated?"[77]

---

[76] Nobel winner Leon Lederman, Ph.D., quoted in *The Washington Post* article "Physicists Plan World's Largest Atomic Machine" by Philip J. Hilts, 16 August 1983, p. A4, col. 1. He was arguing for the expenditure of a stupendous amount of money to construct a new accelerator that might reveal some of those missing facts.

[77] Schmicker, p. 18.

I replied that I was unaware of this fact.

> "It's true. And perhaps the reason is that a better informed person can better comprehend the existence of unknowable things.
>
> "Nevertheless, without some rationale, the evidence for Survival is more difficult to accept. So, if you wish, I can offer a few concepts that might help you understand how it is possible for heaven and earth, and hell also, to exist in the same here and now."

I gave him a "go-right-ahead" motion.

> "Let's start with the seemingly unscientific idea of magic mirrors."

"You mean as in 'Who's the fairest of them all?'?"

> "The use of mirrors to contact spirits has, indeed, been practiced since before Snow White's time. And, by the way, is still being practiced productively today.[78] But mirrors are magical in a more basic way, for they help us to comprehend the concept of all-in-one. Consider this one here."

"I wondered why that was there." It was a cheaply framed full-length mirror such as you might buy at a discount store. He had mounted it on the cedar siding just outside the door to the porch. "Is that a magic one?"

> "As magical as any," he replied. "Look into it and tell me what you see."

I turned and looked into the mirror at the darkening forest: "Just a few trees. Guess I'm not adept at reading mirrors."

> Unperturbed, he asked: "Can you see the tree with the broken limb hanging to the ground."

"Not in the mirror," I said, although I could easily see such a tree off to my other side.

---

[78] See Moody, *Reunions*.

"I can see it quite clearly," he stated, as he stared into the mirror.

"Of course you can; you're at a different angle than I."

"Can you see the entire height of the screen, from floor to ceiling."

"Just barely."

He got up and retrieved a large piece of cardboard that had been cut from a shipping box and leaned it against the mirror, covering the lower half. "Now can you still see the entire screen?"

"No."

"That's strange; I can."

"Okay. I get the point.

"What you can see in a mirror depends on your angle of view. At any given time, there are an uncountable number of views available in that single mirror."

"Correct. And?"

"And, how much you can see in a mirror depends on how close you are."

"What if I were to break the mirror into a dozen pieces and hand you a single fragment? What could you see in that?'

"Well, if I held it close to my eye," I said, demonstrating with the flat of my hand, "I guess I could see most everything."

"Suppose you dropped that piece and it broke into a dozen smaller pieces?"

"I'd have to hold one closer, but I could still see the entire scene within it."

"So the entire scene that you first saw in the whole mirror is actually available in each piece or part of the mirror."

"Yes, I never thought of it before, but mirrors are like 2-dimensional versions of holograms. Or maybe I should say a hologram is like a mirror frozen in time. Wasn't there a book about that?"

> "Yes, by Michael Talbot.[79] You should consider reading it.
>
> "So, could it be that our universe is similar to a mirror or a hologram in that all information exists everywhere and what we experience depends solely on our 'point of view'?"

"I don't know, I guess that helps me accept the possibility of multiple universes all in the here and now, but it doesn't give me much sense of why I'm usually aware of only one of them."

> "For that, we leave the ancient art of mirror gazing and the advanced science of holography for the more conventional technology of the telephone."

"Aha," I interjected, "a telephone between worlds."

> "That, by the way, is actually the title of another interesting little book,[80] but one that's irrelevant to my point."

"Which is?"

> "Which is multiplexing.
>
> "You might be too young to remember having to make sure that none of your neighbors were talking on the 'party line' before you could make a telephone call."

"I was a mere babe, but I remember. You could never be certain that no one was listening to your conversations."

> "In my neighborhood," he sighed, "you usually could be certain someone *was* listening.
>
> "Do you recall how you could tell that a call was for your family?"

---

[79] Talbot,.*Holographic Universe*.
[80] Crenshaw *Telephone*.

"The rings were different, weren't they?"

"Right. Calls to one house might be indicated by two short rings separated by a pause. Calls to the house next door, by one long and then one short ring, and so on. A simple code that allowed multiple users to share one copper wire. A very basic form of multiplexing.

"As telephone equipment became more sophisticated, more advanced forms of multiplexing were developed to allow the limited number of lines between cities to handle a growing number of long-distance calls. What happens is that equipment at both ends of the long-distance lines chops several calls into little coded snippets that are interspersed among the bits of other signals and then sent through shared circuits in rapid-fire sequence. At the other end, the pieces are sorted out, reassembled and sent on as complete conversations. The pulses come so quickly that your brain cannot detect the gaps between them and so the transmission sounds smooth and seamless."

"Cool enough, but what does that have to do ... "

"If, as some spirits claim, the universe blinks, then it could very well be multiplexed. Myriad, totally different and separate worlds or planes could then all co-exist in the same space."

"The universe blinks?"

"On and off, on and off."

"Uh, where does it go when it's off?"

"When it's off, the idea of 'where' is likewise off."

"You mean it no longer exists at all?"

"Think about a strip of motion-picture film. When it is run through a projector, one frame is shown by shining a bright light through it. Then a shutter closes, blocking the light while the film is advanced to the next frame. The shutter opens allowing the light to project the next image and then the process is repeated. At 30 cycles per second, our brains interpret this rush of images as seamless movement. Now, where do the movie characters go between frames?"

"There's no answer to that," I said, "they don't 'go' anywhere because they don't exist between the frames."

"Back when I went to the movies a lot, there was only one theater per building, but now it seems most movie houses are complexes."

"It's more efficient to have only one ticket booth and lobby and such serve multiple theaters," I pointed out.

"Let's carry that idea a bit further and have one projector serve two theaters."

"And how might that be accomplished?"

"Simply by interspersing one movie, every other frame, among another movie. Then, speed up the projector so that it is showing 60 frames per second instead of 30. Use a rotating mirror synchronized to the projector to direct the frames belonging to one movie into one theater and the frames belonging to the other movie into the other theater."

"That would probably work," I commented, "although it doesn't seem very efficient, and both movies would then have to begin and end at the same time, and the audio track would be tough to handle."

"Well, no analogy is perfect," he shrugged. "The important point is that it doesn't matter how much distance there is between frames. There could be one movie interspersed, or a dozen. As long as the film, the projector, and our brains are synchronized, the illusion of reality is maintained.

"In the same way, there could be many universes blinking into and out of existence in sequence. Our senses would detect only that universe with which we were synchronized. We wouldn't normally notice the blinking. A million or more other universes could come into existence and vanish again with each blink and we might be no more aware of them than the characters in one film would be aware of the characters in another, interspersed, film."

"So, you're saying that the universe is multiplexed and ..."

"I'm saying it is *possible*. It would help explain a lot of strange phenomena, especially if our minds and souls were more or less constant."

"You mean that souls don't blink?"

"Again, it would explain much if various aspects of ourselves blinked at different rates. Our brains, being part of the physical universe, would, of course, blink at the same rate as the physical universe. But our minds might be synched with both the physical universe and a mental universe. This could explain where we are when we are dreaming. Then our astral bodies could be synched to blink with the physical, the mental, and the astral universe; thereby spanning all three. And so on, up the pyramid to the Godhead."

"So then, God would be the universal constant; the part that doesn't blink."

"Yep. I reckon you could say that God is always 'on.'"

"That would make a great T-shirt.

"I wonder if there is any way that such a hypothesis could be proved or disproved."

"None that I can think of, although there are numerous reports of anomalous events that could be explained much easier by reference to multiplexing."

"You mean like the folks who claim that they were miraculously transported across an intersection, thus saving them from a collision that was imminent an instant before?"

"Yes, or the many cases of 'missing time' in which people discover that several minutes or hours have passed that they were not aware of."

"Well, whether it explains hiccups in either time or space, I like your analogy."

"Thanks," he smiled, "but most of the credit goes to others."[81]

"The only complaint I have is that 'blinks' sounds like something has been shorted out."

"Would you prefer 'flickers'?"

"That's even worse." I thought for a moment and then my eyes lifted to the star-filled sky and I suddenly knew just the term. "How about 'twinkles'?"

He saw where I was looking and smiled. "Okay then, our first analogy for the operation of the multiverse is that it twinkles."

"First? You have more than one?"

"Oh yes, many. But it's getting late," he said, "so we'll just look at one or two others.

"During our walk today, did you notice the bush out where the driveway meets the road?"

"You mean the one with the gorgeous pink flowers?"

"Yes, and the fact that you saw the pink flowers on the green bush indicates that you do not suffer from the most common form of color blindness."

"Yeah, I knew that. I took those tests when I was in school. You know, the ones where you look at a bunch of colored dots and if you can see one number you are color blind and if you see another number you aren't."

---

[81] See: Roberts, *Unknown Reality*, pp. 87-88, and *Seth Speaks*, pp. 133 & 266; and Mathes, pp. 125-126.

> "Exactly the response I was seeking! Now, imagine a somewhat larger picture consisting of many thousands of dots of various colors so that a person with red-green color blindness would see the word 'EARTH' and a person with blue-yellow color blindness would see the word 'HEAVEN' while a person with full color vision would see the words 'HEAVEN AND EARTH.'"

"I'm not certain that is technically possible, but I can do that in my imagination."

> "Good. Now just make that picture three-dimensional and enlarge it by a factor of a billion-billion or so and you have another way of wrapping your mind around the idea of several different worlds existing, interspersed, within the same space."

I considered this for awhile and then I got an idea that made me convulse with one of those hrrummf-snort-giggle combinations, and he asked what was so funny. And I sighed and said, "Well, I was thinking of all those little colored dots distributed throughout the universe like sprinkles on ice cream and it occurred to me that the two grand analogies you've offered for the comprehension of our universe can be summarized in two words: 'twinkle' and 'sprinkle.'"

> He grinned broadly, shook his head slightly, and said: "I reckon that's all we're likely to accomplish this evening. Tomorrow we consider what heaven is actually like."

And so, muttering and chuckling to ourselves, we made our way to bed.

Sunday Morning I
Time for Breakfast

Here we are, set in the midst of an infinity of time — the chances are infinitely against us that we should be alive at any specific time. But here we are. The only way to get rid of the infinity of chances which are against us is to assume — that we too are infinite.

— J. Paul Williams, essay in the *Yale Review,* Spring, 1945

We enjoyed our breakfast of fruit cup and French toast out at the small table on the screened porch. The aroma of coffee mixing with the fresh scents of summertime in the woods made for a most pleasant morning. Apparently it put him in a speculative mood.

"Let's say that I asked you to meet me on the corner of Twelfth Street and Vine," he said, as he poured himself some apple juice. "And you agreed, but I went and stood on the corner and you failed to meet me. Assume also that we do actually meet again, say … in the lobby of the Hotel California, and I ask you why you failed to show up. What excuse would you offer?"

"Well, you never said which 'Twelfth Street and Vine,' but I well remember the song,[82] so I'm 'going to Kansas City' … Missouri, that is."

"Yep," he agreed, "that's where I was."

"The question, then, is *when* were you standing on that corner? I was there at 3 p.m. and you were no where to be seen."

---

[82] Wilbert Harrison's song *Kansas City* made the Top Ten in 1959. If you want to stand there too, you'll have to use some imagination, as the streets no longer intersect in Kansas City, MO.

"Aha!" he exclaimed, with a bit more enthusiasm than needed. "That explains it. I was there at 2 o'clock.

"We were missing an entire dimension!"

"I've never been real comfortable with the idea of time as a dimension," I said.

"Dimensions are simply labels we use to identify places," he explained.

"I thought they were how we measured the size of things," I replied, "like length, width, and height."

"The size of a thing is calculated or *derived* from its dimensions. For example, to determine the length of that log," he gestured towards a large dead limb on the forest floor, "you would first need to have a starting point and an ending point and then calculate the difference between the two. If you were using a tape measure, your starting point would be zero and your ending point would be whatever number on the tape coincided with the other end of the log. But you could also derive the length of the log using the longitude and latitude of the two ends and a bit of elementary trigonometry."

"Perhaps *you* could," I said, "there's nothing about trigonometry that I consider elementary.

"I do know that longitude and latitude are numbers signifying a certain distance from the Greenwich meridian and the equator. And, I suppose that the corner of Twelfth Street and Vine is distinguished from the corner of Eleventh Street and Vine by its distance from First Street. But, I still am confused about dimensions and size and time."

"The difficulty arises from our use of the term 'dimension' to mean both scale and size. When we say that the dimensions of a rectangle are 4 inches by 6 inches, we are talking about size or quantity. On the other hand, when we say that there are three dimensions in space, we are referring to directions. These directions can be given mathematically according to the x, y, and z axes; or, on a geological map, by longitude, latitude, and height above sea level; or, in everyday terms, as up-down, right-left, and forward-back.

"So, from now on, when we want to talk about length and width or some other indication of size, let's speak of 'proportions' or simply 'size' and reserve the term 'dimensions' for information that tells us where something is on a particular spatial scale."

"And the scale time is on … ?"

"Exactly."

"Exactly? Exactly what?"

"The scale of time is on."

" … Uh, pardon me, but have we slipped into an Abbott and Costello reject?"

"On, as opposed to off," he said with a grin. "Remember what we said last night about the universe blinking, or rather 'twinkling' on and off?"

"Yes."

"Think of each 'on' blink to be one unit of time. Let's call that a 'twink.'"

I was pretty certain he was making this up as he went along, but I just said: "Okay. How long is a twink?"

"A twink is an indivisible unit. It cannot be divided into smaller parts; therefore, its duration is zero."

"So then, no time passes during a twink? How does anything happen?"

"For the universe to actually blink, or twinkle, it would have to be constantly re-created. Movement, or change, comes about because each new creation is a tiny bit different than the previous one.

"Think again of the movie frames. Each frame is static, a still picture. The action in the movie we see is the result of each succeeding frame being different from the last. The main difference between the film analogy and 'reality' is that each twink of the universe has been created fresh, rather than being preordained by the producer."

"So, movement occurs only when the universe is off?"

"No. When the universe is off, physical objects do not exist, so they cannot move. In fact, nothing ever really 'moves.' At each twink, all things are created anew, only in a slightly different position than they were in the preceding twink."

"Just how rapidly does the universe twinkle?" I asked while pouring extra syrup on my French toast.

"That's like asking the characters in a movie to tell you the speed of the projector. We denizens of the physical universe cannot detect the twinks. You would need to be on the outside of the system to do that. Nevertheless, based on Planck's constant, we can assume that the minimum number of twinks that occur in each second of our time is very large."

"How large?" I asked.

"So large that there is no English word for the number, although I believe it could be termed 'one quintillion septillion.' Physicists write it as 10^{43}, if you wrote it out it would be the number one followed by 43 zeros."

"Do you expect me to believe that the entire universe is terminated and regenerated one-quintillion-septillion times each second?"

"If you can accept that something was created once, is it so much harder to believe that it was, and is still, being created many times?

"Perhaps the British astronomer and physicist Sir Arthur Eddington was correct when he said: 'Not once in the dim past, but continuously by conscious mind is the miracle of the Creation wrought.'"[83]

"Aha. — Excuse me for asking, but how do you know all this?"

"I don't. It's just speculative extrapolation. Remember that the whole 'universe blinks' thing was introduced as an analogy to help us understand certain possibilities." He took a sip of coffee.

"But whether our world actually blinks or twinkles or whatever, time is still a dimension because time is a way of locating things in space. Or, rather, time is a way to determine *what* space we are locating things within."

I must have looked a bit befuddled, because he said: "Let's go back to Kansas City. The Twelfth and Vine where I was standing had a blue Edsel parked on the corner. Did you see it?"

"No," I played along, "just a Studebaker and a 1950 Nash Rambler. You know, the kind that the seats folded back into a bed."

"There's an old fella up the hill still has one of those sitting out in his front yard. No tires on it, but the bed still works. I think he sleeps in it when it gets too hot indoors.

"Anyway, the space in which I was waiting to meet you had a blue Edsel on the corner; the space where you came to meet me had a Nash Rambler instead. We are clearly referring to two different Twelfth and Vines."

"But we'll never meet if we have to make dates according to what cars are on the corner. That blue Edsel might be there every afternoon, but it might not."

"Which is precisely why a device that produces nothing and transforms nothing is, nevertheless, one of mankind's most important inventions."

---

[83] Eddington, p. 241.

"Clocks?"

> "Of course. All that clocks do is move in a constant and reliable fashion — unlike the traffic in Kansas City. This allows me to say: 'I'll be standing on the corner of Twelfth Street and Vine at 2 p.m.,' and you will know that I am specifying one particular intersection out of all the gazillion Twelfth & Vines that there have been in the past and will be in the future. I am not talking about the intersection at which the clock's hands point to 3 or 4 or 5. I am specifying that singular Twelfth Street and Vine at which the little hand of the clock is pointing to the 2. And it doesn't matter if the car on the corner is a blue Edsel or a yellow Hummer.
>
> "Time is not something that changes; time is just a scale we use to locate events."

"In that case," I said, "it really makes no sense to speak of the flow of time or the passage of time, does it?"

> "No more sense than it makes to talk about the flow of latitude or the passage of depth."

"Then, do you think time travel is possible?" I asked.

> "Once an event has occurred, I very much doubt that it can be undone," he replied while stacking our empty plates. "On the other hand, it would be imprudent of me to surmise any constraints on what could take place in the gaps between twinks."

"What about the future? Can spirits foretell the future?"

> "I doubt that even God knows the future."

"Then you don't believe Him omniscient?" I asked.

> "To know all doesn't mean knowing what is not," he replied. "Knowledge comes only from experience — it can be the experience of doing, or sensing, or just thinking. There can be no knowledge if the experience has not occurred."

Apparently sensing my dissatisfaction with this idea, he went on: "For anyone, even God, to know anything, there must be some experience of it. And for Him to have experienced something, it must have already happened. To know the future, therefore, would require going through the process twice. I hardly think that the Almighty would have nothing better to do than repeat experiences that He has already had. And, even if He did repeat Himself, what of the initial experience? There's a first time for everything — even for God."

"Well," I said, "could it not be that God knows the future because He has thought it through, and now we are living it?"

"Ah my friend," he sighed. "What are we, but the thoughts of God? And, what is our living, but God experiencing Himself in the form of the world?"

At this point, I switched off my recorder, my experience having shown that it was useless in picking up conversations over the sounds of table clearing and dish washing.

Sunday Morning II
Other Lives

> *In every generation for more than 10,000 years, man has been given overpowering evidence that his personality will survive death. The authenticity of this evidence becomes more convincing the more carefully it is observed. There is no rational reason why a general acceptance of the fact of survival should be delayed any longer.*
>
> — Jerome Ellison[84]

After breakfast we found that the wind had picked up considerably making the porch a less than attractive setting, so we adjourned to the recliners in the main room.

> "Both the ancient Egyptians and the Tibetans created well-known 'Books of the Dead'" he said, "intended to guide the soul on its journey to the afterlife. To the extent that these tomes have influenced the beliefs of readers, they may well have affected the souls' postmortem experiences. This is because in heaven, even more than on physical worlds, what you expect or believe affects what you experience.
>
> "Much of what we know about heaven comes from the descriptions obtained during hypnotic regressions to the time before birth. Thousands of such regressions have been performed. We can rely on this testimony to the extent that it matches the descriptions given by other people likewise regressed. (If everybody is telling the same story, then that story is probably true, providing, of course, that outside influences have been ruled out.)

---

[84] Ford, *Life Beyond Death*, p. 169

"Our knowledge of the afterlife also comes from its current residents (discarnate souls) via mediums. Some of these souls, we should note, have expressed concern that the process of interpreting their reality in physical terms cannot be accomplished without considerable distortion.[85]

"Altogether, hundreds of people have made important additions to our current understanding.

"Any questions before we delve into the heavenly environs?"

"I am now certain that there is an afterlife," I said, "but I'm not real clear on *what* it is that survives."

"Then allow me to try and clarify the situation," he replied. "That which is 'you' is a one-of-a-kind, one-time-only combination of your physical body and a portion of your soul. Your physical body will die and decompose, your brain along with it. Your physical body *will* not be, *can* not be resurrected. [If you disagree, consider that the molecules that now make up your body have formed the structure of other persons in the past.] Thus, no life is lived twice, which means that what is now *you* will not 'live again.'

"But your soul will not die with your body. That portion of your soul that currently resides within your body will be set free and will return to its wholeness in heaven. Your soul will remember being you, as it remembers being all of the entities it has been part of throughout the ages."

I said, "I take it you believe in reincarnation."

"If you don't, you haven't honestly evaluated the evidence," he replied.

"Way back when, I did read the book about Bridey Murphy and I remember being impressed, but I heard that had been discredited."

---

[85] For example, see White, *The Betty Book*, p. 109.

"There certainly was no dearth of critics of Morey Bernstein's *The Search for Bridey Murphy*. And some strange bedfellows they made, too. The atheists, of course, were against it, as were those whose religions do not offer second chances. Tucked in with them, to the surprise of many, were more than a few ardent spiritualists who weren't enthusiastic about normal folk being able to contact spirits on their own."[86]

"But Bridey wasn't a departed spirit," I pointed out.

"Many mediums claimed she was. Despite what their own spirit contacts were teaching, these mediums denied reincarnation, asserting that, rather than being recalled from a past life, the memories were those of deceased spirits being telepathically transmitted to the entranced subject."

"That's a bit of a stretch. But I suppose everybody tends to see things according to their own beliefs."

"A tendency against which we must be constantly vigilant," he said. "Anyway, it turns out that the so-called refutation of the Bridey Murphy case is, itself, full of holes. The 1965 edition of the book showed that emphatically. Of course, I can't blame you for not knowing this; you can bet that long after the public forgets the truth, the überskeptics will continue to repeat the fabrications.

"I suggest you re-read Bernstein's book; it is both entertaining and convincing. The sessions revealed an impressive number of details about the culture Bridey knew in Ireland, details she had no way of knowing in her current life and that could only be confirmed by painstaking research. Nevertheless, it was hardly the first or last good treatise on reincarnation. Solid evidence has been known for centuries, and even stronger evidence continues to be found to this day."

---

[86] For a thorough rebuttal of past and current arguments against reincarnation, see Allen, *Defending Bridey's Honor*.

"Didn't the early Christians believe in reincarnation?"

"For over 500 years, many did, including some very prominent leaders. But then, the petty tyrants — who felt that the threat of eternal damnation was critical to the church's control of its members — won the debate. From then on, believers in reincarnation were branded (and often executed) as heretics."

"But, what about the argument that everyone could not have lived on earth before, because there are more humans alive today than have lived in all our past history — there just aren't enough past lives to go around."

"True enough," he replied, "but that was also true at mankind's beginning. Clearly the first people on earth could not have been reincarnated souls, as they had no predecessors. And their immediate children, at the least, were likewise souls unaccustomed to the earthly plane.

"But, who knows how many souls there are in the universe, either incarnated on other worlds or simply hanging around heaven. Probably more than enough to inhabit many times the number of bodies this planet can hold."

"Good point," I conceded. "I hadn't thought of that. But, if we accept that many people have lived numerous past lives and factor in the recent population growth, then a large segment (maybe even the majority) of those now living on earth are here for the first time."

"Perhaps."

"Why just 'perhaps'? It doesn't add up any other way."

"Well now, I can think of at least three factors that would change your equation. The first is that no one can say for sure how many people *have* lived on Earth. There could well have been extensive populations that pre-date our earliest records."

"You mean Atlantis and Mu?" I queried.

"I mean that our planet is very old and holds many mysteries. Until we solve them all, let's not discount the possibility of unknown civilizations.

"The second possibility," he continued, "is that souls might be able to split as they grow, as do the roots of a tree. If so, then the soul of one ancient forefather might now be incarnated in several current residents of Earth."

"Then two people under hypnosis might be induced to remember the same life," I speculated.

"In theory, although I've heard of no such incident."

"And what's the third factor I might have missed?"

"Ah," he hesitated a moment, "well, that's the one I am least comfortable with … transmigration."

"You mean coming back as an animal?" I exclaimed.

"No. I mean coming *from* an animal. Some cultures fervently believe that souls develop by incarnating first in lower life forms and graduating to higher and more intelligent species as they grow."

"The idea doesn't feel right to me," I said.

"Me neither; but, is our resistence to it based on it being false or simply on human pride? Whatever the case, I've not seen any solid evidence for the reality of it.

"Is something on your mind?"

Apparently he had noticed that distant look I get when impressed by an odd idea. After a moment of thought collection, I said: "Just thinking about the spiritualist viewpoint. Knowing as we do that spirits of deceased humans exist, and that they could well be capable of imparting their memories to humans, how can we tell if a particular experience stemmed from reincarnation or from possession?"

"Indeed, I don't know what the criteria for making such a decision would be. But the fact that spirit possession might account for the reception of any particular information about another life, is not an argument against reincarnation. Just because we can't tell whether something comes from source A or source B, is no proof that there is no source B."

"Granted.

"So, out of all the volumes of evidence that must exist for the soul living more than one physical life, which have you put in your little blue book?" I said, reaching once again for the *Afterlife Casebook*.

"There are a few cases there that appertain. Go ahead and take a look."

And so I did.

Case 18 – Hypnotist's Heaven

There are many reasons for the increase over the past century in the quantity and quality of evidence for Survival. Medical advances, better communications, and faster ambulances have led to far more resuscitations of people who would otherwise have died, thus leading to many more near-death experiences; hospitalizations of the very ill are more common, resulting in better reporting of deathbed visions; and the development of various electronic devices has provided new pathways for spirit communications. But the biggest advance in afterlife investigations is the result of the development of hypnosis and the ensuing improvements in regression techniques. Curious minds shall always be grateful for the pioneering work of Colavida and de Rochas, and the contemporary efforts of Bernstein, Goldberg, Netherton, Sutphen, Wambach, and Weiss.

While almost all regression therapists have concentrated on revealing the previous earth-lives of their subjects, Michael Newton, Ph.D., has chosen a different, and apparently more difficult, route that makes him a pioneer among pioneers. Dr. Newton has developed and implemented regression techniques that allow his subjects to remember the time spent *between* lives — the time spent in heaven. From this has sprung a new branch of regression therapy called LBL, for Life-Between-Lives therapy. Newton has written three books[87] detailing his subjects' experiences. Now semi-retired, he remains devoted to training other therapists to carry on the LBL work.

LBL patients paint remarkably consistent pictures of the afterlife, pictures that neither reflect their religious upbringing nor fulfill their prior expectations. It is difficult to imagine any explanation for this universal agreement except that the memories are what they claim to be — accurate portrayals of a real heaven.

Beyond their inner consistency, we have, of course, no way of confirming the descriptions of lives between lives. One of Newton's cases[88] is worth relating here, however, because it is especially evidential of reincarnation in that it involves two living subjects relating the same story of a past-life incident from two different perspectives.

Maureen and Dale were born near San Francisco, California, almost at the same time; but if they were supposed to live together the fates must have screwed up somehow because they took 50 years to find one another. By then, they were living 3,000 miles apart and had to make their connection in a computer chat room; a room dedicated, appropriately enough, to discussions of life after death. Almost immediately they felt a strong affinity for each other and found that they had an unusual amount in common. Dale had read Dr. Newton's first book and he and Maureen agreed to undergo regression sessions to see if they were friends or lovers in the past.

During Maureen's session, she relived being a woman named Samantha who is getting ready for her 18th birthday party in 1923. She lives near San Francisco, and the party is in a downtown mansion. When she is

---

[87] Titles are: *Journey of Souls, Destiny of Souls,* and *Life Between Lives: Hypnotherapy for Spiritual Regression.*
[88] Newton *Destiny,* pp. 266-274.

moved forward to the party, she tells of dancing with her boyfriend Rick and drinking the liquor that he and his friends smuggled into the party. Rick suggests that they need to be alone and so they sneak out of the house by a side entrance and drive away in his red roadster. For awhile, she feels the warm wind in her hair and the joy of being with the man she loves. But the man she loves is paying more attention to the woman he loves than to the road ahead. He is driving too fast and, when they encounter a sharp curve on the Pacific Coast Road, the car goes over a cliff.

When Dale was regressed, he told the same story from Rick's point of view, the only difference being that his soul abandons his body as the roadster falls through the air, whereas Samantha tells of dying in the cold ocean water.

In follow-up discussions, both Dale and Maureen spoke of being strangely uncomfortable driving on certain roads around San Francisco. It is important to note, however, that neither Dale nor Maureen, prior to their sessions, had any idea of being Rick and Samantha or of dying in an auto accident. Dale had only flown out to meet Maureen for the first time in person on the day before they met with Dr. Newton. Each was regressed individually and privately and there was no communication between them in the interim between Maureen's session and Dale's.[89]

End Case 18

"The fact that Dale and Maureen described the same scenes certainly deflates any theories regarding imagination or subconscious memories," I said. "I wonder if there are any surviving police records of the accident?"

> "Perhaps one of your readers can find out. Per Samantha's account, the accident occurred on the night of June 26th 1923. (Although, according to Dr. Newton,[90] dates given during regressions

---

[89] Per personal correspondence with Newton, May 2005.
[90] Personal correspondence, July 2005.

are not always reliable, as a subject may supply a date with strong personal significance rather than the date of the day in question.)"

"Well, I like the fact that two people both testify to the same events. But I don't think we can rule out the possibility of collusion between Dale and Maureen prior to the sessions."

"There is no reason to suspect it either, but you are correct, the possibility is there and does weaken the case somewhat.

"A small thing that I believe strengthens the case, on the other hand, is that the two souls went their separate ways en route to heaven. If this was a fabrication, or a dream that Maureen somehow telepathically shared with Dale, how could she resist having the two soulmates rise together above the moonlit breakers, astral hand in astral hand?"

"It does make for an enchanting picture."

"Funny you should use that term, for the next case centers around a picture.

"Most of the cases in the hypnotic-regression literature are described by therapists, either directly or via journalists, so this story is special because it is told, and told most convincingly, by the subject himself."

Case 19 – The Policeman and the Painter

Captain Robert L. Snow, Commander of the Homicide Branch of the Indianapolis Police Department, veteran of 30-years on the force, and author of four books on police procedures, thought of himself as a down-to-earth, street-wise, and rational cop. So, when he underwent regression hypnosis — as a result of a colleague's dare — he felt more than a little foolish and a lot like he was wasting his time.

He was astonished, therefore, when, after spending an uncomfortable half-hour on a psychologist's couch, he suddenly found himself standing almost naked on the slope of a mountain. For a brief time, he experienced the life of a primitive man struggling to survive in an ancient forest before dying in a lonely cave.

Soon afterwards, the scene shifted and he was standing before an easel, paintbrush in hand, studying a somewhat hunchbacked woman by gaslight. In briefly living several scenes from this life, Snow discovered that the artist resided in a large city in the late 1800s, spent some time in France, was recognized as a talented portrait painter although he didn't care to paint portraits (he did so only because they paid well), and many other mundane facts. When the hypnosis session was concluded, the image that stuck in Snow's mind most forcefully was of the painting of the hunchbacked woman in a long gown that he had seen, nearly completed, on the artist's easel.

Captain Snow was surprised, to say the least, that he had actually entered a hypnotic trance and experienced several highly realistic creations of his subconscious mind. But that was all that he was willing to admit. Nevertheless, as days passed, he couldn't get his thoughts off of the session. Finally, he decided that the painting he could remember so vividly was the key. If he could prove that he had seen the painting somewhere before in this, his 20th-century-policeman's life, then he might be able to forget about possible past-lives and move on with the present one.

Assuming the task would prove to be simple because the picture must be famous, Snow went to the art section of the city library and commenced to scan the picture books. He failed to find a picture of the painting. In fact, after many months of intense detective work and hundreds of hours spent in art libraries and art galleries, all he found was frustration. So, when his wife suggested that some time off might be useful, he agreed to a short vacation in New Orleans. And there, in a city he had never before visited, off an obscure street in the French Quarter, in the far corner of the front parlor of a small art gallery, Captain Robert L. Snow came suddenly face to face with artist J. Carroll Beckwith's portrait of a slightly hunchbacked woman in a long gown. It was perched there on an easel almost exactly as he had last seen it, some 100 years before. "I stared open-mouthed at the portrait," he later wrote,[91] "reliving an experience I'd had once when I grabbed onto a live wire ... huge voltage surged up and down my arms and legs. ... There was absolutely no doubt at all that this was the portrait I had seen myself painting while under hypnosis." But his no-nonsense side refused to go away; Snow's next thought was: "Now I just had to find a logical explanation for everything."

What he found from the gallery owner was that the painting had been part of a private estate from the time of its creation and was never in the public eye until purchased by the gallery. What he found from several more months of investigation was that Beckwith's career matched the data from the hypnosis sessions in at least 28 particulars and nothing he could find contradicted his impressions except for Mrs. Beckwith's first name (which he had been uncertain of from the first). Most of these facts were preserved only in Beckwith's private journals and had never been published. Finally, even Snow was forced to admit that there really was no "logical explanation" and that, as he said when telling of his visit to Beckwith's grave: "I realized I had nothing to be frightened of ... I knew there couldn't be any ghosts or spirits here because the spirit that had been in Beckwith's body was now in mine."

End Case 19

> "Consider the three possible outcomes of Captain Snow's search for the painting," he suggested, as the sky darkened and the wind began to deliver the rain it had promised since breakfast. "First, it could have been displayed or reproduced in a public venue or document. Second, it could not have existed at all except in Snow's imagination. And, third, it could be real but beyond his access. How do you think each possibility would affect the case?"

"If Snow had found that the painting had been reproduced in a time and place where he could have seen it," I said, "he would have assumed

---

[91] Snow, pp. 79 & 84.

that he had simply forgotten that viewing until his subconscious mind offered it up during hypnosis. In which case, he would never have investigated further and found the other 28 correspondences, and there would be no case.

"If Snow had never found the painting, because it didn't exist or had been destroyed or remained in a private collection, he would never have uncovered Beckwith's name, and sooner or later he would have stopped looking. Again, no case."

> "It would appear, then," he summarized, "that Snow's rather inexplicable obsession with finding the painting had to be combined with his wife's sudden desire to visit New Orleans and the gallery's recent purchase and prominent display of the painting, or we would have no story. I cannot conceive of all this occurring by chance alone. But if, by some stretch, other people can, the remaining cases are bound to change their minds."

"Before moving on," I said, "there is another thing that strikes me as especially evidential in the Beckwith case. The one piece of evidence that Snow got wrong was Mrs. Beckwith's name, yet that surely would be part of the public record, no matter how scanty that record might be. This is a pretty strong indication that Snow's source was indeed the regression, rather than any prior experience or research."

> "Good point," he said, moving to close the windows across the back, where the rain was coming in. "And it brings to mind an interesting footnote to the case. Snow, while in trance and speaking as Beckwith, said that he was in a city and meeting a woman named Amanda. After his book was published, Snow reports,[92] research by a librarian revealed that the young Beckwith dated a girl named Amanda, who moved to New York City at about the same time Beckwith did. So, it wasn't that Snow got the name of his wife

---

[92] Per personal correspondence, October, 2005.

wrong, it was just that he incorrectly assumed that the girl Amanda must be his wife.

"As with so many of these cases, the deeper one looks, the more convincing they become."

I nodded agreement and continued reading.

Case 20 — Death in the Garment District

Dr. Morris Netherton began specializing in what he terms "Past Lives Therapy" around 1970. He does not call what he does "hypnosis" as he relies on word associations rather than the more common types of trance induction, but his methods seem to work well for accessing traumas in past and pre-natal lives. In 1978 he published a collection of his cases that includes several with exceptional verification; one of these is the story of Rita McCullum.[93]

During regression, a patient (whom Netherton does not name) related numerous trials and tribulations of a personality named Rita, who was born in 1903. We shall limit our coverage of Rita's tale to the period beginning in the late 1920s in midtown Manhattan. She and her husband, Keith McCullum, had finally brought their fledgling clothing company to the brink of success. In the winter of 1928, the overwork involved in this accomplishment resulted in Keith contracting pneumonia and dying. Only one year later, Rita's son died of polio. That October, 1929, the stock market crashed and the Great Depression began. Despite her heroic struggles over the next few years, Rita ended up broke and alone and suicidal.

On the 11th of June, 1933, a destitute and despondent Rita McCullum went into the cutting room of her defunct factory, looped a rope over the bars that were used to hold garments, and hung herself.

Such is the tale that was told by a regressed patient in Dr. Netherton's office in the mid-1970s. And such is the tale confirmed by a notarized death certificate that Netherton later obtained from the New York City Hall of

---

[93] Netherton, pp. 166-168.

Records. The certificate states that one Rita McCullum, age 30 (and thus born in 1903) committed suicide by hanging on 11 June 1933 at an address in the heart of the garment district in Manhattan.

End Case 20

So what has Netherton been doing since 1978," I asked. "I don't think I've heard of the man."

> "That's probably because you're not a psychologist. Netherton has been concentrating on helping patients and on teaching other therapists his techniques. As laymen, we're interested in the sensational evidence he uncovers from time to time, but his focus is on healing … as it should be.
>
> "The next case, by the way, certainly qualifies as 'sensational.'"

Case 21 — The Numbers of the Beast

During a training demonstration in Brazil, Dr. Netherton regressed a young woman suffering from agoraphobia (the fear of being in open places). Starting when she was 16 years of age, her fears had steadily grown until she was very uncomfortable when not near her home and she trusted only her immediate family.

While regressed, she recalled a life that ended in a German concentration camp. According to her story, when she arrived at the camp, a guard burned an identification number into her arm. As she told of this, she suddenly began screaming and clutching at her arm. Netherton observed red welts appearing on the woman's arm. These began to resolve themselves into numbers. An elderly psychologist sitting nearby jumped up and rolled up his sleeve to show similar numbers that had been burned into his arm at just such a camp. The man was so excited that it took awhile for Dr. Netherton to calm him down so that the session could continue.

During this session, the recalled personality gave numerous facts identifying herself, her family, and the camp. She said that she died after suffering through several months of exposure to the harsh elements there.

The numbers on the subject's arm faded away when the session ended. But, an assistant at the demonstration had taken a photograph of the numbers and an inquiry was made by sending only that identification number to the Holocaust Museum in Israel. The report sent back by the museum described a young girl whose name, birth date, parent's name, village of birth, and date of death perfectly matched the facts given by the subject.

According to Dr. Netherton,[94] "These facts are unimportant when compared to the effectiveness of the session. It changed the young lady's feelings, and she began returning to her normal life."

End Case 21

As evidence of reincarnation, the facts cited here are anything but unimportant," I said, looking up from the manual.

"Yes, but the therapeutic affect of the session does add validity. What do you think of the appearance of the numbers?"

"A little difficult to take," I admitted.

"But very difficult to fake," he pointed out. "If the female subject were a skilled illusionist and well-practiced at feigning trance, I suppose fraud would be possible. But I can imagine no motivation for achieving such a deception and then not claiming credit for it. In actuality, the woman did not appreciate her sudden notoriety and, for awhile, Netherton even changed the reported locale of the incident from Brazil to the Netherlands in an effort to give her some respite from the curious."

Another bit of information that may make you more comfortable with the strangeness of the numbers appearing on the woman's arm is that the phenomenon has been reported before. Not long after the "birth" of Spiritualism near Rochester, New York, an illiterate

---

[94] Netherton, Morris, *The Psychology of Past-life Regression*, web page: http://www.centrodifusao.hpg.ig.com.br/morris.htm. Additional information per personal conversation with Dr. Netherton, August 2005.

servant girl, working for the family of Mr. and Mrs. Lewis Burtis in that same city, developed a condition in which writings and drawings would spontaneously appear on her arm. These would fade away, once they has been read by a family member, who generally found them relevant to a current issue or situation in the household.[95]

"In 1929, an article in the French *Revue Métapsychique*,[96] presented testimony and illustrations of "skin writing" by the medium Olga Kahl. In front of numerous witnesses, among them the eminent professor Charles Richet, letters of the alphabet would appear on Kahl's forearm in apparent response to the unspoken thoughts of the witnesses. So, as unusual as the "Numbers" case is, it is does not stand alone.

"The next one, though, *is* unique to my knowledge."

Case 22 – The Apprentice Murderer

Dr. Bruce Goldberg has regressed literally thousands of patients in his 30-year career in hypnotherapy. Most all of his cases are interesting and evidential, but two of them, when combined one with the other, offer both a fascinating story and a powerful proof of Survival and reincarnation.

The first case concerns a patient, a retail clerk, who complained of always being dominated and manipulated by co-workers, customers, and even relatives. Several age-regressions were tried, revealing a childhood of being pushed around by most everyone, but no clear initiating incident. Then past-life regressions were attempted and, after four rather unproductive sessions, the man began to speak as a fellow named Thayer, living in Bavaria in the year 1132.

---

[95] Hardinge, p. 196.
[96] Barrington, Mary Rose, "Archive No. 86: Mrs. Olga Kahl – Ideas Expressed as Skin Writing by Dr. E. Osty; Summarized form pages 124 – 136 of *Revue Métapsychique*, 1929," in the *Paranormal Review*, Issue 66, April 2013, Society for Psychical Research.

In the opening scene of this regression, Thayer was eating supper *under* the table. He explained this bizarre situation by saying that he was apprenticed to a goldsmith named Gustave who often beat him, sodomized him, and kept him chained to the table whenever the shop was closed. And, when the shop was open for business, Gustave would humiliate Thayer in front of the customers, especially when Clotilde, a nice girl from a wealthy family, came in to purchase something.

Moved forward to a significant moment in his life, Thayer told a dreadful tale of getting into a fight with his master, being stabbed in the stomach with a metal-working tool, and looking down on his own dead body.

Mainly as a result of reliving these ancient events, Dr. Goldberg's patient rapidly gained self-esteem and confidence and went on to pull his life together. [It is an accepted principle of hypnotherapy that getting such past-life incidents into the awareness of the current mind has the effect of eliminating or greatly reducing their debilitating effects. Why this should be true is unclear.]

About 18 months later, Dr. Goldberg was working with another patient, an attorney, whose major complaint was that he felt overwhelmed by urges to manipulate and dominate people. It seems his guilty conscious was causing insomnia and eating disorders. As with the above case, normal hypnotic suggestions and age-regressions met with only limited success. As you have probably already surmised, past-life regression revealed that this man had been a master goldsmith named Gustave in early 12th-century Bavaria. He complained about his incompetent apprentice and, when asked for the fellow's name, said it was Thayer. "At this point," Goldberg reports, "my skin began to crawl. However, my obligation was to my current patient, and it was important to continue this regression as if nothing unusual had happened."[97]

---

[97] Goldberg, pp. 112-125.

Without any coaching from Goldberg, Gustave proceeded to say that he enjoyed beating his apprentice, that a certain girl named Clotilde was a distraction to the boy, and many other facts that exactly complemented the story that "Thayer" had told while reclining on the same couch over a year earlier. The culmination, too, was identical in all pertinent particulars: Gustave told of his apprentice resisting attempts to chain him to the table, getting into a fight, and then killing the boy by stabbing him in the stomach.

Of course, Goldberg never breached his patients' confidence by telling either about the other, so, unless they happened to recognize themselves in Goldberg's book or this one, neither man currently is aware that his nemesis of the past is his neighbor today.

End Case 22

"That's a really impressive story," I said. "The number of specific details (including unusual names and uncommon activities) given by both subjects certainly rules out any idea of coincidence or lucky guesses. The fact that these details are part of a time and place alien to the patients makes it even more convincing. Altogether, this is one of the most evidential cases I have yet seen. I'm not certain, however, why you referred to it as 'unique'?"

> "As far as I am aware," he replied, "this is the only case in anyone's files in which two hypnotic subjects describe the same incidents without either knowing of the other's existence."

"Can we be certain of that? Could it be a hoax?"

> "Any suggestion of trickery is fatuous for several reasons:
> 1. the effort and skill needed to fool a seasoned hypnotherapist twice would be monumental,
> 2. there was no reason to wait several sessions to begin their fabrications,

3. the time delay between the two appearances is overly long, and
4. the subjects have gained neither notoriety nor money from their efforts. In fact, the sessions would have been rather costly to them.

"I agree with you that the story of Thayer and Gustave is one of the strongest proofs of reincarnation, that is why I saved it until the end ... or almost the end," he said, and nodded one last time towards the book in my lap.

Case 23 – A Town Reborn

Those who teach reincarnation often speak of souls traveling in packs. Your spouse today might have been your best friend in some yesterday, your current neighbor could be a teacher in a past life, and so on. These configurations are intentional, having been carefully planned by the souls involved during their time between lives. A subject undergoing hypnotic regression may say that so-and-so in their current life is the reincarnation of some principal person in their past life, but such claims almost always lack supportive testimony. This is because friends and relatives typically are not invited to observe the sessions.

There are exceptions to every rule, however, and one such uncommon observance led to what is probably the best corroborated collection of past lives ever revealed. Marge Rieder, Ph.D., practices hypnotherapy in the town of Lake Elsinore, California. She had a patient named Maureen, who was reliving a past life as a woman in Virginia during the American Civil War. Maureen invited a friend named Barbara to attend one of the sessions and Dr. Rieder, who was also a friend of Barbara, allowed her to observe. Midway through the session, Barbara passed a note to the therapist that said: "Ask her if I was there." Rieder reports that she was shocked to hear Maureen say that Barbara was her mother-in-law in that life.

To make a complex and fascinating story overly simple, the long-term results of that one hypnosis session led Rieder to become the only hypnotherapist known to have uncovered almost an entire town full of people reincarnated together. During a 17-year investigation, one subject after another named others who currently lived in the vicinity of Lake Elsinore but who had also lived in the little town of Millboro, Virginia in the mid 19th century. So far, more than 50 people have remembered lives in that time and place, although only three had visited the state of Virginia in their current lives and none had ever heard of Millboro. At least, they hadn't heard of it until Rieder's first book[98] was published. Afterwards, several people contacted Rieder and asked to be hypnotized because they were certain that they, too, were part of the story. Remarkably, hypnosis often revealed that such convictions were merely wishful thinking; they actually could recall no lives as "Millboreans."

The name of the town itself provides significant support to the case, as it was pronounced "Marlboro" by most of the regressed. The reality of the town at first seemed doubtful when no "Marlboro" could be found on maps of Virginia. But when one entranced subject was induced to write down the name, she wrote "Millboro." There was a town named Millboro on the map and it appeared to fit the descriptions perfectly. Upon investigation, Rieder discovered that many residents of the area around Millboro pronounce the name as "Marlboro" to this day.[99]

A majority of the subjects who are part of the group had not met when they first underwent hypnosis, yet they have all told consistent stories and described the same locations, without any overlap of personalities. Most evidential, are the buried rooms and tunnels that several subjects described as being utilized by the underground railway in aiding slaves and orphaned Union soldiers to travel north. Although no resident in the current town of Millboro was aware of these, and they were not described in

---

[98] Rieder has written three books on the subject: *Mission to Millboro, Return to Millboro,* and *Millboro and More.*
[99] Rieder, *Mission to Millboro,* p. xvii.

any document nor located on any known map, excavations revealed them to exist precisely as described by Rieder's entranced subjects in California — right down to the uncommon color of the walls.

End Case 23

I was especially impressed with the fact that some people undergoing regression fully expected to relive a life in Millboro, but failed to do so."

"Yes," he agreed, "it goes to show that preconceptions have nothing to do with the results.

"Another interesting twist is that Rieder had another hypnotist regress her subjects, but the results were the same."

"Well, if I wasn't already convinced of an afterlife, I sure would be now.

"But we have yet to address the problem of distinguishing actual past lives of the current subjects from memories being telepathically received from discarnate souls."

"Okay. Here are my top ten reasons for believing in the reincarnation hypothesis," he said, handing me a typewritten sheet of paper. While I read, he busied himself preparing a snack of sliced apples and cheese.

```
          The Top Ten Reasons
 For Reincarnation Not Being an Illusion
       Caused by Discarnate Spirits
```

```
     10. If there is no reincarnation, then the evi-
dence we have of past lives would have to be the
result of thousands of discarnate spirits deceit-
fully projecting their memories into the minds of
hypnotized humans. It is unlikely that there could
be so many souls both able and willing to commit
such fraud.
```

9. Since humans may elect to undergo past-life regression at any time, a fiction of reincarnation could only be maintained if each human had a discarnate soul assigned to hang around just in case. And being available just once isn't enough, for most therapies access the same life numerous times. Actually, each human would require several souls in constant attendance, as most regressions uncover more than one past-life.

8. The difficulties raised in number 9 are vastly increased with group reincarnations. For example, are we to believe that the soul of Samantha managed to transfer its memories into the mind of Maureen while the soul of Rick hung around waiting for the opportunity to try and transfer his memories into the mind of Dale? When we consider the 50 some souls involved in the Millboro case, the idea becomes transparently ludicrous.

7. Then there is the question of motivation. Why would a soul want its personal memories to be claimed by someone else? Such a transference goes against everything we know about the psychology of personal identity. As has been demonstrated over and over again during mediumistic communications, souls adamantly want to be known as themselves.

6. Our understanding of mental telepathy is stretched close to, and perhaps beyond, the breaking point by the idea of communicating memories of subjective experiences -- the feeling of being in love, the intention to accomplish a goal, etc. -- that are so often part of the regression scene.

5. In hypnotic regressions using relatively light trances, both men and women recall past lives as males more often than lives as females. This makes sense when you consider that the lives of males tend, on average, to be more dramatic (more

competitive, more daring, more active, etc.) than female lives, and that lives with more drama are more easily remembered. On the other hand, deeper trances tend to access lives without regard to their intensity, including the truly boring ones, as in:

> "What are you doing now?" "Weaving baskets."

> "Okay, go forward five years. What are you doing now?" "Weaving baskets."

> "Okay, go forward ten years. What are you doing now?" "Teaching my granddaughter to weave baskets."

And deeper trances reveal an equal number of male and female lives.[100] There is no known reason for such correlates to arise if the life stories were being dictated by discarnate souls.

4. Additional regressions may reveal additional past-lives, but the original cast always remains. Subjects never claim to be Napoleon one week and Nelson the next. This makes perfect sense if reincarnation is valid, and no sense if the regressions rely on the whims of discarnate souls and the vagaries of telepathy.

3. Regressions reveal only one personality per era. If a subject recalls several lives, they will occur before or after one another, virtually never simultaneously.[101] Telepathically "remembering" the lives of some other souls would not be likely to result in the same degree of exclusivity.

2. A whole bunch of psychiatrists, psychologists, and other trained hypnotherapists have confirmed for themselves that past-life regressions

---

[100] TenDam, p.188.
[101] Claims have been made that, in rare circumstances, a soul will divide its essence among two physical bodies simultaneously. See TenDam, p. 321 and Newton, *Destiny of Souls*, p. 116.

and LBL regressions are almost always therapeutic. We have no reason to think that remembering someone else's memories would likewise be so effective in alleviating symptoms.

1. And the number one reason that reincarnation is not a deception of discarnate spirits is that the spirits say so! For awhile, many Spiritualists scorned the idea of reincarnation. But then, several of those who were against the idea in life became ardent supporters in their post-mortem communications via mediums. Today, you would be hard pressed to find an astral entity who denies the reality of reincarnation.

After studying these reasons briefly, I handed the sheet back to him and he tucked it into my copy of the *Casebook,* saying that I would need it later.

> "Are you convinced that reincarnation is the most reasonable and likely explanation for the phenomena?" he asked.

"I am so convinced."

> "Then have some apple and let us return to our exploration of heaven."

The remainder of the morning was essentially a Q and A session. My questions were neither as cogent nor as well organized as they appear here, but I felt that a bit of editing would make for easier reading.

Note added for 2015 revision of this book: In order to make *The Hereafter Trilogy,* a more manageable size, a large portion of the following chapter, titled "Celestial Q and A," has been excised. Readers are assured that far better and more complete descriptions of the multifaceted realms in the afterlife are provided in, *Astral Intimacy.*

Sunday Morning III
Celestial Q & A

If we harden our hearts against dogmatism in some quarters, sentimentalism in others, and wishful-thinking in ourselves; if we carefully scrutinize the evidence (especially the odder and more unexpected items); if we try to develop a reasonable theory of what is likely to be going on, and check it wherever possible against any relevant facts obtainable, I believe we shall gradually form a pretty clear conception of what post-mortem conditions are like, and why.

— Whately Carington[102]

Q. Why would some souls have been on Earth more than others?

A. The Source expresses Itself in many dimensions, some are physical like Earth, others are not. Thus, prior to coming to Earth, a soul may have spent several millennia incarnating on other planets or as a spirit in other realms. Our Earth, by the way, is one of the more recently opened venues; which is one reason it is currently such a popular destination.[103]

Also, new souls are still being created. Thus, some souls are older than our physical universe, others were born this morning.

Q. Sounds like souls have a life cycle. Do souls grow old and die?

A. To me, it seems right and reasonable that (as many theologies teach) souls ultimately return to the Source from which they came (in as much as they ever really left). But we have no way of knowing what happens at such levels.

---

[102] Carington p. 12.
[103] Homewood, p. 76.

I should point out here that Survival and immortality are not necessarily the same thing. We might live many lives and then simply cease to reincarnate. We might enjoy heaven for ten thousand years and then go "poof." Even the wisest spirit guide has no way of knowing. So we're really just speculating when we speak of ultimate destinations.

Q. When souls incarnate on other physical planets besides Earth, do they reside in human or human-like bodies? For that matter, can we come back as animals or insects?

A. At this time, no one seems to have gathered much information on the type of bodies a soul might inhabit elsewhere. One explanation for this lack is that the images are blocked because we would find them too creepy or repulsive. A more probable — and palatable — reason is simply that no soul who has spent any amount of time incarnated on another planet and then come to Earth has yet undergone a regression extensive enough to reveal such information.

As far as souls inhabiting animals, the short answer is "no." To understand the full answer you must understand that souls created the universe. It was souls that created matter, and stars, and planets. It was souls that created bugs and trees and chimpanzees. This is not blasphemy because <u>souls are parts of the Source</u> (call it God, Allah, Creator, All That Is, or whatever name you wish). Souls are the mechanisms that the Source uses to express Itself. In the process of doing all this creating and expressing — which occupied untold eons and was certainly performed according to the laws of nature — individual souls often semi-merged with their creations for brief periods. I use the prefix 'semi' because bugs and trees and chimpanzees are not suitable for containing more than a small bit of a soul for a brief time. Who hasn't wondered what it would be like to be an eagle or a lion? Well, the souls had the opportunity to find out, so they did. And that is why memories of past lives sometimes include sensations of being an animal or, in very rare cases, the feeling of being a plant.[104]

Q. Were humans created in the same way?

A. Yes. After many millennia of creative play with millions of solar systems and billions of life forms, some souls decided to create an animal suitable for housing a major portion of a soul for an indefinite period. Tired of temporary excursions, they wanted to experience what it was really like to live fully immersed in a physical body. So they modified an existing animal (giving it a larger brain, different hormonal structure, etc.) and merged with the result.

They soon discovered, however, that the pretense of being a human (or a Klingon or whatever) was tough to maintain, especially in the face of pain or immediate threat to life. Every time a cave bear took a swipe at a man, the inhabiting soul would pop out in fright, leaving the man rather disoriented. (A lot of cave folks were lost that way.) The souls' solution was to hide their memories and sense of 'soulness' deep in their unconscious mind when they entered a biological body. This conditional amnesia also allowed for a fresh approach to life's challenges.

As time went on, this 'incarnation game' became one of the most popular pastimes throughout the universe.

Only in the past century (a mere moment to the Source) have humans of our era developed reliable techniques to temporarily overcome our self-imposed amnesia and access the soul's hidden memories of itself.

Q. Are there other reasons that recall of our past lives is repressed?

A. Yes, several.

For an actor to convincingly play a character on stage, he must focus fully on that role. If you were playing the role of Romeo, your

---

[104] Knight, pp. 82-87, and Newton, *Journey*, p. 168.

performance would be seriously degraded if you let your mind wander to the list of items that your wife asked you to pick up from the all-night grocery on your way home. Imagine how much greater a problem if you attempted to play Romeo while rehearsing in your head your lines from *Hamlet*!

There may be times when knowledge of a past-life event can benefit us in this life, but full and constant awareness of another life would seriously interfere with the living of this one. There will be plenty of opportunity between lives to compare and contrast our previous incarnations. It's best to focus on the present, and be happy that we're not asked to live more than one life at a time.

Another reason becomes apparent when we consider the immense frustration that would be faced by a fully conscious adult trapped within an immobile and generally incapable infant body for several years.

There could be other reasons as well. For example, if we knew what awaited us, we might be too ready to leave when things started getting tough on this side.

I am particularly fond of a rationale offered by Rudyard Kipling as he tells of a young man whose recall of his past lives fades rapidly when he meets his first love in this life. Musing about the impact on the reproduction of our species if people could remember their very first loves from their very first lives, Kipling wrote: "Now I understand why the Lords of Life and Death shut the doors so carefully behind us. It is that we may not remember our first wooings. Were it not so, our world would be without inhabitants in a hundred years."[105]

Despite all these impediments, sometimes people *do* recall part of a past life, even without being hypnotized. Dr. Ian Stevenson has dedicated his career to studying such occurrences.

---

[105] Kipling, Rudyard, "The Finest Story in the World," in *Many Inventions*, 1893.

Q. What are angels?

A. At times, a soul in spirit can get the opportunity to assist a soul in flesh, and so be perceived as angelic. But angels are not a special class of beings. In fact, there are no 'classes' of beings. There ain't nobody here but us souls. Some souls are old, others are young; some are advanced, others are novices; some have incarnated, others have not; all are of equal value to God.[106]

Q. To what extent is our next life planned?

A. The evidence shows that no life plan is specified completely. The plan presents the patterns; we fill in the details as we live out our biological lives. Free will always trumps destiny. The decisions of others can change your options (but never without your acquiescence at some level).

Q. Many books speak of teachers and students. Is heaven a school?

A. Numerous entranced people speak of classes and learning as a major activity in the afterlife, but they also insist that souls are never forced to do anything and always have choices. I believe the references to classes stem from our natural desire to learn and to express ourselves, so I wouldn't worry about an eternity of class work.

Perhaps a quote from *Conversations with God* would be relevant here: "School is a place you go if there is something you do not know that you want to know. It is not a place you go if you already know a thing and simply want to <u>experience your knowingness</u>."[107]

Q. Many spiritualists posit several levels of heaven — the astral, the causal, the mental, etc. Must all souls pass through these as do students through elementary, middle, high school, and college?

---

[106] Crenshaw, p. 45.
[107] Walsch, p. 21. Emphasis added.

> A. Let us say that your home was on a mountain top and you left to go exploring. You traveled down the mountain slope, penetrated the encircling jungle, crossed a desert, sailed an ocean, traversed a great forest, and ended up visiting a little house on the prairie. When you decided to return to your aerie, there would be many paths to take you home; but all would require first leaving the prairie, going back through the forest, re-crossing the ocean, the desert, and the jungle, and climbing back up the mountain. So it is with souls, who first left the Source as pure consciousness and then progressively enveloped themselves in denser and denser energy bodies in order to operate at lower and lower frequencies, all the way down to the physical. Although there is some speculation involved in the nature and naming of these various soul wraps, it seems certain that a return to the Source would involve shedding them in reverse order, and thus living at higher and higher frequencies or "levels" until the Origin is reached.
>
> Whether or not a return to the Source is mandated, desirable, or even possible (you can't come back if you never left) is debatable.

Q. Before we end this, I have one last question. You stated that your answers are synthesized from numerous sources. Are all your sources in 100-percent agreement?

> A. No.
>
> There are some differences in the details reported. Frankly, I'd be surprised if there weren't. For one thing, as we discussed last evening on the way to dinner, discarnate entities have not been goof-proofed. Neither are they all-knowing (at least not the ones available for conversations with us Earthlings), nor are they necessarily immune from natural human tendencies to speculate beyond their current knowledge. For another thing, the truth may not be the same in all the various realities that make up the totality of God's being.

Nevertheless, the reports sent back from beyond death's door are sufficiently consistent on important matters to provide a high degree of confidence in the mosaic we have been assembling.

Sunday Lunch
Why This Could Be

> *The stream of knowledge is heading towards a non-mechanical reality; the universe begins to look more like a great thought than a great machine.*
>
> — Astrophysicist Sir James Jeans,
> *The Mysterious Universe*, p. 148.

It had been a long and intense morning, so most of our lunch was spent resting and refueling. Towards the end, however, we dove briefly but deeply into the meaning of what we had spent the weekend discussing. Here, as best as I could reconstruct it, is our conversation on why God created the universe and what man's role in it is. Please note that neither I nor the old man pretend any special knowledge of, connection to, or revelation from the Almighty Creator. The concepts presented herein are those revealed by discarnate souls or deduced from their revelations.[108]

I believe I had made some rather awkward statement about the purpose of life when he said to me:

> "Have you ever considered the conundrum of omnipotent desire?"

"You mean, if God is perfect, He cannot lack anything; therefore He cannot desire anything?"

> "Exactly."

---

[108] See Walsch, pp. 21-28; Knight, p. 79; Roberts, *Seth Material*, pp. 240-244; TenDam, p. 285; Newton, *Destiny*, p. 132.

"And without desire," I continued, "there could be no motivation for God to make the rather stupendous effort necessary to create the universe."

> "Very good," he gave me one of his charming but all too rare grins, "but imagine, if you will, that you have spent most of the last 5 years in a gym developing your chest and arm muscles."

"Oooookay," I replied, raising my eyebrows just a bit, "I don't know if my imagination is up to such an outlandish idea, but I'll try."

> "Well, challenge it a bit more by imagining that one day you and your super-sized chest are walking down the street and, because you aren't used to being so wide, you bump into a man and knock him to the ground. Turns out this man is really a dark wizard. (I dare not say his name.) He becomes very angry, pulls out his wand and zaps you."

"Ouch!"

> "Not only 'ouch,' but you suddenly find that you can hardly move your arms. You look down and confirm that all your muscles are still there, but you barely have the strength of an infant. You see, the wizard is also psychic and he knows how upset you'll be to have great strength but be prevented from experiencing the use of that strength."

"It's difficult to think of 'having' anything if you can't make use of it," I agreed.

> "And, just as there is no value in being extremely strong if you cannot experience the exercise of that strength, so there is no value in being extremely wise if you can never experience the application of your wisdom. Likewise, no joy ensues from perfect love without experiencing the process of loving. The characteristics generally at-

tributed to God — omniscience, omnipotence, over-arching compassion, etc — are of no consequence without a mechanism of experiencing their employment.

"You see, there is one thing, and only one thing that Perfect Allness lacks, that it *must* lack, by definition, and that is an outside viewpoint. If God is all, than God cannot 'see himself as others see him' because there *are* no others.

"The key word is 'separateness.' God, the Universal Mind, The Prime Force, All That Is — by virtue of being God — lacks that separate viewpoint that is necessary to *experience* being God."

"So, you're saying that God's purpose for the universe is to enable God to experience being God."

"I can't imagine any other. And from that" he continued, "we can extrapolate with fair assurance that each soul, being a tiny bit of God, inherits a like purpose: to experience that small section of the universe that is available to it. We humans are some of the mechanisms employed to have these experiences. Or, to phrase it another way, we are experiential parts of God."

"Most teachers who speak of mankind's purpose put it in terms of 'meeting challenges,' 'fulfilling karma,' or 'learning lessons.' How do such activities mesh with this experiential purpose?"

"Well, it's only natural that teachers see the world in terms of learning something, just as politicians think in terms of righting wrongs and priests are biased in favor of connecting with God. But, God is an explorer, not a prospector."

I must have looked puzzled at this, for he continued, "By that I mean there is no particular experience God is seeking, all the experiences He has are valuable to Him. So, as far as I can tell, our physical world is neither school, prison, nor temple. We are not here to learn, nor to be rehabilitated, nor to worship."

"Just to experience?"

"To *create* and experience. But don't say 'just.' This is the most important job there is, for it is getting to know God. Or, at least, it is one way for God to experience a little bit of Himself."

Then we once again provided God with the experience of clearing the table and washing the dishes.

Sunday Afternoon
Goodbye and Best Evidence

I know how weighty the word "fact" is in science, and I say without hesitation that individual personal continuance is to me a demonstrated fact.

— Sir Oliver Lodge[109]

I put my overnight case in my truck and returned to sit beside him on the front stoop and say my goodbyes. When I eased down next to him he handed me a cold can of Coke and said:

"Did my little course meet with your expectations?"

I told him I thought it was excellent and most convincing, then added: "The only thing I foresaw that didn't happen was me staring into the flickering fire while you told hair-raising tales of haunted houses and spectral encounters."

"I suppose a bit more atmosphere wouldn't hurt," he replied. "I'll have to consider adding a ghost story or two. Trouble is, those tales that cause the most shivers are rarely well documented, while the more evidential accounts seem rather mundane."

"Then you don't think that ghostly encounters are all hallucinations?"

"Oh no. There are numerous cases with multiple witnesses, both sequentially and simultaneously. These witnesses report observing the identical locations, clothing, actions, and expressions. Some ghosts have been seen head-on by those facing it and in left

---
[109] Lodge, *Why I Believe*, p. 1.

and right profile by those standing to either side.[110] Of course, some reports of ghosts probably are the results of hallucination, but all or even most reports certainly cannot be so easily explained away."

"Just how *would* you explain ghost sightings?"

"As I said yesterday, I cannot say for certain how any part of this old world actually works; but, I can most easily imagine the phenomenon as a matter of bleed-through caused by an overlapping of twinks. The majority of sightings don't demonstrate life after death so much as *energy* after death."[111]

"Any final questions before you hit the road?"

"I think you've pretty well covered the subject," I said, "but there is one thing that concerns me a bit."

"And that is?"

"How can I be certain that I will be me? After I die, that is."

"Imagine that we have the power to reach back in time and find you as you were at the age of 7," he said, "and that we magically transport that 7-year-old you onto this porch right now."

"Okay."

"We'll calm him down, and give him a soda, and sit him right there next to you. Then we look him over carefully and have a little chat with him."

"You know, I don't recall anything like that happening to me."

Ignoring my feeble attempt at humor, he continued: "In this *imaginary* situation, I have super x-ray vision. I can see the finest structures of this boy's body, and of yours. After careful comparison, I can attest that not a single molecule is the same. Over the years sep-

---

[110] Gauld, pp. 238-239.
[111] Myers, p. 209.

arating the two of you, your body has totally changed. And, in talking with the boy, I am hard pressed to discover any non-physical similarities between him and the person I know to be you. Your voices are different, as is your vocabulary. Your outlook on life ... virtually every aspect of who you are today seems markedly different from the 7-year-old version of yourself. Indeed, should a stranger walk up the drive and speak at length with you both, she would never suspect any link beyond a slight familial resemblance."

"But we'd have the same memories of being a child."

"You think so? You'd be surprised how much your memories have morphed over the years."

"You're probably right," I mused. "I was watching *The Wizard of Oz* with my grandson Dylan the other night, and I kept thinking they must have changed the movie, because I remembered it being different."

"Now," he went on, "you didn't die as a young man ..."

"Not that I recall."

"Yet, in most every way we can measure, the you that was 7 years old no longer exists.

"Just as you did not mourn his passing, so you need not be concerned about future life changes. Memories become muddled and faded, but our sense of self continues to grow stronger. All of the evidence we have points to the next life being most joyous and satisfying.

"Do you remember dreams?"

""Sometimes when I first wake up I do. But only the most recent one, and only for a moment," I replied. "Very few make a lasting impression."

"Have you ever been going about your daily business when some small event — some piece of conversation overheard or some action or scene observed — triggered the sudden recall of a dream? Not one of the dreams you ever remembered, but one you never knew you had dreamed until that moment. And you are a bit startled, and you think 'Hey, I had a dream about this!'"

"Yeah, that's happened to me a few times. It's a pretty weird feeling."

"So then, you have at least a fleeting familiarity with the experience of realizing that there has been more to your life than you had thought up to that moment. That dream was a part of your previous experience, part of who you were, yet you were going through life without any awareness of it. So," he lifted his eyes directly to mine, "which was the true you?"

I returned his gaze with a befuddled stare.

"You are your memories, are you not?"

I managed to nod and say: "At least partially."

"Then the 'you' that existed before your recall of that dream was at least somewhat different than the 'you' that existed afterwards, because your memories were different. So, at the point you gained the new memory, did you become less 'you'?"

"Well, no," I said, wondering where all this was going. "I was still the same me ... maybe just a tiny bit more."

"Indeed. And a similar feeling awaits you on the other side of this life. Soon after your body's death you will wake up to the memory of who you really are, and your reaction will be a mixture of relief and consternation. You'll exclaim things like 'Oh, wow ... of course! ... How could I have forgotten all of that?' Then, you will realize how much more of 'you' you are.

"And at some point in the far future, that greater 'you' will move on to another plane of existence and you will meet up with even more of 'you.' And once again you will be taken by surprise and feel chagrined to remember that larger self that you really are. And so the process will go on and on through successive stages, at each of which you will realize a continually grander 'you.'"

"Are you saying that I will merge with other souls?" I asked.

"I am saying that you will come to remember that you and other souls are, and always have been, one soul. That you will overcome the forgetfulness that now makes you feel separate and alone.

"I will be going through the same process, of course. And there will come a time when we will both remember that we are each other. Then we'll recall, fondly I hope, this conversation we once had with ourself.

"You will never be less than you are right now. There will never be any diminishment of your current personality, no loss of any sense of self ... just continued merging with more and more parts of you, gaining more and more memories, until, at long last, all of our journeys are complete. Until we remember being All That Is.

"Even when you become God again, you will still remember being you."

For awhile I could think of nothing to say, so I just sat there in the sunlight letting his words sink in. Then, I realized there was nothing more I could say, so I stood and grasped his hand. "Thank you so much for an enlightening weekend. Now that I've got a book-full of the most convincing evidence for Survival, I feel a bit less anxious about dying."

"Don't expect to ever get over that anxiety completely," he said, shaking my hand warmly. "The human animal you reside within will never 'go gentle into that good night,'[112] it was programmed to keep itself physically alive, else we wouldn't be standing here today.

"I'll tell you a secret about that book, though. In my opinion, the very best, most convincing evidence isn't in there."

Now, *that* got my attention real good. "Why would you hold out on me?" I stammered. "Are you saving the best for another weekend?"

---

[112] Thanks to Dylan Thomas for that memorable phrase.

"Oh no. I'm not holding out on you. The very best evidence isn't one colossal case that would suffice as proof to everyone; the best evidence is an amalgam of millions of personal incidents.

"Polls show that most people believe in life-after-death and in some sort of heaven.[113] Much of this belief is based on personal experience. Almost everyone could tell a story about themselves or some member of their family that suggests the reality of an afterlife. We don't generally hear these stories unless we probe for them and, by themselves, they rarely rate publication. But if you could stand back and grasp the huge volume of experiences, you'd see that the evidence is overwhelming.

"And, we should not forget the work of the many hundreds of unheralded but talented psychics out there. Most are honest, sincere, and dedicated to helping souls on both sides communicate with one another."

"Having been convinced by the major cases you've shown me," I said, "I'll certainly be more open to such less prominent stories in the future."

"As well you should. But don't go to the extreme and blindly accept every story and claim that you hear either. The certainty that there really is a spiritual or astral plane populated by living souls does not negate the fact that some souls, both here and there, are liars and frauds who seek to drain your energy or your wallet. As they go about making their own hell, don't let them come between you and heaven.

"Be open to the spirit, but don't disengage your critical mind."

"Sounds like excellent advice," I said, starting my truck and putting it in gear. "Be assured, I shall try to follow it." I thanked him again, and he wished me a safe journey, and I drove off down the tree-shadowed drive.

---

[113] Gallup, pp. 139 & 143.

The last glimpse I caught of him, in my "magic" rear-view mirror, he was throwing a stick for Dasher to retrieve.

As I headed towards my in-law's to pick up my wife and continue our vacation, I began to recap the weekend. Of course, I had my recordings and the *Afterlife Casebook*, so I knew I had a lot of reviewing and analyzing and writing time ahead. (In fact, it took almost a year to put it all together.) Nevertheless, I couldn't help considering what, of all the great evidence I had received, was the most convincing. Then, while sitting at a traffic light and weighing which route to take, it occurred to me that pieces of evidence are very like paths to a destination — which one is best depends upon where you start out.

Since each reader had his or her own beliefs when they came to this book, there isn't likely to be a consensus on what evidence is strongest. Obviously, I thought all the cases were worthy of inclusion, and these are only a small portion of the evidential material that has been collected over the past few decades. Perhaps the children's near-death experiences had the greatest effect on you, or the OBEs of people blind since birth. I will always remember the malefic goldsmith and his abused apprentice; but, all things considered, the buried crosses impressed me most.

I trust that you have been equally impressed, and thus reassured by these 23 cases, but they hardly begin to present the totality of the evidence available today.

The "Old Man" and I look forward to meeting you in this life or the next.

Appendices

The original version of *The Survival Files* contains several appendices that have been removed to conserve space. The bibliography has been combined with those of the other books in this trilogy and appears as the final section. The documents titled "The Scientific Fallacy" and "The Skeptical Quagmire" may be accessed online at www.survivaltop40.com.

The Hereafter Trilogy
Vol. II: The Afterlife Confirmed

The public was being protected against all knowledge of the inexplicable, the weird, the surrealistic. All part of the usual governmental pretense that human affairs were rationally administered by experts who knew what was really going on. They feared that if people ever discovered that those in power were as confused by this inexplicable universe as those out of power, then the whole charade might collapse.

— Robert Anton Wilson, *Schrodinger's Cat*

Chapter One
A Gettysburg Gathering

*It seems like a sunset
but in reality it is a dawn;
when the grave locks you up,
that is when your soul is freed.*

— Rūmī [114]

The rain had stopped in the morning, but the sunshine on the green fields and split-log fences did little to brighten our somber mood. For the moment, there were no busses on the gravel pullover and no crowds of school children or camera-toting tourists milling about beside us; we stood quietly alone, reluctant to challenge the majestic silence of the lands that stretched before us. They were anything but silent during the first three days of July in 1863 as more than 51,000 soldiers died or were wounded here.

Two years and more had passed since I spent a weekend being tutored by "the old man" not so far from here, at his cabin in the Appalachian hills. We had kept somewhat in touch, meeting occasionally at charitable functions in D.C. Today, we were visiting the battlefields as a prelude to a conference on the afterlife being held in historic Gettysburg, Pennsylvania. It seemed to me only fitting to speak about the Survival of death at a place known for the deaths of so many in such a brief time. Finally, the old man broke the somber mood.

---

[114] Ode number 911 by Jalāl ad-Dīn Muhammad Rūmī , 13th century Sufi poet.

"Remind you of anything?" he asked, looking down at two dead mice semi-submerged in a small pool of rainwater at the bottom of a grassy slope.

They were lying in a line, nose to tail, as if they had been playing follow-the-leader and the first one had died so the second followed suit. They had wandered pretty far from the McPherson barn to have dined on poison there, but I could think of no other reason for their demise. I was tempted to say something about them being overcome with grief at the horrendous loss of life on this field where the battle of Gettysburg had started, but the place didn't seem right for any form of levity. So, I just gave him a questioning glance.

"At the cabin, we considered several OBEs. We decided to call them 'Other-Body Experiences'."

"I recall being especially impressed with the OBEs of the children and folks who are blind."

"Just so. And do you recall also why we thought that OBEs in the blind might provide special evidence for Survival?"

"I do. We speculated that the experiential referents necessary for the blind to recognize physical images must have been learned prior to their birth."

"Your memory is excellent," he said.

"Well, maybe, but I don't recall any link between OBEs and dead rodents."

He reached over and patted my forearm in such an avuncular manner that I half expected him to say "Tut, tut, my good man." But he just smiled a bit and, after looking a while longer at the grassy hills, asked "What do you think of the OBEs of sighted adults as evidence for a life beyond?"

I considered this as we turned and walked back towards our rental car. Best I could recall, when at his cabin, we hadn't talked much about the evidential value of OBEs. When I wrote up our conversation, I included a quote from Robert Crookall to the effect that being able to temporarily leave one's body was a good indication that one could perform the same feat after the body died.[115] Beyond that, I hadn't thought much about the matter, and I told him so.

> "Let's say that you live in Orlando and have the sensation of leaving your physical body and traveling to Osaka. It is true that being able to accomplish this feat while your body is alive does not guarantee that you will be able to repeat the performance after the body's demise. No, it does not guarantee it, but it does suggest it very strongly. If the very existence of your mind was dependent upon your physical body being alive, then there would have to be some physical mechanism of dependence operating between your body in Florida and your mind in Japan. But such a connection doesn't exist. There are neither blood-filled arteries nor strands of nerves stretching across the Pacific. No electrical signals or light rays flicker between your mind and the body it left behind. There can be no physical dependency if there is no physical connection."

"But there does seem to be some sort of connection," I pointed out. "Many astral travelers have reported that a disturbance or discomfort of their body causes their mind to snap back from wherever it has journeyed."

> "Which indicates that the OBEr's mind remains somewhat aware of their body; but awareness isn't the same as dependence.
>
> "Any observation mechanism must have a viewpoint and perspective and scale. But this mechanism cannot be physical or we could detect it with physical instruments."

"I well remember the astral eyes," I said.

---

[115] "If a man can leave his physical body temporarily and continue to exist as a self-conscious being, the fact would prove a strong presumption that eventually when he comes to leave his physical body, *i.e.*, to die, he will then also continue to exist as a self-conscious being in that second body." Quoted in Ebon, p. 116.

"Indeed. And if something isn't physical, how can it be dependent upon a physical process? I really don't see any good reason to suspect that the cessation of physical processes in the body (which we call death) should have any effect upon these non-physical (astral) mechanisms."

"So the ability of some people to travel out-of-body is, truly, additional evidence for the ability of us all to survive the grave."

"Seems a fair and reasonable conclusion to me.

"And that grave we will survive brings us back to the mice."

We had reached the car, so I took advantage of the time to get it started and fasten my seatbelt to consider that reference, then: "Ah, yes! Now I remember. I shall have to include that story in my next book."

Here is the case we were referring to. I present it exactly as it was written by Robert Dale Owen, just after the U.S. Civil War ended.[116]

The Two Field-Mice

"In the winter of 1835-36, a schooner was frozen up in the upper part of the Bay of Fundy, close to Dorchester, which is nine miles from the river Pedeudiac. During the time of her detention she was intrusted to the care of a gentleman of the name of Clarke, who is at this time captain of the schooner Julia Hallock, trading between New York and St. Jago de Cuba.

"Captain Clarke's paternal grandmother, Mrs. Ann Dawe Clarke, to whom he was much attached, was at that time living, and, so far as he knew, well. She was residing at Lyme-Regis, in the county of Dorset, England.

"On the night of the 17th of February, 1836, Captain Clarke, then on board the schooner referred to, had a dream of so vivid a character that it produced a great impression upon him. He dreamed that, being at Lyme-Regis, he saw pass before him the funeral of his grandmother. He took note of the chief persons who composed the procession, observed who were the

---

[116] Owen, pp. 178-180.

pall-bearers, who were the mourners, and in what order they walked, and distinguished who was the officiating pastor. He joined the procession as it approached the churchyard gate, and proceeded with it to the grave. He thought (in his dream) that the weather was stormy, and the ground wet, as after a heavy rain; and he noticed that the wind, being high, blew the pall partly off the coffin. The graveyard which they entered, the old Protestant one, in the center of the town, was the same in which, as Captain Clarke knew, their family burying-place was. He perfectly remembered its situation; but, to his surprise, the funeral procession did not proceed thither, but to another part of the churchyard, at some distance. There (still in his dream) he saw the open grave, partially filled with water, as from the rain; and, looking into it, he particularly noticed floating in the water two drowned field-mice. Afterward, as he thought, he conversed with his mother; and she told him that the morning had been so tempestuous that the funeral, originally appointed for ten o'clock, had been deferred till four. He remarked, in reply, that it was a fortunate circumstance; for, as he had just arrived in time to join the procession, had the funeral taken place in the forenoon he could not have attended it at all.

"This dream made so deep an impression on Captain Clarke that in the morning he noted the date of it. Some time afterward there came the news of his grandmother's death, with the additional particular that she was buried on the same day on which he, being in North America, had dreamed of her funeral.

"When, four years afterward, Captain Clarke visited Lyme-Regis, he found that every particular of his dream minutely corresponded with the reality. The pastor, the pall-bearers, the mourners, were the same persons he had seen. Yet this, we may suppose, he might naturally have anticipated. But the funeral had been appointed for ten o'clock in the morning, and, in consequence of the tempestuous weather and the heavy rain that was falling, it had been delayed until four in the afternoon. His mother, who attended the funeral, distinctly recollected that the high wind blew the pall partially off the coffin. In consequence of a wish expressed by the old lady shortly before her death, she was buried, not in the burying-place of the family, but at another spot, selected by herself; and to this spot Captain Clarke, without any indication from the family or otherwise, proceeded at once, as directly as if he had been present at the burial. Finally, on comparing notes with the old sexton, it appeared that the heavy rain of the morning had partially filled the grave, and that there were actually found in it two field-mice, drowned.

"This last incident, even if there were no other, might suffice to preclude all idea of accidental coincidence.

"The above was narrated to me by Captain Clarke himself;* [Footnote in Owen's text: * In New York, on July 28, 1859. The narrative is written out from notes taken on board his schooner.] with permission to use his name in attestation of its truth."

On the way back to Lincoln Square, we agreed that Captain Clarke's tale is not strong evidence of Survival, as it could simply be the result of an other-body experience. But OBEs such as his certainly support the idea of an independent spirit and thus of its ability to endure beyond the demise of the physical body. When the vast amount of such supporting evidence is considered, those cases that do provide solid evidence for Survival become even more convincing. Throughout this book, I will present some of the most convincing evidence for an afterlife as listed in the current Survival Top 40. (See www.survivaltop40.com for more about this list and Survival evidence in general.) Interspersed among these top cases, I shall relate our discussions of some implications and intriguing aspects of evidence of the supporting type.

A note on the organization of the following material: Throughout our three-day stay in Gettysburg, the old man and I had several opportunities to discuss matters both weighty and mundane. Unlike the course of instruction that I was privileged to receive at his cabin, these talks were unscheduled and unstructured, so presenting them as they happened would likely be more confusing than enlightening.

We parked in the garage behind the hotel and walked up the shady side of the street towards the main entrance.

"Being in this historic city," he said, as his walking stick tapped along the concrete walk, "it occurs to me, that you might set the scene for this new book of yours with a bit of history."

"The history of psychic phenomena is a huge subject," I replied, as we rounded the corner into the sunlight and started up the wide brick stairs. "Did you have any particular approach in mind?"

"Well, I suppose you could start with the prophets of old, but you'd likely lose half your readers before you got to Delphi. Perhaps a few words about rapping would be both enlightening and entertaining," he said, punctuating the word "rapping" by tapping the head of his stick on the frame of the large glass doors to the lobby of the Gettysburg Hotel.

Chapter Two
Knock, Knock ...

When faced with evidence against their will,
They keep the same opinion still.

— Anonymous

Unexplained physical activities – knockings, flying objects, and such – have been reported throughout history. So numerous and common are they, that several languages have coined words specifically to denote them, including the German "poltergeister" — meaning "rumbling (or noisy) spirit" — from which, of course, English speakers have derived "poltergeist."

There are three popular explanations for poltergeist activity. Fans of contemporary horror movies might agree with Catholic priests of previous centuries that poltergeists are manifestations of Satan or, at least, of one of his demonic hoard. As organized efforts in occult research were getting underway in the 19th century, investigators noted the rather playful aspect of many outbreaks and tended to think in terms of "tricksy elves" or "imps of frolic and misrule." As the new science of psychology came of age in the 20th century, the focus shifted to a supposed correlation between the disturbances and the presence of pubescent youths. The idea here being that repressed sexual energy was being released in bursts of kinetic activity. This approach remains popular in contemporary thought; though an examination of the facts reveals that frustrated libidos alone are insufficient to explain the phenomena.

Let's look at a few representative, and fascinating, cases occurring over the past 450 years. [Note: To save space and move this narrative along more smoothly, two of the original case descriptions ("Terror at Tedworth" and "A Confounding Castle") have been excised. They may be viewed on the web at www.SurvivalTop40.com.]

An Excitement at Epworth[117]

Here we have a report written by a 17-year-old Englishman, the fifteenth of nineteen children born to a highly educated and immensely respected family. Because this young man was away at boarding school during most of the occurrences, his report is based on interviews of, and written testimonies he collected from, his own family members and neighbors. I have attempted to shorten the account a bit by deleting minor and repetitive statements, but the majority is well worth quoting — and studying.

The young man writes:

"On December 2, 1716, while Robert Brown, my father's servant, was sitting with one of the maids, a little before ten at night, in the dining-room, which opened into the garden, they both heard one knocking at the door. Robert rose and opened it, but could see nobody. Quickly it knocked again, and groaned. 'It is Mr. Turpine,' said Robert: 'he has the stone, and uses to groan so.' He opened the door again twice or thrice, the knocking being twice or thrice repeated; but, still seeing nothing, and being a little startled, they rose up and went to bed.

"When Robert came to the top of the garret stairs, he saw a handmill which was at a little distance whirled about very swiftly. When he related this he said, 'Nought vexed me but that it was empty. I thought if it had but been full of malt he might have ground his heart out for me.' When he was in bed, he heard as it were the gobbling of a turkey-cock close to the bedside, and soon after the sound of one stumbling over his shoes and boots; but there was none there: he had left them below.

---

[117] This presentation is based on numerous documents, foremost among which are Robert Dale Owen's *Footfalls on the Boundary of Another World*, and Dudley Wright's *The Epworth Phenomena*.

"The next day, he and the maid related these things to the other maid, who laughed heartily, and said, 'What a couple of fools are you! I defy any thing to fright me.' After churning in the evening, she put the butter in the tray, and had no sooner carried it into the dairy than she heard a knocking on the shelf where several puncheons[118] of milk stood, first above the shelf, then below. She took the candle, and searched both above and below, but, being able to find nothing, threw down butter, tray and all, and ran away for life.

"The next evening, between five and six o'clock, my sister Molly, then about twenty years of age, sitting in the dining-room reading, heard as if it were the door that led into the hall open, and a person walking in that seemed to have on a silk night-gown, rustling and trailing along. It seemed to walk round her, then to the door, then round again; but she could see nothing. She thought, 'It signifies nothing to run away; for, whatever it is, it can run faster than me.' So she rose, put her book under her arm, and walked slowly away.

"After supper, she was sitting with my sister Sukey (about a year older than her) in one of the chambers, and telling her what had happened. She made quite light of it, telling her, 'I wonder you are so easily frighted: I would fain see what would fright me.' Presently a knocking began under the table. She took the candle and looked, but could find nothing. Then the iron casement began to clatter, and the lid of a warming-pan. Next the latch of the door moved up and down without ceasing. She started up, leaped into the bed without undressing, pulled the bed-clothes over her head, and never ventured to look up until next morning.

"A night or two after, my sister Hetty (a year younger than my sister Molly) was waiting as usual, between nine and ten, to take away my father's candle, when she heard one coming down the garret stairs, walking slowly by her, then going down the best stairs, then up the back stairs, and up the garret stairs and at every step it seemed the house shook from top

---

[118] A puncheon is a cask that holds about 84 gallons (318 liters).

to bottom. Just then my father knocked. She went in, took his candle, and got to bed as fast as possible. In the morning she told this to my eldest sister, who told her, 'You know I believe none of these things: pray let me take away the candle to-night, and I will find out the trick.' She accordingly took my sister Hetty's place, and had no sooner taken away the candle than she heard a noise below. She hastened down stairs to the hall, where the noise was, but it was then in the kitchen. She ran into the kitchen, where it was drumming on the inside of the screen. When she went round, it was drumming on the outside, and so always on the side opposite to her. Then she heard a knocking at the back kitchen door. She ran to it, unlocked it softly, and, when the knocking was repeated, suddenly opened it; but nothing was to be seen. As soon as she had shut it, the knocking began again. She opened it again but could see nothing. When she went to shut the door, it was violently thrust against her; but she set her knee and her shoulder to the door, forced it to, and turned the key. Then the knocking began again; but she let it go on, and went up to bed. However, from that time she was thoroughly convinced that there was no imposture in the affair.

"The next morning, my sister telling my mother what had happened, she said, 'If I hear any thing myself, I shall know how to judge.' Soon after she begged her to come into the nursery. She did, and heard, in the corner of the room, as it were the violent rocking of a cradle; but no cradle had been there for some years. She was convinced it was preternatural, and earnestly prayed it might not disturb her in her own chamber at the hours of retirement; and it never did. She now thought it was proper to tell my father. But he was extremely angry, and said, 'Sukey, I am ashamed of you. These boys and girls frighten one another; but you are a woman of sense, and should know better. Let me hear of it no more.'

"At six in the evening he had family prayers as usual. When he began the prayer for the king, a knocking began all round the room, and a thundering knock attended the Amen. The same was heard from this time every morning and evening while the prayer for the king was repeated.

"Mr. Hoole, the vicar of Haxey (an eminently pious and sensible man) — said, 'Robert Brown came over to me, and told me your father desired my company. When I came, he gave me an account of all that had happened, particularly the knocking during family prayer. But that evening (to my great satisfaction) we had no knocking at all. But between nine and ten a servant came in, and said, "Old Jeffrey is coming," (that was the name of one that died in the house) "for I hear the signal." This, they informed me, was heard every night about a quarter before ten. It was toward the top of the house, on the outside, at the northeast corner, resembling the loud creaking of a saw, or rather that of a windmill when the body of it is turned about in order to shift the sails to the wind. We then heard a knocking over our heads; and [your father], catching up a candle, said, "Come, sir, now you shall hear for yourself." We went upstairs; he with much hope, and I (to say the truth) with much fear. When we came into the nursery, it was knocking in the next room; when we went there, it was knocking in the nursery. And there it continued to knock, though we came in, particularly at the head of the bed (which was of wood). He then said, sternly, "Thou deaf and dumb devil! Why dost thou fright these children, that cannot answer for themselves? Come to me, in my study, that am a man!" Instantly, it knocked his knock (the particular knock which he always used) and we heard nothing more that night.'

"Till this time my father had never heard the least disturbance in his study. But the next evening, as he attempted to go into his study (of which none had the key but himself) when he opened the door, it was thrust back with such violence as had like to have thrown him down. However, he thrust the door open, and went in. Presently there was a knocking, first on one side, then on the other, and, after a time, in the next room, wherein my sister Nancy was. He went into that room, and, the noise continuing, adjured it to speak, but in vain."

There is more to this account, but the incidents described therein are of essentially the same character as those related above. And who was this young gentleman who tells such haunting tales? He was John Wesley, later to be known as the patriarch of the Methodist church. His father was the Reverend Samuel Wesley, the rector of Epworth, England, and the disturbances took place at the parsonage there. The testimony above has been extensively corroborated, mainly by a journal that Samuel Wesley kept at the time and by numerous letters written by eyewitnesses. A few incidents described in those documents may be of interest here.

Samuel Wesley's journal entries include two occasions when the knockings seemed to respond in kind to knocks made by he and his children. On three occasions, he notes, he was "pushed by an invisible power, once against the corner of my desk in the study, a second time against the door of the matted chamber, a third time against the right side of the frame of my study door, as I was going in." His entry on Christmas Day states that their household dog, a mastiff, "came whining to us," as he did at every occurrence except for the initial incident when the dog "barked violently." That mastiff, Samuel wrote, "seemed more afraid than any of the children."

Mrs. Susanna Wesley, in a letter to John, wrote that once she had the idea that if the intruder was a spirit it might answer her, and so she stamped several times on the floor. In return, she says, "it repeated under the sole of my feet exactly the same number of strokes, with the very same intervals."

Emily Wesley later wrote in a letter that the presence "would knock when I was putting the children to bed, just under me, where I sat. One time little Kezzy, pretending to scare Polly, as I was undressing them, stamped with her foot on the floor; and immediately it answered with three knocks, just in the same place. It was more loud and fierce if any one said it was rats, or any thing natural."

It is difficult for the fair-minded person to disagree with one of Wesley's biographers who concluded: "The accounts given of these disturbances are so detailed and authentic as to entitle them to the most implicit credit. The eye- and ear-witnesses were persons of strong understandings and well cultivated minds, unmuddled by superstition, and in some instances rather skeptically inclined."[119]

The entire Wesley family ultimately concluded that the cause of the phenomena was supernatural. John considered it the work of the devil but today's readers will likely prefer Mrs. Wesley's explanation. She supposed that the disturbances portended the death of her brother, who was working abroad for the East India Company. This gentleman, having recently acquired a large fortune, had suddenly disappeared and was never heard from again.

Or was he?

The Troublesome Tenant

Now we briefly consider an unusually spirited relationship between a tenant and his landlord. In May of 1835, a Captain Molesworth rented one side of a duplex home from a Mr. Webster, who resided in the adjoining half. This was in Trinity, two miles from Edinburgh, Scotland.

Within two months of he and his daughter moving in, the captain began to hear noises that, he believed, must be coming from Mr. Webster's side of the home. His landlord denied these complaints, saying he certainly wouldn't do anything that might damage the reputation of his own house, or drive a responsible tenant out of it; and retorted that Molesworth must be causing the strange noises.

Meanwhile the disturbances continued both day and night. Sometimes there was the sound as of invisible feet; sometimes there were knockings, scratchings, or rustlings, first on one side, then on the other. Occasionally the unseen agent seemed to be rapping to a certain tune, and would answer, by so many knocks, any question to which the reply was in numbers; as, "How many persons are there in this room?"

---

[119] Clarke, Dr. Adam, *Memoirs of the Wesley Family*, Vol. 1, Tess, 1823, p. 245.
   [This quote has been translated into contemporary English by the author.]

So forcible at times were the poundings that the wall trembled visibly. Beds, too, were occasionally heaved up, as by some person underneath. Yet, search as they would, no perpetrator could be discovered. Captain Molesworth had the floorboards removed in the rooms where the noises were loudest and most frequent, and perforated the wall that divided his residence from Mr. Webster's; but without the least result.

Sheriff's officers, masons, justices of the peace, and the officers of the regiment quartered at Leith, all came to Molesworth's aid, in hopes of detecting or frightening away his tormentor; but in vain. Suspecting that it might be someone outside the house, they formed a cordon round it; but caught no intruder.

Finally fed-up with the constant disturbance, the landlord sued the tenant for damages to the property's reputation as well as for the lifted floorboards and the holes in the walls, not to mention the time that the captain fired a bullet into the wainscoting in a frustrated attempt to shoot the spirit. At the trial, all of the above facts, and more, were elicited by the plaintiff's attorney, who spent several hours in examining numerous witnesses. The published details of this case are based on the testimony of this attorney, a Scottish solicitor named Maurice Lothian.[120] The trial dragged on for at least two years, and apparently was never settled to anyone's satisfaction.

Once Molesworth moved from the premises, the commotion ceased. Soon afterward his daughter, who had been ill for some time, passed on.

---

[120] Later, Lothian became the Procurator Fiscal of the county of Edinburg.

Chapter Three

... Who's There? ...

Everything of which we are ignorant appears improbable, but the improbabilities of today are the elementary truths of tomorrow.

— Charles Richet[121]

The poltergeist cases presented in the previous chapter are just the tip of the iceberg, for there are records of scores of such cases prior to the mid-19th century, and hundreds up to the current time. In many, if not most, of these incidents, rappings, knockings, drumming, or similar percussive sounds are heard. And in more than a few these knocks have demonstrated sufficient awareness and intelligence to understand queries and provide correct answers. At Tedworth, the mysterious drum beats would mimic raps made by observers and sometimes seemed to play requested pieces. The Wesley family received several intelligent responses to both their verbal requests and their own knocks. And whatever was disturbing Captain Molesworth's domicile would answer any question "to which the reply was in numbers."

Testing the Spirit

Despite the evidence that, in almost every case, some sort of intelligence was responsible for the disturbances, no one took the next step — and from our vantage point, the obvious step — and actually asked the "spirit" who it was. That didn't happen until 13 years after Molesworth's troubles began and an ocean away, in the small village of Hydesville, New York. And it only occurred then because a nine-year-old-girl's curiosity and verve overcame her natural fear of the unknown.

---

[121] *30 Years of Psychic Research*, p. 9.

This child was one of two daughters living with their parents in a rented house while their new home was being built nearby. The year was 1848, the girl's name was Catherine (Kate) Fox, and this is her family's story:[122]

The Fox family were reputable farmers, members in good standing of the Methodist Church, and much respected by their neighbors as honest, upright people. Mr. John D. Fox was born in America of German descent. Mrs. Margaret Fox's ancestors were French and there was some history of psychic powers on her mother's side of the family. Mr. and Mrs. Fox had six children, of whom the two youngest — Margaret, twelve years old, and Kate, nine — were residing with them when, on the 11th of December, 1847, they moved into their temporary quarters.

Soon after their arrival, they began hearing many strange noises; but they assumed that rats and mice were the source. During the next month, however, the noises began to assume the character of slight knockings heard at night in the bedroom; sometimes appearing to sound from the cellar beneath. At first, Mrs. Fox sought to persuade herself this might be but the hammering of a shoemaker, in a house close by, sitting up late at work. But further observation showed that the sounds originated within the house. For not only did the knockings gradually become more distinct, and not only were they heard first in one part of the house, then in another, but the family noticed that these raps, even when not very loud, often caused a motion, tremulous rather than a sudden jar, of the bedsteads and chairs, and sometimes of the floor. This motion was quite perceptible to the touch when a hand was laid on the chairs, was sometimes felt at night in the slightly oscillating motion of a bed, and was occasionally perceived as a sort of vibration when standing on the floor.

Toward the end of March, the disturbances increased in loudness and frequency. Mr. Fox and his wife got up night after night and thoroughly

---

[122] Much of this text comes from the works of the Hon. Robert Dale Owen and Sir Arthur Conan Doyle.

searched the house; but they discovered nothing. When the raps came on a door, Mr. Fox would stand, ready to open, the moment they were repeated. But this expedient, too, proved unavailing. Though he opened the door on the instant, there was no one to be seen. Next, he stationed himself outside of the door while his wife stood inside; but the knocks were heard on the door between them.

The only circumstance which seemed to suggest the possibility of trickery or of mistake was that these various incidents never happened in daylight. And thus, notwithstanding the strangeness of the thing, when morning came they began to think it must have been but the fancy of the night. Not being given to superstition, they clung, throughout several weeks of annoyance, to the idea that some natural explanation would at last appear. They did not abandon this hope until the night of Friday, the 31st of March, 1848.

The day had been cold and stormy, with snow on the ground. In the course of the afternoon, their son David came to visit them from his farm, about three miles distant. His mother then first recounted to him the particulars of the annoyances they had endured; for until now they had been little disposed to communicate these to anyone. He heard her with a smile. "Well, mother," he said, "I advise you not to say a word to the neighbors about it. When you find it out, it will be one of the simplest things in the world." And in that belief he returned home.

Wearied by a succession of sleepless nights and of fruitless attempts to penetrate the mystery, the Fox family retired very early on that Friday evening, hoping for a respite from the disturbances that harassed them. But they were doomed to disappointment.

The parents had moved the children's beds into their bedroom, but scarcely had the mother seen her daughters safely beneath the blankets, and was retiring herself, when the children cried out, "Here they are again!" Their mother chided them, and lay down. At which point the noises became louder and more startling. The children sat up in bed. Mrs. Fox called in her husband. The night being windy, he thought it might be the rattling of the sashes. He tried several, shaking them to see if they were loose. It was then that Kate pointed out that as often as her father shook a window sash the noises seemed to reply. Being a lively child, and in a measure accustomed to what was going on, she turned to where the noise was, snapped her fingers, and called out, "Here, old Splitfoot, do as I do!" The knocking instantly responded.

Others, as we have seen, had also noticed that their noisy ghosts would sometimes follow their lead and rap responses to their own raps, but Kate Fox next went where no man, or girl, had gone before — she raised her hand and moved her finger across her thumb in a snapping motion but she made no sound. Immediately a knock was sounded to this "silent snap." Clearly the maker of the noises could observe what was happening in the room! Kate called her mother's attention to this phenomenon. And as often as she repeated the noiseless motion, just so often responded the raps.

This at once arrested her mother's attention. "Count ten," she said, addressing the noise. Ten strokes, distinctly given! "How old is my daughter Margaret?" Twelve strokes! "And Kate?" Nine! "What can all this mean?" was Mrs. Fox's thought. Who was answering her? Was it only some mysterious echo of her own thought? But the next question which she put seemed to refute that idea. How many children have I?" she asked, aloud. Seven strokes. "Ah!" she thought, "it can blunder sometimes." And then, aloud, "Try again!" Still the number of raps was seven. But then she remembered something. "Are they all alive?" she asked. Silence, for answer. "How many are living?" Six strokes. "How many dead?" A single stroke. She had lost a child.

Then she asked, "Are you a man?" No answer. "Are you a spirit?" It rapped. "May my neighbors hear if I call them?" It rapped again.

Neighborly Ingenuity

Thereupon she asked her husband to call a neighbor, a Mrs. Redfield, who came in laughing. But her attitude was soon changed. The answers to her inquiries were as prompt and pertinent as they had been to those of

Mrs. Fox. She was struck with awe; and when, in reply to a question about the number of her children, by rapping four, instead of three as she expected, it reminded her of a little daughter, Mary, whom she had recently lost, the mother burst into tears.

Other neighbors, attracted by the rumor of the disturbances, gradually gathered in, until the house was crammed with folks. Mrs. Fox left for the home of Mrs. Redfield, and the children were taken home by another neighbor. Mr. Fox remained in the crowded home.

Having formed a sort of informal committee of investigation, the crowd, in shrewd Yankee fashion, spent a large part of the night probing for information. They began to question the rapper using a "twenty questions" methodology wherein a response signified "yes" and the lack of a response meant "no." To ensure accuracy, each question was repeated in a reversed manner. For example, if the query "Were you a man?" received a positive response, the next question would be "Were you a woman?" And each time, the answer was properly the opposite of the initial response.

In this way the sounds alleged that they were produced by a spirit; by an injured spirit; by a spirit who had been murdered in that house; between four and five years ago; not by any of the neighbors (whose names were called over one by one) but by a former resident of the house, a certain John C. Bell, a blacksmith. His name was obtained by naming in succession the former occupants of the house.

The spirit alleged, further, that he had been murdered, at the age of 31, in the bedroom, for money, on a Tuesday night, at twelve o'clock; that no one but the murdered man and Mr. Bell were in the house at the time; that the body was carried down to the cellar early next morning, not through the outside cellar door, but by being dragged through the parlor into the pantry and thence down the cellar stairs; that it was buried, 10-feet deep, in the cellar, but not until the night after the murder.

Thereupon the assembled party adjourned to the cellar, which had an earthen floor. Mr. Redfield stood in various places and asked, each time, if that was the spot of burial. There was no response until he stood in the center. Then the noises were heard, as from beneath the ground. This was repeated several times, always with a similar result, no sound occurring when he stood at any other place than the center. One of the witnesses describes the sounds in the cellar as resembling "a thumping a foot or two under ground."

To double check this burial spot, on the following evening a group went into the cellar and all but one stood motionless while one person, Mr. Carlos Hyde, moved about to different spots. While this was going on, another neighbor, Mr. William Duesler, sat in the bedroom above and kept repeating the question: "Is anybody standing over the place where the body was buried?" In every instance, as soon as Mr. Hyde stepped to the center of the cellar the raps were sounded loudly enough to be heard in both the bedroom and the basement; but as often as he stood anywhere else, there was silence.

Although we have no record of who thought up the idea, it was also Duesler who, on that first night, sought to obtain information that could not be determined by single yes-or-no answers: the identity of the murdered man. He did that by calling out the letters of the alphabet, asking, at each, if that was the initial of the murdered man's first name; and so of the second name. The sounds responded at C and B. An attempt to obtain the entire name did not then succeed. At a later period the name "Charles B. Rosma" was given in the same way in reply to queries from David Fox.

It took four months of such tedious questioning before it was thought to ask the spirit to spell out answers by rapping once for the letter A, twice for B, thrice for C, etc. rather than having the questioner go through the alphabet over and over. Mr. Isaac Post will forever hold an honored place in the history of spirit communications because he made that suggestion.

The report of the night's wonders at Hydesville spread all over the neighborhood and beyond. On Saturday, the house was beset by a crowd of the curious. That night there were some three hundred people in and about the house. Various persons asked questions; and the replies corresponded at every point to those formerly given.

Then it was proposed to dig in the cellar; but, as the house stands on a flat plain not far from a small sluggish stream, the diggers reached water at the depth of less than three feet, and had to abandon the attempt. In the summer of 1848, when the water level was much lower, David Fox, Henry Bush, Lyman Granger, and others, recommenced digging in the cellar. At the depth of five feet they came to a plank, through which they bored with an auger, when, the auger-bit being loose, it dropped through out of sight. Digging further, they found several pieces of crockery and some charcoal and quicklime, indicating that the soil must at some time have been disturbed to a considerable depth; and finally they came upon some human hair and several bones, which proved to be portions of a human skeleton, including two bones of the hand and certain parts of the skull. But they found no corpse.

Supporting Testimony

Within a few weeks of the March 31st disturbances, a 40-page pamphlet[123] was published in which many of the neighbors gave testimony as to what they had witnessed.

Duesler stated that he inhabited the same house seven years before, and that during the term of his residence there he never heard any noise of the kind in or about the premises. He added that no other residents prior to Bell had any such experiences either. Apparently, the same cannot be said for the Bells themselves, for a near neighbor, Mrs. Pulver, claimed that Mrs. Bell once complained of not having slept at all during the previous night because she seemed to hear someone walking about from one room to another. Pulver further deposed that she heard Bell, on subsequent occasions, speak of unexplained noises.

Pulver's daughter, Lucretia, stated that she worked for and boarded with the Bells for three months during the winter of 1843-44 (which would

---

[123] *A Report of the Mysterious Noises heard in the house of Mr. John D. Fox, in Hydesville, Arcadia, Wayne County, authenticated by the certificates and confirmed by the statements of that place and vicinity*, E.E. Lewis Publishers, Canandaigua, New York, 1848.

have encompassed the time that the peddler claimed to have been murdered). She was 15-years old then and going to school. She stated that the Bells "appeared to be very good folks, only rather quick-tempered." Furthermore, she recalled that one afternoon a peddler, apparently about thirty years of age and having with him a trunk and a basket, called at the Bell's. Mrs. Bell informed Lucretia that she had known him formerly. Shortly after he came in, Mr. and Mrs. Bell consulted together for nearly half an hour in the pantry. Then Mrs. Bell told Lucretia — very unexpectedly to her —that they did not require her anymore; that she was going that afternoon to Lock Berlin,[124] and that Lucretia had better return home. Accordingly, Mrs. Bell and Lucretia left the house, the peddler and Mr. Bell remaining. Before she went, however, Lucretia looked at a piece of delaine[125] and told the peddler she would take enough to make a dress from it if he would call the next day at her father's house, which was nearby. He promised to do so, but he never showed up. In fact, none of the villagers could recall seeing the peddler since that time. Three days after she had left, Mrs. Bell returned and, to Lucretia's surprise, sent for her again to stay with them.

A few days after this, Lueretia began to hear knockings in her bedroom. The sounds seemed to be under the foot of the bed, and were repeated during a number of nights. One night, when Mr. and Mrs. Bell had gone to Lock Berlin, and she had remained in the house, she heard footsteps. It sounded as if someone crossed the pantry, then went down the cellar stairs, then walked part of the way across the cellar, and stopped. About a week after this, Lucretia, having occasion to go down into the cellar, fell down near the middle of it. Mrs. Bell heard her yell and, when she came upstairs again, asked what was the matter. Lucretia exclaimed, "What has Mr. Bell been doing in the cellar?" Mrs. Bell replied that the soil must have been soften by rats. A few days afterward, at nightfall, Mr. Bell

---

[124] A town about seven miles east of Hydesville.
[125] Delaine is a light all-wool cloth of plain weave, usually printed.

carried some earth into the cellar, and was at work there some time. Mrs. Bell said he was filling up the rat holes.

A couple that occupied the house for 18 months after the Bells moved out, Mr. and Mrs. Weekman, deposed that, one night as they were going to bed they heard knockings on the outside door; but when they opened there was no one there. This was repeated, until Mr. Weekman lost patience; and, after searching all round the house, he resolved, if possible, to detect these disturbers of his peace. Accordingly, he stood with his hand on the door, ready to open it at the instant the knocking was repeated. It was repeated, so that he felt the door jar under his hand; but, though he sprang out instantly and searched all round the house, he found not a trace of any intruder. From then on until they moved out, they were frequently disturbed by strange and unaccountable noises. One night Mrs. Weekman heard what seemed the footsteps of someone walking in the cellar.

As for Mr. Bell, he had moved to the town of Lyons, in the same county. On hearing the reports of the events, he showed up at his former residence, and got several of his prior neighbors to sign a certificate setting forth that "they never knew anything against his character." Of course, most of the worst serial killers of the past century would have been able to elicit similar testimony from their neighbors, prior to the exposure of their crimes. Bell's statement is dated only six days after the initial communications and weeks before the publication of most of the damning testimony. No charges were ever brought against Bell, however. And, apparently, no official ever asked him any hard questions, such as: "What was the name of the peddler with whom you were so friendly and where is he now?" and "Why did you let Lucretia go and then re-hire her three days later?"

Not every "statement" made via the raps could be verified. No record of a Charles B. Rosma could be located, despite the claim that the peddler had five children living in New York. And, most significantly, no skeleton was found in the cellar.

Bones Revealed

That is, no skeleton was found in the cellar until 56 years had passed. In November of 1904, children playing in what had become known as the "Spook House" noticed bones that led to the discovery of an entire skeleton buried between the earth and the crumbling cellar walls.[126] A tin "peddler's box" was found alongside the remains.

Although absolute certainty is impossible at this point in time, it's a good bet that John Bell did murder the peddler for his money (supposedly a substantial amount) and buried him quickly in the center of his cellar. Because of his haste and the high water table, the grave was likely shallow. Yes, the rappings said it was 10-feet deep, but a just deceased spirit cannot be expected to have an accurate sense of physical distance. Fearing that the hasty burial would be discovered, Bell very likely dug up the corpse a day or two later and re-interred it behind a cellar wall. This double digging would explain the soil being so soft that a young girl would sink into it.

And, the reader might wonder, why didn't the spirit of the peddler inform the citizens of Hydesville of his final resting place? Perhaps because no one asked. Once the inquisitors had ascertained that the body had been buried in the cellar (which it had been), they wouldn't have thought to ask if it had been later disinterred and buried elsewhere. And when Carlos Hyde walked about the space, William Duesler, in the room above, kept asking if anyone was standing "where the body was buried"? He didn't ask about where the body might have been sealed in a wall. Before discounting such an argument, consider the difficulty of inserting an entirely new line of thinking into a game of Twenty Questions. The spirit could only indicate yes or no, it had no way to say "Yes, but …" or "Well, maybe …" so how could it communicate that "yes" it had been buried in a certain spot, but "no" the body was no longer there?

Another possible reason for the spirit's failure to fully inform is that it simply didn't know that its body had been moved. The act of leaving

---

[126] *Boston Journal*, November 22, 1904, quoted by Doyle, p. 73.

your body doesn't make you omniscient. After the trauma of being murdered and the experience of watching his physical remains being buried in the dirt, it would be perfectly understandable if the peddler's soul abandoned the locale for a while and never witnessed the morbid resettlement of his bones.

Word Spreads

The Hydesville disturbances caught the attention of the entire country and, in a short time, of Europe as well. It is the seminal event in the history of Spiritualism. What made this event exceptional certainly was not any of the rather mundane messages received from beyond, nor the level of proof of an afterlife provided; rather, as Sir Arthur Conan Doyle has so well explained, its impact was so great because it "occurred within the ken of a practical people who found means to explore it thoroughly and to introduce reason and system into what had been a mere object of aimless wonder."

Of course, many people questioned why the spirit world would elect a murdered peddler as the herald of this new religion and why a backwater hamlet like Hydesville was chosen as the venue. One of the earliest psychical researchers of high-standing, Robert Hare, M.D., actually asked those questions during a séance. He was told "that the spirit of a murdered man would excite more interest, and that a neighbourhood was chosen where spiritual agency would be more readily credited than in more learned or fashionable and conspicuous circles, where the prejudice against supernatural agencies is extremely strong; but that the manifestations had likewise been made at Stratford, in Connecticut, under other circumstances. Nor were these the only places. They had been made elsewhere, without much success in awakening public attention."[127]

As for the evidence that the events in Hydesville provide for Survival: there is the fact that something unseen was capable of observing and affecting the environs of the house. The pivotal issue with poltergeist activity

---

[127] Hare, p. 85.

is the possibility that the disturbances are actually telekinetic effects, generally unconscious, of a living person (usually a pubescent girl or boy). To those who are unfamiliar with the facts, the Fox sisters seem likely sources for such energies. But the knockings were heard in the house by the Weekmans and Lucretia Pulver long before Kate and Margaret came on the scene. Also, at the time that the crowd was asking questions in the cellar, the girls had been sent to stay with a neighbor. Therefore, those who would explain the case in terms of unconscious forces from living minds must posit at least four different people as sources — a far more incredible explanation than the survival of the peddler's spirit.

Nevertheless, to be truly convincing, the evidence should include the transmission of information from the supposed spirit to the living — information that the living would have no way of knowing otherwise. In this case, there is the information that a peddler was murdered by John Bell in the house; but all the physical evidence and testimony does not totally confirm that information.

And so, the evidence from the Hydesville case is strongly suggestive of Survival, but not absolute. If it stood alone, it would convince few people. As we have seen, though, it does not stand alone. It was preceded by numerous similar cases and, because this case received such fame, it was followed by a veritable explosion of spirit communications as the public woke up to their psychic potential.

Even though the citizens of Hydesville had never read the books of arcane history that told of disturbances at Tedworth, Epworth, Silesia, Edinburgh, and scores of other disturbed places, they applied their famous Yankee ingenuity and practical sense in examining the phenomena clearly and extracting the real meaning behind the spectacle. Because of their ground-breaking efforts, common folks throughout the world have learned that it is indeed possible to communicate directly with departed souls. The Fox family and their neighbors should forever be honored for their key role in reconnecting physical man with his spiritual essence.

Chapter Four
... The Alien Rapper!

Through studying scientists in action, sociologists of science have revealed that scientists are indeed like other people. ... They usually ignore what they do not want to deal with.

— Rupert Sheldrake,
Science Set Free

The Fox Family case clearly is key to the development of spirit communications throughout the ensuing century and a half. Of course, if little Kate Fox had not triggered it all with her silent mimicking of finger-snaps, sooner or later someone else would likely have taken her place in history. But it *was* Kate, and so a 9-year-old girl gets the credit for shaking up the world. It is fitting then, that 126 years later, another little girl became the central figure in the next major development of spirit-rap dialogue.

Like Kate Fox, Theresa Andrews was one of six children and shared a bedroom with an older sister in a rented house. At the time the knockings started, on 12 April 1974, Theresa was three years older than Kate was (in 1848) and the Andrews' home was in the Andover suburb of London rather than upstate New York.

The girls' bedroom was upstairs and shared a wall with an adjoining house. It was within this wall that the initial knocks were heard. Naturally, Theresa and her 20-year-old sister, Maria, first thought that the sounds were being made by their neighbors. They soon abandoned that idea, however, because they found that the knocks responded to Theresa's questions, even when she whispered the questions so softly that Maria could barely hear them from the adjacent bed.

The knocking usually began as the girls were about to sleep and seemed to be centered mostly around Theresa, although it sometimes occurred when no one was in the room. Soon, the girls developed a code in which one knock meant yes, two meant no, and three meant that the answer was unknown. It only took a few days before the code had been enhanced so that letters could be indicated by a number of raps indicating their position in the alphabet. Via this method, the rapper communicated that his name was Eric Waters. Despite never having experienced such events, nor even hearing of such things, the Andrews' family all took part in the questioning as if it were a game. The source of the sounds remained mysterious, but there seemed nothing sinister about the messages. At least at first.

Others, including neighbors, clergy, and police, were shortly called in to witness the events. All of them heard the raps but none could explain their origin. A woman claiming to have psychic powers visited the home and declared that the raps were caused by the spirit of a young boy who was murdered in the house and whose body was buried under the floorboards. (We are not told if this woman was familiar with the tale of the peddler in the cellar of the Fox home.) This revelation bothered the family and their discomfort seemed to infect Eric,[128] for the sessions became more erratic afterwards. Then, about 6:30 in the evening on April 29th, the knocking became unusually loud and continued far into the night despite the family's pleas for it to stop.

The next day, Barrie Colvin,[129] an investigator who had conducted one prior interview with the family, was called back to the house in the hopes that he might find a means to bring an end to the disturbances. Altogether, Colvin visited the Andrew's household nine times, the last being on the 10th of June. Sometimes there was more activity than others. On one

---

[128] For ease of reference, the source of the raps shall hereinafter be referred to by the name it claimed for itself.

[129] Colvin. "Andover." This report was not published for 30 years at the request of the family involved. All family names are pseudonyms.

occasion, the banging was so loud and prolonged that, when Colvin arrived, a score of neighbors were gathered outside the Andrew's home listening to the racket, which could easily be heard from 50 yards down the street.

During his investigations, Colvin witnessed a number of intriguing performances by Eric. On the 2nd of May, at the suggestion of Colvin, Mrs. Andrews asked Eric to shift the location of his rapping from the wall to the headboard of Theresa's bed. Colvin reported the result thusly: "She then said: 'Eric, please try to knock on the headboard.' This was followed by a very soft tap, which was heard by us all. I was at that moment standing very close indeed to the headboard, with my ear about 15 cm from it. As Mrs. Andrews repeated the request, I put my hand on the headboard to see whether I could feel any sensation. Eric rapped progressively louder on the headboard and I could clearly feel the vibration. I noted, however, that on each occasion the onset of the vibration appeared to be slightly before the moment when we heard the rapping sound. (It is possible that this effect was purely subjective, but it felt real enough for me to make a note of it.)"[130]

Upon hearing that Theresa had discovered that Eric could correctly name whatever number she was thinking of, Colvin shuffled together four sets of cards numbered from 1 to 10. He picked a card at random, showed it to all in the room, and then held it facing the wall. When he asked Eric to rap the number on the card, Eric did so accurately. This test was run five times with the same correct results. Next, Colvin repeated the test, only without anyone but himself seeing the number prior to holding the card up to the wall. Out of a run of seven tries, Eric was correct each time. Then another run of ten tries and Eric was correct eight times and one number off two times. Lastly, for a run of ten tries, Colvin held the card to the wall without himself or anyone seeing it; Eric was correct eight times.[131] It's possible that the fewer people who were thinking of the number, the more

---

[130] Colvin, "Andover," p. 9.
[131] _____, p. 12.

difficulty Eric had ascertaining it; or it could simply be that, as he grew tired, Eric was less able to discern the number correctly.

Finally, Colvin attempted to gain some details about Eric's life. Many of his questions, though, were answered by the three knocks which signaled a lack of knowledge. Colvin reports, "Despite an apparent willingness to produce raps in reply to our questions, we were unable to find out much about Eric and concluded that he seemed to know very little about his life." To explain this lack, Colvin offers the explanation that Eric's manifestations are "derived from the mind of Theresa" and that "if she had a rather incomplete picture of Eric's family history, it was perhaps to be expected that Eric would be unable to formulate answers to some apparently simple questions."[132] I suggest that another explanation might better fit the facts.

Often during the rapping sessions, Eric would seem to get angry over minor things. At times he would get silly, giving responses just the opposite of what was requested. If he was slighted or ignored, Eric would suddenly go quiet, sometimes refusing to respond for several days. In short, Eric's actions were consistent with those of a child: sometimes sincere, sometimes needy, sometimes petulant. And while a child might be good at numbers or the alphabet, it's no surprise that he would have trouble with dates and the names of people and places from long ago.[133]

Whatever the truth about Eric's origins, he was unable to supply any useful information about his life and Colvin was unable to find any record of an Eric Waters ever residing in the Andover neighborhood. (Of course, Eric never claimed to be from that neighborhood.)

If that were the end of the tale, Theresa and Eric would be little more than curious footnotes in the literature of the paranormal. Despite Eric's

---

[132] _____, p. 13.
[133] In fact, the names of people are notoriously difficult for the spirits of adults to recall and/or communicate.

claims and his ability to see cards held up to a wall, the case provides rather weak evidence for Survival.

The true value of this story did not become apparent until Colvin subjected recordings of the rapping and knocking sounds to analysis using modern acoustical-research tools. In April 2010, he published a 29-page report[134] of his tests on both the Andover rappings and several similar cases. The technicalities are far too complex to accurately relay here, so the following simplified synopsis will have to do. The simplicity of my explanation should not be allowed to lessen the great importance of the findings.

When one object is struck upon another – such as a knuckle upon a wall, a stick upon a board, or a hammer upon a gong – the sound wave will taper off differently depending upon the objects, but the wave always begins abruptly. For example, a bell will ring for some time after it is struck by its clapper, but before it is struck it makes no noise and when it is struck the sound produced is instantly as loud as it's going to get. That is, the sound wave reaches maximum amplitude immediately. The waveform in Figure 1 illustrates this characteristic.

---

[134] Colvin, "Acoustic Properties," pp. 65-93.

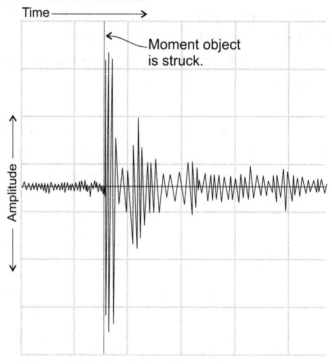

Figure 1. Typical waveform of normal rap.

This characteristic has been shown to hold no matter what the objects are, including knuckles on a wall, a spoon tapping a wine glass, and a rubber mallet striking a rubber mat.[135]

But waveform analysis of the recordings made of the Andover raps shows a marked difference: instead of reaching maximum amplitude immediately, the sound builds to a peak over time. See Figure 2.

---

[135] _____, pp. 72-73.

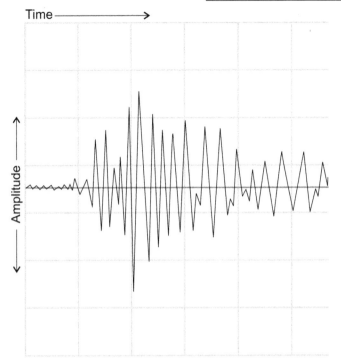

Figure 2. Typical waveform from Andover raps.

When Colvin noted that he seemed to feel a vibration in Theresa's headboard prior to hearing the knock, he was correct!

Other researchers have made similar observations and numerous recordings have been made by investigators of poltergeist phenomena, but the Andover case inspired Colvin to go a step or two further. He managed to obtain recordings of supposed paranormal sounds from ten separate cases that were investigated between 1960 and 2000. These he subjected to careful acoustical analysis, and, in every case, he discovered the same waveform patterns. Every rap known to be made by living humans reached maximum loudness instantly; every knock, rap, or bang of apparent paranormal origin exhibited a more gradual rise to maximum amplitude.

These ten cases were not picked because anyone thought they were the strongest or most evidential, but simply because they were the ones for which recordings were available. This means their selection for analysis was essentially random and indicates a high probability that most, if not all, similar claims of paranormal raps should be assumed true until proven otherwise. In other words, because ten cases selected essentially at random all displayed a common attribute, the odds are excellent that all well-documented cases will also share that attribute. If you were to reach blindly into a bag of marbles and pull out a blue one, you couldn't attach any meaning to it. But if you reach into the bag ten times in a row and get ten blue marbles, then you can be pretty sure that the remaining marbles are also blue. We can't be absolutely certain in every case, but it seems fair to assume that raps that exhibit this gradual rise to maximum amplitude indicate the exercise of physical powers that reside beyond the bounds of the material world.

[Note: Further research[136] has created the need to qualify this statement somewhat. Tests done by Roemer, *et. al.*, demonstrated that by placing the microphone on a solid surface a fair distance from the impact site, the immediate rise in amplitude could be softened enough to mimic the psi raps in a few cases. This effect is likely due to vibrations traveling through the floorboards, the walls, and the support structure prior to reaching the microphone. Thus, it would be more accurate to state that "raps recorded via a microphone held in the vicinity of the apparent source that exhibit this gradual rise to maximum amplitude indicate the exercise of physical powers that reside beyond the bounds of the material world."]

In the future, investigators might be able to save a great deal of time using this approach instead of spending hours peering behind doors and under tables. Likewise, we no longer have to suffer skeptics claims of hidden accomplices or popping toe joints. If acoustical analysis says the sounds aren't of incarnate origin, the argument should be settled.

Perhaps even more important to the human race is that Colvin seems to have developed convincing evidence, if not absolute proof, of the existence of a heretofore unknown source of energy. For decades we have been

---

[136] See the, *JSPR*. Vol. 75.1, pp. 61-63; and Vol. 75.3, p. 175.

reading about the search for whatever it is that powers UFOs, while all the time a truly alien energy source has been right under our noses, or inside our tables and walls. The topic is outside the scope of this book, but it is such an interesting concept that I couldn't help mentioning it.

To get back to the subject at hand ... demonstrating that a sound was not made by any physical action does not prove that it was made by the dead, but it does demonstrate the existence of mental/spiritual powers capable of affecting our physical world. Replication of Colvin's work by other scientists is required, but these special waveforms certainly appear to qualify as what Alex Imich calls "The Crucial Demonstration" of the existence of paranormal phenomena.

Given the fact that some intelligence is proficient at discerning our actions, responding wisely and sometimes wittily to our questions, providing information unknown to us, and manipulating physical matter in ways we cannot, it seems both illogical and presumptuous of us to reject its claim of being an independent spirit who once lived on Earth.

Chapter Five
— Cases from the Survival Top-40 —
Visions and Dreams

I start from the position that most people tell the truth as they believe it to be. It would be difficult to get through life if you took a different view. ... Even science would fall apart, because we can't all verify everything for ourselves. ... If a physicist wants to leave square one he has to rely on other people's eye-witness statements, and believe that the instrumental data they produce in support of their anecdotes are authentic.

— Mary Rose Barrington[137]

In this chapter, and in chapters 7, 9, 11, 13, and 15, you will find cases taken from the Survival Top 40 and grouped by type. This chapter features those spirit contacts that are either unsolicited or uncontrolled.

Case 33 — The Wealthy Wall[138]

A Houston businessman named Charles Vance experiences an unusually vivid and memorable dream in which he sees a man standing in front of a brightly painted cottage. He recognizes the man as a fellow named Murphy who, many years before, had been a mentor and father figure to Vance. After Vance married, he and his wife often visited Murphy and his wife, Lorraine; but the couples had drifted apart a few years before Murphy's death.

---

[137] "Broken Threads in the Fabric of Physical Reality," *The Paranormal Review*, October 2009, pp. 27-28.
[138] Arcangel, pp. 74-82.

In the dream, Murphy says that it is important for Vance to tell Lorraine "to look in the hall — just south of the bedroom, to the right of the light socket — inside that wall." Vance tells his own wife of the dream, but refuses to call Lorraine, being sure that she would think him nuts. But the dream is repeated four or five times and, finally, Vance's wife, seeing how disturbed Vance is becoming, calls Lorraine herself and tells her about the dreams. Shortly, a very excited Lorraine calls back to say that she had broken into the wall indicated by her husband's spirit and found a cache of "thousands and thousands of dollars."

Lorraine also informed the Vances that her house was scheduled to be remodeled during the following week and the money might well have been found by one of the laborers. Of course, he might have turned it over to Lorraine, but perhaps not. Thus, the urgency of Murphy's message was most reasonable at that time. Lorraine claims that she had absolutely no idea that any money had been hidden in the house.

When Lorraine called her daughter in Florida to tell her about the fortunate discovery, the daughter replied that she had been having the same dreams as had Vance, but had ignored them. The woman was Murphy's step-daughter and the Vances had never met her.

This story was revealed, rather reluctantly, to its author after a friend had urged her to contact the Vances.

Case 25 — The Ramhurst Revenants

In 1866, Alfred Russel Wallace,[139] described this case as one in which the evidence for the appearance of spirits was "as good and definite as it is possible for any evidence of any fact to be." One hundred and thirty-three years later, author Susy Smith claimed it was her favorite ghost story.[140] The text here is taken from a book by Robert Dale Owen. A former member of the Indiana Constitutional Convention, a U.S. Congressman

---

[139] Wallace, *Scientific Aspect*, p. 21.
[140] Smith, S., p.53.

(drafter of the bill to establish the Smithsonian Institution) and an American Minister at Naples, Owen was the author of many works, including *The Policy of Emancipation*. He was an outspoken skeptic of paranormal events until he witnessed a few astounding phenomena for himself. He then set himself the task of collecting the best evidence for Survival available at the time.

Owen writes[141]: "In October, 1857, and for several months afterwards, Mrs. Reynolds,[142] the wife of a field officer of high rank in the British army, was residing in Ramhurst Manor House, near Leigh, in Kent, England. From the time of her first occupying this ancient residence, every inmate of the house had been more or less disturbed at night — not usually during the day — by knockings and sounds as of footsteps, but more especially by voices, which could not be accounted for. These last were usually heard in some unoccupied adjoining room; sometimes as if talking in a loud tone, sometimes as if reading aloud, occasionally as if screaming. The servants were much alarmed. They never saw anything; but the cook told Mrs. Reynolds that on one occasion, in broad daylight, hearing the rustle of a silk dress close behind her, and which seemed to touch her, she turned suddenly round, supposing it to be her mistress, but, to her great surprise and terror, could see nobody. Mrs. Reynolds's brother, a bold, light-hearted young officer, fond of field-sports, and without the slightest faith in the reality of visitations from another world, was much disturbed and annoyed by these voices, which he declared must be those of his sister and of a lady friend of hers, sitting up together to chat all night. On two occasions, when a voice which he thought to resemble his sister's rose to a scream, as if imploring aid, he rushed from his room, at two or three o'clock in the morning, gun in hand, into his sister's bedroom, there to find her quietly asleep.

---

[141] Owen, pp. 414-427.
[142] All names here are pseudonyms. Owen was personally acquainted with both "Reynolds" and "Stevens."

"On the second Saturday in the above month of October, Mrs Reynolds drove over to the railway-station at Tunbridge, to meet her friend Miss Stevens, whom she had invited to spend some weeks with her. This young lady had been in the habit of seeing apparitions, at times, from her early childhood.

"When, on their return, at about four o'clock in the afternoon, they drove up to the entrance of the manor-house, Miss Stevens perceived on the threshold two figures, apparently an elderly couple, habited in the costume of a former age. They appeared as if standing on the ground. She did not hear any voice; and, not wishing to render her friend uneasy, she made at that time no remark to her in connection with this apparition.

"She saw the appearance of the same figures, in the same dress, several times within the next ten days, sometimes in one of the rooms of the house, sometimes in one of the passages — always by daylight. They appeared to her surrounded by an atmosphere nearly of the color usually called neutral tint. On the third occasion they spoke to her, and stated that they had been husband and wife, that in former days they had possessed and occupied that manor-house, and that their name was Children. They appeared sad and downcast; and, when Miss Stevens inquired the cause of their melancholy, they replied that they had idolized this property of theirs; that their pride and pleasure had centered in its possession; that its improvement had engrossed their thoughts; and that it troubled them to know that it had passed away from their family and to see it now in the hands of careless strangers.

"I asked Miss Stevens how they spoke. She replied that the voice was audible to her as that of a human being's; and that she believed it was heard also by others in an adjoining room. This she inferred from the fact that she was afterward asked with whom she had been conversing.* [*Footnote in Owen's text:* * Yet this is not conclusive. It might have been Miss Steven's voice only that was heard, not any reply — though heard by her — made by the apparitions. Visible to her, they were invisible to others. Audible to her, they may to others have been inaudible also. Yet it is certain that the voices at night were heard equally by all.]

"After a week or two, Mrs. Reynolds, beginning to suspect that something unusual, connected with the constant disturbances in the house, had occurred to her friend, questioned her closely on the subject; and then Miss Stevens related to her what she had seen and heard, describing the appearances and relating the conversation of the figures calling themselves Mr. and Mrs. Children.

"Up to that time, Mrs. Reynolds, though her rest had been frequently broken by the noises in the house, and though she too has the occasional perception of apparitions, had seen nothing; nor did any thing appear to her for a month afterward. One day, however, about the end of that time, when she had ceased to expect any apparition to herself, she was hurriedly dressing for a late dinner, her brother, who had just returned from a day's shooting, having called to her in impatient tones that dinner was served and that he was quite famished. At the moment of completing her toilet, and as she hastily turned to leave her bed-chamber, not dreaming of any thing spiritual, there in the doorway stood the same female figure Miss Stevens had described — identical in appearance and costume, even to the old point-lace on her brocaded silk dress — while beside her, on the left, but less distinctly visible, was the figure of her husband. They uttered no sound; but above the figure of the lady, as if written in phosphoric light in the dusk atmosphere that surrounded her, were the words 'Dame Children,' together with some other words, intimating that, having never aspired beyond the joys and sorrows of this world, she had remained 'earthbound.' These last, however, Mrs. Reynolds scarcely paused to decipher; for a renewed appeal from her brother, as to whether they were to have any dinner that day, urged her forward. The figure, filling up the doorway, remained stationary. There was no time for hesitation: she closed her eyes, rushed through the apparition and into the dining room, throwing up her hands and exclaiming to Miss Stevens, 'Oh, my dear, I've walked through Mrs. Children!'

"This was the only time during her residence in the old manor-house that Mrs. Reynolds witnessed the apparition of these figures.

"And it is to be remarked that her bed-chamber, at the time, was lighted, not only by candles, but by a cheerful fire, and that there was a lighted lamp in the corridor which communicated thence to the dining-room.

"This repetition of the word 'Children' caused the ladies to make inquiries among the servants and in the neighborhood whether any family bearing that name had ever occupied the manor-house. Among those whom they thought likely to know something about it was a Mrs. Sophy Osman, a nurse in the family, who had spent her life in that vicinity. But all inquiries were fruitless; every one to whom they put the question, the nurse included, declaring that they had never heard of such a name. So they gave up all hopes of being able to unravel the mystery.

"It so happened, however, that, about four months afterward, this nurse, going home for a holiday to her family at Riverhead, about a mile from Seven Oaks, and recollecting that one of her sisters-in-law, who lived near her, an old woman of seventy, had fifty years before been housemaid in a family then residing at Ramhurst, inquired of her if she had ever heard any thing of a family named Children. The sister-in-law replied that no such family occupied the manor-house when she was there; but she recollected to have then seen an old man who told her that in his boyhood he had assisted to keep the hounds of the Children family, who were then residing at Ramhurst. This information the nurse communicated to Mrs. Reynolds on her return; and thus it was that that lady was first informed that a family named Children really had once occupied the manor-house.

"All these particulars I received in December, 1858, directly from the ladies themselves, both being together at the time.

"Even up to this point the case, as it presented itself, was certainly a very remarkable one. But I resolved, if possible, to obtain further confirmation in the matter.

"I inquired of Miss Stevens whether the apparitions had communicated to her any additional particulars connected with the family. She replied that she recollected one which she had then received from them, namely, the husband's name was Richard. At a subsequent period likewise, she had obtained the date of Richard Children's death, which, as communicated to her, was 1753. She remembered also that on one occasion a third spirit appeared with them, which they stated was their son; but she did not get his name. To my further inquiries as to the costumes in which the (alleged) spirits appeared, Miss Stevens replied 'that they were of the period of Queen Anne or one of the early Georges, she could not be sure which, as the fashions in both were similar.' These were her exact words. Neither she nor Mrs. Reynolds, however, had obtained any information tending either to verify or to refute these particulars.

"Having an invitation from some friends residing near Seven Oaks, in Kent, to spend with them the Christmas week of 1858, I had a good opportunity of prosecuting my inquiries in the way of verification."

[At this point in his testimony, Owens relates how he visited the nurse, Sophy Osman, and she confirmed Reynold's story of strange voices, footsteps, and the incident with the cook hearing a silk dress rustle behind her. A nice corroboration, but we need to trim this tale somewhere.]

"But as all this afforded no clew either to the Christian name, or the date of occupation, or the year of Mr. Children's death, I visited, in search of these, the church and graveyard at Leigh, the nearest to the Ramhurst property, and the old church at Tunbridge; making inquiries in both places on the subject. But to no purpose. All I could learn was, that a certain George Children left, in the year 1718, a weekly gift of bread to the poor, and that a descendant of the family, also named George, dying some forty years ago, and not residing at Ramhurst, had a marble tablet, in the Tunbridge church, erected to his memory.

"Sextons and tombstones having failed me, a friend suggested that I might possibly obtain the information I sought by visiting a neighboring clergyman. I did so, and with the most fortunate result. Simply stating to him that I had taken the liberty to call in search of some particulars touching the early history of a Kentish family of the name of Children, he replied that, singulary enough, he was in possession of a document, coming to him through a private source, and containing, he thought likely, the very details of which I was in search. He kindly intrusted it to me; and I found in it, among numerous particulars regarding another member of the family, not many years since deceased, certain extracts from the 'Hasted Papers,' preserved in the British Museum; these being contained in a letter addressed by one of the members of the Children family to Mr. Hasted. Of this document, which may be consulted in the Museum library, I here transcribe a portion, as follows:

> 'The family of Children were settled for a great many generations at a house called, from their own name, Childrens, situated at a place called Nether Street, otherwise Lower Street, Hildenborough, in the parish of Tunbridge. George Children of Lower Street, who was High-Sheriff of Kent in 1698, died without issue in 1718, and by will devised the bulk of his estate to Richard Children, eldest son of his late uncle, William Children of Hedcorn, and his heirs. This Richard Children, *who settled himself at Ramhurst*,[143] in the parish of Leigh, married Anne, daughter of John Saxby, in the parish of Leeds, by whom he had issue four sons and two daughters, &c.'

"Thus I ascertained that the first of the Children family who occupied Ramhurst as a residence was named Richard, and that he settled there in the early part of the reign of George I. The year of his death; however, was not given.

---

[143] Emphasis is Owen's (I assume).

"This last particular I did not ascertain till several months afterward; when a friend versed in antiquarian lore, to whom I mentioned my desire to obtain it, suggested that the same Hasted, an extract from whose papers I have given, had published, in 1778, a history of Kent, and that, in that work, I might possibly obtain the information I sought. In effect, after considerable search, I there found the following paragraph:

> 'In the eastern part of the Parish of Lyghe (now Leigh), near the river Medway, stands an ancient mansion called Ramhurst, once reputed a Manor and held of the honor of Gloucester." ... "It continued in the Culpepper family for several generations." ... "It passed by sale into that of Saxby, and Mr. William Saxby conveyed it, by sale, to Children. Richard Children, Esq., resided here, and died possessed of it in 1753, aged eighty-three years. He was succeeded in it by his eldest son, John Children, of Tunbridge, Esq., whose son, George Children, of Tunbridge, Esq., is the present possessor.'* [Footnote in Owen's text: *That is, in 1778, when the work was published. See, for the above quotation, *Hasted's History of Kent*, Vol. i, pp. 422 and 423.]

"Thus I verified the last remaining particular, the date of Richard Children's death. It appears from the above, also, that Richard Children was the only representative of the family who lived and died at Ramhurst; his son John being designated not as of Ramhurst, but as of Tunbridge. From the private memoir above referred to I had previously ascertained that the family seat after Richard's time was Ferox Hall, near Tunbridge.

"It remains to be added that in 1816, in consequence of events reflecting no discredit on the family, they lost all their property, and were compelled to sell Ramhurst, which has since been occupied, though a somewhat spacious mansion, not as a family residence, but as a farmhouse. I visited it; and the occupant assured me that nothing worse than rats or mice disturbs it now.

"I am not sure that I have found on record, among what are usually termed ghost-stories, any narrative better authenticated than the foregoing. It involves, indeed, no startling or romantic particulars, no warning of death, no disclosure of murder, no circumstances of terror or danger; but it is all the more reliable on that account; since those passions which are wont to excite and mislead the imaginations of men were not called into play.

"It was communicated to me, about fourteen months only after the events occurred, by both the chief witnesses, and incidentally confirmed, shortly afterward, by a third.

"The social position and personal character of the two ladies to whom the figures appeared preclude, at the outset, all idea whatever of willful misstatement or deception. The sights and sounds to which they testify did present themselves to their senses Whether their senses played them false is another question."

[At this point, Mr. Owen begins his analysis of the case. He first points out that Miss Stevens first saw the figures, "not in the obscurity of night, not between sleeping and waking, not in some old chamber reputed to be haunted, but in the open air, and as she was descending from a carriage, in broad daylight." He mentions the numerous encounters, both visual and auditory, and the multiple witnesses. His major point, of course, is the precise information (names and dates) communicated by the spirits, information that was confirmed only later by his own research in obscure places.]

Cloak & Danger[144]

Vincent and Ivan Idanowicz lived in the house of their employer, Joseph Kronhelm. One November day in 1894, Vincent[145] traveled to the nearby town of Gajsin seeking a new fur cloak to keep the Russian winters at bay. While he considered various fabrics in the shop of Izloma Sierota, the tailor brought out an almost new cloak that, he said, had belonged to a gentleman named Lassota. The low asking price of 45 rubles convinced

---

[144] Johnson.
[145] I will use first names for ease of distinguishing between the brothers Idanowicz.

Vincent to buy this cloak instead of ordering a new one, and he went home with his purchase, pleased with the bargain he had gotten.

That night, however, Vincent was awakened from a sound sleep by "a gentleman dressed in black." Even though the door to the bedroom was locked, and his brother slept undisturbed nearby, Vincent felt only surprise, not fear. The visitor warned Vincent to return the cloak immediately as it was infested with tuberculosis bacteria. The cloak had come, he said, from a judge who had recently died of TB, not from Mr. Lassota, as the tailor had claimed. And then, the visitor simply vanished.

Vincent woke up his brother, who only laughed at his story. And, since a careful check revealed no way that anyone could have entered the bedroom, Vincent came to accept that he had experienced a hallucination. He spoke not a word of the vision throughout the following day. That night, however, the visitor came again. This time, the brothers were discussing family matters when the man in black came banging through the door and said: "You are both awake. Well, this time, Mr. Vincent, you will not say that my appearance yesterday was a hallucination. I come, therefore, to repeat to you: Go and ask Mr. Kronhelm to allow you to go to Gajsin tomorrow, and return the fur to Sierota, who is deceiving you in saying that it belonged to Mr. Lassota. I repeat that it belonged to a judge, who died of tuberculosis at Gajsin. It is infected with tuberculosis bacilli. I was a Government official at Lipowice, and died there in 1892; but as my mission is to watch over you, I warn you of what will happen if you do not follow my advice." So saying, the apparition vanished.

Kronhelm reports that he was awakened at 5:00 a.m. by two pale and frightened brothers. Upon hearing their story, he decided to accompany them to Gajsin.

When questioned by the three men, the tailor insisted that he had been truthful when he told Vincent that he had bought the cloak from a Mr. Lassota. So, the trio went to see the current judge at Gajsin, who confirmed that his predecessor had died of tuberculosis, but knew nothing about his effects. The judge directed them to a dealer in second-hand goods named

Fonkonogy. This man told Kronhelm that he had bought all the effects of the late judge, except for a fur cloak, which had been bought by the tailor, Sierota. The men showed him the fur cloak and he recognized it at once. Later he signed a written affirmation of his testimony.

Written statements were also signed by both of the brothers and by the priest in attendance at the judge's death. What happened to the cloak, or to the tailor, was never reported.

Discussion

The author of the article from which this case is derived, took a supercautious approach that was typical of the early SPR members. In her attempts to offer explanations other than Survival, she repeatedly piles "might be's" on top of "could have's" on top of "may have's"; cobbling together arguments so unlikely and ungainly as to be laughable. An example of this is her suggestion that Vincent "may have" been in the habit of visiting Gajsin, and that the judge "may have" been pointed out to him, and "could have" been wearing the cloak, and it "might have" some identifying mark, that Vincient's subconscious mind "may have" registered and so "might have" recognized, and something in the tailor's manner "might have" seemed suspicious, and then, in response to all that, Vincent's subconscious "could have" created an elaborate dramatic presentation (*i.e.* the ghost). But even if every one of these assumptions were not completely unfounded, they fail to explain three things: (1) how Vincent's subconscious linked the cloak to tuberculosis, (2) why the ghost was of a complete stranger rather than the judge himself or someone Vincent trusted, and (3) how it was that brother Ivan saw and heard the same apparition.

Regarding the visitor's identity, Johnson points to the lack of verification of the name it gave and she suggests that the case is somehow weakened thereby. But spirits are known to adapt an image and name acceptable to their audience. Who they "really are" could well interfere with the reception of their message. If, for example, the spirit had admitted that he was a Hindu, or a Cherokee, or something equally outlandish to someone raised in the Greek Orthodox church, his warning would most likely have never been heeded.

The Reticence of Scientists

It is unfortunate that learned men, who see the phenomena for the first time, commit the error of supposing that their entry into the arena marks the beginning of the proper investigation of mediumistic phenomena.

— Baron Albert von Schrenck-Notzing, M.D.[146]

Sooner or later, any student of psychic phenomena is bound to wonder why the scientific and academic communities are so reticent to investigate the subject. When scientists who have made disparaging remarks about psychic phenomena are asked what actual investigation they have done to reach such an opinion, their answer will not only be "none" but, more often than not, that answer will be expressed in a disdainful tone suggesting that any such effort would be a waste of their valuable time.

The ignorance these scientists thereby demonstrate is partly the fault of those researchers who have investigated and yet have been restrained in proclaiming the results of their investigations. Professor James Hyslop, PhD., LL.D., once wrote that most of the leading members of the Society for Psychical Research "who have conducted personal investigations have become convinced that man survives bodily death; but it has been regarded as not always good policy to avow the conviction with any missionary zeal. Hence, conviction on the point appears to the public to be less strong than it actually is."[147] If the experts are not pressuring academia to accept their conclusions, it's no surprise that scientists shy away from personal investigation, especially in light of what I call "conversion phobia."

---

[146] von Schrenck-Notzing, p. 292.
[147] Hyslop, *Contact*, p. 35.

Simply put, conversion phobia is the worry that if one opens oneself to a new idea, one might be forced to agree with it. And, in the case of Survival, the penalties for doing so can be severe. Scientists generally are not stupid. They know that the history of science is littered with the carcasses of their brothers who have felt compelled to investigate the afterlife with an open mind and report their findings honestly.

Scattered throughout this book are short "Conversion Phobia" sections containing quotes from a few of the scientists who were brave and honest enough to publicly admit their change of mind.

Conversion Phobia I
Robert Hare

In 1818, Hare was called to the chair of chemistry and natural philosophy at the College of William and Mary and that same year was appointed as professor of chemistry in the department of medicine at the University of Pennsylvania, where he would remain until his retirement in 1847. He was awarded honorary M.D. degrees from Yale in 1806 and Harvard in 1816. In 1839, he was the first recipient of the Rumford Award for his invention of the oxy-hydrogen blow-pipe and his improvements in galvanic methods. He was a member of the American Academy of Arts and Sciences, the American Philosophical Society, and an honorary life member of the Smithsonian Institution.

In His Own Words:

"In common with almost all educated persons of the nineteenth century, I had been brought up deaf to any testimony which claimed assistance from supernatural causes, such as ghosts, magic, or witchcraft, [and] I was at that time utterly incredulous of any cause of the phenomena excepting unconscious muscular action on the part of the persons with whom the phenomena were associated."[148]

"I sincerely believe that I have communicated with the spirits of my parents, sister, brother, and dearest friends"[149]

"The most precise and laborious experiments which I have made in my investigation of Spiritualism, have been assailed by the most disparaging suggestions, as respects my capacity to avoid being the dupe of any medium employed. Had my conclusions been of the opposite kind, how much fulsome exaggeration had there been, founded on my experience as

---

[148] Hare, , p. 37.
[149] _____, p. 12.

an investigator of science for more than half a century! And now, in a case when my own direct evidence is adduced, the most ridiculous surmises as to my probable oversight or indiscretion are suggested, as the means of escape from the only fair conclusion"[150]

---

[150] Hare, p. 13.

Chapter Six
Spontaneous Spirits

> *We are so far from knowing all the agents of nature and their various modes of action, that it would not be scientific to deny any phenomena merely because, in the current state of our knowledge, they are inexplicable.*
>
> — M. le Marquis de La Place[151]

We had just sat down in the anteroom to enjoy a cup of afternoon tea when he said:

> "You know, we have spent considerable time examining reports of NDEs [Near Death Experiences] and we have spoken briefly of the NDA [Nearing Death Awareness] but we would be remiss if we didn't also pay some attention to those interactions with the spirit world that are unsought, unplanned, and unpredictable. Authors Bill and Judy Guggenheim have named these 'After-Death Communications' (ADCs), and that name seems to be most popular. Author Diane Arcangel refers to them as 'Afterlife Encounters' (AEs). Personally, I prefer Spontaneous Trans-dimensional Contact or STC."

"Oh great, another acronym," I complained, while writing 'S-T-C' in my notebook. "Just what the world needs. What's wrong with 'ADC' anyway?"

> "Call them what you want," he said. "I happen to think that names should be both clear and descriptive. After-death communications or encounters could just as well refer to interactions *between*

---

[151] *Théorie analytique des Probabilités,* p. 43.

souls within heaven. And both terms could cover intentional contacts initiated through mediums."

"Okay, then. I'll accept one more acronym for the sake of clarity. When Jane Q. Public is sitting in her kitchen and suddenly hears the voice of her deceased daughter calling from the toaster, we'll chalk it up to another case of STC.

"Do these contacts supply strong evidence for Survival?"

"For the most part, the stories are just the sort of anecdotes that scientists blithely ignore and skeptics gleefully spotlight because they are rarely corroborated and are often subject to alternative explanations such as coincidence and hallucination. But not all anecdotes are created equal. A few are worthy of being added to the Survival Files.

"Now, don't get me wrong," he cautioned, "I doubt neither the accuracy nor the sincerity of the percipients in other cases, especially since so many of them were hard-nosed skeptics prior to their experience. Furthermore, as a firm believer in an afterlife, I have no problem assuming that most of the events related to Arcangel and the Guggenheims did involve communications with the deceased. Nevertheless, if I were attempting to convince a non-believer, I wouldn't find more than a half dozen of the tales worth relating."

"What do the tales-worth-telling have in common? Are the visiting spirits especially solid and life-like?"

"No. Opacity is irrelevant," he replied. "Although many people falsely assume that there is a direct correlation between realism and reality."

I gave him a questioning tilt of my head.

"Over and over again, in book after book, people adamantly deny that their experience was a hallucination because it was 'too real.' Apparently, most folks don't know the meaning of the term.

A 'hallucination' is, by definition, an experience that seems absolutely real — but isn't. If the experience seems unreal, then it isn't a hallucination, it's a dream or a fantasy or a bad trip.

"It isn't uncommon for the human brain to be tricked into believing false data. So, when evaluating the strength of evidence, one should ignore all statements of personal belief in 'how real' the event seemed.

"The more evidential stories in *Hello From Heaven*, *Afterlife Encounters*, and similar compilations of testimony, are those wherein the manifesting soul conveys information of some sort that is not available to the percipient via normal channels. In one case related by the Guggenheims, for instance, a friend, whom a woman had last known to be entering the priesthood, appeared to her, a decade later, inexplicably dressed in a Navy uniform. She only found out afterwards that he had become a Navy chaplain and had been killed on the day she saw his spirit.[152]

"In another case, a young woman, who thought her father was in excellent health, had a vision of him in spirit and heard him laugh and claim that now he wouldn't have to pay for the new furniture. Then the phone rang and she was told that her father had died. Later on, she found out that her mother had bought an extravagant amount of new furniture just before her father's unexpected heart attack."[153]

"These are good evidence for paranormal phenomena of one sort or another," I pointed out, "but I don't see them as unequivocal support for the survival of a conscious personality. I mean, there were bound to be lots of people who knew the woman's old friend during the time he was a Navy chaplain. She could have been reading their minds, couldn't she? Likewise, the daughter could have been reading her mother's mind about both the furniture and her father's death."

---

[152] Guggenheim, p. 244.
[153] _____, p. 246.

"I reckon. Although you might recall a discussion we had earlier about the significance of telepathy. But," he continued, "there are several cases the Guggenheims cite in which deceased loved ones appear and give directions to find money, stocks, insurance policies, and the like that the mourners did not know existed."

"That sounds familiar," I said.

"It should. The literature of the paranormal contains many such cases. One of my favorites was reported back in 1891."[154] He carefully placed his tea cup and saucer on the glass atop the Sheraton console table between us and sat back in a contented manner. I prepared myself for a nice long story.

The Farmer's Daughter

"It was on February the 2nd of that year …"

"Tell me," I interjected, "do you think that those who die on Groundhog Day can see their shadow when they come out of the tunnel into the light?"

Amazingly, he didn't even crack a smile at my brilliant wit.

"On the second day of February, 1891," he repeated and then continued, "Michael Conley, a farmer from Ionia, Iowa, suffered the indignity of crossing over while sitting in an outhouse in the town of Dubuque, some 110 miles from his home. His body was taken to the local coroner's office and prepared for shipment to his family. In the process, his soiled and rather smelly clothing was removed and thrown on the ground out back of the morgue.

"When Conley's son brought the coffin home, one of his sisters (that is, a daughter of the deceased) fainted and could not be revived for several hours. When she finally awoke, she reported that the spirit of her father had appeared to her and told her that he had sewn a considerable amount of money inside his gray shirt. He had used, she said, a piece of red fabric from an old dress of hers.

---

[154] Myers, p. 228.

"Well, the family was most dubious, but on the advice of their doctor, they tried to placate the nearly hysterical daughter by calling the morgue and asking if the farmer's clothing was still in their possession. On being located in the rubble, the seeming pile of rags was bundled up and given to the son when he arrived to fetch them. As you surely have guessed by now, a rather large roll of bills was soon discovered, wrapped in a red cloth and sewn to the inside of Conley's discarded shirt."

"Well, that's certainly one of your more earthy stories," I said. "Can we trust anything that comes from that period in mid-America? I understand that editors of the time were wont to make up tall tales in the hope of boosting the circulation of their newspapers."

"I cannot deny that possibility," he replied, "although there are a couple of reasons to think this story more credible. First of all, the newspaper involved had already carried the story of Conley's death a week before it reported the incident of the money being found in the shirt. Secondly, F.W.H. Myers, one of the most respected and hard-headed investigators of psychic claims, wrote that the case seemed to have been 'carefully and promptly investigated.'"

"Well then," I continued playing devil's advocate, "perhaps the daughter had sewn the money into the shirt for her father. After all, the pocket was made from her dress. Perhaps she and her dad were hatching some nefarious plot and, when she realized the money was gone, she faked a faint until she could invent a story that would retrieve the shirt."

"That's good skeptical analysis, but it seems that the investigators considered this possibility, for they made special note of the fact that the stitches on the inner pocket 'were large and irregular, and looked to be those of a man.' Furthermore, the woman fainted as soon as she saw her father's coffin. (Her brother, wanting to be certain of the corpse's identity before alarming the rest of the family, had not told her why he was traveling to Dubuque.) At the time she asked about the clothing, she had not seen how her father's body was dressed, so she wouldn't have known that his gray shirt had been removed."

"Okay. I accept it, but I wouldn't call it one of the strongest cases."

"I didn't say the story was the most evidential," he avowed, picking up his teacup once more, "I merely said it was one of my favorites."

Grave Mistakes

After a moment quietly contemplating the universe and savoring his tea, the old man got back to the subject at hand.

"As for my favorite cases in the more current literature, I am particularly impressed by the story of Cody in *Hello From Heaven*. Cody was a boy who passed on at the age of two and came back to tell his mother that his tombstone had been put on the wrong grave and that his name was 'backwards.'[155] His mother, who had not been to the cemetery since the monument was supposedly installed, checked and discovered that, indeed, the stone had been mistakenly placed on the grave of a little girl who had died 2 weeks prior to her son."

"I can see why you like that one. Unless the installers intentionally screwed up, the improper placement was a fact known to no living person."

"Not only that," he elaborated, "but it was information about a situation that only existed after the death of the communicator. You know, so many of the cases which entail 'knowledge unknown to any one living' involve info that *was* known to someone at one time. Those folks who are willing to swallow any explanation other than Survival — no matter how unlikely, or preposterous — might claim that the knowledge somehow lingered in the atmosphere (or the Akashic Records, or some such arcane place) until sensed by the percipient. The information that Cody communicated to his mother, on

---

[155] Guggenheim, p. 285.

the other hand, was never known to anyone at any time until Cody's discarnate mind observed a situation and deduced a conclusion. Thus, it demonstrates the ability of a discarnate soul, not only to communicate with us, but to be aware of events on this plane, to rationally analyze those events, and to emotionally react to them."

"Yes," I agreed, "that is extremely evidential. Why do you speak of Cody reacting emotionally? Did he seem upset when he appeared to his mother?"

"The book doesn't say, but the fact that he made the effort necessary to communicate suggests a high level of concern. Although he likely cared more about soothing his mother's grief than about the placement of a stone."

"Was the boy's name actually backwards?"

"It was not spelled backwards, but it was facing backwards. Once his mother located it, she noticed that the stone was oriented opposite from all the others in the cemetery."

"So," I wondered, "a 2-year-old was able to read well enough to know which way the letters on the stones were oriented?"

"The boy's body may have been young, but I think his soul must have been a bit older — perhaps a few millennia or so."

"You know, there's something very familiar about those switched tombstones."

"Perhaps you are remembering the tale of the elderly man who died and was buried in West Sussex, England, but whose ghost kept haunting the dreams of his daughter, complaining that his fine tombstone had been erected on another man's grave. When asked, the sexton insisted that such a mistake was impossible because his own brother had died just after the old man and was buried in the very next plot. This assurance failed to placate the spirit and, finally, to save the daughter's sanity, an exhumation order was obtained and the markers were, indeed, found to be on the wrong graves.

> Once the mistake was corrected, the daughter was no longer haunted.
>
> "It makes for an entertaining story, but it comes to us secondhand[156] and lacks corroboration, so it has no value as evidence."

"As I recall, Arcangel's book also contains a case centering around a grave marker."

> "Yes, and an especially interesting case it is.[157] A man has a lucid dream in which a friend who died one year previously is standing beside a headstone. 'Call my mother,' the friend says, 'and tell her I love my headstone.' When the man awakes, he draws a picture of the stone and then calls his friend's mother. She tells him that the stone was just set the day before. He immediately drives to the cemetery and discovers that his sketch has captured the actual stone in every detail."

"Well, this could be a case of astral travel," I pointed out, "although the precise timing of his vision argues in favor of spirit involvement. I'm not sure why the case is of such special interest, though."

> "The specialness lies in the fact that the man's dream was his second contact with his friend's spirit. In the first, which occurred six months earlier, he could only see blackness as he heard his buddy saying that he was in hell. (Apparently this was due to a crime he had committed.) About two years after the headstone incident, the man had a third dream in which he asks his buddy how he managed to escape from hell. 'I got out,' the friend replied, 'the moment I forgave myself!'"

I nodded my support of that concept, which was in line with the picture of the afterlife we had examined previously. "Do any more of Arcangel's cases stand out?"

---

[156] "Correspondence Concerning Evidence for Survival," *Journal of the Society for Psychical Research*, Vol. 24, 1928, p. 336.
[157] Arcangel, pp. 93-95.

He thought for a moment and said: "Do you recall the case of Uncle Jerry's watch?"

"I certainly do. It involved the medium Leonora Piper and the spirit of a man who told of various things he and his brothers did as youths in England. He was Sir Oliver Lodge's uncle and his spirit responded to a gold watch that had belonged to him."

"A most accurate summary," he said. "Now we shall segue from the case of Uncle Jerry's watch to the case of Granddaughter Jerri's watch.[158]

Grandma's Gift

"This tale is related by a young woman whose best friend, Jerri, excitedly showed her a watch she had received as a Christmas present from her grandmother. It seems that the grandmother had purchased the watch, wrapped it, and hidden it away — and then departed for heaven just before the holidays. Jerri found the watch only because she had an STC in which her grandma gave her very specific directions: 'Look in the bottom of my big sewing box in the back of the closet in the spare bedroom. … it's wrapped in a red and green box.' Both Jerri's mom and grandpa dismissed the encounter as merely a dream. They were most amazed when the watch was found just as indicated."

"I like your favorite stories," I said. "While we're on the subject of STCs, do you have a least-favorite case?"

Jumping to Confusion

"Well, there are certainly many cases reported that add nothing to the body of evidence for Survival. That doesn't mean that they aren't sincere, however, and they are often entertaining. The only gripe I have about some instances of spirit contact — whether via

---

[158] Arcangel, pp. 8-9. The author admits to altering some of the names to protect the privacy of the percipients, so this might not be such a coincidence after all.

STCs, NDEs, mediums, or whatever — is the way in which the messages can be distorted by the percipients to endorse their own particular ideology."

"You mean how some people jump to the conclusion that the loving being of light they perceive is actually Moses or Mohammed or whoever is the major figure in their religion?"

"Yes, even though the entity never actually makes such a claim.

"Perhaps the most extreme example I've ever read of this didn't even involve a loving light. It is the case of a mail carrier named Glen.[159] Early one morning, according to his account, Glen had a vision in which his son and his ex-wife appeared looking healthy and happy. Glen, who up 'til that moment had been an atheist, realized that his son was in heaven and, he says: 'All of sudden, I believed! I knew that God, Jesus, the Holy Ghost, the saints, and everything that I had been taught was true!'

"Now, neither Glen's son nor his ex-wife mentioned anything about God or Jesus, let alone 'the saints.' But, once Glen's mind accepted the evidence for an afterlife it blindly jumped to the conclusion that all the associated religious concepts it had been taught in Sunday school must also be correct. This sort of overreaction is all too typical of new converts. Perhaps this is another reason that more people don't experience STCs."

"How so?" I asked.

"The spirits might be afraid that their appearance will reinforce latent, and erroneous, religious beliefs, thus contributing to the already plethoric zealotry and divisiveness in this world."

I decided to shift focus slightly. "Aside from the matter of evidence, are STCs useful in learning about heaven?"

"Not very. Many, if not most, communications are from souls who are still earthbound. And even if they have gone on, apparently

---

[159] Guggenheim, p. 372-3.

it takes a while for souls, even old souls, to become adjusted to their new surroundings and remember who they really are. Only then are they able to accurately perceive the higher realms. So, the recently deceased can't provide us much information about the conditions in heaven, and they almost never mention reincarnation. Nevertheless, what they do describe fits well with the picture of heaven we have built up from other sources.

"One intriguing point of agreement, by the way, is not with the destination but with the means of entrance and egress. Several of the folks interviewed by the Guggenheims told of visions in which they traveled through a tunnel to reach heaven and to return to this plane."[160]

"Wow! That further weakens the überskeptic's argument that all those tunnels reported in near-death experiences are merely an effect of brain cells expiring ."

"Well, that argument was dead anyway," he said. "But I suppose these tunnel experiences of healthy folks are additional nails in its coffin."

Resisting Review

"These souls you speak of that are earthbound, why do you suppose there are so many of them?" I asked. "Why would so many spirits not be attracted to a warm and loving light? Why would they want to avoid heaven?"

"I'm sure there are quite a few who just haven't gotten around to focusing on that light because they are so concerned with monitoring, and possibly trying to influence, events in the physical world. As for the others, well, it may not be that spirits are afraid of going to heaven; it could be that what they truly dread is the entrance exam."

"The entrance exam?"

---

[160] Guggenheim, pp. 174-181. Also, see Botkin, pp. 149-152.

"Over and over, both spirit contacts and NDErs report that each soul undergoes a life review as part of the process of entering heaven. During this review, the souls experience the effect they have had on other people. According to many reports, this experience is from the other person's point of view. It is not actually an 'exam,' but it can be a dreadful experience. Imagine that you were a bit of a bully in your youth and liked to tease, beat-up, and otherwise terrorize those smaller and weaker than you. After you've met your demise — and once you accept the fact that you are still a conscious being — you realize that in order to move on, you must go through a process in which you will feel all the horror and hurt that you inflicted upon others. Plus, you will feel it much more strongly than your victims did, because disembodied spirits are far more sensitive to all emotions than embodied ones are."

"Yes, we touched on that in our previous conversations."

"Well, it bears emphasizing. If *you* were such a bully (and the world has certainly had its share of them) how anxious would *you* be to cross that threshold?"

"The world has had its share of much worse than that," I pointed out. "Child molesters, rapists, axe murderers, and the like must be especially fearful of experiencing the pain they caused."

"And then there are those who face even tougher life reviews," he said.

"Even tougher than child molesters and serial killers?"

"Imagine what awaits those who, for their own advancement or to promote their own causes, have brought war upon the world. Even the hardiest would tremble at the thought of having to experience all the pain of all the soldiers dead or mutilated in battle, not to mention the anguish of their widows and loved ones."

"Ouch! And some say there is no such thing as punishment."

"Don't think of the life review as punishment," he remonstrated. "Remember that we are all tiny parts of God and God is not a masochist. He has no interest in punishing Himself in any form or for any reason.

"Think of it more as making the most of the experience. The life review brings the cause and the effect together into an easily comprehended whole. The pain and the perpetrator become one. The agony is merged with the ecstasy. Thus, the experience is clarified and the gestalt is closed."

"But if all these souls avoid the life review by hanging around the physical plane, there must be an awful lot of unfinished business."

"There is — for the moment — but our moments are very brief in the celestial time frame. Sooner or later, everybody moves on. At least, that is what the spirits assert and what we all hope."

Conversion Phobia II
Alfred Russel Wallace

British naturalist and explorer, co-originator with Charles Darwin of the natural selection theory of evolution, and known to many as the "Grand Old Man of Science." Wallace was awarded honorary doctorates by both the University of Dublin and by Oxford University, and important medals from the Royal Society, the Société de Geographie, the Royal Geographical Society, and the Linnaean Society. Also, he received the Order of Merit from the British Crown. The fact that he never had to protect a tenured position at a major university may explain his willingness to challenge establishment views.

In His Own Words:

"Up to the time when I first became acquainted with the facts of Spiritualism, I was a confirmed philosophical sceptic, rejoicing in the works of Voltaire, Strauss, and Carl Vogt, and an ardent admirer (as I am still) of Herbert Spencer. I was so thorough and confirmed a materialist that I could not at that time find a place in my mind for the conception of spiritual existence, or for any other agencies in the universe than matter and force.

"Facts, however, are stubborn things. My curiosity was at first excited by some slight but inexplicable phenomena occurring in a friend's family, and my desire for knowledge and love of truth forced me to continue the inquiry. The facts became more and more assured, more and more varied, more and more removed from anything that modern science taught or modern philosophy speculated on. The facts beat me. They compelled me to accept them as facts long before I could accept the spiritual explanation of them; there was at that time no place in my fabric of thought into which it could be fitted. By slow degrees a place was made; but it was made, not by any preconceived or theoretical opinions, but by the continuous action of fact after fact, which could not be got rid of in any other way."[161]

---

[161] Wallace, *Miracles*, pp. vi-vii.

Chapter Seven
— Cases from the Survival Top-40 —
Invited Spirit Conversations

I dismiss the whole question of fraud from the phenomena so emphatically that I should not waste any time on the skeptic who still insists on that point of view. He is either too ignorant or too indolent for us any longer to attach any value to his convictions. ... Our business is not with him, but with honest people.

— Professor James H. Hyslop[162]

The following three cases taken from the Survival Top 40 all involve information intentionally sought from a specific spirit and delivered via a medium who had no normal access to that information.

Case 48 — Friends and Strangers[163]

George Pellew was trained as a lawyer and was the author of at least six books, including a well-known biography of the first Chief Justice of the United States, John Jay. Pellew was a member of the Society for Psychical Research but, in common with many SPR members, he did *not* believe that the human personality survived the demise of its physical body. He and Richard Hodgson, one of the chief researchers for the SPR, were closely acquainted and had enjoyed several lengthy discussions on metaphysical matters. In February, 1892, at the age of 32, Pellew was killed in an accident in New York City.

---

[162] Hyslop, *Proceedings*, p. 2.
[163] Source: Hodgson, pp. 295-334.

On March 22, a little over a month after Pellew's death, Hodgson began to arrange sittings for Pellew's friends with the trance-medium Leonora Piper – sittings in which Pellew made himself known. For these, and in all published materials, Pellew was referred to by the pseudonym "George Pelham" or, simply "G.P." Apparently influenced by the Victorian sense of propriety, a great deal of care was taken not to identify people or reveal any personal matters that were discussed. The result was that a great deal – probably the bulk – of evidence developed in the Pellew sessions was never made public. Even so, a significant amount was published, as the spirit of George Pellew actively participated in virtually all of Piper's sessions for more than five years. The majority of Pellew's communications were achieved via automatic writing.

Throughout his tenure, over 150 persons participated in sessions with Piper, of whom about 30 were friends or acquaintances of Pellew. Remarkably, he seemed always to recognize with "the appropriate emotional and intellectual relations" those he knew in the past, and to treat as strangers those whom he had never met.

There were actually two exceptions to Pellew's "always" recognizing only those whom he knew. One occurred on January 7, 1897. The sitter, a young woman given the name "Miss Warner," had attended a session the day before and mentioned that she had known Pellew, yet he had not acknowledged her. During this second session, he asked her who she was. Hodgson spoke up and told Pellew that the woman's mother was a friend of his. The conversation proceeded:

[G.P.] "I do not think I ever knew you very well."

[Warner] "Very little. You used to come and see my mother."

"I heard of you, I suppose."

"I saw you several times. You used to come with Mr. Rogers."

"Yes, I remembered about Mr. Rogers when I saw you before."

"Yes, you spoke of him."

"Yes, but I cannot seem to place you. I long to place all of my friends, and could do so before I had been gone so long. You see I am farther away. … I do not recall your face. You must have changed."

[At this point Hodgson asked, "Do you remember Mrs. Warner?" Immediately Piper's writing hand showed excitement.]

"Of course, oh, very well. For pity sake. Are you her little daughter?"

"Yes."

"By Jove, how you have grown. I thought so much of your mother, a charming woman."

"She always enjoyed seeing you, I know."

"Our tastes were similar."

"About writing?"

"Do you know Marte at all?"

"I've met him once or twice."

"Your mother knows. Ask her if she remembers the book I gave her to read."

"I will."

"And ask her if she still remembers me and the long talks we used to have at the home evenings."

"I know she does."

"I wish I could have known you better, it would have been so nice to have recalled the past."

"I was a little girl."

"

Hodgson asks his readers to remember that "these sittings were held five years after the death of G. P., and that G. P. had not seen Miss Warner for at least three or four years before his death, that she was only a little girl when he had last seen her, that she had not been, so to say, a special friend of his, and that she had, indeed, changed very much in the intervening eight or nine years. This non-recognition, then, by G. P. is a perfectly natural circumstance."

The second (apparent) exception to Pellew's perfect memory also adds to the strength of the evidence, but in the opposite way. It occurred when a man known as "Mr. Savage" was a sitter. Hodgson believed that Pellew was meeting Savage for the first time, a belief in which Savage concurred. Nevertheless Pellew seemed familiar with the man. Hodgson asked, "Do you know this gentleman, M. J. Savage?" Pellew replied, "Yes. I do. How are you, sir? Speak to me. This is too delightful. I am so pleased to see your face again." Hodgson persisted, "You remember meeting him in the body?" "Oh yes, well. I do, well."

Hodgson reports that he was "surprised at the amount of feeling indicated both by the words written and the excitement of the hand." Later, however, Hodgson recalled that George Pellew had, while living, attended one sitting with Piper and that Savage was an SPR Committee Officer who was present officially at the sitting. At that time, Pellew was not introduced under his real name, and it was noted in the report of the sitting that he was unknown to Savage. Clearly, though, Pellew's spirit recalled with some excitement meeting Savage some six years previously when he was in the position of the sitter, instead of his current position as communicator.

The Pellew sessions thus offer excellent evidence that Piper's success was not due to reading the minds of the living. All the strangers attending a session certainly held their own names clearly in their conscious minds yet, when Pellew was acting as control, he never greeted them by name. Even when the sitter held a memory of meeting Pellew, he could not derive her name because he did not recognize her physically as a past acquaintance. But he did greet all those he knew, even one who had forgotten he knew him. It is this last point — the insistence by the spirit of a truth counter to the thoughts of both the sitter and the witness — upon which hinges the uncommonly high rating for the case.

All this indicates a human personality acting precisely as would be expected of one who had survived death. Or, as Hodgson put it, "This recognition of friends appears to me to be of great importance evidentially, not only because it indicates some supernormal knowledge, but because, when all the circumstances are taken into consideration, they seem to point, in G. P.'s case, to an independent intelligence drawing upon its own recollections."

Case 39 — A Mysterious Death[164]

Edgar Vandy was a brilliant young engineer and inventor who lived in London with his family (mother, sister, and two brothers). At the time of his death, in 1933, Edgar[165] was involved with several engineering projects involving telephony, radio, and other electro-mechanical devices. His largest and most promising project was known as the Lectroline Drawing Machine, a machine that could precisely create lines and lettering on plates suitable for use on printing presses. The Lectroline could enable one person to do the work of several craftsmen. A lot of time and family money had been expended in the creation of this machine, and the details of the prototype's operation were a closely guarded secret.

On August 6, 1933, Edgar went for a ride in the country with a friend, referred to only as Mr. Jameson[166] or "N.J." and Jameson's sister. They ended up at an estate in Sussex owned by the sister's employer, who was not there at the time. It being a particularly hot and very sunny day, the trio decided to go for a swim in a pool on the estate grounds. The pool was lined with concrete and had a diving board, but the bottom was coated with slime and sediment that, when stirred up, made the water so cloudy that one could see no more than a few inches beneath the surface.

Such a condition of dense turbidity was what confronted Edgar's would-be rescuers when they arrived in response to Jameson's summons. Although only seven feet down, the body could not be seen, even when the pool was half-drained.

---

[164] Sources: Gay, pp. 2-61; MacKenzie, pp. 166-173; Keen, Montague, pages 247-259.
[165] First names are used here to distinguish among Edgar and his brothers.
[166] A pseudonym.

At the inquest, Jameson testified that he and Edgar had gone behind heavy shrubbery some ways from the pool to change into swim wear. Edgar had not brought a swimsuit so Jameson's sister loaned him one. Edgar changed quicker and went ahead. When Jameson arrived he saw Edgar floating face down in the water. Jumping in immediately, Jameson tried to save him, but he slipped from his grasp and sank. Jameson then retreated from the pool and went to find help, which did not arrive until an hour later.

The doctor who was present when Edgar's body was pulled from the murky water, noted that there were slight abrasions beneath the chin and the tongue had been bitten through. Some scrapes were also found on the body's left side and right shoulder. Also, there was less fluid in the lungs than usual in drowning victims. These facts led to the theory that the young man had struck his jaw while diving into the pool and been knocked unconscious. The coroner accepted all of this testimony and returned a verdict of "Death by Drowning by Misadventure."

Edgar's two brothers, Harold and George Vandy, were not satisfied with this verdict. From a contemporary standpoint, in a world full of forensic TV dramas, it is easy to sympathize with their doubts. Actually, we can only marvel at their restraint in not raising specific questions. How, for instance, did the pool water get so stirred up that it was still impenetrable an hour after Jameson climbed out? Or, was the water always so turbid? If so, is it conceivable that a highly intelligent man would have dived into it without any idea what lay beneath? (Edgar, by the way, was a poor swimmer and was never known to dive into anything.)

Perhaps most out of the ordinary is that a man unfamiliar with a place would "go ahead," leaving his friend to finish changing alone. Also difficult to believe is that Jameson could not manage to drag Edgar, who was not a large fellow, to safety in such a small and fairly shallow pool with no currents or other endangering conditions. And what would possess someone to think that they could find help in less time than it would take for a man to drown?

Then there is the matter of the sister who clearly instigated the visit to her boss' home, encouraged Edgar to enter the pool by providing him with a swim suit from who-knows-where, and then seems to have disappeared forever. She did not appear to help her brother rescue Edgar; she did not appear at the inquest, and couldn't be traced later. The fact that she worked for a very wealthy (and thus influential) man who likely didn't appreciate any bad publicity sullying his estate is more than cause for suspicion that the inquest was not entirely above board.

The Vandy brothers, however, voiced no such misgivings, at least not publicly. Their only stated goal was to clear up "some doubts" regarding the cause of Edgar's death. Although they did not at first believe in an afterlife, they hoped that a trance medium might be able to tap into some mind or another and uncover the truth via ESP.

George had once heard the Reverend Drayton Thomas lecture on proxy sittings whereby a person who knows little or nothing of a case "sits in" for a more involved person. (This should rule out the medium pulling key information from, or otherwise being influenced by, the mind of the sitter.) So George wrote to the Rev. Thomas asking him to proxy sit with the medium Gladys Osborne Leonard. This sitting was granted but it could not be scheduled for several weeks, and the brothers made other arrangements in the interim. Altogether, over a period of a year, nearly a dozen separate sessions were held with at least four mediums. (An additional sitting was held some 23 years later with yet another medium.)[167]

In the archives of psychic research one would be hard pressed to find any other case of a private citizen's death being so thoroughly and repetitively investigated. The inordinate number of mediums and sittings makes for a complex case that can be difficult to grasp in its entirety. For our purposes, we'll consider all the evidence as coming from one "super séance" and present only key statements therefrom. Nevertheless, it is important

---

[167] In order of consultation, the mediums were: Miss Frances Campbell, Mrs. Gladys Osbourne Leonard, Mrs. Mason, Miss Naomi Bacon, and Mrs. Bertha Harris.

to note that the repetition of many descriptions and ideas among the various mediums makes an excellent counter to those who claim that a medium's correct statements are simply lucky guesses. Those who strongly resist the idea of a spirit world may be able to credit one correct statement to fortune, but when three or more mediums all come up with the same information, only the most desperate überskeptic will dare claim luck or coincidence.

Of course, some would claim collusion. This is why the Vandy brothers went to such lengths to conceal their identities. Each initial appointment was made under a false name by mail from a different address. They never attended sessions together and they did not look at all alike. There was no normal way in which any medium could have known the identity of either Harold or George. They even hired different note takers to accompany them to each new medium. Furthermore, during the sessions they were most reticent to answer the medium's requests for confirmation of her statements.

Making the extent of the case even more exceptional is the underlying skepticism of the brothers. Although deeply desirous of information, they persisted in assuming that recognized facts were gleaned via telepathy from the minds of the living and unrecognized statements were false until proven true. Ultimately, though, they seemed to accept that some part of their brother Edgar had survived the murky water.

Each medium consulted seemed to make contact with the spirit of Edgar Vandy. Out of all the hundreds of statements made by the various mediums, a few of those demonstrating paranormal knowledge appear below. Each statement by a medium (or her control, or a contact) is followed by the relevant facts.

Statement: (As the medium points to her front teeth) He is showing me a little gap in his mouth as if a tooth were missing. Now he shows me an old scar and says 'That's my identification mark!' [Sitter: "Where is the scar?"] On his face.

Facts: The cutting edge of one of Edgar's upper teeth had broken off, leaving a small gap between that and the corresponding lower tooth. He also had a large scar on the right side of his forehead, obtained by being thrown from a trap as a child. George had heard him make the remark, "This scar will always identify me."

Statement: Now he is showing me a cigarette case, and that's funny, because he did not smoke. [Sitter: "I don't think he had a cigarette case."] He tells me where to find it — in his room — it seems to be at the end of a passage — there's a chest of drawers near the window. In one of the drawers you will find his things carefully folded up. I think you will find it there. [Sitter: "He didn't have a cigarette case."] Put it down and check it up.

Facts: True, Edgar did not smoke.[168] The evening after the sitting Harold and George looked in the chest of drawers (which was near a window) and found Edgar's underwear carefully folded as described. They did not find a cigarette case, but in a corner at the bottom there was a new aluminum soap box. This, when held in the hand as shown by the medium, looked exactly like a metal cigarette case.

Statement: This young man had a lot of papers that he kept in a kind of flat book form... there was quite a pile of them. But there was one of them that had both writing and drawings in it that he had done ... some of them had brown, and some it looks almost like black covers on them.

Facts: These notebooks were unknown to the brothers until George found them while clearing out a storeroom more than 30 years later. All had black stiff covers except one, which had brown.

Statement: Now he's showing me a tennis racquet. He is holding it up like this (holding her two hands diagonally), and that's strange, because he didn't play tennis. He doesn't look like a fellow who would play tennis. [Sitter: "I don't understand the racquet. He didn't play tennis."] Make a note of it and check it up.

---

[168] In that era, the odds were that the young man *did* smoke cigarettes.

Facts: Edgar did not play tennis or possess a racquet. When the incident was mentioned to their sister, she related that, a few weeks previously, she had a spare exposure on a spool of film and she used it to take a photograph of Edgar in the garden. It was a bright sunny day and he was dressed in tennis shirt, trousers, and shoes. To complete the picture, his sister fetched her racquet and asked him to pose with it. He joked about it and said the picture would delude people into thinking he was a player.

Statement: Do you know why he was interested in wireless [radio]? He seems very interested in it. In fact he keeps using wireless terms; he calls this a transmission. He is showing me the letters B.B.C.

Facts: Edgar was keenly interested in wireless and had an expert knowledge of the subject. In the early days of the industry he ran a small manufacturing business. He and George were founding shareholders in the original British Broadcasting Company.

Statement: Would lithography or something of that work come into it? He says lithography or something to do with printing and I think he was clever in something he was helping to do. There were more machines, but he did a particular thing, and I do not know whether photography comes into it as well, but he is trying to show me plates or something. It seems to be very fine work, but in the actual room he is in I do not get many machines, but one special machine. In other parts of the building there are more, but he had a special thing.

Facts: The primary output of the machine was lithographic plates. "The last attachment Edgar made for the Lectroline was a device for ruling very fine lines. In order to test how fine and close together he could draw the lines he used an old photographic negative and replaced the pen by a razor edge he specially made. In an adjoining room of the premises are seven copper-plate printing presses and an engraving machine." — Harold Vandy

An important counter to the idea that all was done by reading the minds of the living should be noted here. One brother, Harold, was in the real estate business and totally ignorant of the operations of Edgar's inventions; the second brother, George, was an engineer who was generally familiar with the machines; Edgar's assistant, John Burke, also had one sitting with one of the same mediums. Burke was an engineer who had worked on the equipment from the start. If the mediums were reading minds to gain their information, one would reasonably expect the more technical information to result from sittings with the more technically oriented and knowledgeable sitters. Exactly the opposite was the case. The séances with Harold produced the most attempts to describe machinery. The session with Burke, who was well versed in every aspect of the equipment, produced nothing technical whatsoever.

As for *how* Edgar died, many intriguing comments were passed along by the mediums. Some examples are:

"He passed out through water, and yet it seems it need not have happened. I do not think it was a swimming bath. I am in a private kind of pool, and I am getting diving and things like that. Yes, I am out-of-doors, I am not enclosed — it is like a private swimming pool."

"He did not commit suicide, and he says he was not foolish, it was not his fault. He was after a definite object. There was somebody else. There was another person? His death was quite sudden."

"Your brother is talking a little as if he were afraid. That is curious, he is telling me that there is a woman who can tell you more about him (he is pointing to himself). This will puzzle you very much, as you cannot in any way connect it up. 'I tell you she was frightened and went away,' he says. When I ask him to explain more, he just nods. 'That is right, it was to do with my passing over, but no one knew she was there.'"

"It is something about having to get his clothes. He had taken some of his clothing off. He gives me exactly the condition he was in, he was ill for only two or three minutes before he passed out, dazed, I get a quick drop. Even in the time he took to fall, the whole mind seemed to be upon his clothes. Your brother was very shy by nature."

"It was not his fault, he says 'It was not my fault.' There was a funny feeling in his head, a woolly head, muddled, I feel; he gives me that feeling purposely after what you said — it was something he felt before, while, and even now, when he thinks of his passing."

"He certainly had a blow, and I am getting as though he were semi-conscious when he was in the water. From what I see of the conditions it is as though it were strange that he was drowned. I feel that he can tell me more than he will tell me, but he might implicate someone else. That is what I feel, and he does not want to give it."

"Is it right that you cannot get accurate information as to what happened, and that they did not tell you, and there is something being hushed up, because he is saying 'I do not think you will be able to prove it on Earth. It is something which was done and I do not know whether you will really get the truth about it.'"

"If this other person who was with him had not been cowardly, it would not have happened. This other man knows about it and will not say. I do not know if he was frightened and got out of the way and left him, because he is asking me to tell you that."

"I am not sure if someone was diving at the time. There was a diving board and whether someone knocked him or not I do not know, because he remembers going under and feeling a distinct blow on the head. He could not come up, as he apparently lost consciousness under water. This water should have been transparent, and it is very extraordinary nobody saw that, but he distinctly said there was another man there at the same time who should have known he was hurt."

And so, the cause of Edgar Vandy's physical demise seems destined to remain mysterious. One of the mediums opined: "I do not think he is capable yet to give the evidence that I wanted him to." But was he incapable or unwilling? And, if unwilling, who was he protecting?

Case 24 — New Meaning for "Soul Mate"

If you've spent any time puttering around chess sites on the Web, you might have encountered a story about a game played between two chess masters, only one of whom was alive at the time! Those telling the tale generally assume that it is bogus or was an April Fool's joke or they find some other way to disassociate themselves from such an outrageous idea. Their ignorance is quite understandable, for the full story was only available in the German language until quite recently.

There are two parts to this story: the interview and the game. The interview contains a great deal of compelling evidence; nevertheless, the game is the more unusual and therefore interesting aspect, so we'll cover it first.

The Game

When an acquaintance came up with the idea for a chess match played across the great divide, Wolfgang Eisenbeiss, Ph.D., thought that a medium named Robert Rollans might be able to facilitate the competition. Eisenbeiss had worked with Rollans for several years, and felt that the medium had the two necessary qualifications: he was trustworthy and he knew nothing of chess. So, a list of deceased Grandmasters was drawn up and Rollans' spirit control was asked to see if any of them could be located in the spirit realms and persuaded to play a game. While that search went on, Dr. Eisenbeiss sought an earthbound champion willing to compete against a ghost. Perhaps the most amazing thing about this remarkable story is that someone was willing to risk ridicule in the chess world by agreeing to do so. That person was Grandmaster Viktor Korchnoi, who was ranked third in the world at the time.

On the 15th of June, 1985, the challenge was accepted by a spirit claiming to be Géza Maróczy (the name is pronounced GEH-zaw MAHR-ot-see) a Hungarian who had passed from this mortal plane in 1951. Maróczy was also ranked third in the world — during the early 1900s — so the pairing promised to be competitive. [This presentation will refer to this combination of the medium Rollans and the spirit Maróczy as Maróczy/Rollans, or simply M/R.]

Maróczy/Rollans moved first. (It isn't clear how the opener was selected; perhaps it was because ghosts are generally envisioned as being white.) The move was communicated through Rollans via automatic writing, forwarded to Eisenbeiss, who passed it on to Korchnoi. When Korchnoi determined his response, he told Eisenbeiss, who told Rollans. Rollans would then go into his home office, write the move on a piece of paper, and make the move on a small chessboard. (Eisenbeiss, an amateur chess enthusiast, had to give Rollans lessons on chess moves and notation so that the medium would understand enough to move the pieces properly.) The communication of each move typically required about 10 days, but Korchnoi was often out of touch (grandmasters travel a lot) and so the entire match took 7 years and 8 months. Maróczy resigned after 47 moves. Just in time too, as Rollans fell ill toward the end and died only 3 weeks after the match's conclusion.

And how well did the spirit master acquit himself? About as well as one might expect from any champion with Maróczy's training and background. Those readers proficient at chess play and knowledgeable of chess history can judge for themselves by examining the game. The rest of us will have to rely on the testimony of experts. His opponent, Korchnoi, made the following observation after the 27th move: "During the opening phase Maróczy showed weaknesses. His play is old fashioned. But ... I am not sure I will win. He has compensated the faults of the opening by a strong end-game. In the end-game the ability of a player shows up, and my opponent plays very well." Helmut Metz, a well known chess commentator, observed that Korchnoi's opponent "controlled the end-game like the old masters from the first half of the century."[169]

---

[169] See Metz's Website: http://www.rochadekuppenheim.de/ meko/meko1a/m12.htm.

The Moves

1. e4 e6	13. Bxc6 Bxc6	25. a4 Rxg3	37. Rf5+ Kxg4
2. d4 d5	14. Bg5 d4	26. fxg3 b6	38. h6 b3
3. Nc3 Bb4	15. Bxe7 Kxe7	27. h4 a6	39. h7 Ra8
4. e5 c5	16. Qh4+ Ke8	28. g4 b5	40. cxb3 Rh8
5. a3 Bxc3+	17. Ke2 Bxf3+	29. axb5 axb5	41. Rxf6 Rxh7
6. bxc3 Ne7	18. gxf3 Qxe5+	30. Kd3 Kg6	42. Rg6+ Kf4
7. Qg4 cxd4	19. Qe4 Qxe4+	31. Rf1 Rh8	43. Rf6+ Kg3
8. Qxg7 Rg8	20. fxe4 f6	32. Rh1 Rh7	44. Rf1 Rh2
9. Qxh7 Qc7	21. Rad1 e5	33. Ke2 Ra7	45. Rd1 Kf3
10. Kd1 dxc3	22. Rd3 Kf7	34. Kd3 Ra2	46. Rf1+ Rf2
11. Nf3 Nbc6	23. Rg3 Rg6	35. Rf1 b4	47. Rxf2+ Kxf2
12. Bb5 Bd7	24. Rhg1 Rag8	36. h5+ Kg5	0—1

Playing chess well enough to make a grandmaster unsure of victory is an extremely rare skill. (Chess playing computers that could threaten a grandmaster were not readily available during those years.) Doing so in an "old fashioned" style could only be accomplished by a handful of geniuses ... if by anyone alive today. Not to accept these events as convincing evidence of Survival would require believing that some unknown player of immense skill and knowledge would be willing to put his reputation at risk by committing fraud over and over again for almost a decade — and without any recognition or compensation!

Mind reading, even on a grand scale, can't explain things either. Picking up impressions may be common, and discerning an occasional message from another's mind is not unheard of, but no one has ever demonstrated an ability to learn a complex skill via telepathy.

But wait ... there's more!

The Interview

At various times over the course of the match, Eisenbeiss asked Maróczy/Rollans to provide information about Maróczy's tournaments and personal life. M/R's initial response was to produce 38 hand-written pages of biographical information. From these pages, Eisenbeiss compiled a list of 39 points (later subdivided by his co-author, Dieter Hassler, into

92 discrete statements) that he thought might be subject to verification.[170] These points were sorted into five categories according to the likelihood of the medium being able to guess or discover the information without spirit help. These categories ranged from the sort of facts that could be gleaned from an ordinary encyclopedia (such as Maróczy's birthplace) through more specialized facts (such as the place Maróczy won in a Monte Carlo tournament in 1903) up to private information shared by few and not known to be written down (such as the level of chess-playing skill displayed by Maróczy's children, and the sort of job that Maróczy took after he finished school[171]).

Eisenbeiss then set about checking the validity of the spirit's statements. First, he asked Korchnoi to verify the statements, but the Grandmaster declined the task, saying that he did not know the facts and it would take too much time and effort to learn them. So, Eisenbeiss put the statements into question format and obtained the services of historian and chess expert László Sebestyén to find the answers. Not told anything of the case and never meeting Rollans or Korchnoi, Mr. Sebestyén worked under the assumption that his research was for an article on Maróczy. Consulting numerous specialized libraries and interviewing Maróczy's two surviving children and a cousin, Sebestyén managed to answer all but seven of the questions. And only three of the historian's answers differed from the statements given by M/R.

Of perhaps greater significance, when only the more difficult questions — 33 pieces of private or hidden information — are considered, 31 were verified and the answers to the remaining two could not be found.[172] None contradicted the spirit's testimony. This gives a confirmed accuracy

---

[170] The *Journal* report of 91 points was corrected in an Erratum sent by Hassler to the author on 23 November 2006.
[171] The spirit had correctly stated that Maróczy was a draftsman for a company that designed municipal water mains.
[172] These unanswered questions asked the name of Maróczy's first love and the name of a café he liked to frequent in Paris.

rate of 94 percent, but if more information could be discovered the rate could well be 100 percent!

Impressive statistics aside, there are a couple of exchanges worthy of special attention. The first revolves around a spelling dispute.

One of the questions involved a match in San Remo, Italy, in which Maróczy made a surprising move that thrilled the spectators and saved a game thought to be lost. For this reason, Eisenbeiss speculated that the game might be recalled by Maróczy, even though it was played almost 60 years earlier against a relatively unknown player from Italy named Romi.

As with the chess move that prompted the question, Maróczy/Rollans' response was unexpected — and exceptionally evidential. Maróczy said that he never knew anyone named Romi, but that, as a youth, he did have a friend named Romih (with an "h" at the end) and that this was the man whom he had defeated in San Remo. So, Eisenbeiss asked Sebestyén to determine the correct spelling of the name.

The historian found a German book and a Russian book that mentioned Romi (sans h) but another one by a Hungarian spelled the name Romih, so he felt the matter could not be settled. Eisenbeiss then took up the hunt himself and discovered two more references to Romi, and was about convinced that M/R was incorrect, when he managed to obtain a copy of the official program of the 1930 San Remo Tournament. Therein, the Italian player was mentioned in several places and his name was always spelled Romih. So Maróczy had remembered the name correctly.

Why this spelling discrepancy had occurred was not revealed until Eisenbeiss found a chess expert from Italy who remembered that Max Romih was of Slavonic origin and had emigrated to Italy in 1918. He hadn't dropped the "h" off the end of his name until after the San Remo tournament. Thus, there was no discord in Maróczy claiming to have known this Italian player as a youth in Hungary.

The second of Maróczy/Rollans' statements that deserve special attention concerns a female chess champion named Vera Menchik. On the 4th of

August, 1988, an ad in a chess magazine asked readers to answer the question: "Who was the Austrian founder of the Vera Menchik Club?" This club was formed as a lark by players who had lost tournament games to Menchik. As Menchik was known to have been one of Maróczy's pupils, Eisenbeiss put the question to M/R.

On the 8th of August, M/R offered two names as possibly the club's founder; neither was correct. On the 11th, he again expressed uncertainty and mentions a Dr. Becker, but rejects him because Becker had moved to South America. Furthermore, M/R described the club as a "silly joke" that had not captured his attention at the time. On August 18th, the magazine answered its own question: the founder of the Vera Menchik Club was, indeed, Dr. Becker.

During a session on August 21st, the subject was again raised and, despite the fact that the answer was now public knowledge (at least to those who read that particular chess magazine), M/R remained uncertain of the founder's identity. Instead, he changed the subject and told a most revealing story involving the wife and mistress of another world champion. This story is also quite evidential — as are several others in the report — but only the strongest evidence can be examined here.

The difficulty of emulating the play of a Grandmaster from the early 1900s makes any source other than Maróczy's spirit virtually inconceivable. Add to that the knowledge demonstrated of Maróczy's life and his insistence on spelling Romih with a final "h" (despite being contradicted by most available reference works) and one can eliminate the qualifier "virtually." Nor, in light of Maróczy's inability to name the founder of the Vera Menchik Club, is it justifiable to claim the employment of some theoretical and baseless "Super ESP."

Following the publication of this case, Vernon M. Neppe MD, PhD, FRS(SAf), who is both Director of the Pacific Neuropsychiatric Institute and a chess champion, did an extensive analysis of the game that further strengthens the case. Neppe carried out a detailed computer stimulation in addition to his own analysis and consulted with other chess experts.

Chess enthusiasts are encouraged to study his article that was published in the *Journal of the Society for Psychical Research*. For those not so familiar with the game, here are some of Neppe's insights and conclusions:[173]

"The game was analyzed in detail by comparing the moves with those of a computer that played at approximately low Master level. The author assiduously consulted with an outside independent International Chess Master, Leon Pliester, validating ideas, correcting obvious errors of computer judgement and move rankings, and assessing stylistic aspects of the play.

"Maroczy played at least at the Master level, ... This level could not have been achieved by the medium even after great training, assuming the medium was not a chess genius. ... not many living chess players could produce this kind of game.

"A chess computer could not reproduce this game as of the 1980s. Nor is it likely that it could replicate Maroczy's play even today because of the stylistic elements.

"The availability of expert outside validators by March 1987 (e.g. the Swiss chess champion, as reported to me by Dr Eisenbeiss), when the bulk of the game had been played, is a distinct plus against any hypothesis of fraudulent collaboration. The provision of outside evidence early on and the involvement of the news media in that regard is a definite plus."

It should also be noted that the medium, Rollans, received no compensation for his participation throughout the almost eight years of the match. Neither, by the way, did Korchnoi.[174]

Some have suggested that Rollans could have played as he did by reading the mind of Korchnoi. There are three problems with this idea. First, it does nothing to explain the interview data. Second, it requires that Rollans access Korchnoi's thoughts to an unheard-of degree. And third, if Rollans knew what his opponent was thinking ... he should have won.

---

[173] Neppe, pp. 129-147
[174] According to correspondence from Eisenbeiss to the author on 13 November 2006.

Conversion Phobia III
Sir William Crookes

An esteemed British physicist and chemist, Crookes taught at the Royal College of Chemistry before becoming a meteorologist at the Radcliffe Observatory, Oxford. In 1861, he discovered the element thallium, and later invented the radiometer, the spinthariscope, and the Crookes tube, a high-vacuum tube which contributed to the discovery of the X-ray. He was founder and editor of *Chemical News* and later served as editor of the *Quarterly Journal of Science*.

Crooks was knighted in 1897 for his scientific work, and awarded the Order of Merit in 1910. A Fellow of the Royal Society, he received honorary degrees in law and science from Birmingham, Oxford, Cambridge, Ireland, Cape of Good Hope, Sheffield, and Durham universities.

In His Own Words:

"When I first stated [in the *Quarterly Journal of Science*, October, 1871] that I was about to investigate the phenomena of so-called Spiritualism, the announcement called forth universal expression of approval, [it was said] that 'if men like Mr. Crookes grapple with the subject, taking nothing for granted until it is proved, we shall soon know how much to believe.' These remarks, however, were written too hastily. It was taken for granted by the writers that the results of my experiments would be in accordance with their preconception. What they really desired was not the truth, but an additional witness in favor of their own foregone conclusion. When they found that the facts which that investigation established could not be made to fit those opinions, why – 'so much the worse for the facts.' "[175]

---

[175] Crookes, p. 13.

Chapter Eight
Qualities Of Evidence

Of all the men professionally of science who have seriously and persistently investigated and studied the alleged phenomena of 'spiritualism,' the overwhelming majority have drawn the conclusion, as a result of their patient researches, that there is personal survival of death.

— Booth Tarkington[176]

We were finishing some fine pasta at Mama Ventura's when he took a sip of his Chianti, sat his glass down on the checkered tablecloth, and asked:

> "The cases at the end of *The Survival Files* are clearly more evidential of an afterlife than those that you described near the beginning, are they not?"

"Yes, I felt that you were saving the most impressive for your finale. But all of my readers haven't agreed with the order," I replied.

> "Nor would I expect them to. Decisions that are entirely subjective will never be unanimous."

"Do you think," I wondered, "that it is possible to develop an objective way of evaluating the evidence for Survival?"

> "We could give it a try," he said, pulling a pen from his pocket.

"I'll be happy to," I said, "but I'm not certain that my readers are going to be interested in such a dry subject as evidence evaluation."

---

[176] Introduction to *Neither Dead Nor Sleeping*, by May Wright Sewall.

"Oh, you can put the tedious stuff in an appendix," he said as he moved aside his empty plate, flipped over his placemat, and began writing. "But you ought to try and get the basic concepts across, because it's really important that people understand what makes good evidence and what doesn't."

"Well, there sure are a lot of books out there full of pretty weak cases."

"Then let's try to figure out what sort of occurrences are truly evidence of an afterlife," he said and he continued to write for a while as I stared through the front window, trying to imagine the streets crowded with Union soldiers instead of tourists.

In only a few moments, he interrupted my reverie with: "Let's start with a person who goes to see a medium. Assume that the medium doesn't know the sitter. She goes into a trance and tells the sitter these various things." And he handed me the list he had just written.

After I translated his scratchings, filled in the blanks, and cleaned it up a bit, the list looked like this:

- The name of the departed friend's fiancé, whom the sitter was not thinking about.
- That the departed friend had a brother who died in infancy; a fact the sitter had never known.
- Where the departed friend had hidden some money; a fact that no one else but the friend knew.
- The name of a departed friend from whom the sitter hoped to hear.
- That the departed friend's grave marker had been damaged by lightning the day before; a fact that was not known to any living person.
- The name of the departed friend's first dog, which the sitter had forgotten.

"Some people would say that each of these is proof of Survival, some would say none are. Some would admit one or more to be proof, but not all," he said. "Let's deal first with those who claim

> that none of these situations offer proof of Survival. They have only two arguments available to them. First, that the mental powers of the living are sufficient to account for the occurrences. Second, that the report was inaccurate or the phenomena fraudulent.
>
> "Those who assume that all evidence must be the result of mistakes or trickery — even though they cannot discover the mistake or detect the trickery — are essentially taking a religious stance. Since nothing can shake their firm belief in the impossibility of Survival we can move on, leaving them to their cold devotions.
>
> "Now, the idea that feats typically attributed to discarnate spirits are actually within the capabilities of the human mind deserves some attention. After all, we cannot be certain what the limits of the mind are."

"Yes," I agreed, "as far back as 1903, Myers wrote an excellent book[177] on that subject."

> "Absolutely, but for those who posit powers of mind as an explanation for some, if not all, incidents indicating Survival, we should reiterate that the act of mental telepathy is, in and of itself, strong evidence for the existence of a non-physical plane of consciousness, and thus, indirectly, of Survival."

He was referring to a conversation we had at his cabin, the gist of which was: It isn't so difficult to accept that we can mentally send and receive thoughts; the tough part is figuring out how a mind could sort through all the billions of thoughts that are being sent out at any given moment and read only the sought for message. The problem is not in the transmission or the reception, but in the tuning. Without some structure, all any mind could ever receive is the "white noise" created by the intermingling of the thoughts of every being in the universe. This argues strongly for the existence of some sort of universal mind or discarnate communications system that routes and delivers mental images according

---

[177] *Human Personality and Its Survival of Bodily Death.*

to our intention or desire. Such a system couldn't be limited to our own minds; it would have to exist in a mental plane independent of the physical.

> "In fact," he continued, "we can't be sure that there is any such thing as mental telepathy. The "Universal Mind" or "Cosmic Consciousness" required to properly route mental messages may, by itself, be sufficient to explain all mediumistic and psychic talents."

"Do you mean that all psychic phenomena could be the work of spirits?"

> "That doesn't seem likely, does it? But it seems more likely than the idea that all 'spirit' effects are caused by mental powers of the living."

"It occurs to me," I mused, "that if we must choose between accepting that a bit of information was communicated from the mind of a spirit or that it was derived from the mental feats of the medium, our decision might hinge on just how difficult a task the medium would have had to perform."

> "I can go along with that," he agreed. "The more demanding and complex are the mental gymnastics necessary to garner the information or create the effect, the simpler, more rational, and intuitively easier it is to believe that a discarnate entity is the true cause."

"Well, then, looking at your list, the first thing that strikes me is that receiving thoughts seems an easier task than reading minds. If a sitter was concentrating on a large blue star, it would be somewhat impressive for a psychic to describe the star. How much more impressive it would be, though, if the psychic could also tell the color of the pajamas that the sitter wore the previous night. Even though both bits of data exist in the sitter's mind, I can accept the possibility of thought reception more readily than the ability to read the entire contents stored in another's mind. Therefore, if a spirit testifies to a fact on which the sitter was concentrating (such as the name of a deceased friend) the evidence for the spirit actually being that deceased friend is not as strong as if the spirit were to give the name of the deceased friend's fiancé which the sitter knows but was not thinking of at the time."

> "Okay, we'll rank these in order of difficulty, with the simplest on top, and place the 'name' entry above the 'fiancé' entry." And he drew an arrow indicating that shift of position.

"Likewise, reading information stored only in someone's unconscious mind should be more difficult than reading the memories that they can normally recall. Thus, spirit testimony of a forgotten fact that resides only in the sitter's subconscious (such as the name of a deceased friend's first pet) is more evidential than giving a consciously remembered fact."

> "So, we put the 'pet' entry below 'fiancé'," he said, drawing another arrow.

I was on a roll now, so I continued: "Research has shown that mental telepathy is not affected by physical distance; thus, the possibility that a medium might be reading the mind of a person across the country should be given no more weight than reading the mind of a person across the table. But relationships matter, even if proximity does not. The fewer connections that can be found between a medium or the sitter and the person whose mind contains the information, the less probable that mind-reading will be a satisfactory explanation. For instance, revealing a fact only known by people not involved in the sitting (such as the lost infant) is more evidential than giving facts known (consciously or unconsciously) by the people involved."

> "You're saying that the information about the friend's deceased brother, if it didn't come from the friend's spirit, would have to have been pulled from the minds of the friend's parents."

"Yes, and their relationship with the sitter is weak or non-existent, so the medium, if she were not actually in contact with the spirit of the deceased friend, would face the herculean tasks of locating the friend's parents when there was no reason to do so nor any overt hint as to where they might be ... and then reading their minds to discover memories of a lost child."

> "Of course, the medium wouldn't have to read both parent's minds; but having the ability to find and plumb even one is still incredible."

"True enough, but that makes me think of a situation you haven't described for our deceased friend. Sometimes the information received is only partially known by one person while the remainder is known by another."

> "Okay," he said, "I'll place 'brother' beneath the 'pet' entry and add a line for 'multiple targets.'"

"So, now we come down to information known only by the spirit — the hidden money and the singed tombstone. Why did you make that two separate entries?"

> "Well, you are correct that obtaining information only known by the spirit cannot be attributed to mental telepathy. But if the knowledge was possessed before death, some might claim that it became part of the Akashic Records or some sort of cosmic data bank and that the medium could access it there."

"I've always thought that to be a really big stretch."

> "A really big stretch, indeed! Especially when the person propounding that theory also claims that individual minds do not survive the body's demise.
>
> "Nevertheless," he continued as he drew more arrows, "the most powerful evidence of all is the reception of information that was uniquely obtained by a spirit after it left its physical body."

When he had finished, the list looked like this:

Relative Strength of Evidence (from weakest to strongest):
- The name of a departed friend from whom the sitter hoped to hear.
- The name of the departed friend's fiancé, whom the sitter was not thinking about.

- The name of the departed friend's first dog, which the sitter had forgotten.
- That the departed friend had a brother who died in infancy; a fact the sitter had never known.
- Information divided among two or more people's minds.
- Where the departed friend had hidden some money; a fact that no one else but the friend knew.
- That the departed friend's grave marker had been damaged by lightning the day before; a fact that was not known to any living person.

"You know, mental telepathy and cosmic data banks aren't the only alternatives. Some of my readers might think that clairvoyance or remote-viewing could account for discovering buried objects or observing stormy graveyards."

> He laid down his pen and said: "There is some evidence that remote-viewing, or whatever you want to call it, does work — sometimes; but successful procedures require that a target be consciously selected and then carefully concentrated on. If a skilled practitioner were given the coordinates of a particular grave, he might be able to 'view' it and report back as to whether the headstone appeared to have been struck by lightning. But even then, the ability to wend one's mental way through the vastness of the universe to a specific spot demands the existence of some sort of map and navigation system. So, we're right back to the requirement for a cosmic consciousness.
>
> "Without being given a specific target, though, there is simply no way that a medium's mind, operating solo, could first sense that something had been struck by lightning, then identify what it was and who it belonged to, and then discover its placement. Such a feat could only be achieved with the guidance of someone who had observed the damage and knew the location."

"So, it's pretty clear," I summarized, "that mental telepathy, clairvoyance, and maybe other psychic powers could be the proper explanation for some evidence given for Survival, but they certainly cannot explain all cases."

> "This is very true," he affirmed as he stood and brushed a scattering of crumbs from his ample stomach. "And since the spirit explanation must be accepted in some cases, then it is very likely a factor in most."

The Case of the Missing Information

We paid our check and walked . . .

"Okay, so we've got a good start on a way to objectively determine which cases make the best evidence for Survival. Trouble is, our approach is only useful for revelations of information."

> Squinting in the afternoon brightness, he nodded: "This is true."

"So, what about incidents that seem to involve spirits but that don't have messages? The kind of events that are messages in themselves?"

> "Do you have a particular one in mind?" he asked, halting to look into a shop window.

I didn't really, but when I stopped beside him, I noticed an angel figurine of hammered copper that was wedged between the wooden hearts and the plaques lettered with homespun aphorisms. "Well," I said, "there's that woman who was vacuuming and found an angel on her carpet.

"As I recall the story, she was in the habit of vacuuming her carpets weekly, and had done so many times since the Christmas ornaments were put away in the basement, when suddenly she almost ran over a golden angel in the middle of the living room. Unbeknownst to her, her husband had just discovered another angel lying on the basement floor. They agreed that the ornaments' appearance was the sign they had been seeking that their son had survived his body's death."

"Ah, yes. A most provocative tale."

"And famous too." I added. "I first learned of it when it was the subject of a segment on the *Unsolved Mysteries* TV show nearly a decade ago."

"Most believers no doubt think it's obvious that the appearance of the angels was just the sign that the parents were seeking, and was thus a powerful affirmation of the son's continued life in heaven."

"I gather you're not so sure."

"Oh, that might very well be the proper conclusion … but then again, it might not be. The problem is that we have no solid knowledge of how a spirit could manage such a feat. We do know that physical effects such as apports, rappings, and flying and falling objects seem to require the presence of humans; but we have no idea what portion of the effect is typically caused by the human and what portion, if any, by a spirit.

"If the mind of a discarnate youth is capable of de-materializing a metal object from inside a cardboard box on one level of a home and re-materializing it on the surface of the carpet on another level, then would the minds of his living parents be any less capable? Is it reasonable to attribute certain powers to the dead yet deny them to the living?"

He stepped from the store window and turned down the street, letting his question hang in the air and giving me time to formulate an answer.

A block or so later I said: "Actually, yeah, I think there might be a couple of reasons."

"I'm glad to know the summer sun hasn't sapped all of your brain power," he said as he stepped into the shadow of a canvas awning. "What might these reasons be?"

"Well, for one, there are many cases in which the physical manifestations are used to transmit information. Rappings, table tilting, direct voice … all these have a physical component. We have strong evidence that they are often associated with spirit forces. Therefore, it seems reasonable to assume that at least some of those manifestations that don't transmit information are likewise caused by spirits.

"Secondly, as far as I know, no one has managed to consciously perform telekinetic acts that show anything like the power and complexity of the typical poltergeist haunting — at least not in a laboratory. Yes, it might be possible for a mother or father to mentally teleport ornaments around their home, but such abilities are far beyond anything yet demonstrated. In fact, the only times that such extraordinary physical effects are reported are in cases where spirits are thought to be involved."

> "You make some good points," he said. "You might also have reasonably claimed that the style of the ornaments chosen — angels rather than stars or icicles — was so appropriate to answering the parent's current concerns that it *was* information, although not verifiable information.
>
> "Even so," he continued, "how do we rate such cases as evidence. Is an angel apport more evidential than a rainbow? Is it more difficult to psychically create sounds or to produce visual images? Is slamming a door a tougher trick than levitating a skillet?"

"I suppose we could develop some distinguishing criteria; but, since they each involve the movement of inanimate things — even a noise is just the movement of air molecules — we probably ought to simply rank all of them equally? Where we could make a distinction is between effects on living and non-living things."

> "Which do you think are the more evidential?" he asked.

"Well, we generally consider mental telepathy to be more common than psychokinesis, so wouldn't it be more difficult to mentally influence a skillet than a hummingbird?

> "I reckon it would. What about plants?"

"Ah yes, a lot of after-death communications do involve flowers blooming out of season or popping up where they were never planted," I noted. "I suppose that organisms without a brain would be more difficult to influence than conscious animals but easier to affect than inanimate matter."

"Seems like we're well on our way to another rating system. Why don't you write it up when we get back to the hotel?"

"I'll do that," I promised.

"And, while you're at it, you might want to share the 'refrigerator' story with your readers as a good example of strong evidence for the presence of a spirit without the communication of information."

That I can do right here:

Case 34 — A Different Sort of "Cold" Case[178]

Promises to contact a living friend after one's death are often made but rarely kept. Even rarer are those that are fulfilled in a way that provides solid evidence of Survival.

In the final days of her battle with cancer, Mary Jasen made such a promise to her friend Christina. They had been friends for several years and Christina took Mary seriously, even though Mary's proposed method for announcing her spirit presence was a bit unorthodox. She said that she would knock loudly on the refrigerator to get Christina's attention. When Christina asked why the refrigerator, Mary jokingly pointed out how much she loved food and said that the refrigerator was her "favorite place." Then she told Christina to keep their arrangement a secret between them. A few months later, Mary passed on, and Christina awaited the signal.

Some five years later, Christina had pretty much given up any hope of hearing from Mary. Then, she had a dream in which she saw Mary and Len, who was Mary's husband, sitting at a picnic table in an unfamiliar park. In the dream, Mary turned toward Christina and said that she was fine and no one should worry about her. This was not the contact that Mary

---

[178] Martin, p. 96 - 100.

had been wishing for, but it made a vivid enough impression that, the next time she visited Len, she described her dream to the widower.

Len was more impressed with the dream because the park that Christina described was exactly like an area where he and Mary had often eaten lunch. This revelation lifted Christina's spirits, but the next thing that Len said was far more astonishing. A few days before, Len related, he had been in his kitchen when he had been startled by a banging sound as if rocks were being thrown at his windows. He could discover no culprit; but, when the sounds were repeated, he realized that the noises seemed to be caused by some unseen visitor banging loudly on the refrigerator door. He was perplexed but did not feel fear. In fact, he said that he somehow knew that his wife's spirit was responsible for the disturbance and he felt comforted.

If Mary's husband had dreamed of a picnic with his wife at a familiar location, no one would consider it indicative of anything — except, perhaps, that he loved his wife, or that he went to bed hungry. The fact that Christina dreamed of an area she had never visited is certainly suggestive, yet telepathy could explain it and unconscious knowledge cannot be ruled out. But if she had not had the dream, Len would not have been encouraged to tell Christina about the rapping sounds.

In almost every case of alleged spirit rappings, the evidential value comes from the information communicated, not the means of communication. This is because we cannot be 100-percent certain that living humans have less psychokinetic power than deceased humans. But, such an explanation simply doesn't wash in this case. If Christina's unconscious mind were going to generate loud raps on a refrigerator door, it would no doubt do so on her own appliance, not on that of someone who would not understand the significance of the disturbance. And, the husband is not a feasible source of the noises, as he was unaware of the friends' pact. This sort of "cross correspondence" leaves us with either accepting Mary's spirit as the source or conjecturing a psychic communication between Len and

Mary, and vice versa, that triggered a psychokinetic outbreak by the unconscious mind of a 68-year-old man. In this case, Occam's razor is greatly in favor of the spirit explanation.

Touched By The Past

Wandering among the cannon balls, belt buckles, and tattered uniforms in the next shop on the street, we stopped to examine some coins, both Union and Confederate. "Looking at old coins often makes me think of psychometry. Wouldn't it be great to be able to read their history just by touching them?"

> "Oh, I don't know," he replied. "I have enough trouble handling the sense impressions of the here and now. Can't say that I would appreciate being constantly bombarded by the then and there of everything I bumped into."

"As I recall, King Midas had a similar complaint," I mused. "But, if one could control it, what an entertaining and educational talent to have!"

> "Or what a depressing talent," he replied. "Does not your study suggest that the impressions one can obtain seem strongest when linked to powerful, and usually negative emotions? To what horrors might these coins be linked? More than 30,000 soldiers were seriously wounded at Gettysburg alone; uncounted legs and arms were amputated (without anesthesia), thousands of young men deafened, or blinded, or paralyzed for the rest of their lives. No, as far as I'm concerned, these coins and all their siblings and cousins can keep their anguished history to themselves."

For a long moment, neither of us spoke as our minds skirted the edges of the intolerable sadness of civil war.

> He turned toward the shop door. "Unfortunately, terror and suffering are much more likely to fill a psychometry session than peace and joy."

"But how does psychometry fit into our picture of the world and the afterlife?" I wondered. "How could it work?"

> "Goodness! my young friend. You surely don't think that I have the answer to that?"

But, I just followed him out into the sunshine and said nothing.

> "I doubt that any resident below the seventh heaven actually comprehends how such things work. If I may quote one of the first researchers into the paranormal, even advanced spirits can never 'understand the hidden sphere of cause.'[179]"

I maintained an expectant stillness. ... He snapped a pair of shades over his steel rims and turned his steps back to our hotel. ... I followed quietly.

> We hadn't even reached the end of the block when he broke the silence. Turning towards me with a resigned grin that I took as confirmation that he was aware that I knew that he could not resist any opportunity to speculate on such deep subjects, he said, "But if I *was* going to speculate on the workings of that hidden sphere, I would say that the best analogy we have for the universe would be a stupendously large and powerful computer network. Each conscious being is a tiny node in an almost infinite network of consciousness. And, at some level, every node is connected to, and can share information with, every other.
>
> "So, I don't consider it useful to assign any consciousness or even memory to inanimate objects. When a psychometrist focuses on a coin or other object, he or she can trace the links through the network to the mind or the memories of others who have possessed it." With that, we hurried our steps towards the hotel, for the lunch break was almost over.

---

[179] Hare, p. 95. The full statement is: "Although advanced spirits are much more conversant with the forces operating in nature than the most intellectually developed man in the form, still they do not, nor can they ever, as long as eternity rolls on, understand the hidden sphere of cause."

As we sat in the conference room awaiting the inevitable stragglers, he pointed to a program item concerning super-ESP and said softly, "You know, there is a counter argument to the super-ESP theory that we haven't mentioned yet. Those who deny the existence of independent spirits usually claim that mediums get their information by tapping into the minds of the living."

I nodded my agreement.

"Why then, would the information virtually always be about dead people? If we picture the medium somehow traveling around in mental space, picking up impressions that people have of each other, then shouldn't at least half of those impressions be about living persons?"

"Well," I said, "sitters don't generally pay mediums to provide information on folks that are still alive."

"A valid point. But what about 'drop-in' communicators?"

"You're referring to those entities that neither the medium nor the sitters know, who interrupt a session for reasons of their own? Like the captain of that English blimp?"

"Ah, yes. few drop-ins are as well known as Flight-Lieutenant Irwin, but you don't have to crash a dirigible to crash a séance. Unexpected strangers might make their presences felt whenever and wherever the living attempt to contact the dead. And, in almost every case, those strangers are not currently alive. If Survival is erroneous and super-ESP is the true explanation, then those drop-ins should be representations of living people at least as often as they are of the dead."

"Not bad," I said, "not bad at all. Is this something you came up with?"

"No," he replied, "I first came across it in an academic paper. But I do take credit for digging it out of the middle of a 36-line footnote on the 56th page of that paper."[180]

"Well, I've got several good cases involving drop-in communicators; this will give me a fine intro."

---

[180] Gauld, "A Series,"pp. 273-340. Remarkably, the old man had the page and line numbers correct.

Chapter Nine
— Cases from the Survival Top-40 —
Talking To Strangers

You and I may not have the power to bring about sensational happenings, but at least we can, in our small way, help in the furtherance of the knowledge that there are vast horizons quite beyond our perception, stretching limitless into the infinite.

— F.W.H. Myers via G. Cummins

These three cases involve information given by a spirit previously unknown to anyone involved in the séance. These are generally considered to be more evidential than when information is supplied from a spirit that is somehow linked to the medium or the sitters.

Case 46 — The Rationalist Spirit[181]

In 1959, Dr. Alan Gauld participated in seven meetings of a "home circle" in Cambridgeshire, England. This group consisted of a few core people and assorted visitors who gathered in a private home to attempt contact with the spirit world, mostly via the talking board. The group met, with various participants, on and off from 1937 to 1964. Careful records were kept of the majority of the circle's sessions. Based on these records and a great deal of personal investigative work, Gauld produced a report titled "A Series of 'Drop In' Communicators." The term "drop-in" refers to spirits who are strangers to anyone in the circle and who arrive uninvited. Such intrusions are thought to be especially evidential because of the presumed difficulty of any participant reading the information from the mind of a person whose identity and whereabouts are unknown.

---

[181] Gauld, "Drop In Communicators," pp. 273-340.

This case is of special interest because it reveals a rude and belligerent spirit; it is of even more interest because it shows a rude and belligerent spirit transforming into a polite and friendly one. To best demonstrate these characteristics, the dialogue is given verbatim, with the exception of a few irrelevant passages whose absence is indicated by " * * * ". The comments in [brackets] are Gauld's, those in {braces} are my attempts to clarify a passage.

A note on voice and formatting: The messages spelled out on the board are printed here in a different typeface. "Peter" was a frequent spirit presence who served as a kind of control or astral traffic manager for the circle. Comments in normal (serif) typeface generally come from a male observer referred to as "R.W." but occasionally other members interject a comment. In the opening lines, Peter is referring to a session held by some of the participants in another home a few days previously.

> ['Peter' writes:] A little later I am going to let the eel slip through. He slipped along on Thursday [*i.e.,* at the previous sitting] so I kept control. Stanley [R.W.'s deceased brother] and son will help me. Stan will help you son. Talk to him.

Is it a man, then?

> Yes. Humour him. Get to know him. We can then deal with him from here – big job. We do not know him so I am wanting to make contact through you. Humour him. Thank you all – I am leaving now. No worry. No harm.

> {At this point, the new spirit is allowed to take control.}

> M.p.m.p. {meaningless?} I know all the ladies.

> {The spirit recognizes women in the group from the previous session.}

What is your name?

> Lady I am Molly.

How can we help you?

> I am helping you. You like me to talk. I help the ladies but kind Nell [Mrs D.] does not like me. She says I am Elsie.

[*i.e.,* Miss E., Mrs D.'s customary partner on the talking board].

You are helping both ladies?

Yes. I do and I bring them lots of people.

What makes you come to them? What is your job?

Talking.

You know you are on the spirit plane?

Yes. I am.

Why do you come to these ladies?

They wanted people from here. I am all the people really.

It must be hard to be all those people at once?

I am only one at a time.

Then you find you change from one to another?

Yes. Do not really change.

What is your real name, do you remember?

Yes. I will not say.

We want to help you.

I do not want your help.

But we would like to help you.

Why?

Because we are taught to help those who need it.

Wrong teaching.

I have a feeling you are a man.

I was happy with the ladies and I am not going to be bloody well pally with you. Mind your own business. I did not come to talk to you. Shut up.

[Mrs. W.G.] What is your name?

Mollie.

You spelt it differently a little while ago.

Rats. My friends talk to me.

[R.W.] I'm going to talk to you.

Mind your bloody business.

You must take your business elsewhere and not worry these dear people.

Surely you don't use language like that to your lady friends.

Men friends.

What sex are you?

> Mollie.

Can you see anyone standing near you?

> Yes. Man.

Well, that is my brother and he is a good chap. He will help you.

> No. I cannot pretend here.

Isn't it better not to pretend, but to be yourself?

> You know a hell of a lot.

Do you remember your earth life?

> Yes.

What was your business?

> Not yours. I was a man who always kept to himself.

Oh, so you are a man?

> Damn. Like lady. Do you like religion?

Yes, but not over fond of it. Do you?

> Bloody rot.

That's only your opinion. You will be happier if you will be yourself and stop all this nonsense.

> Don't you talk. Let the ladies. I don't damn well like you.

I don't mind that, we want to stop you worrying our friends.

> Go now.

You will not go.

> I go.

Be reasonable.

> Shut up, buggar you.

There are people who will help you.

> Only Hitler can help. He is the master mind.

What is your real name?

> What has that to do with you? Shut up blast you. I am going.

There is only one master mind, God, and you cannot alter that.

> You make me sad. Go away.

I'd rather make you pleased.

> Keep quiet.

I want you to promise to stop worrying our friends here.

> Sorry.

That's better. That's the reply of an intelligent man, which I am sure you are.

> I go now.

Go with the thought of friendship from us.

> Shut up.

Go where you will, but be intelligent.

> I come with my heart full of love.

You certainly do not, what do you take us for? What you are doing is a cad's trick.

* * *

You are not to worry our friends any more with your pretence. There is a Power which will stop you. You are afraid of it. That Power protects them.

> Pray until your head falls off. I am German and my name is Gustav.

That's a French name.

> Liar. You are mad. Gustav German.

What is your surname?

> You say you help. I am Gustav Adolf Biedemburg. If I come and say Gustav would you like me better?

Not until you are sincere. Go with my brother, he will help you.

> Will he like me?

He will help you.

> I am not pretending about German.

What made you come to us? Why not to a German circle?

> I lived in London. It is better as myself. You welcome me.

You may come again if you first ask permission of the greater power, Peter or Bob.

> I must ask greater power first.

Yes, that's the idea.

> Yes. I am myself now.

Did you pass in air raid?

> No. My house was Charnwood Lodge.

What address?

    Let me think for next time I come.

Ask Bob and Peter to help you.

    I am going now with a kind friend who will listen and talk.

Give that friend my kind regards.

    ['Peter' writes:] Many thanks son.

Was he really sorry?

    Yes and he is German.

January 7, 1943

[Operators: Mrs W.G. and Mrs G.J. Recorder: L.G. Also present: R.W.]

    I offer my humble apologies and add to them my grateful thanks.

We are only too glad to have been of help. Come when you like, you will find friends here, and Mrs D. and Miss E. will welcome you too.

    I want to help. I am not lonely now. I will tell you my correct name. Adolf Biedebmann. I always was known and called Gustav.

Shall we call you Gustav?

    Please. I was a rationalist.

What exactly is that?

    A type of religion to follow only the reasoning of one's own mind. It puts a barrier around.

That is why you have been so lonely and found no companions?

    Yes. Partly.

* * *

    I had my own business.

What was it, do you remember?

    No. In some remote way I am associated with the Lond[on] University.

When did you pass over?

    Year ago.

Was your business a bookshop?

    No.

Publishers?

    Rationalist Press.

Do you want to remember your earth life?

Yes. I am happy though. I am forgiven for my lapse?

Yes, of course, it was no fault of yours.

Thank you all. Goodnight. ▶

In investigating this case, Gauld discovered no "Biedemburg" or "Biedebmann" but changing only one letter gives "Biedermann" and there can be no doubt that is the name the spirit attempted to communicate. Dr. Adolf Gustav Biedermann was a German-born, naturalized citizen of England who lived at Charnwood Lodge on the outskirts of London until he died at the age of 73. He was a fairly wealthy businessman who also worked in the Psychology Department at London University.

Those who knew Biedermann described him to Gauld as an arrogant, obstinate, and aggressive man who, nevertheless, could be a pleasant companion when one got to know him. He seemed to revel in his German heritage and never dropped his accent. One acquaintance portrayed him as "an out-and-out rationalist" who may well have been attracted to the idea of Aryan superiority. Biedermann once wrote a sarcastic letter to the London Times about experiments on telepathy. His disdain for religion is demonstrated by his will, which instructed that his children be brought up without any religious instruction whatsoever, and that he himself should be cremated without any religious ceremony. Also in this will, Biedermann bequeathed money to the Rationalist Press Association.

A spirit using crude and aggressive language is not unheard of, but it is rare and does not seem to have occurred at any of the other sessions held by this home circle. Thus, it cannot reasonably be attributed to either of the operators.

The Murder of Jacqueline Poole[182]

The gruesome slaying took place on the 11th of February 1983. The killer was identified within a few days. He was tried and convicted 18 years later.

The delay was not the fault of Ms. Christine Holohan of Ruislip Gardens, West London.

Holohan called the police in response to their broadcast request for information that could shed light on the murder of a bar maid named Jacqueline Poole. Although Holohan had never met the victim in life and knew none of her family or friends, she had read something about the crime in the local paper and she had a feeling that the presence she had been sensing might be the spirit of Poole. When it actually appeared to her, however, the spirit identified herself as Jacqui Hunt.

The different name than that published in the media was the first thing that got the attention of Police Constable Tony Batters when he and Detective Constable Andrew Smith called on Holohan a day or so later. But the knowledge of Poole's maiden name was only the first drop in a flood of information supplied by her spirit via Holohan. Poole's spirit had come to Holohan for justice, and she provided 131 separate facts concerning her murder. These included:

- On the evening she was murdered, Poole was supposed to go to work but did not because she felt ill.
- Two men had come by intending to take her to work.
- After they left, another man came by to visit her.
- She knew this man through friends, but she did not care for him.
- She let him into her flat.
- She thought he had a message for her from her boyfriend.
- Her boyfriend was currently in detention.
- When the police arrived at Poole's flat, there were two coffee cups visible in the kitchen. One clean and one with coffee remains.
- Also visible were a black address book, a letter, and a bottle of prescription medicine.

---

[182] Playfair, pp. 1-17.

Holohan went on to describe the attack, struggle, and murder in what the police referred to as graphic details, but those details were not released to the public. She said that there were rings missing from the body. Furthermore, she mentioned five names associated with the victim: Betty, Terry, Sylvia, Barbara Stone, and Tony.

Because Constable Batters had been the first on the scene of Poole's murder, he was aware of the coffee cups, address book, and other such details of the location. Of the other facts transmitted via Holohan, all but 10 were verified by the time the case was closed, and all but one of those were consistent with the known facts. The single at-variance item was Holohan's mention of Sunday, from which it was inferred that she thought the murder to have taken place on Saturday rather than on Friday.

"Betty" was Jacqui Poole's mother. "Terry" was her brother. "Sylvia" was her boyfriend's mother. "Barbara Stone" was a friend of Poole who had died several years previously, but the police did not make the connection at the time.

As for "Tony," when Holohan tried some automatic writing in her attempt to name the murderer, the only person's name she wrote was "Pokie." The constables immediately recognized that as the rather uncommon nickname of one of their key suspects, Anthony (Tony) Ruark.

Ruark, who had a history of criminal, but not violent, behavior, had already been interviewed by the police; however, no solid evidence of his guilt could be found. Based on Holohan's revelations, the man was detained and grilled at length and various items were confiscated during a search of his home. Nevertheless, no incriminating evidence was uncovered and Raurk was again released.

With nothing further for the police to go on, the Jacqueline Poole case grew cold, and what items had been collected as possible evidence were placed in storage. There they remained for 18 years until an informant claimed knowledge of the killer and the investigation was reopened. As it turned out, this new informant named the wrong man, but in the process of going over the stored evidence using the latest in DNA technology, the truth was revealed. A pullover that had been taken from "Pokie's" trash was found to have skin cells, body fluids, and clothing fibers that conclusively linked him to the murder.

In August of 2001, Anthony Ruark was convicted of Poole's murder and sent to jail for the rest of his life. Justice for Jacqui Poole was delayed, but her efforts to communicate via Holohan were not in vain, for it seems that it was the medium's prolific and accurate statements that triggered the search of the killer's home and resulted in the collection of the damning evidence. If that contaminated shirt had not been found in Ruark's trash, he would most likely have remained a free man.

The typical case in which mediums claim to have helped the police has little corroboration from the police themselves. Poole's murder investigation is most uncommon in that the detectives involved agreed to be interviewed by the researchers, supplied the researchers with copies of their original notes, and signed statements[183] affirming the accuracy of the researchers' report on which this article is based.

Psychic detective work is not, of course, the focus of The Survival Top-40. Therefore, the issue here is not how impressed the police were, but whether or not Holohan could have obtained her information from sources other than Poole's discarnate mind.

Some critics have claimed that it is not impossible for Holohan to have obtained her information through normal means. When each fact is considered separately, their arguments make some sense ... sometimes. For instance, it is possible, as one critic suggests, that Poole's father, who was allowed access to the murder scene momentarily to identify the body, happened to pry his eyes away from the mangled body of his daughter long enough to note that there were two coffee cups sitting out in the kitchen.

---

[183] Declaration: I confirm that the above account agrees with my recollection of my interview with Christine Holohan and with my knowledge of the case. (Signed) Anthony Paul Batters. Metropolitan Police Warrant No. 153617. 27.11.2002; (Signed) Andrew Smith, Detective Sergeant. Metropolitan Police Warrant No. 91/167901. 27.11.2002.

It is also possible that he felt the necessary curiosity and had the presence of mind to examine these cups and determine that one was clean and one still had some coffee in it. And it is just possible that in his grief-stricken state he thought to describe these cups to someone else. And, yes, it is possible that that someone was sufficiently impressed by two innocuous coffee cups to pass on the information and that — somewhere down the line of gossip — "news" of the cups reached Holohan. Possible ... but extremely unlikely.

To posit a long string of such outlandish possibilities for scores of other trivial facts is either being disingenuous or downright silly.

And then there are the facts that Holohan simply had no way of knowing, such as the name of Poole's deceased girlfriend, Barbara Stone. Even the police didn't make that connection for nearly 20 years.

Other critics might claim that Holohan was gleaning the information via mental telepathy. The coffee cups and such she could have pulled from Constable Batter's mind; the murder details from Ruark's mind; knowledge of the two who came to escort Poole from their own minds, and so on. Pulling just the relevant facts from so many different minds is theoretically possible ... say, about as possible as winning the lottery ten times in a row. But even those willing to swallow the idea of such super-ESP must choke on Holohan's mention of Barbara Stone — a girl who had nothing to do with the murder and wasn't even alive at the time.

The one mistake that Holohan possibly made actually strengthens her credibility, because the one thing that everyone involved in the case knew was that Poole was killed on a Friday. If Holohan was such a brilliant weaver of lies and guesses, she surely wouldn't have been wrong about the day of the week. Discarnate spirits, on the other hand, generally display a poor comprehension of time and dates.

Fire and Iceland[184]

It took 103 years for the facts about the Jensen case to fully emerge ... the wait was totally worth it!

The name Indridi Indridason might seem strange to most readers, but for a period of five years, this young man was the best-known medium throughout his native Iceland. So varied, prolific, and amazing were the manifestations of his power that a special committee of highly respected professionals was formed to study him.

The committee was called The Experimental Society and its 70-plus members included a professor of theology at the University of Iceland and a newspaper editor who later became Prime Minister of the country. In addition, Dr. G. Hannesson, an honored scientist who was appointed Professor of Medicine at the University of Iceland, studied Indridason over several months. Despite his initial skepticism, Hannesson concluded by stating his "firm conviction that the phenomena are unquestionable realities."[185]

So meticulous was the Experimental Society that they had a house designed and built in Reykjavik that featured living quarters for Indridason and a secure hall for séances. The hall was generally filled with up to 100 observers, even though attendance was by invitation only. Much of his mediumship was physical (involving lights, levitations, and such) but there were some mental phenomena, *i.e.* information presented from inexplicable sources.

The most written about mental phenomena of Indridason's brief career concerned a spirit who told the séance audience about a fire taking place in Copenhagen. These statements were made on November 24, 1905, and, on their own, do argue strongly for the Survival hypothesis. Information uncovered in 2008, however, raises the case to an entirely different level.

---

[184] Haraldsson, pp. 195-223.
[185] Hannesson, p.29.

In brief, the events of 1905 unfolded as follows. Around 9 p.m. the medium began to speak as a spirit claiming to be a deceased man named Jensen who said that he had been to Copenhagen and observed a fire raging in a factory there. About an hour later, Jensen came through once more and stated that the fire was under control.

Three of the witnesses have given public testimony to these facts and, within a day, a record was entrusted to the Bishop of Iceland to keep until these statements might be confirmed. Copenhagen is about 1300 miles distant from Reykjavik. Lacking access to telephone or telegraph connections between the two cities, the Committee thought that the fire might be reported in a newspaper when it arrived by ship from Copenhagen.

When the paper did arrive, it contained a story confirming the four facts given in the séance. There was one large fire in Copenhagen on the night of November 24th. It was in a factory on Kongensgade (a main street). It had been reported about the time given by Jensen, and was brought under control in about an hour.

Many commentators have remarked on the similarity with the famous report of Swedenborg's announcement of the great fire in Stockholm (in 1759) while he was visiting Gothenburg, some 245 miles away. Swedenborg, did not claim that that specific piece of information came from a spirit, only that he had seen a vision, so his experience is not evidential of Survival. Also, there was a strong connection, at least theoretically, between the fire and the seer, as the fire consumed the homes of several of Swedenborg's friends and was not extinguished until it had almost reached his own. No such connection was apparent between Indridason or Jensen and the fire on Kongensgade — at least no connection was realized at the time.

The hand-written records of Indridason's séances filled many large volumes, all of which were presumed lost for the past half-century. In 1991, however, two of the missing volumes were discovered in the estate of a former president of the Icelandic Society for Psychical Research. Even so, it wasn't until another 17 years had passed that a professional researcher carefully examined these records. Dr. Erlendur Haraldsson,[186] the author of numerous books and papers on psychic phenomena, calls his unexpected discovery "perhaps the most memorable finding of [my] life."

Scattered among the thousands of notes in these records are several, hitherto unknown, facts about the earthly life of Mr. Jensen, including that:

- His first name was Emil.
- He was a manufacturer.
- He was unmarried and childless.
- He died when he was "not young."
- He had several siblings.
- All of whom outlived him.

Haraldsson tried to corroborate these statements by combing through old business directories, census data, and birth and burial records at the Royal Library, the National Archives, and the City Archives in Copenhagen — and he was 100-percent successful!

Here is what the professor discovered:

- There was one, and only one, Emil Jensen listed as a manufacturer in Denmark (despite Jensen being one of the most common surnames in the country).
- This Emil Jensen lived almost his entire life within a few blocks — much of the time within a few yards — of the factory that burned.
- He never married.
- He had no children.
- He died at age 50.
- He had four sisters and two brothers.
- All of whom died after 1905.

Between his report of the fire and his statements about his personal life, we count 12 distinct facts stated and confirmed by the spirit of Jensen, and no statements contradicted or challenged by careful research. This is

---

[186] Professor emeritus of psychology at the University of Iceland.

made all the more convincing by the physical isolation of the séance from Copenhagen, the direct connection between Jensen and the location of the fire, and the lack of any link between the séance attendees and the events described or the participants therein.

We are left with no feasible conclusion other than that the spirit of Emil Jensen detected a serious fire near his earthly residences and immediately communicated that news via the most accomplished medium holding a séance at that hour.

Conversion Phobia IV
Cesare Lombroso

Lombroso obtained his doctorate in medicine from the University of Turin and became a neuro-psychiatrist; then served as an army physician. In 1862, he was appointed professor of diseases of the mind at Pavia, then took charge of the insane asylum at Pesaro. Later he became professor of medical law and psychiatry at Turin.

The son of a long line of rabbis, Lombroso founded the Italian School of Positivist Criminology and is considered a key originator of the science of criminology.

In His Own Words:

"If ever there was an individual in the world opposed to spiritism by virtue of scientific education, and I may say, by instinct, I was that person. I had made it the indefatigable pursuit of a lifetime to defend the thesis that every force is a property of matter and the soul an emanation of the brain."[187]

"I am ashamed and grieved at having opposed with so much tenacity the possibility of psychic facts – the facts exist and I boast of being a slave to facts. There can be no doubt that genuine psychical phenomena are produced by intelligences totally independent of the psychic and the parties present at the sittings."[188]

---

[187] Lombroso, p. 1.
[188] Fodor.

Chapter Ten
The Darkness Dialogue

There are no miracles that violate the laws of nature. There are only events that violate our limited knowledge of the laws of nature.

— Saint Augustine

The grand conference room of the Gettysburg hotel was once the lobby of an elegant bank. There are chandeliers hanging from the intricate tray ceiling and, near the current entrance, a massive door guards the opening to the bank's now-empty vault. Sitting near that steel behemoth, while awaiting the start of the next session, the old man and I shared a few thoughts about what a neat setting the vault might provide for a séance. Would the tons of steel and concrete deter the spirits? There certainly would be no problem restricting access, or achieving the total darkness that so many spirits seem to require.

> "I note," he said, "that the system by which you propose to rank cases for the Survival Top-40 excludes any incident that is not sufficiently illuminated to be observed clearly. Do you think all of the reports from darkened séance rooms are fallacious?"

"It isn't what I think that matters," I replied. "As you know, the cases in the Top-40 are supposed to be those that are most likely to convince the reader that we do live on. Since most folks, quite rightly, are suspicious of what might occur under cover of darkness, I am reticent to include such cases, even if I have no reason to suspect fraud."

> "But have you ever considered that total darkness can reveal as well as hide?"

"No. Can't say that I have."

"Well, consider that if you've been sitting in the dark for a long time so that your eyes are as well adjusted as they can get and you still can see absolutely nothing, then anyone or anything that moves easily and precisely about the room must possess inhuman powers of sight.

"We have testimony from scores of participants in hundreds of pitch-dark séances that something intelligent was capable of moving about rapidly without bumping into any furniture or person. Likewise, many sitters have spoken of being deftly touched, tapped, and even kissed in a way that no human could duplicate without sufficient illumination. In addition, comments revealing a clear view of the room are often made by seemingly disembodied voices."

Later, I retrieved this passage from Findlay's *On the Edge of the Etheric*[189] in which he is discussing sittings with the medium John C. Sloan:

"[A spirit] reprimands someone for sitting with his legs crossed, which is one of the first things a novice at a séance is told not to do. The novice, thinking that as we are sitting in the dark no one will see him, sometimes disobeys this injunction, but forgets that the darkness is no darkness to them, that they see us clearly, and everything we do. A tap by the trumpet on the culprit's head, and a polite request not to cross his legs, invariably proves this; in fact, I have never known a mistake to be made. … Other instances have occurred, quite apart from the regular voice phenomena, to show that the etheric intelligences present can see in the dark. I shall mention a few.

"At the close of a sitting, just before the farewells are said, I have often held out my watch and asked the time, and on every occasion, when the lights have been turned on, I have found the reply correct almost to the minute, and this be it remembered is done in the dark and when no luminous watches are in use. This correct time telling, moreover, occurs after a

---

[189] Findlay, pp. 135-136.

sitting of from two to three hours. Again, if I hold my finger in any direction it will, on request, be gently touched with the trumpet; no fumbling, a clean gentle touch. Any part of the body, on request, will be cleanly and gently touched, either ear, the nose, the left or right knee—an impossible thing, as I have proved, for any human being to do in the dark."

And all this long before the invention of night-vision goggles.

> "Furthermore," my companion pointed out, "there is another aspect of darkness that argues for the reality of spirit intelligences. That is the impossibility of a medium carefully studying a sitter's demeanor and posture in order to seemingly read her mind. As Findlay states, 'It might be possible for a human being with the deductive faculty of a Sherlock Holmes to have some idea of our thoughts in daylight, from a study of our facial expressions, but in the dark, never.'[190]
>
> "Finally, the inability of séance participants to see in the dark sharpens their aural acuity and eliminates visual cues that could be misleading. The right clothing, a pair of spectacles, maybe even a beard, in dim light, combined with the desire to believe, can result in a false recognition. But the voice alone is not so likely to be misidentified.
>
> "To us, darkness is blindness. If spirits see 'with their minds' then everything would seem to be illuminated whether or not there was any light present."

Even though I do not plan to eliminate the requirement for clear observation from the Top-40 ranking system, I see the validity of these points, and so include them here for further consideration by both researchers and skeptics.

---

[190] Findlay, p. 173.

Not Seeing Is Believing

Cases that depend upon eyewitnesses are, of course, seriously weakened when the witnesses cannot see clearly. But, when the medium or percipient is blindfolded or otherwise in the dark, the evidentiary value can be greater. The best examples of this effect are probably cases involving the "Ouija" board.

Boards covered with letters and numbers that could be pointed to with a small triangular table known as a "planchette" or "traveler" were often used by spirit seekers during the early 1880s. On February 10, 1891, Elijah J. Bond was granted the first patent on such a board. His business partner, Charles Kennard gave their version the name "Ouija," which he falsely believed was Egyptian for "luck." Parker Brothers bought the rights to the name in 1966, so I will use the generic "talking board" from here on.

Of all the diviner's devices, the talking board is the most popular. Perhaps this is because its low cost and ease of use appealed to many who wouldn't think of buying a crystal ball or learning to read tarot cards. Also, using the board is a social thing requiring at least one person and usually two people to touch the traveler and another to copy down the messages being spelled out. Before the advent of horror movies on late-night television, many young folks sought answers to burning questions ("Will I marry a handsome man?" "Does Frankie love me?") from the board. This proved especially thrilling on dark and stormy nights amid flickering candles.

Unfortunately, not all encounters with the powers behind the board have been so innocent or harmless. Many people claim that playing with a talking board can open portals to other dimensions, letting in immoral or amoral spirits who revel in encouraging nasty deeds and may even try to possess the naive planchette pusher. The recommendations made for dealing with such interlopers range from prayer to envisioning white auras to trashing the board altogether.

Nevertheless, the talking board is hugely important because several of the best mediums and channelers employed it to make their initial contact with the spirit realms.

This author would, therefore, advise those trying out the talking board to exercise caution and common sense. Any messages coming through the traveler should be evaluated in the same manner as would commentary or advice received from any other stranger. As the Bible commands, "Do not trust any and every spirit, test the spirits to see whether they are from God."[191]

Skeptics are quick to claim that the only thing coming through talking boards is the inner self of the user and that the results are either fantasy or repressed memories. These critics are often correct; but when the operators have no link to the information sources, the evidence is very convincing. And it gets even more convincing when the operators are kept in the dark as to the location of the letters.

The Honorary Secretary of the S.P.R. for Russia, Michael Solovovo wrote an article describing how a certain Lieutenant Colonel Starck obtained previously unknown information while ensuring that the operators of the board could not be influencing the messages. Prior to each session, Stark would bandage the eyes of both women so that they could see nothing. Then he would write the letters of the alphabet in random order on a piece of paper and place it on a table between the women. He would next place their hands on the traveler — in this case, a small over-turned saucer with a pointer attached. As he asked questions, the traveler would move quickly and precisely to spell out the answers.

A similar approach was used by the Unitarian minister, Dr. Horace Westwood. This is his description of how his 11-year-old daughter, Anna, got started with the board: "So we let them try, one by one, and each pulled a blank, much to their chagrin, until Anna placed her little hand on the

---

[191] 1 John, 4:1. See "The Sin of Speaking with Spirits" at www.TheSurvivalTop40.com for more on Biblical injunctions regarding communicating with the dead.

planchette. She had hardly touched it, when the indicator began to move with startling rapidity and with equally startling accuracy, spelling out words and sentences in complete and intelligent sequence." Turning the board around had no effect on Anna's remarkable ability, nor did blindfolding the girl. The next day Westwood drew the letters of the alphabet "higgledy-piggledy" on a large piece of paper. "Indeed," he explains, "they presented such a confused picture that if I wanted to spell out any word, and with my eyes wide open, it was an effort to find the letters." Such precautions proved pointless. When Anna was blindfolded and led to the scrambled board, the planchette flew just as rapidly and the messages came just as intelligently as before.[192]

One of the most inventive and certain methods of preventing operator input was devised by a circle of friends in Dublin, Ireland. They created a board consisting of letters on individual cards that could be arranged in any order. This display was then covered with a sheet of glass 22-inches square. The various arrangements had no effect on the rapid movements of the traveler or on the precision with which it spelled out meaningful messages. Neither did blindfolding the operators have any deleterious effect; nor did placing opaque screens between the blindfolded operators and the board. In other words, there was absolutely no way that either person touching the traveler could have any idea — via their normal senses — of what letters were being pointed to or what messages were being spelled out. Often, in fact, the operators distracted themselves with light talk and laughter even when serious messages of disaster or despair were being communicated through their darting fingertips.

In each of the three situations described above, the message(s) contained accurate information unknown at the time to anyone involved. But it should be emphasized that the ability to rapidly spell out *any* meaningful message when the location of the letters is hidden is, of itself, strongly indicative of spirit influence.

---

[192] See pages 362-369 for more about Anna's psychokinetic abilities.

Conversion Phobia V
Horace Westwood

Born in Yorkshire, England, Westwood became an ordained minister of the Methodist Episcopal Church in 1906 and pastored at Sault Ste. Marie, Michigan. In 1910, he joined the Unitarian Church and was pastor successively at the First Unitarian Church, Youngstown, Ohio; All Soul's Church, Winnipeg, Manitoba, Canada; and First Church, Toledo, Ohio. He was minister at large for the Unitarian Church (1927-1933) and for the First Unitarian Church, Berkeley, California, ending his career as pastor of the oldest Unitarian church in the South, in Charleston, South Carolina. He was the author of 20 books on religion and morality.

In His Own Words:

"To be concerned with the question of individual survival beyond death when there is so much misery and suffering upon earth is the essence of selfishness."[193]

"The entire thing is utterly foreign to the world of fact I think I know. Also, it leads to an outlook upon life which I regard as inimical to the best interest of mankind. Such a possibility is entirely beyond the range of any consideration I could entertain, even for a moment."[194]

"I am scientifically convinced that thought and personality can manifest themselves apart from a brain and body as we now conceive them. This I hold to be true, because the phenomena upon which the inference is based can be repeated ... they are verifiable."[195]

---

[193] Westwood, p. 9.
[194] _____, p. 3.
[195] _____, pp. 196-197.

"I am convinced that the truth of immortality may ultimately prove itself to be the only cornerstone upon which a decent and humane society can really depend."[196]

---

[196] _____, p. 199.

Chapter Eleven
— Cases from the Survival Top-40 —
Spirit Possessions

From the moment that I had understood the overwhelming importance of this subject and realized how utterly it must change and chasten the whole thought of the world when it is wholeheartedly accepted, I felt ... that all other work which I had ever done, or could ever do, was nothing compared to this.

— Sir Arthur Conan Doyle[197]

Possession, for our purposes, involves the apparent take-over of one person's body by the spirit of a deceased person without the living person's knowledge or consent. The possession may last only a few minutes, or go on for weeks, or even for as long as the possessed body remains alive.

Case 66 — The "Deadicated" Reporter

The description of events given below was written out by A.A. Hill, of New York City, and published by businessman and researcher Isaac Funk[198] (the publisher of the Funk and Wagnalls dictionaries). Mr. Hill was known to Funk and described by him as a man of character and intelligence. At the time he wrote the story – at Funk's urging – Hill was the editor of *The Amateur Sportsman* magazine.

"Some twelve or fifteen years ago, I was the editor of the *New York Sunday Dispatch*, a newspaper well known at that period and for many years before.[199] One of our reporters was a man named Williamson, a

---

[197] Carr, p. 268.
[198] Funk, Class V, Case 1.
[199] One well-known contributor to this paper was poet Walt Whitman.

son of the former owner, then deceased. He was about thirty years of age, and having long been connected with the paper, was retained on the staff by the new owner, more because of his faithfulness and loyalty and out of respect for his lamented father, than because of his journalistic or intellectual ability. It was his duty to take care of the city fire-department news and gossip, and his interest in the fire department and its affairs was unusual – I could almost say, phenomenal. Moreover, if to his faithfulness and zeal for his work had been added average talent, he would have been a treasure as a reporter. It used to wound his feelings greatly whenever I found it necessary to curtail or otherwise edit the copy he turned in concerning what seemed to me to be rather trivial fire-department matters.

"But he was suddenly stricken with illness and died within a few days. In casting about for someone to fill his place, I bethought myself of a quiet, modest, but very bright young journalist who had previously been in my employ in another city. In engaging him I was careful not to inform him that a member of the staff had died or that he was to fill a vacancy. The position did not warrant paying a large salary, and a bright young man could take on other work. So I wrote my young friend that I could find work for him if he would come on and be willing to do anything called upon to do. He arrived the following Wednesday afternoon, and being a stranger in the city, I met him at the railway station and took him to the office. I gave him the desk formerly occupied for a good many years by his predecessor, who had then been dead for about a week, telling him he need do nothing that day, and if he would excuse me for a time while I finished some writing, I would then take him up-town and find him a place to board.

"In about fifteen or twenty minutes he suddenly appeared at my desk, looking astonished and agitated. He laid two sheets of manuscript before me, written on the usual copy paper of the office, with the remark: 'I did not write that.' I could not see much sense in the remark, but replied: 'Well, if you didn't, who did? Some of it looks like your handwriting.' His reply was: 'I don't know; as soon as I sat down I never felt so peculiar and drowsy in my life. I must have gone to sleep and when I was awakening I found myself writing, but it doesn't all look like my handwriting.'

"Now, I should explain that this young man's handwriting was nervous, small, and not clearly legible, while his dead predecessor had written a large, round hand that could be read easily. But the writing in question varied between that of the two; some of it was like the writing of the dead man and some like that of the new reporter, and other parts of it were a composite or intermixture of both. The last few words were undecipherable, and the sentence was apparently unfinished. It should likewise be stated that the deceased reporter had for years begun his report of the meetings of the fire commissioners in this form: 'The regular weekly meeting of the fire commissioners was held last Wednesday, Commissioner in the chair.' The manuscript the young man had placed before me began that way, altho if he himself had been the author of it in his normal condition, it would by no means be the form he would begin a newspaper story of that kind. It purported to state what had been done at a fire commissioners' meeting, and altho it was not all clear or complete, there was enough to puzzle me.

"Now comes the most singular fact: I preserved the two pages of manuscript, and the next day ascertained what had been done at the fire commissioners' meeting, held perhaps an hour or two before it had been written. I was astonished to find that, so far as it went, it was a correct report of what had actually taken place.

"What was the agency by which this information was conveyed? Was it thought-transference or mind-reading? It could not have come from me. I certainly neither knew nor cared what they did at the meeting, and I had intended to omit publishing the report for that week altogether, or get an abstract for publication from some other paper, not sending the new man for the report until the following week. The information could hardly have been 'thought transferred' by any living fire commissioner from another part of the city; none of them was especially anxious that the *Sunday Dispatch* publish their reports, even if he were able to thus 'project' the information through space in this way. It could have been no one in the newspaper office, for no one had such information to impart, and there was only an office boy and a bookkeeper on the floor. It could not have been any trick or duplicity on the part of the new reporter himself. He knew nothing about the fire commissioners, or their meetings, or that they were published in the paper which was to employ him, even tho he had possess the miraculous power of reporting a meeting several miles away and when not attending it.

"Could the man who had just died, and who had always taken such a vital interest in the fire department and in the reports in the *Sunday Dispatch* concerning these meetings, have returned in spirit and through the new reporter communicated the report for publication?

"I will leave the solution to the reader. I have only stated the absolute facts."

Being that these events took place over a hundred years ago, it's easy to assume that they are somehow less valid than cases described in more recent books, but on close examination, the evidence for Survival presented here is quite strong. Anyone who has read Isaac Funk's works could have no doubt of his integrity and perspicacity. Hill correctly points out that telepathy offers no enlightenment. Some might fall back on other extra-sensory explanations, but there was no link between the new reporter and the meeting's venue – no path for a mind, or thoughtform, or whatever to follow. So the theoretical possibilities of clairvoyance, an OBE, or remote viewing just aren't feasible. Also, the new reporter had neither the means, motive, nor opportunity to trick his new boss, even if he were crazy enough to try. The absolute facts that Hill has so succinctly provided point directly to the Survival of the human personality and to naught else.

Case 45 — The Return of Mary Roff[200]

Teenage girls are the focal point of many strange stories. What makes this tale really weird is that it involves two girls, both teenagers, who were born 12 years apart.

Although she was often a loved and loving child, from the time she was six-months old Mary Roff had been afflicted with seizures that gradually increased in violence. As she grew into a young woman, Mary started hearing voices and began to complain of a "lump of pain" in her head. To relieve her headaches, she would repeatedly draw out her blood with leeches. Whatever was causing her agonies seemed also to bestow psychic powers, as it was claimed that she could read sealed envelopes and closed books while tightly blindfolded. She became known throughout her hometown of Watseka, Illinois, and her alleged powers are said to have been carefully investigated by prominent citizens, including newspaper editors and clergymen.

Mary's special talents could not save her, however. After slicing her arm in an apparent suicide attempt, she was committed to a mental hospital, where she died on the afternoon of July 5, 1865, at the age of 18.

Some 12 years later, another girl named Mary, living at the other end of the same town, began showing similar symptoms. There were two main differences between the Marys. For one thing, this second girl was named Mary Lurancy Vennum, and she was known as Lurancy or simply

---

[200] The case was first published in 1879 as "The Watseka Wonder" in the *Religio-Philosophical Journal*, and published in pamphlet form in 1887 titled *The Watseka Wonder: A Narrative of Startling Phenomena Occurring in the Case of Mary Lurancy Vennum*, by E.W. Stevens.

Additional evidence was obtained by Dr. Hodgson in personal interviews with some of the chief witnesses and printed in the same journal in December 1890.

The editor of the journal, said by F.W.H. Myers to be well known as a skillful and scrupulously honest investigator, endorsed Stevens and claimed that great pains were taken before and during publication to "obtain full corroboration of the astounding facts from unimpeachable and competent witnesses."

"Rancy." For another, Lurancy had seemed perfectly healthy until she was nearly 14. Then one day, July 11th, 1877, to be exact, Lurancy had some sort of seizure and lost consciousness for five hours. A similar episode occurred the following day, except that the seemingly unconscious girl began speaking of seeing dead people. This sort of thing happened several times daily for the ensuing six months, leading many friends and family members to suggest commitment to an asylum. No doubt these suggestions would have been followed, were it not for the interference of Mary Roff's father.

Since the death of his daughter, Mr. Asa Roff had sat with a couple of mediums, had received material he thought came from his daughter, and had come to believe in the existence of a spirit world. Furthermore, he suspected that sending his daughter to an asylum had been a mistake. When he heard of the tribulations of Lurancy, Roff was concerned that the same mistake might be repeated. So, he contacted the Vennum family – with whom he was distantly acquainted – and persuaded them to allow a friend to try and assist the girl.

Roff got considerably more than he bargained for.

The friend was Dr. E.W. Stevens of Janesville, Wisconsin, who was skilled in hypnotism. Stevens traveled to the Vennum home in Watseka and Roff introduced him to Lurancy in the presence of her family. Much of what we know about this case comes from material published later by Stevens, although others also did follow-up investigations.

When Stevens first saw Lurancy she was sitting in a chair with the posture of an old hag. He drew-up a chair and she savagely warned him not to come nearer. She identified herself as a woman named Katrina Hogan and she was reticent and sullen, but she said she would talk to the doctor because he was spiritual and would understand her. Then, suddenly, that personality was gone and she claimed to be a young man who had recently run away from home, gotten into trouble, and lost his life. Finally, Stevens managed to induce a hypnotic trance and "was soon in full and free communication with the sane and happy mind of Lurancy Vennum herself." She claimed that she had been influenced by evil spirits but that now there were angels around her and one of them wanted to come to her. On being asked if she knew who it was, she said: "Her name is Mary Roff."

Mr. Roff, although surprised, naturally thought that was a great idea. He encouraged Lurancy to let Mary come through, saying that his daughter was good and intelligent, and would be likely to help Lurancy since she used to suffer from a similar affliction. Lurancy, after seeming to discuss the matter with her attending spirits, agreed that Mary would take the place of the former wild influences.

Mr. Roff, apparently thinking that Lurancy would now be in control with Mary's aid, said to her: "Have your mother bring you to my house, and Mary will be likely to come along, and a mutual benefit may be derived from our former experience with Mary." But, the next morning, the first day of February, 1878, the girl who awoke in Lurancy's bed and body claimed to actually *be* Mary Roff. She showed no recognition of the Vennum home or any of the family members. She just wanted to go home "to see her pa and ma and her brothers."

The next day, there was no change; nor the day after that. Mrs. Roff and her daughter, Mrs. Minerva Alter (Mary's mother and sister) came to see the girl at the Vennum home. As they came in sight, far down the street, "Mary"[201] spied them from a window and exclaimed, "There come my ma and sister Nervie!" – the name that Mary had called her sister in their childhood. For over a week, although she remained docile and polite, "Mary" constantly pleaded to go "home" and showed no signs of leaving Lurancy's body. Finally, on February 11th it was agreed that she could go and live with the Roff family. This was not intended to be a permanent arrangement, though, as "Mary" said that she would only be allowed to remain in control until "some time in May."

---

[201] To minimize confusion, the name Mary (printed plainly) indicates the original Mary Roff and the name "Mary" (in quote marks) indicates the apparently possessed Lurancy Vennum.

And so, for the next 14 weeks, the Roff's were visited by a person who, except for her physical appearance and the lack of seizures and despondency, was in every way the daughter they had lost over 12 years previously. "Mary" immediately recognized every relative and family friend that Mary had known since infancy. She always called them by the names that Mary would have been familiar with; but she treated the Vennum family as total strangers.

These affirmations of her true being started on the way to the Roff home across town. As they traveled, they passed by the house where they had been living when Mary died. "Mary" demanded to know why they were not returning there and they had to explain that they had moved a few years previously.

She proved herself familiar with hundreds of incidents, both major and trifling, that had occurred in her previous life; sometimes spontaneously and sometimes in response to careful questioning. She knew what articles of clothing belonged to Mary and which ones Mary had made. She knew exactly where her brother was scarred when a stovepipe fell on him. When asked if she remembered a certain dog, she immediately pointed out the precise location in her sister's home where it had died. Never did any statement, or way of talking, or gesture give the slightest hint that she was not who she claimed to be.

"Mary" was thoroughly familiar with the horrid "treatments" that Mary was subjected to in attempts to cure her supposed insanity. She remembered cutting her arm, but when she started to pull up her sleeve to show the scar, she suddenly stopped and said, "Oh, this is not the arm; that one is in the ground." She then spoke of watching her own funeral and of sending messages to her father during his séances and she gave the exact times and locations of those sessions and correctly repeated the messages transmitted.

And then, around 10 o'clock on the night of the 20th of May, "Mary" came down from her sleeping quarters and lay down with Mr. and Mrs. Roff, hugged and kissed them and wept, saying that she must leave them again. The next morning, after bidding goodbye to her friends and neighbors, "Mary" was driven by the Roffs back to the Vennum home. By the time they arrived, Lurancy was back in control of her own body, where she remained, whole and healthy, until her death in the late 1940s.

A Country Revival

This story concerns two women, Susan Singer[202] and Sharon DeMint, who lived about 60 miles apart and never met or heard of one another prior to the occurrences detailed here.

Singer was raised on a tobacco farm near Owingsville, Kentucky. She never attended school, picked up her very basic reading and writing skills from a friend, got married at 15 to Jacob Singer, moved into his parent's home and, 3 years later, gave birth to a son.

In contrast, DeMint's father was a college professor in Berea, Kentucky, and she took advantage of the complementary tuition to get her bachelor's degree in home economics. She was married at 18 and had two sons.

Only 6 months after the birth of her second child, on the 19th of May, DeMint's dead body was discovered lying between the tracks of the local railway.

One of DeMint's uncles had visited her the evening before and reports that she had been crying over mistreatment by her in-laws, but that she had not seemed suicidal. DeMint's father accused her in-laws of murder, but a police investigation failed to find compelling evidence thereof. No doubt this failure was partly due the fact that her husband had her body cremated immediately, so there was no way to confirm eye-witness testimony that the corpse did not appear to be mangled as would be expected if hit by a train.

---

[202] All people and place names in this discussion have been changed for reasons explained later.

A few months prior to DeMint's rather suspicious demise in Berea, Singer began to suffer periods of loss of consciousness that lasted from a few minutes to an entire day. On two occasions she was seemingly possessed briefly by discarnate personalities. One of these claimed to have been a local Owingsville woman who had drowned herself in a well; the other asserted that he had been a man from Muncie, Indiana.

Although the ministrations of a local healer did seem to calm Singer at times, they did not stop her intermittent trances. During one mid-summer episode, she predicted her own imminent demise, and 3 days later she seemed to have achieved that state. Her respiration and pulse were undetectable and her face became drained of blood like that of a dead person. A considerable group of persons surrounding her were convinced that she had died, and some began to cry. There was no doctor available to make a declaration, so we'll never know whether or not Singer was clinically dead. All we know is that, when she revived several minutes later, she recognized neither her surroundings nor her family. She said little or nothing for a day after her revival. Then she announced that her name was Sharon DeMint, and she demanded to be taken to her two sons in Berea. By that time, the actual body of Sharon DeMint had been naught but a pile of ashes for nearly two months.

Singer's in-laws thought that she had become possessed by a wandering discarnate personality who could be exorcised away or might leave spontaneously as had previous ones. But they made no attempt to verify that any such person had ever lived in Berea. Whatever efforts they made to banish the invading personality were clearly failures as the spirit of Sharon DeMint remained in control of Singer's body for 13 years, until she died – or died again.

It took a month before DeMint's father got wind of a story about a young girl claiming to be his deceased daughter. On October 20th, he traveled to Owingsville and tracked down the girl, who immediately recognized him as her father.

These incidents soon caught the attention of the press, and folks sent clippings from two different newspapers to the best-known investigator of such cases, Dr. Ian Stevenson. Within a month, Stevenson and his colleagues began interviewing witnesses. Over the next three years, interviews were conducted, and re-conducted, with 24 family members and another 29 folks who were in a position to furnish background information, especially concerning the communities and the intercourse between them. About 22 years later, a follow-up investigation was done by other researchers that involved interviewing some 15 surviving witnesses and examining a couple of previously unavailable letters that Singer/DeMint had written to DeMint's father. Rarely, if ever, has an apparent case of possession been so thoroughly investigated.

The pertinent facts these researches revealed are:

- All those who were part of, or had knowledge of, Singer's family testified that they had no previous acquaintance with DeMint's family.
- All those who were part of, or had knowledge of, DeMint's family testified that they had no previous acquaintance with Singer's family.
- When DeMint's father heard a rumor that his dead daughter had taken possession of a girl in Owingsville, he did not even know where the town was located.
- The revived Singer/DeMint (hereinafter referred to as "DeMint"—in quote marks) had knowledge of several of DeMint's possessions, including a particular yellow dress, and a watch and the box in which it was kept.
- "DeMint" knew the respective order of birth of DeMint's maternal uncles (although one who was younger actually looked older than one of the older uncles).
- "DeMint" knew which two colleges DeMint had attended.
- "DeMint" knew both of DeMint's pet names (as used by her family) and the names of her two children, two brothers, two of her sisters, two of her maternal uncles, a maternal aunt, and a nephew.
- When DeMint's father showed "DeMint" a photograph taken 18 years earlier, she correctly identified all six persons, including "herself," saying "This is me."

- "DeMint" was equally accurate in identifying the people in several other photographs, none of which had ever been available to the public or the press.
- In one of these photographs, she identified DeMint's sister-in-law, describing her additionally as the person "who hit me with a brick."
- On the other hand, "DeMint" recognized no member of the Singer family and none of the locations in which Sharon Singer had lived.
- Letters written by DeMint and "DeMint" were analyzed by a handwriting and fingerprint expert who concluded that there was "an overwhelming preponderance of probabilities that these letters have been written by the same person."
- Although Singer had virtually no education and could barely write, "DeMint" demonstrated a degree of literacy and knowledge one might expect from a college-educated spirit working through an unfamiliar body.
- Once she awoke, it soon became apparent that "DeMint" was unaccustomed to having to leave the house to relieve herself. Unlike the Singer home, the DeMint home had indoor toilets.

The number of witnesses, the number of researchers, and the number of facts presented, combine to make this a most convincing case for possession. Some might argue that it does not add to the proof for Survival after death because the spirit of DeMint was operating not from the grave but from a living body. The proper rejoinder to that is to ask: Where was the spirit of Sharon DeMint during the two months between the time her body was cremated and the time she awoke in the body of Susan Singer?

As stated in the initial footnote, the names of the people and locations described in this case have been changed. The reason for this is rather unusual; it wasn't done to protect anyone's privacy, but to facilitate comprehension of the facts of the case. The events described took place in India, not Kentucky. The research papers[203] from which this case was derived used, quite naturally, the actual names of the people and villages involved. The strangeness of these terms to my English-educated ear and eye greatly

---

[203] Stevenson, "Case of the Possession Type," pp. 81-101, and Mills.

increased the effort required to sort out who did what to whom and where. On the assumption that others might face the same resistance to absorbing the facts — and thinking that this difficulty might explain why the case has not been more widely recognized — I took the step of "translating" the names into those more easily digested by western readers. I certainly do not mean to denigrate the ancient and honorable languages of the Indian sub-continent. Neither, by the way, do I mean to suggest any ill regard for the people of Kentucky. In fact, my maternal ancestors were from the areas mentioned and I choose Owingsville to honor the memories from visiting there in my youth — tobacco fields, outhouses, and all.

Conversion Phobia VI
Sir William Fletcher Barrett

Barrett lectured on physics at the Royal School of Naval Architecture before becoming professor of physics at the Royal College of Science in Dublin in 1873. He taught there for 37 years, retiring in 1910. Knighted in 1912.

Barrett developed a silicon-iron alloy used in the development of the telephone and transformers, and did pioneering research on entoptic vision, leading to the invention of the entoptiscope and a new optometer. He was a fellow of the Royal Society, Philosophical Society, and Royal Society of Literature as well as a member of the Institute of Electrical Engineers and the Royal Irish Academy.

In His Own Words:

"In a paper I read before the British Association in 1876, [I wrote] that where fraud did not explain these physical phenomena, and the observers were men of unimpeachable integrity ... the witnesses thought they saw what they describe, owing to mal-observation or some hallucination of the senses such as occurs in incipient hypnosis. In fact I began the whole investigation of these phenomena convinced that this was their true explanation"[204]

"It was not until after stretching this hypothesis to illegitimate lengths that I found the actual facts completely shattered my theory"[205]

---

[204] Barrett, *Threshold*, p. 37.
[205] _____, p. 38.

"I am personally convinced that the evidence we have published decidedly demonstrates (1) the existence of a spiritual world, (2) survival after death, and (3) of occasional communication from those who have passed over."[206]

---

[206] Barrett, *Death-Bed Visions*, p 162.

Chapter Twelve
Angels Or Aliens?

> *"Unfortunately, those interested in flying saucers had no interest at all in psychic phenomena, and vice versa. Those who were busy trying to trap a Bigfoot frowned upon all other forms of the weird and supernatural. Yet sea serpents, Abominable Snowpersons, poltergeists, frog rainfalls, and UFOs are all interrelated. You can't possibly investigate one without some knowledge of the others."*
>
> – John Keel[207]

McClellan's Tavern looks just like it's name suggests, subdued lighting on the imported mahogany bar and frosted glass on the doors. They likely served the same beer here as anywhere, but it somehow tasted especially good on this night. Perhaps it was the friendly crowd and the even friendlier bartender that heightened our appreciation, or maybe it was the satisfaction of capping off a most productive day, sitting on a comfortable leather stool beside a good friend. We had just ordered our second round of summer ales when I overheard someone sitting at a small table behind me make a comment about the "weirdoes invading the place next week." At first, I was taken aback and started to wonder if I should be insulted, then I remembered seeing a placard in the lobby announcing an upcoming conference on UFOs. Apparently the old man heard the comment also.

> "The most salient thing about the psi/UFO connection," he said, "is that virtually no one involved wishes to recognize it. There is

---

[207] Quoted from a publication of the New York Fortean Society, 1991, excerpted in *Fate*, September 2007, page 12.

hardly any intercourse between the 'angels-are-real' community and the 'aliens-are-real' community."

"Perhaps this is because each is convinced of their subject's authenticity and dubious of the other's," I speculated. "Each is fearful of being tainted by too close an association — as if their truth would somehow become less true if the other were found fallacious."

"This fear of contagion is not uncommon among groups on the fringe of society. Take nudists, for example. Instead of 'hanging together lest they be hung separately,' many nudists (not all, by any means, but many) are intolerant of any deviation from society's norms, except, of course, lazing around the pool in their birthday suits."

"Don't tell me you're against social nudism."

"Oh no!" he replied. "I always say that if God had wanted people to run around naked, He would have made them that way."

Once I figured out what he meant, I replied: "But, that's a two-edged sword. You could just as well say that if God had wanted people dressed, He would have inspired them to make clothing."

"But of course! God wants to experience both states — that, you may recall, is what this old world is all about: God experiencing being Himself through us. And that is why all preferences should be kindly tolerated." He took a sip from the glass just set before him, wiped a bit of foam from his beard and added, "… except, of course, a preference for <u>in</u>tolerance."

"So you don't think that the investigation of angels and aliens should be kept separate?"

"There certainly is value in focus;" he stated, "nevertheless, I believe much benefit could be derived from investigating where and why the two fields overlap."

Common Factors

"The first thing that comes to my mind, is that both UFO and psychic phenomena seem able to affect electrical and electronic equipment."

> "Yes. This is so common, in fact, that lights, radios, engines, and other devices turning on and off 'by themselves' have become clichés in the literature of both groups. If the witness is at home, such phenomena will likely be interpreted as ghostly; if in an automobile, flying saucers will likely be blamed, especially if strange lights appear in the sky.
>
> "And strange lights," he continued, "are likewise construed to be either angels or aliens depending upon where they manifest. A ball of light swooshing through one's bedroom will generally seem mystical, while one outdoors will probably trigger thoughts of cosmic invaders."

"Unless," I pointed out, "the out-of-doors phenomena occur over a cemetery ... at midnight ... on Halloween."

> "Ah yes," he grinned, "expectations are always important.
>
> "Perhaps the most striking effects shared by psychic and UFO manifestations involve the apparent utilization of other dimensions. Ever since our previous meeting, I have been thinking of these as 'twink links.'"

[Author's note for those who may not have perfect recall of that conversation: We commented that it is possible that our universe rapidly blinks into existence and out of existence and that other universes or dimensions exist within our `off' moments. Such multiplexing could help explain many otherwise inexplicable phenomena. In that earlier conversation, I suggested that 'twinkles' was a better term than 'blinks,' so he now refers to each 'on' period as a 'twink.']

"There are at least two possibilities here," he continued. "The first seems to involve a time displacement in which persons suddenly find themselves in another world. They may experience this alternate reality for only a few brief moments or for what seems to be several hours. However long they stay away, the length of time they experience in that place is not congruent with the time that has passed in this world. It is as if they were re-created in the wrong dimension where they stay until the 'mistake' (if such it was) is discovered and they are then re-inserted into their proper world, but not quite at the proper twink. Reports of such incidences are not common, but they're not all that rare either. Whether or not they are interpreted as the work of spirits or spacemen (or fairies) is pretty much a matter of who is doing the interpreting.

"A second type of event is more of a space displacement than a time warp. Often termed 'teleportation,' this phenomenon involves something or someone disappearing from one place in our physical world and reappearing instantaneously (or almost so) in another physical location. When people are involved, they generally have no sense of time passing, so that one moment they are in one location and the next moment they are somewhere else. Again, the twinkle paradigm would suggest that the teleportee somehow was de-created at one place and re-created at a far different location."

"I'm not sure I can buy this twinkle thing," I said, "even if I did come up with the name."

"Well, whatever the truth may be, I think such metaphors are useful in helping us grasp some very real phenomena. Both time and space displacements have been reported numerous times in both UFO and psi literature."

I took out a pen and started jotting notes on a cocktail napkin. "It strikes me as rather unlikely that the same sort of experiences are actually caused by different factors," I said. "So, either a lot of supposedly psychic occurrences are the result of alien technology or many UFO encounters are really spiritual events."

> "Or there is some common bond between the two that we have yet to fathom." he added.
>
> "Another commonality between spirit entities and space entities is the postulate of other planets and planes being occupied by souls. If we answer the questions: 'Where are these beings coming from and how do they travel from one plane or planet to another?' for aliens, we may well answer for angels also."

"You don't mean that heaven is up-there, somewhere, in outer space?"

> "Probably not. The hypothesis that would explain most observations is that both angels and aliens travel extra-dimensionally rather than that both reside in Alpha Centauri. But further research is definitely needed on the matter.
>
> "Another strange characteristic of both spirits and spaceships is that they are sometimes seen in photographs but not by the naked eye. In almost all cases of ghostly images and many cases of shiny disks appearing on negatives, the photographer was unaware of anything unusual when the shutter clicked. Investigators really should give more consideration to the differences between the sensitivity of camera film and the human retina."

"Most of the so-called 'ghost pictures' that I have seen are just fuzzy blobs and streaks of light," I said.

> "Yes," he agreed, "but have you noticed that the figures in many pictures taken with early cameras back in the 1800s are much more clearly delineated?"

"I always assumed that those were simply fakes."

"You should examine the evidence closely before judging them all so harshly. If you did, I believe you would conclude that many are not so easily dismissed."

"Why would photographs taken with antique cameras register ghostly forms more clearly than modern equipment?"

"I've been considering that very question," he replied, "and I'm wondering if it might have more to do with the lenses than with the film emulsions."

"But, early cameras had much simpler lenses, some little more than pin-holes."

"What if the energy that is imprinting the ghost images onto film is not 'light' as we normally think of it? What if this energy — call it 'ghost light' — was capable of affecting film emulsions but was not as easily refracted as light waves? That would mean that the lenses that focus the light would have little or no effect upon such emissions so the image of the ghost or spirit would register on the film but would be blurred."

"I see what you mean. A pin-hole camera (having no lens at all) would cast regular light and this 'ghost light' equally well onto the film plane. But the more complex the lens, the larger the difference between the focused regular light and the less refracted ghost light. So, earlier cameras and simpler cameras could be better tools for ghost hunters than more advanced ones."

"It does seem an idea worth further investigation," he concluded, "but we probably ought to get back to the subject at hand."

[Comments added later: Upon reading over my notes of this conversation, it occurred to me that there is another major difference that could possibly account for the clearer images in early photographs – the length of the exposures. Today's cameras, both film and digital, take pictures in a small fraction of a second; in the 19th century, taking a picture indoors without a flash could require exposures of 15 minutes or more. Could it be that the qualities of our speculative "ghost light" require extra long exposures despite today's improved sensors? I also wonder if the partial transparency of many ghostly appearances might result from the spirit only being manifested intermittently – say every third twink or so.]

"Okay," I said, referring to the scribbles on my napkin, "so far we have seven areas of overlap between survival research and UFO investigations: electronic effects, mysterious lights, temporal displacements, spatial displacements, place of origin, means of travel, and photographic effects. Any others?"

> "Two that I can think of right now," he responded. "The first is the fact that animals often react strangely in the presence of both psi manifestations and UFO visitations. Brave dogs are often known to cower and hide; cats hiss at the air, cattle panic, and so on. Frequently, these occurrences are a human's first hint of an unusual presence.
>
> "The other similarity that comes to mind is that both spirits and spacemen claim to be the source of channeled messages to us earthlings. The number of mediums who claim psychic contact with physical beings from other star systems is much smaller than those who seem to speak for discarnate spirits, but there have been a few."

"I think that Uri Geller once made such a claim."

> "Yes, he asserted that aliens from a far distant planet called 'Hoova' were the source of his psychokinetic powers. Of course, this sort of talk didn't make him any points with parapsychologists. The überskeptics loved it, naturally, as they could easily avoid dealing with Geller's phenomenal abilities by throwing up a screen of derision centered on the 'little-green-men.'
>
> "But Geller is not the only psychic to connect with beings claiming to be aliens rather than angels. Ken Carey and Lenora Huett are two that come immediately to mind."

Reciprocal Recognition

"Speaking of communications, are there any channeled teachings that touch on the subject of UFOs?"

> "I'm hardly familiar with all the information that has ever come from the mouths of mediums, but I do recall that Roberts had something to say on the subject, and Walsch also."

[Note: I looked it up later and found his memory accurate. The Seth entity, channeled by Jane Roberts, made several statements about the reality of non-Terran civilizations and alien craft, including: "I am quite sure — I know for a fact — that beings from other planes have appeared among you, sometimes on purpose and sometimes completely by accident."[208] The origin of these beings, he claims, may be physical or nonphysical.[209] For those readers concerned about invasions, it may be reassuring that Seth does not believe we "will have any saucer landings for quite a while" {because} "These vehicles cannot stay on your plane for any length of time at all."[210]

As for Neale Donald Walsch, a fair portion of Book 3 of *Conversations with God* is devoted to the characteristics of various cultures throughout the galaxy. Walsch's 'god' claims that there are thousands of civilizations more advanced — and a much smaller number less advanced — than ours.[211] Furthermore, he states that such highly evolved beings refrain from directly assisting mankind because humans tend to worship them as gods.[212] If so, then they must have visited earth in the past.]

"We haven't covered past-life regressions," I pointed out. "Do subjects under hypnosis ever speak of living lives as aliens?"

---

[208] Roberts, *Unknown*, vol. 2, p. 754.
[209] Roberts, *Seth Speaks*, p. 473.
[210] Roberts, *Unknown*, vol.2, p.755.
[211] Walsch, *Conversations Book 3*, p. 271.
[212] _____, p. 323.

"It's pretty rare, but it does happen enough to rate mentioning. In his life-between-lives regressions Dr. Michael Newton has encountered a handful of people who recall visiting Earth from other star systems.[213] But all such contact was in the far past. Apparently souls do not jump back and forth between species."

"You mean 'once a human, always a human'?" I asked.

"Oh no. Just that all of one's lives as a human seem to be grouped together, rather than mixed in with alien existences."

I paused a moment to consume a slice of the bruschetta sitting before us. I was glad we had ordered something that was good at room temperature, as it was difficult to find a moment to eat during our conversations. Washing it down with a swallow of beer, I asked him: "Do you think it's possible that aliens are the sole cause? That all phenomena we now think of as psychic are really a result of advanced technology from other galaxies?"

"Do you recall the ten reasons that reincarnation is not an illusion caused by discarnate spirits?"

I nodded yes.

"Well, most of those reasons make equally strong arguments against the 'illusion-caused-by-aliens' idea. For instance, to accept such a hypothesis would mean believing that each of us has one or more aliens watching over our shoulders, ready at all times to relate consistent stories of past lives, just in case we decide to be hypnotically regressed."

"That is rather inconceivable," I agreed.

---

[213] Newton, "Early Visitations," pp. 26-27.

"And just as reincarnation is supported by those who speak from the afterlife, so the idea of Survival is supported by the testimony of aliens. If you look up that book on Uri Geller that we mentioned earlier, I believe you'll find a good example of this."

[Note: In this book, the esteemed scientist Andrija Puharich, who was investigating Uri Geller, tells of several communications from entities claiming to be from a far-distant planet. They spoke via a tape recorder and the tapes either were erased afterwards or simply vanished in front of Puharich's eyes. {These same entities claimed that they were the power behind Geller's ability to make objects disappear.} In response to the question "What is the nature of the soul?" they stated: "It inhabits different worlds at different times in its existence. When the physical body dies, it goes with all of its being to its own world. There it carries on with the next phase of its existence. It may go on to other spaces, or it may even return to an earth physical body for another round of existence — what humans call reincarnation may occur."[214]]

Well then," I responded, "what about the other way round? Could UFO's actually be spirits?"

"As in God is my starship's co-pilot?" he asked while motioning for our check.

"Not exactly. If reports from the other side are true, then many souls find themselves in a place where thoughts easily become things. You know, like in that movie where Robin Williams is trying to rescue his wife from her self-imposed hell."

"What Dreams May Come."

---

[214] Puharich, p. 211.

"Yeah. So what if someone with a love of science fiction movies dies on this plane and awakens on one like that and decides to create a reality of silvery flying disks. And then, suppose that one of these inter-dimensional bleed-throughs occurs and his creation is seen, for a moment or so, by witnesses in our physical reality. That would explain a lot, wouldn't it?"

"Actually, that could explain a phenomenon that has puzzled UFO researchers – and delighted their critics – for a long time: Strange craft seen in the skies often seem to be one step ahead of current technology. Before hot air balloons were first launched, there were reports of mysterious balloon-shaped objects hovering near the earth. Before airplanes officially flew, bi-planes were witnessed landing on the prairies. And triangular craft were seen in several locations years before stealth bombers were built.

"Perhaps, in some cases at least, these phantoms were the heavenly manifestations of the dreams of those inventors who passed on before their plans were physically constructed. Yep, you could be on to something there."

Rational Witnesses

For awhile, he seemed to be mulling over this idea, but then he took a new tack. "Your agile thinking reminds me of another similarity between reports of psychic phenomena and aerial anomalies, and that is the type of person making the reports. Those who testify to having these strange experiences are generally above average in intelligence, education, and income.[215] And they have a minimal interest in organized religion."

"That sure is contrary to what the überskeptics would have the public believe," I commented.

---

[215] Steiger, pp. 52-56.

"Yes, and that false image — a gaggle of ignorant fanatics claiming visitations by Martians or visions of Mary — is too often the one propagated by the media in search of a titillating tale. The very same media," he added, "that blithely ignore the constant stream of research reports and other valid evidence in support of both Survival and UFOs."

With that, we tipped our bartender and made our way to the elevator. We found a fellow conferee awaiting its arrival, so we felt comfortable continuing our discussion as we boarded.

"It occurs to me that there is one final characteristic shared by angels and aliens."

"And that would be?"

"That would be that they have both been visiting Earth since ancient times."

"Ahh," I said, "you must be referring to the clay tablets that tell of beings from space arriving in Sumer some 6,000 years ago."

"Those are the oldest writings we know of — at least so far — and they tell a remarkable tale of strange beings, spaceships, and genetic engineering. But they're not the only examples. The Judeo-Christian Bible contains several reports of seemingly physical beings coming down from the skies and interacting with humans. And such stories can be found in the folklore of almost every culture around the world."

"I've always thought of such stories as merely myths."

"Easy enough to so dismiss one or two," he replied as we stepped out of the elevator, "but when you learn how widespread and similar they are, you realize that there must be some truth behind the tales."

"So," I attempted to summarize, "the spirits claim that ETs are real, and the aliens believe in souls, yet the earthly manifestations of both are almost the same. That's more than a bit puzzling."

> "The same in many ways and yet different in some. Tell me," he asked, stopping my stroll with a hand on my arm, "what do you hear?"

I listened for a moment. Only one other person was walking down the corridor ahead of us. Then the guy turned and entered a room. "Just that fellow's footsteps and the door closing," I answered.

> "Well, according to the reports I've read, if that figure was not a human, then he was likely a spirit, not a space brother. The sound of footsteps is virtually always a ghostly phenomenon."

Listening to our own footfalls as we resumed walking, I thought about various alien-sighting, encounter, and abduction reports I had heard or read. UFOs are almost always reported as moving soundlessly, even when performing high speed aerobatics right over the observers' heads. Greys and other beings seem to glide silently over the ground and never speak aloud. I realized that sound of any sort was uncannily rare in all UFO reports.

Then, another thought occurred to me. "But ghosts and spirits are likely two different phenomena. I know that poltergeists are noisy but aren't most spirits just as quiet as aliens?"

> "Tell that to the Fox family," he said.

As discussed at the beginning of this book, the Fox family gained fame in 1848 when a spirit began communicating with them via loud rapping sounds.

"You're right. I never heard of aliens rapping ... although," I grinned at him, "some rappers do seem pretty alien to me."

> He rolled his eyes at that, but he couldn't totally suppress a smile. We had reached his room and he swiped his keycard in the

lock. "When you're ready for breakfast, come and *rap* on my door," he said, his grin getting wider.

At a loss for a witty repartee, I just grinned back and headed on down to my room.

Note: An excellent source of information on UFOs is the website: http://www.paradigmresearchgroup.org/
A few of the better books on the subject are: *Above Top Secret* by Timothy Good; *Clear Intent* by Lawrence Fawcett; and *Confrontations* by Jacques Vallee.

Conversion Phobia – VII
Charles Richet

A physiologist, chemist, bacteriologist, pathologist, psychologist, and aviation pioneer, Richet received his doctorate in medicine in 1869 and in science in 1878. He served as professor of physiology at the medical school of the University of Paris for 38 years.

Richet was awarded the Nobel Prize for his research on anaphylaxis, he contributed much to research on the nervous system, anesthesia, serum therapy, and neuro-muscular stimuli. He served as editor of the *Revue Scientifique* for 24 years and contributed to many other scientific publications.

In His Own Words:

"The idolatry of current ideas was so dominant at that time that no pains were taken either to verify or to refute Crookes' statements. Men were content to ridicule them, and I avow with shame that I was among the willfully blind. Instead of admiring the heroism of a recognized man of science who dared then in 1872 to say that there really are phantoms that can be photographed and whose heartbeats can be heard, I laughed."[216]

"To ask a physiologist, a physicist, or a chemist to admit that a form that has a circulation of blood, warmth, and muscles, that exhales carbonic acid, has weight, speaks, and thinks, can issue from a human body is to ask of him an intellectual effort that is really painful.

"Yes, it is absurd, but no matter – it is true."[217]

---

[216] Richet, p. 31.
[217] _____, p. 544.

Chapter Thirteen
— Cases from the Survival Top-40 —
Memories of Home

Near-death experiences may suggest an afterlife, but other lines of evidence more directly prove false the arguments against survival. These lines include the evidence for reincarnation.

– Chris Carter[218]

Case 61 — Family Lost & Found

'Tis an oft-told tale, both sad and inspiring: a woman driven by guilt and worry strives to locate the family she was forced to abandon years before. There's a most uncommon twist to the tale Jenny Cockell tells, however, for when she finally finds her lost children, they are all several decades older than their mother.[219]

From a very young age, Jenny Cockell (pronounced ki-KELL) was plagued by unexplained dreams and visions in which she was a woman named Mary. She seemed to be reliving Mary's life or, more often, re-dying Mary's death. Night after night, Jenny's dreams were filled with the panic of a 30-something woman lying in a hospital bed, racked with pain yet suffering even more from the thought of dying and forsaking her children. During the day, Cockell's visions were of more pleasant times with the woman's numerous children – she could envision at least seven of them, but she felt that there may have been more.

In addition to Mary's children and her final hours, the young Cockell had visions (which seemed like memories to her) of a home and village that, although she had never traveled outside England, she somehow

---
[218] Carter.
[219] Cockell.

knew were located in Ireland. As a child, she often drew maps of this village and described her home as a two-room cottage, sitting first on the left of a country lane and turned sideways to it. She envisioned where the cottage's windows were and what pictures hung on the interior walls. She felt that Mary had two older brothers who had gone away from the area. Altogether, Jenny Cockell had memories involving scores of minutia about a place far away and a life that ended some 21 years before she was born.

At school, Cockell studied a map of Ireland and felt drawn to the town of Malahide about 10 miles north of Dublin. She longed to travel there and confirm her visions, but it was not until she was 33 years of age and a married mother with two children of her own that she managed to get the money, the time, and the confidence to make the trip. Once she discovered that her inner-knowledge of the town did actually match quite well with current reality, Cockell was emboldened to begin a determined quest to locate and contact Mary's children.

She scoured libraries, spoke with priests, wrote letters to historical societies and orphanages, placed newspaper ads, underwent hypnosis, and even made calls to names found in Ireland's phone books. Her search went into high gear when she located a man who had lived in Malahide as a youth. He had gone to school, he said, with some children whose mother's name was Mary and who had lived with a large number of siblings in a two-room cottage that sat sideways, first on the left from the start of Swords lane. The family's last name, he said, was Sutton. This surname, which Cockell had never been able to recall, was the key that enabled her to locate, contact, meet, and ultimately befriend five of Mary's children.

The story of Cockell's search and the discovery of innumerable bits of confirming evidence is well told in her book. Also, she has appeared, either alone or with Mary's 60- and 70-something children, on several televised programs including, in the U.S., *20/20 with Barbara Walters*, *Donahue*, *Sightings* and *The Unexplained*.[220]

As far as the evidence is concerned, the maps Cockell drew as a child are virtually the same as those anyone might hand-draw of the same roads today. Likewise, the largest church in the town could easily be picked out by anyone who had seen her sketches. Cockell's descriptions of her childhood dreams and drawings have been publicly backed up by testimony from her mother.[221] And then, we have the downright amazing fact that several siblings have testified that Jenny Cockell demonstrated to them a knowledge of their early home life so intimate and detailed that they are convinced that she incarnates the spirit of their long-dead mother. This despite their lifetime immersion in a religious doctrine that denies any such possibility.

Today, a search on the Net for "Jenny Cockell" will get many thousands of hits, including a few informative videos. Also, of course, there are skeptical commentaries claiming to explain or expose the case, but I have found none of these to be either factual or objective. Just to take one example, an article in the *Skeptical Inquirer* says, in part:

> "She turned then to actual research, publishing an ad in a Mensa magazine, sending out numerous form letters, acquiring maps, and so on. Eventually she turned up a village (Malahide), a road (Swords Road), and finally a woman named Mary Sutton who roughly fit the target. ... Unfortunately, Cockell's intriguing and no doubt sincere saga does not withstand critical analysis. First, consider the overwhelming lack of factual information provided by the dreams and hypnosis. Unknown were Mary's surname, either maiden or married,

---

[220] The television program segments mentioned first aired on ABC in 1994, on CBS and NBC in 1995, and on A&E in 1998 respectively. Cockell's story was also the inspiration for a made-for-TV movie titled *Yesterday's Children*, which was first broadcast in October 2000.

[221] A&E *Sightings* on reincarnation, available on DVD from A&E.com.

or the names of her husband or children. Similarly, the village's name and even its location were a mystery."[222]

Apparently, this critic had not taken the trouble to actually read the book he is denigrating, for it clearly states that Cockell, while still a young girl, had selected the town of Malahide using a map of Ireland in her school atlas. A map that was far too small of scale to allow any matching with the sketches she had made. So, the village was not "turned up" as part of her adult research and neither its name nor its location "were a mystery." Furthermore, while it is true that every name could not be recalled, this critic manages to avoid mentioning the many "unknowable" details that Cockell *did* know about the children and the events in the family's life. The eldest boy was in his seventies when he stated on record that she knew things about his childhood that even his brothers and sisters did not know.

As for possible alternative explanations, clairvoyance and cosmic databases clearly have no parts to play. Although all of the confirmed information did exist in one mind or another, the idea of super-duper mental telepathy is negated: first, because there was no earthly link between Cockell and any of those minds, and second, because the children had been separated at their mother's death and had little or no contact since – the youngest did not even know she had siblings.

The Rebirth of Bridey Murphy

The phrase "a household name" has rarely been more truly applied than it was to the name Bridey Murphy during the late 1950s and early '60s. The impact of Morey Bernstein's book, *The Search for Bridey Murphy*,[223] was felt in virtually every city, town, and hamlet in the Western world because it suggested that the theretofore alien concept of reincarnation was a demonstrable fact. In the media frenzy that followed the book's release – it was even made into a movie – numerous falsehoods were circulated as

---

[222] "A Case of Reincarnation — Reexamined," by Joe Nickell, *Skeptical Inquirer*, Vol. 8.1, March 1998.
[223] Bernstein.

debunkers and überskeptics attempted to undermine the evidence. These days, the idea of reincarnation is not so novel and the brouhaha over Bernstein's book seems almost a bit of quaint Americana; nevertheless, the evidence remains strong and the tale fascinating.

Only a brief summary of that tale can be told here. For the full story, read the 1965 version of Bernstein's engrossing book. This is referred to as "the counter-attack version" as it includes full rebuttals to all the misinformation spread by overzealous critics. Also, Bernstein had LP records made from the session tapes and some may still be available via the Internet.

Before looking into who was Bridey Murphy, it is important to know who was Morey Bernstein. Some detractors like to picture the man as a dabbler in occult arts and/or an opportunistic seeker of fortune and fame. In fact, Bernstein was a well-to-do and highly respected businessman in both New York and Colorado, where he served on the board of directors of four leading firms. Bernstein was a pragmatic man who had once walked out on a stage demonstration of hypnotism because he wanted to make certain that his friends knew that "this silly business" was beneath his intelligence. Not until years later, when he witnessed a demonstration in a friend's home, did he decide that hypnotism was a subject worth pursuing. Over a period of 10 years, he became highly skilled at his new avocation. Often the local medical community would request his services to hypnotize a patient and he always complied without accepting any compensation. Furthermore, he did not seek publicity. When a friend of his suggested that a newspaper reporter write an article about his experiences, he was quite resistant to the idea.

Why Bernstein, a materialistic scoffer who laughed at hypnotism and was repulsed by the concept of reincarnation, came to champion both, is a story well told in his book. Suffice it to say that on his very first attempt to regress someone back beyond her infancy, his patient, Virginia Tighe, recalled several previous lives — one of which was as an Irish girl named Bridget Kathleen Murphy who referred to herself as "Bridey." In that session, and five more ensuing, she provided a richly detailed description of her life during the first half of the 19th century. Hundreds of facts were given that were most unlikely to be known by Tighe.[224] More than a few of these were thought wrong by scholars but were proved correct through diligent research.

Particularly striking examples of "impossible-to-know" facts are Bridey's statements that, while living in Belfast, she brought "foodstuffs" at "John Carrigan's" and at "Farr's." No one living in Belfast, or anywhere else, could confirm that such establishments ever existed, until a local librarian, after weeks of searching, found a directory for 1865 that listed both as greengrocers doing business in the same sector of the city. The two grocer's names were given during different sessions and, by themselves, constitute powerful evidence that Bridey's story is exactly what it claims to be.

Another convincing piece is Bridey's statement that, in her youth in Cork, she lived "outside the village" in a place called "The Meadows" where she had no neighbors. Again, the "Meadows" was unheard of at the time of the regressions, but researchers later found an 1801 map of the Cork area that shows a large pastoral area called "Mardike Meadows" just to the west of the city. This is the only "meadows" on the map. No more than eight buildings are shown, spread throughout 82 acres of land. Thus the area perfectly fits Bridey's description in location, population, and name.

No one, living or dead, could reasonably be expected to recite hundreds of details about their life and never make a mistake, but, so far, none of Bridey's statements have been proved false and no contradictions discovered. Time and again, the "experts" have claimed that Bridey was wrong about one arcane point or another, only to see her vindicated by further research. Her use of the term "slip" to mean a child's frock, or

---

[224] In an attempt to protect her privacy, Bernstein calls his subject "Ruth Simmons," but her actual name was soon made public. Virginia Tighe had to be cajoled to participate in the sessions as neither she nor her husband had any interest in pursuing past lives, and they both shunned the public eye.

"linen" instead of handkerchief, are just two of many such instances. According to William J. Barker, a journalist who spent weeks in Ireland investigating various statements: "Bridey was dead right on at least two dozen facts 'Ruth' (Virginia Tighe) could not have acquired in [America], even if she had set out deliberately to study up on Irish obscurities."

As for the possibility of there being other information sources in Tighe's life, despite the fanciful inventions of those desperate to undermine her story, the fact is that no source other than a past-life memory is either feasible or credible.[225]

Case 60 — The Strangers Were Lovers

As far as I can tell, this case is unique in reincarnation literature. Most cases involve one hypnotherapist and one subject who recalls one or more past lives. Sometimes there is solid evidence to precisely confirm the recalled events; often the evidence is merely supportive or suggestive. The evidential basis for a very few cases comes from the agreement of two or more subjects recalling participation in the same past-life event while being separately regressed by the same hypnotherapist. The case discussed here goes a step beyond the others in that it involves two different subjects recalling the same lives while being regressed by two different therapists in sessions that were both many miles and several years apart.

Entirely unknown to one another, a woman in Georgia in 1984 and a man in Florida in 1989 recalled associated lifetimes in Ohio in the early 1900s. During a unique joint session, their love affair and tragic deaths were recounted by both, to the amazement of several witnesses. There could be many similar occurrences, but most will never be known due to the privacy typically observed by therapists and patients. The exceptional nature of this case only came to light because Jack Turnock happened to be watching a rerun of *Unsolved Mysteries*[226] in which a woman named

---

[225] Allen, *Bridey's Honor*, pp. 140-143.
[226] *Unsolved Mysteries*, season 2, episode 21, first airing on 14 February 1990.

Georgia Rudolph was recalling a past life. Her name in that life, she remembered was Sandra Jean Jenkins and she had a boyfriend named Tommy Hicks. As he watched the show, Turnock says, he began to have strange feelings. When the name Hicks was mentioned, he reports, "Even though I knew what she was going to say, it still felt like I was punched in the solar plexus."[227]

Turnock, now a university professor, had undergone hypnotic regression at his wife's request because she was considering giving a session to her mother as a birthday present. During his session — with Dr. Bruce Crystal in Jacksonville, Florida — Turnock found himself re-living scenes from the life of a boy in Ohio around the turn of the last century, a boy named Tom Hicks.

Since early childhood, Georgia Rudolph had been haunted by unexplained memories and recurring dreams in which she seemed to be a young girl – some of the times the girl was about 8 years of age, other times about 18 – living an upper-middle-class life around the turn of the century. She could picture the girl vividly and used to spend hours with her crayons trying to capture her face. The memories were often so realistic that she could feel the icy cold air as she seemed to ride in an open carriage, could smell the horses and the leather of their harnesses, could hear their hoofs striking the pavement.

As she knew that she had been adopted at the age of 5, Rudolph at first assumed that these images must be associated with her earliest childhood. When she queried her birth relatives, however, they could recall no correspondent experiences.

At the age of 33, determined to uncover the cause of her dreams and memories that had troubled her so long, Rudolph consulted Dr. Douglas Smith, a clinical psychologist who was the deputy director of a mental

---

[227] Details of Turnock's involvement are taken largely from a written statement he submitted to the author on 17 February 2010. Miscellaneous facts were gleaned from telephone interviews with Rudolph and with Turnock.

health center in Macon, Georgia. At the time, Rudolph did not believe in reincarnation. In fact, she says that the idea frightened her because it "went against everything that I have ever been taught as far as religion goes." Smith wasn't expecting a past-life recall either. He states that, when he began to treat Rudolph, "reincarnation was probably the last thing in my mind about what had happened to her."

During the initial session, after Smith had regressed her to the approximate age of 2, she suddenly stopped responding. When he persisted in calling her name, she said "I don't know who you're talking too." So Smith said, "Well, if you aren't Georgia, who are you?" And she responded, "My name is Sandra Jean Jenkins."

Throughout this and subsequent sessions, "Jenkins" provided an abundance of information about her life as a girl who was born in 1895 and raised in or near a small city beside a river. Although she never specifically identified the town, the name "Marietta" kept surfacing and she deduced that Marietta, Ohio was the location of the recalled events. When the sessions were concluded, Dr. Smith testified: "Georgia seems to me a very down-to-earth person ... I think that she's a very stable individual ... She is not faking or pretending." As further testament to her character, the producers of the television segment stated, "What's definite about Georgia's story is that, meeting her and spending the time we spent with her while we were doing this story, you know she wasn't making this up."[228]

Rudolph's memories of special significance include:

- Many scenes on a stern-wheel riverboat, and a feeling that it belonged to her family.
- Her fiancé named Tommy Hicks by whom she was pregnant.
- Tommy's parents were named Tom and Jennie Hicks.

---

[228] Quoted from commentaries by John Cosgrove and Raymond Bridgers on the *Unsolved Mysteries: Psychics* compilation DVD.

- Walking from a church through a graveyard to a specific tombstone. She could not read the name on the stone, but she saw that it was near the statue of an angel with one arm upraised.
- A large white house that felt like home.
- The death of Hicks just prior to their wedding when his boat hit a sandbar in a storm and he was swept from the deck.
- Her grief at his death and her shame over her pregnancy leading her to suicide by drowning.

In 1985, Rudolph traveled the 640 miles to Marietta, Ohio. While touring Marietta with Ted Bauer (a lifetime resident who was the retired City Editor of the local newspaper) Rudolph demonstrated an intimate familiarity with the town. Whatever Bauer couldn't confirm from personal knowledge he researched and he uncovered no inaccuracies in Rudolph's descriptions. The television production featured a scene in which Rudolph stopped in front of an insurance office and described an ice-cream parlor that used to be in that location. Bauer stated, "She described the interior [as it was when Jenkins lived] almost perfectly. I checked this with the son of the man who had run it for years." That interior had been re-done in 1937.

Driving 5 miles north to Newport, Ohio, Rudolph found a house that felt very much like the one in her dreams. Around the turn of the century, the house had been owned by a family named Greene. These same Greenes owned a fleet of stern-wheelers.[229] Then she found the church that she had so often seen while asleep. When she walked the path – so familiar from her dreams – twixt the church and the grave, Rudolph found that the surname on the tombstone was Greene. And, yes, clearly visible nearby was the statue of an angel with one arm pointing heavenward.

---

[229] A photograph of the sternwheeler from which Tommy Hicks is thought to have fallen is viewable in the case file at www.SurvivalTop40.com.

Altogether, a most evidential case that argues strongly for the reality of reincarnation, even without considering the factor that makes it so special.

The apparent link between his own past-life recollections and those of Georgia Rudolph stunned and perplexed Turnock. "I didn't know what to do with the information," he says, so he "decided to deal with it by not dealing with it." And so, six months passed until one day he happened to turn on his television only to be confronted by yet another re-run of the disturbing *Unsolved Mysteries* segment. Once again, Turnock was both fascinated and agitated by the show. This time, his wife decided to do something about this disruption to her household, so she wrote a letter to Dr. Smith describing the situation. Smith contacted the show's producers who ultimately decided that Turnock was for real and that a follow-up show should be made in which Rudolph and Turnock would be videotaped during a joint hypnosis session.

The filming (or rather, the attempted filming) was done in Smith's office in Macon, Georgia. Turnock was not allowed to meet Rudolph until after he was regressed. During his regression, Turnock (as Hicks) recalled many details about his life and death on a riverboat named the N.B. Forrest. Afterwards, Rudolph asked him where Hicks had proposed to Jenkins and where they were when she had gotten pregnant. Turnock replied that the proposal took place on a bench by the river. As for the conception: "You walk from Gordon Green's house away from town on the road by the river. When you get to a corn field turn right. There's a small bluff overlooking the river where they used to go. That day they had a picnic in the corner of the field and that's where they made love and Sandra Jean got pregnant." According to Turnock, "Rudolf's jaw nearly hit the floor. What I described was exactly what she had seen in her hypnosis sessions."

In the afternoon, Dr. Smith hypnotized both Rudolph and Turnock together. Turnock describes the experience as being the weirdest part of all. "We both went under fairly easily and we began talking to each other as Tom and Sandra Jean. It was the most surreal experience of my life. It was as if another person had taken over my body and I was watching it happen. Tom told Sandra Jean how he was sorry he left her that way. She forgave him. They/we held hands, reiterated our love and said goodbye. It was incredibly emotional. I was so drained I couldn't move for half an hour. Jim Lindsey, the *Unsolved Mysteries* director was literally dancing around, saying it was the best sequence they ever filmed."

Trouble was, they did not actually film the session. Although the equipment was turned on, the cables were connected, and the scene was showing on the monitor, the videotape recorded nothing but static. How and why this bewildering failure occurred is perhaps the biggest unsolved mystery of all.

No written record of a Sandra Jean Jenkins has been found in Marietta or Newport, Ohio, but there is a record of a Tom and Jennie Hicks (who could well have been Tommy's parents) buying a farm in Newport in 1906. Rudolph thinks that no records were kept of Jenkins because the girl committed suicide. Perhaps that is correct, or perhaps the records were accidently destroyed, or perhaps they will be uncovered yet. It is also conceivable that the name "Sandra Jean Jenkins" is some sort of spiritual pseudonym intended to protect the reputation of the Greene family. Whatever the case, the evidentiality of the case must rest on something other than public records.

Those skeptics who rely on some imagined form of super-ESP to explain what they cannot otherwise understand, should consider the lack of links between the house, the boats, and the grave. Since Rudolph had not been able to discern the Greene name in her dreams, neither telepathy nor clairvoyance could have associated the grave site with the house – or the river boats with either. Her inability to read the stone, therefore, strengthens the case considerably.

The most convincing aspect of Rudolph's recall is her intimate knowledge of Marietta, Ohio. On first considering the evidence, Rudolph's description of the pre-renovation interior of the ice-cream parlor seems the highlight of the tour. One cannot rule out, however, that she was simply lucky that her idea of a turn-of-the-century parlor (perhaps gleaned from an old movie) just happened to match reality. Of course, that doesn't explain how she knew that there ever *was* an ice-cream parlor at that location, or how she knew so many other minor details about an unsung little city she had never visited. Even her tour guide, a tough old reporter whom the TV producers called "as skeptical a person as you will ever see,"[230] admitted that he was baffled because she knew more about the place than most lifelong residents.

As for the joint regression session, the unrecorded tape will, no doubt, provide fodder for the skeptics who will view the missing video as suspicious; perhaps even attempting to dismiss the entire case because one part of it was not recorded. I suspect, however, that if the videotape had recorded perfectly, these same skeptics would simply claim (or, at least, imply) that the whole session had been faked for television. The important validation is the number of participants and crew who either have corroborated or have never contradicted the facts presented here.

The evidence from Rudolph's regressions is impressive in its own right; the agreement between Rudolph and Turnock on the details of the marriage proposal and the love-making between Jenkins and Hicks makes this case truly exceptional and exceptionally convincing.

---

[230] Quoted from commentaries by John Cosgrove and Raymond Bridgers on the *Unsolved Mysteries: Psychics* compilation DVD.

Chapter Fourteen
An "Eary" Dinner

Souls don't return promiscuously to any body, in any family. There is a sequence in their lives that necessitates their coming to one particular environment. It is part of the natural law, and works automatically.

— Kelway-Bamber[231]

We were tucked in a corner of the hotel dining room under a picture of President Lincoln and his son that hung above the mantle of a large fireplace. Our two dinner companions had been discussing the old man's presentation on various reincarnation cases when Jenny Cockell's search for her elderly children was mentioned. I took this opportunity to bring up a related subject.

"Although I accept the Cockell case as providing convincing evidence for Survival and reincarnation, there is one aspect of it that bothers me."

"What's so special about that case?"

"Not really special. In fact, it's something that pops up a lot in reincarnation cases — it's the claim that the person today physically resembles the person they recall being in a past life. On the Donahue show, Mary's 75-year-old son made a big deal of how Jenny has the same eyes as his mother has in an old photograph. I just don't get it. People look like their parents or their grand-parents, or maybe the milk man or the …"

"You're really showing your age there; it's been many decades since anyone delivered milk to my stoop."

---

[231] Kelway-Bamber, p. 31.

"Actually, dairy deliveries have been making a bit of a comeback lately. But whether the milkman, the postman, the pool boy, or whomever, it's DNA that determines how we look. Are we to believe that genetics can be overruled by the spirits of lives past?"

> "I sympathize with your skepticism," he said, as a waitress distributed menus around our table, "and I cannot endorse such a connection, but there is a rather fascinating story that argues for it."

"We're all ears," I said, glancing around the table for confirmation.

> "How apropos," he grinned, "for in my punnier moments I think of this as an 'ear-ry' tale.[232]
>
> "In the early part of the 20th Century, in a small village in France, a man and his wife enjoyed passing many evenings by experimenting with a talking board. The wife — let's call her 'Marie' — sat at the table in a sort of trance, her fingers lightly touching the planchette as it moved, seemingly of its own volition from letter to letter. Meanwhile her husband — 'Pierre' — would ask questions and take note of the answers as they were spelled out."

"A most typical arrangement," I observed, peeking at the menu and hoping that this tale would not much delay the satisfaction of my growing hunger.

> "Yes; women are generally more adept at tuning in to the spirit plane. But the spirit communication that makes this case atypical occurred one evening in 1924 when a name was spelled out that the husband did not recognize. After some consideration, the wife recalled that her father had once had a servant by that name, a servant whose right ear stuck out in a most conspicuous way. During an ensuing session, the spirit returned and acknowledged that he had

---

[232] This case was first published in *La Revue Métapsychique* in 1948 by Dr. Maurice Delarrey. For further information in English, see Ian Stevenson's book *European Cases of the Reincarnation Type*, pages 42-44.

served as a servant to that family and he announced that he was preparing to return to the same.

"Pierre was intrigued by this revelation and quizzed the spirit further. It seems that the spirit had selected a relative of theirs who lived in a distant town and already had two daughters. This time, the spirit said, they would have a son and he provided the exact date of the birth to come – some four months in the future.

"'All very well,' said Pierre, who was unaware that his relative was pregnant, 'but how shall we know that the boy is you? After all, you might just be good at predicting the future.'"

"Don't tell me," I interjected. "Let me guess … by his ear!"

"Ahh, such an intelligent lad you are," he observed in a tone that suggested a matronly pat on the head. "Yes, the spirit replied that Marie would easily recognize the babe by its ear."

"And, would my exceptional intellect be accurate in predicting that ensuing events proved the spirit correct?"

"It would indeed. On the morning specified, a son was born to the named family. But it was not until three months later that Pierre and Marie were invited to a family reunion at the new infant's household. Upon arrival, the couple were at once escorted into the nursery by the new mother who warned them that the child was in an unusual mood, breaking out into tears every time she brought someone new to the side of the crib.

"Well, as you have likely guessed, when Marie approached, the babe began to smile and stretched out his hands toward her. The mother actually exclaimed 'Look at that! One might have thought he knew you.'"

With that, the old man opened his menu and stared down at it.

I played along, took a drink of my iced tea, waited several seconds, and then coughed and said, "Uh … the ear?"

> "Oh yes, the ear." He peered over the menu for a moment, eyes twinkling, and then continued. "Well, there was a bandage over the infant's right ear. When Pierre asked about it — trying to sound as if he knew nothing — the mother replied that it wasn't anything to be concerned about; that the fetus must have developed in a 'bad position' in her womb, causing his ear to stick out from his head. The doctor had assured her that the ear would look perfectly normal in a few months.
>
> "Whether or not it did, was not revealed by the researcher who reported the case."

"Fascinating," I remarked. "That suggests the possibility that birthmarks corresponding to wounds and injuries are imprinted on the babe intentionally rather than being a natural consequence of the re-birth process."

> "Now that is a wide-open field for research. As you know, Stevenson published a two-volume set on the links between biology and reincarnation, although I don't recall the good doctor consulting any spirits as to what the intent is behind these appearances."

"Well," I said, setting down my menu as I saw the waitress approaching with pad in hand, "Stevenson faced derision enough from mainstream science for even bothering to investigate such occurrences. It's too bad, really, that researchers don't try more often to hypnotically regress people who have spontaneous recall of a past life to see if their waking memories are matched by their entranced ones.

"I believe I'll have the Chicken Chesapeake …"

Conversion Phobia VIII
Julian Ochorowicz

Professor of psychology and philosophy at the University of Warsaw, Ochorowicz was the leader of the Positivist movement in Poland, and one of the founders of the Polish Psychological Institute.

He received his doctorate from Leipzig University and became assistant professor at Lwów University in 1881, subsequently spent several years in Paris, where he was co-director of the Institut General Psychologique.

In His Own Words:

"I found I had done a great wrong to men who had proclaimed new truths at the risk of their positions. When I remember that I branded as a fool that fearless investigator, Crookes, the inventor of the radiometer, because he had the courage to assert the reality of psychic phenomena and to subject them to scientific tests, and when I also recollect that I used to read his articles thereon in the same stupid style, regarding him as crazy, I am ashamed, both of myself and others, and I cry from the very bottom of my heart. 'Father, I have sinned against the Light.'"[233]

---

[233] Tweedale, Charles, *Man's Survival After Death*, The Psychic Book Club, 1925, p. 470.

Chapter Fifteen
— Cases from the Survival Top-40 —
Memories of War

> *How soon does an entity reincarnate? This is not a set pattern or rule. It is dependent on the free will of that particular entity. Also upon the needs of that entity. If it is one that has been greatly damaged or hurt in one particular incarnation ... it is then incarnated rather quickly.* [234]

Of the thousands of past lives that entranced subjects have recalled, only a few have provided evidential statements that can be corroborated. This is mostly because the average time between lives is so long that any specific information recalled is historically obscure, if available at all. Today's better record-keeping bodes well for a higher rate of confirmation in the future. This may not increase the rate of acceptance, however, since better records mean easier access by non-psychic means.

One factor that can shorten the time spent between earthly visits is sudden, violent death, such as so-often occurs in wartime. This means that the detailed records kept by military organizations in the 20th century can be examined to corroborate the recollections of past lives as soldiers and sailors. The following are three of the best examples of such confirmed recalls.

Case 63 — Round Trip to Allentown

Unlike the typical subject of hypnotic age regression who seeks relief from symptoms unexplained in their current life, Tim Stewart sought only

---

[234] Boulton, p. 71.

to write an article for a national magazine. A computer programmer and freelance journalist, Stewart was living in Albuquerque, New Mexico, when he was given the assignment to write about past-life therapy. To research the subject — about which he was more than dubious — he underwent several hypnotic regressions.[235]

During his fourth session, Stewart experienced being a soldier, and seemed to be reliving battles somewhere in North Africa during the second world war. Now, it is not unusual for hypnotized subjects to recall emotional scenes of fighting and dying, but Stewart went way beyond such general descriptions. He not only gave the soldier's name — William Max— but named his army unit — the 47th Infantry, 9th Division — and gave his blood type, his date of death, and his army ID number. Furthermore, Stewart recalled that Max was born on May 27, 1919 and had grown up in Allentown, Pennsylvania.

And so, as any good journalist would, Stewart called the main library in Allentown and inquired as to the existence of a previous resident named William Max. One month later, Stewart received a copy of an obituary from the local Allentown newspaper dated April 11, 1943. It read, in part, "Fun-loving Bill Max, popular basketball player on the Jewish Community Center team and the 6th Ward Democratic Club team, went down fighting in defense of his country. ... The official War Department message sent to his father, Jacob Max, read: 'The Secretary of War desires that I tender his deep sympathy to you in the loss of your son Private William Max.'"

These facts and others confirmed in the obituary encouraged Stewart to make inquiries of the Department of Defense. Yes he was told, the identification number Stewart had seen on Max's dog tags while entranced did, indeed, belong to an army Private named William Max, who was killed while fighting in North Africa, in 1943.

This story presents strong evidence for Survival, but there is an epilogue that might make it even more convincing to those doubters who

---

[235] The information in this case was adapted from a segment of the television show *Sightings* broadcast on CBS on 6 May 1995.

would grasp at the straw of super-ESP and claim that Stewart got all the information by clairvoyantly accessing old newspaper clippings and military archives. In 1993, Stewart returned to Pennsylvania — a place he had not been since he was a toddler — to attend the funeral of his favorite uncle. While at the funeral, Stewart encountered an elderly woman who was a stranger to him, yet she insisted that he looked familiar to her. In response to her queries, he told her his name and the names of various relatives, but she could not make the connection she sought. Then Stewart asked her name and she replied, "Thelma Max."

Further conversations revealed that Thelma Max was the widow of the brother of William Max. Once she made the connection, she realized that it was her deceased brother-in-law she was reminded of when she looked into Stewart's eyes. Stewart and Max do have similar features, but an outsider would never think they were the same man.

Because of this "chance" encounter, Stewart met other members of the Max family, visited his childhood home, and wandered the neighborhood where William had grown up. Harold Schentzle, a boyhood friend of William Max heard about Stewart's incredible story and arranged a meeting. Schentzle had serious doubts about Stewart's claims and he thought he had the perfect way to settle the matter. After admitting that there was some resemblance, Schentzle asked Stewart if he could recall the last thing that Max said to him prior to embarking for the war. In reply, Stewart told Schentzle that Max had said, "In 1940, I had a dream that if I went into the service and I got shipped overseas, I would never make it home. I'd be killed." Schentzle, who was convinced that Max had never told that dream to anyone but him, fell back in his chair as the blood drained from his face. "To be honest with you," Schentzle reported, "I got goose pimples."

In the ensuing years, most of the Max family has come to accept Stewart as one of them.

Case 59 — A Submariner Resurfaces

Some phobias can be fairly simple to live with. Many folks have a fear of spiders, for instance, and manage to get by well enough. A fear of enclosed spaces, on the other hand, is a true handicap in this modern age of elevators and airplanes. Likewise, a fear of water can be most inconvenient when one wants to join friends at the beach ... or needs a bath. According to a recent article,[236] claustrophobia and aquaphobia (a.k.a. hydrophobia) are two of the six most commonly experienced phobias. Woe unto the poor soul who suffers from both of these simultaneously.

Bruce Kelly, of Glendora, California, was just such a soul in November of 1987, when he showed up at the office of hypnotherapist Rick Brown. Kelly disclosed that, whenever he was on an airplane, he was overwhelmed with terror the moment the cabin doors were latched. He could think of no reason for this fear. Nor could he explain why he was so very, very afraid of water. He could only shower if his back was to the spray and he was simply unable to force himself to climb into a bathtub. On the few occasions when he had been immersed in water he had become dizzy, nauseous, and suffered from trembling and cramps. On top of all that, he was regularly troubled by stabbing pains in his stomach and chest that no doctor had been able to explain.[237]

Rick Brown was a Certified Hypnotherapist who had successfully treated many patients complaining of inexplicable maladies. Although only about one percent of his patients experienced past-life recall while regressed, he felt that Kelly could well be reacting to events that had occurred in a previous lifetime. Brown hypnotized Kelly and asked him "to recall the time and place where he was first affected by the terror."

The entranced Kelly responded, "I'm in a submarine ... I'm dying."

---

[236] *The Ten Most Common Phobias* on phobias-help.com.
[237] Brown, pp. 62-71. See also: "The Reincarnated Submariner," segment of *Unsolved Mysteries* television series, this is included in the DVD collection: *Unsolved Mysteries: Psychics*.

His name, he said, was James Edward Johnston. Then he told a fearsome story of death by drowning in a small, lightless, metal chamber, on the 11th of February, 1942. He said his submarine, the Shark, SS-174, was submerged near Celebes Island when it was attacked by depth-charges for the second time in two days. This time, he was not on duty because he had been confined to his bunk with two broken ribs suffered during the first attack. This time, the Japanese were more accurate, and Johnston was caught in a rush of seawater as he tried to reach his station. He and all the crew were dead before the submarine had settled on the ocean floor.

These specific details and more were revealed during Kelly's first past-life regression. Not only were all of them confirmed by extensive research,[238] the session was successfully therapeutic — his fears of closed spaces and water faded away and he no longer experienced the pains in his torso (apparently caused by his past-life rib injuries).

Despite the goal of the hypnotherapy having been achieved, the therapist was intrigued by the case and wanted to see what else might surface. Although he was a born-again Christian at the time, and could not accept the idea of reincarnation, the subject was likewise curious and agreed to further sessions.

These sessions filled out the life of James Johnston with confirmable facts in a way rarely accomplished before or since. Brown was able to confirm the Johnston-personality's description of the battle theater that included such facts as the names or numbers of four other U.S. subs nearby, their base of operations, the mission of the Shark, and the full names of two other crewman who went down with him.

That's hardly the end of the story, however. In trance, Kelly/Johnston described much of his youth and the events that led up to his enlisting in

---

[238] Prior to the Internet, Brown was required to spend many hours searching in libraries, the U.S. Navy Historical Center and Operational Archives, and the Military Reference and Service Branches of the National Archives, in Washington, DC. Of course, the precise whereabouts of Johnston when he died could not be confirmed, as the submarine was not salvaged.

the Navy. He spoke of his joining the Civilian Conservation Corps and being sent to Tule Lake in California, and Scottsboro and Guntersville in Alabama.

Born in Jacksonville, Alabama on February 1, 1921, [All dates and places were confirmed.] he was raised, he claimed, by his unwed mother in one rented bedroom of a company-owned house in the Profile Cotton Mill Village. His mother died young in March of 1936, he said, and he recalled a cousin named Elizabeth in Alabama and a girlfriend named Molly Lassiter, in California. Also, he remembered being especially fond of eating the ends of bread loaves, just as Kelly is currently.

Rick Brown made three trips to Alabama researching the case; on the third, he was accompanied by Bruce Kelly. This trip was filmed, and was shown, in part, on a segment of *Unsolved Mysteries*. When Kelly visited the house where Johnston was raised, he recalled that he (Johnston) was only allowed to enter or leave the house via the back door. When they met Johnston's cousin, whose name was, indeed, Elizabeth, she confirmed that the boy was not allowed to use the front door. Then she asked if he remembered always eating the ends of bread loaves.

It is hard to imagine a more evidential regression case than this one. Kelly's memories of being Johnston are strong and clear. Brown noted Kelly's extreme and realistic discomfort when reliving Johnston's death. With the exception of the name of one crew member, no statement out of hundreds has been contradicted by research. The three full names of crewmen, the ship's name and number, and the date and location of the sinking were all recalled during the first regression session, before anyone had the chance to look up anything. The scores of facts and intimate details brought to light in later sessions and confirmed by independent investigation negate all feasibility of conspiracy or misrepresentation. Add the rapid alleviation of Kelly's symptoms and this is one of the most convincing cases yet examined.

Case 65 — One More Mission

Ian Stevenson, Dr. Jim Tucker, Carol Bowman and other researchers have uncovered hundreds of cases of children who inexplicably can recall living and dying as other people. The most impressive and thoroughly documented case yet, however, was brought to light not by the efforts of believers or even open-minded, objective scientists, but by a no-nonsense businessman, a stringent Christian, whose upbringing had hardened his mind against the idea of reincarnation.[239]

Bruce Leininger reveled in research, a trait which served him well as a human-resource executive, handling personnel crises and developing corporate compensation and insurance packages. When James, his two-year-old son, started screaming and thrashing about in the middle of the night, Bruce dismissed it as no more than a nightmare, likely triggered by the unfamiliarity of his son's bedroom in their new home. James had been moved before; just after his birth (on April 10th 1998) the Leininger family had relocated from the San Francisco area to Dallas, Texas, but he was too young to remember that. Then, two months previously, they had followed Bruce's job to Lafayette, Louisiana. Some sort of reaction could be expected. The screams were nothing to worry about, except that Bruce needed his sleep.

Andrea Leininger, being expected to supply motherly comfort and, therefore, an eyewitness to her toddler's nocturnal hysterics, could not so easily write them off as a normal childhood nightmare. Up until that night, James had been an unusually happy and contented child who rarely cried or even fussed. The next morning, she shared her concern with her husband, describing James' piercing shrieks and violent kicking and flailing at the covers, but Bruce was indifferent.

His lack of concern would, no doubt, have been proper if James' performance hadn't been repeated "with terrifying regularity and increasing

---

[239] Leininger. See also: videos of interviews with the Leiningers, available on YouTube.

frenzy." They didn't happen every night – sometimes a night or two would be skipped – but when one's sleep is disturbed four or five nights out of seven, the expectation of a reoccurrence can ruin one's rest as well as the event itself. Andrea called her pediatrician, who told her the nightmares were normal night terrors and would soon diminish. She talked with friends; they agreed with her pediatrician. She conferred with her sisters, who echoed her friends and her pediatrician. Perhaps surprisingly, at least in retrospect, two months passed before Andrea realized that James was doing more than shrieking and thrashing about, he was also screaming words. When she caught the gist of what he was yelling, she ran down the hall and got her husband.

Bruce's annoyance at being dragged from bed evaporated quickly once he heard the words: "Airplane crash! Plane on fire! Little man can't get out!" These phrases were repeated over and over as little James flung his head back and forth and kicked upward wildly. Kicking, Andrea suddenly realized, just like a fighter pilot trying to kick his way out of a cockpit. Both mother and father were stunned; neither had any explanation.

Life went on as before.

The next bewildering incident occurred when Andrea gave James a toy airplane to distract him while she was shopping. "There's even a bomb on the bottom," she pointed out. "That's not a bomb, Mommy. That's a dwop tank."[240] Andrea didn't know what a drop tank was. Bruce did. Neither had any idea how their toddler in diapers could identify one, even though he couldn't pronounce it properly.

On August 27th, after a long day playing with a friend from his pre-kindergarten class, James was being read a bedtime story when he casually said, "Mama, little man's airplane crash on fire." The Leiningers, having been told not to interrupt James' nightmares, had been waiting for an opportunity to question him while he was awake. Now, Andrea hurried to bring Bruce into the room.

---

[240] A drop tank is an extra fuel tank that can be jettisoned when empty.

Andrea asked, "Who is the little man?" James replied, "Me." Andrea asked, "Do you remember the little man's name?" James replied, "James." Thinking this was fruitless, Bruce tried a different tack, "Do you remember what kind of airplane the little man flew?" His son immediately replied, in the same conversational tone, "A Corsair." And from where did your plane take off? "A boat."

Now, perhaps James had seen a television program about Corsairs and aircraft carriers; although his mother claims he never watched anything but shows for little kids. And who's to say that James hadn't seen a drop tank when he and his dad visited an airplane museum back in Dallas? Of course, even if he had taken notice of such an unobtrusive thing, he couldn't read signs, so he wouldn't have known what it was called. Nevertheless, all of this has been suggestive at best; not really proof of anything … so far.

Skeptics and debunkers should only proceed to read further at peril of their preconceptions.

Bruce asked his drowsy toddler the name of the boat he flew from. "Natoma," James replied. Bruce thought that sounded like a Japanese name and said so. Little James grew indignant and said no, it was American! Bruce, a bit taken aback that he had been challenged by someone who wasn't even potty trained, went to the Internet and discovered, to his amazement, that an American aircraft carrier called *Natoma Bay* had battled the Japanese in the Pacific.

Feeling that his religious beliefs and his role in the family were under fire, Bruce began a campaign to reaffirm both. He used the tool he knew best – tenacious research. Over the next few years, as little James revealed more and more about James the pilot, Bruce filled his dining room with letters, books, and boxes of documents about the war in the Pacific Theater. He traveled thousands of miles by car and plane and spent many hours on long-distance calls. Using the pretense of writing a book, he infiltrated the reunions of veterans of the *Natoma Bay* and its sister ships. He interviewed scores of old sailors and their family members. He was almost desperate to uncover some rational explanation for his son's memories — anything but the heresy of reincarnation. Andrea, although more accepting of reincarnation as an explanation, nevertheless spent considerable time helping to track down facts and people.

The following paragraphs summarize some of what was said by the child, James M. Leininger, and the confirmation his parents ultimately discovered.

Statement: The pilot's name was James, just like his. He often drew battle scenes with propeller-driven planes; he signed them "James 3" and explained, "Because I am the third James."

Fact: The only pilot on the *USS Natoma Bay* whose first name was James, was James M. Huston, Jr. [The second James?]

Statement: The American planes in his pictures were Wildcats and Corsairs.

Fact: Both were names of U.S. aircraft on carriers in WWII. The Wildcat was the plane Huston was piloting when he died. [Note: Several photographs relevant to this case are included in the write-up at www.SurvivalTop40.com.]

Statement: The red suns on some planes in his drawings meant they were Japanese.

Fact: The rising sun, depicted as a red circle, was the symbol of Imperial Japan.

Statement: The American sailors called Japanese fighters by boy names (such as Zekes) and bombers by girl names (such as Bettys).

Fact: Correct

Statement: He had a friend named Jack Larsen onboard the *USS Natoma Bay*.

Fact: Jack Larsen served on the *USS Natoma Bay* and was a friend of James Huston.

Statement: Unprompted, James pointed to a picture of Iwo Jima in a book and said that was where his plane was shot down.

Fact: James Huston's plane was the only one from the *Natoma Bay* that was shot down during the battle for Iwo Jima. [Huston was supposed to ship home the following day. He was not scheduled to make that run; he volunteered for one last mission when another pilot couldn't fly.]

Statement: Corsair planes had two defects: they often got flat tires and they wanted to turn left when they took off.

Fact: The Corsair's poor sight lines and heavy engines made for unusually rough landings on carrier decks, which blew an inordinate number of tires. The exceptional torque from their single front-mounted prop caused a drift to the left on takeoff. James Huston had served as a test pilot for Corsairs.

Statement: Three fellow crewmen, named Billy, Walter, and Leon, met him when he arrived in heaven. (He gave these names to his G.I. Joe action figures.)

Fact: In addition to James M. Huston, Jr., the names Billy Peeler, Walter Devlin, and Leon Conner were on the official list of men killed from the VC-81 Squadron aboard the *USS Natoma Bay*. Huston was killed on March 3, 1945. The other three died shortly prior to that, in late 1944.

Statement: His plane had been hit in the engine. (As soon as he could after receiving a new toy airplane he would crash it into the coffee table or some other hard surface and break off the propellers.)

Fact: An eyewitness to the crash of James Huston's plane said that the anti-aircraft fire blew away his propeller and his engine exploded as it went down.

Statement: While touring the Nimitz Museum, he saw a 5-inch cannon and announced that it was just like the gun on the fantail of the *Natoma Bay*.

Fact: The *USS Natoma Bay* had a 5-inch cannon on its fantail (the area of the hanger deck at the stern).

Statement: While watching a television program about Corsairs, James corrected the narrator by pointing out that the Japanese plane seen being shot down was a Tony, not a Zero. He explained that the Tony was a Japanese fighter that was smaller than a Zero.

Fact: True.

Statement: During his first telephone conversation with James Huston's sister, Anne Barron, who was 86 at the time, the 5-year-old James:
- Called her Annie, even though his mom thought that disrespectful.
- Said she had a sister "Roof" who was 4 years older than she.
- Said her brother James was 4 years her junior.
- Talked intimately and at length about the senior Huston's alcoholism and the devastating effects it had on the family.
- Asked her what had happened to a picture of her that had been painted by their mother.

Fact: Only her long-dead brother, James Huston, Jr., ever called Anne Barron "Annie." She did have a sister (now deceased) named Ruth who was 4 years her senior. The painting, which no one else knew about, was in her attic. In short, everything little James said over the phone was correct and Anne Barron came to accept that the child was truly her brother born again.

As little James Leininger was encouraged to talk about his memories, the nightmares decreased in frequency, but continued sporadically for several years.

The evidence presented here should be more than enough to convince any open-minded person. The juxtaposition of "Natoma Bay" and "Jack Larsen" in the mind of a 2-year-old is, by itself, inexplicable by any other means than reincarnation or possession, either of which require Survival of the human memory and personality beyond the death of the body.

I will wrap this up by relating one more incident that may be the most intriguing of all. One day in October of 2002, in response to a hug from his father, James commented, "When I found you and Mommy, I knew you would be good to me." (Note that this statement indicates that souls are independent, conscious beings prior to being born on earth, and so, on its own, is strongly suggestive of reincarnation.) "Where did you find us?" asked his father. "In Hawaii," James replied, "at the big pink hotel." Then he added that he had found them one night when they were eating dinner on the beach.

Five weeks before Andrea became pregnant with James, she and Bruce had celebrated their fifth wedding anniversary at the Royal Hawaiian, a landmark hotel easily recognized by its bright pink facade. On their last night there, they had eaten a dinner by moonlight on Waikiki Beach.

Epilogue
Moving On

In interviews and discussions, I am often asked, "Do you really believe this stuff?" To which, my answer is, "No. I don't believe any of it."

My statement is met with varied looks and exclamations — sometimes of consternation (as if I was crazy), sometimes of triumph (as if the interviewer had finally gotten me to admit to fraud).

But, in the next moment, I always add, "Believing is thinking a certain thing when there are insufficient facts to back up your thoughts. So, no, I do not *believe* in the continuation of the human personality after the demise of the physical body. Rather, I have carefully examined the evidence and rationally reached the logical conclusion that the afterlife is real — beyond a reasonable doubt!

That phrase — "beyond a reasonable doubt" — is important, for it suggests a legal venue for any arguments about the validity or acceptability of the evidence. In such a courtroom setting, there is no place for statements as to whether or not there is "scientific" proof of an afterlife. Science is a most useful system for evaluating purely physical events; but it does not deal in "proofs" (other than in mathematics) and is useless when nonphysical factors (such as spirits) may arbitrarily and surreptitiously affect its experiments.

Instead, the search for the truth in matters of the spiritual and the psychic must and should depend on well-established legalistic tests of the strength of evidence and the reliability of witnesses. These procedures have been employed for centuries to determine guilt or innocence; to set men free or send them to the gallows. When we apply them to the vast array of solid evidence for Survival, the verdict is clear: Death is but a doorway to other realms of existence.

At Gettysburg, on the 3rd of July 1863, General Robert E. Lee commanded his troops to charge across Seminary Ridge into the teeth of the Union lines. In the next 60 minutes, some 5,000 Confederate soldiers died in what became known as Pickett's charge. This was the beginning of the end of one of the bloodiest wars in history. I wonder if Lee, or any commanding officer, would ever send another man into battle if they fully comprehended the process of self-judgement and empathic agony that awaits us all on the other side of death. For that matter, how could anyone ever agitate for war if they have any inkling of what awaits them in the next realm? How could they ever condone slavery or ignore poverty if they understood that we spirits come back to live on earth again and again in every race and every role? Can you imagine a world in which everyone realizes that they are part of one, vast spiritual family?

Each of us could pursue no activity more worthy than affirming this great truth.

Appendices

The original version of *The Afterlife Confirmed* contains several appendices that have been removed to conserve space. The bibliography has been combined with those of the other books in this trilogy and appears as the final section. The documents titled "The Sin of Speaking with Spirits" and "The Evidence Scoring System" may be accessed online at www.survivaltop40.com.

The Hereafter Trilogy,
Vol. III: Top 40 Remains

History shows that every intelligent man who has gone into this investigation, if he gave it adequate examination at all, has come out believing in spirits; this circumstance places the burden of proof on the shoulders of the skeptic.

– James H. Hyslop[241]

---

[241] Hyslop, *Contact*, p.480.

Introduction

The presentation of cases in *The Survival Files* (volume one of this trilogy) began with those that showed the ability of the human personality to operate independently of the physical body. Then cases were added that demonstrated the lack of a requirement for the body to be alive at all. Finally, several cases suggested that souls return again and again to live life in Earthly bodies. After completing *The Survival Files*, I continued to research the available evidence and found many more cases, some of which seemed even stronger and more convincing than those I had previously presented. Rather than being just another person proselytizing about their favorite cases, I decided that an objective system was needed to determine which ones were the most evidential. After all, I reasoned, getting a bunch of independent and strong-willed researchers and writers to agree on a particular set of cases as the best would never happen; but it might just be possible to gain consensus on a set of rules we could employ to determine those cases. And so, I spent the better part of two years developing the Evidence Scoring System.[242] From this, the Top-40 was born.

The idea of a "top-40" has a history that may be of some interest. During World War II, an American soldier named Todd Storz noticed that customers in restaurants tended to feed nickels into the jukeboxes to play the same songs over and over; and, when the place had emptied out, the waitresses would play those same few songs again. After the war, Storz bought a floundering radio station in Omaha, Nebraska, and the changes he made

---

[242] This can be seen at www.SurvivalTop40.com, along with an up-to-date listing of the cases in Acrobat format.

brought him unheard-of success. Instead of programming a little bit of music amid news and network shows, he began giving the people the music they wanted to hear, when they wanted to hear it. This led to his creation of the "Top-40" hits, a set of records that were played over and over throughout the day. Although criticized harshly by other station owners who thought their tastes ought to determine the public's listening fare, Storz soon owned five of the most successful stations in the country and "The Top-40" revolutionized the radio industry.

By the time I was approaching my teenage years, in the 1950s, top-40 stations filled the A.M. dial on every car radio from hot rods to station wagons.[243] So, when considering how many cases there should be on my list of the most convincing evidence, 40 was the obvious choice. Out of the thousands of cases to choose from, ten was clearly inadequate and 100 too intimidating ... 40 seems just right.

Due to the difficulty of comparing cases based on communications with cases based on recollections, and to make the list easier to grasp, it is divided into two sections: "The 20 Most Convincing Spirit-Contact Cases," and "The 20 Most Persuasive Reincarnation Cases." The table on the following page shows these, in alphabetical order by case name, with each entry suffixed by the number of the volume of this trilogy in which it appears.

The Survival Files and *The Afterlife Confirmed*, together presented 53 cases, of which 24 currently remain on the Top-40 list.[244] This, third, volume devotes a chapter to each of the other 16 cases that qualified for the Top-40 as of Super Pi Day.[245]

---

[243] These are called "crossovers" today, but to me they will always be station wagons.
[244] When the score of a new case earns it a place on the list, the lowest ranked case is moved to the Honorable Mentions list.
[245] 3.14.15.

The 20 Most Convincing Spirit-Contact Cases	The 20 Most Persuasive Reincarnation Cases
The A.B.C. Séances – III	The Apprentice Murderer – I
Anna's Amazing Abilities – III	Coming Back Down Under – III
A Cameo Reappearance – III	Death in the Garment District – I
Cloak and Danger – II	Dying To Meet Each Other[247] – I
A Country Revival – II	Ex-Actor Makes Comeback – III
The `Deadicated' Reporter – II	Family Lost and Found – II
Fire and Iceland – II	Guns and Rebirth – III
Friends and Strangers – II	Having a Friend – III
The Ghosts in the Machines – I	Keeping Them In the Family – III
The Mysterious Death of Edgar Vandy[246] – II	My Mother's Brother Is My Father's Son – III
The Murder of Jacqueline Poole – II	The Numbers of the Beast – I
New Meaning for 'Soul Mate' – II	One More Mission – II
The Picture of Raymond Lodge – III	The Policeman and the Painter – I
The R-101 Disaster – I	Scotland Redux – III
Relics Revealed & Revisited – I	The Rebirth of Bridey Murphy – II
The Return of Mary Roff – II	Round Trip to Allentown – II
Soule Proves the Soul – III	The Spirits Seller's Spirit – III
A Tale of Two Tattoos – III	The Strangers Were Lovers – II
The Unforgotten Coin – III	A Submariner Resurfaces – II
An Untimely Valentine – III	A Town Reborn – I

---

[246] Titled "A Mysterious Death" in *The Afterlife Confirmed*.
[247] Titled "Hypnotist's Heaven" in *The Survival Files*.

Chapter One — Case 35

An Untimely Valentine

On the first day of September, 2002, Bailey Ginsberg and her brother Jonathan were in a terrible automobile accident; Jonathan was in a coma for several days afterwards; Bailey did not survive the crash. Her parents, Bob and Phran Ginsberg, were, of course, devastated. As they fought to maintain a loving and stable environment for their injured son and their remaining daughter, they also struggled to comprehend why their bright, vivacious, and talented teenager had been taken from them.

Over the ensuing weeks, Ginsberg noticed several unusual phenomena that she felt might indicate the presence of Bailey's spirit, but her rationalist husband could not accept that his daughter could be the cause, neither could he gain any solace from the idea. Then, while sipping coffee in a bookstore awaiting an appointment with their son's rehabilitation team, they noticed a book on the rack near their table. It was *The Afterlife Experiments*, by Dr. Gary Schwartz. They purchased and read the book, and were so impressed that they contacted Schwartz, hoping to have readings with the mediums he studied.

On February 14, 2003, Valentine's Day, Schwartz contacted the Ginsbergs. As a result of their conversation, they had a telephone reading with medium Laurie Campbell and, later, participated in another experiment at Schwartz' lab in Tucson, Arizona. Phran found the experiences "wonderfully healing" ... Bob remained unconvinced.

A few weeks later, they got a call from Dr. Julie Beischel at the Arizona laboratory, inviting them to participate in a rather unusual telephone experiment. A three-way connection would be made between Beischel, Ginsberg, and an unnamed medium. The medium would not be told Ginsberg's identity. Once the connection was made, Ginsberg was to hang up without saying a word. For the next half-hour, the medium would note her impressions, then the call would be connected again. This time, Ginsberg was to stay on the line, but say nothing. The final segment would consist of a "normal" reading in which she could provide feedback.

This arrangement was accepted and, on the appointed day, Ginsberg eagerly awaited the call. She describes the commencement of the session thus:

"I held on as Julie dialed another number to 'conference' the call. The soft-spoken, sweet voice with a western drawl at the other end said 'Hello.'"

"Hi, Allison, it's Julie. When we hang up, you are to begin part 1a," said Julie, and everyone hung up. ... By the time the phone rang again a half-hour later, I was filled with anticipation. Allison [DuBois] was now introduced to me, but I was introduced to her only as "the sitter" and the discarnate was introduced as "Bailey, daughter to the sitter." I was then reminded to remain silent.

The messages then came "fast and furious." Ginsberg took 19 pages of notes. Dubois described the accident and Bailey's fatal head injury. Then she talked about the sports Bailey enjoyed, and the green vegetables she didn't, her shyness, the way she loved to sit in the kitchen and watch her mom cook, and many other personal matters. DuBois described a photograph of Bailey and another girl—"her best friend or sister" — with their arms around each other, smiling towards the camera. She said Bailey was aware of a new puppy a cousin had just gotten, and that she remembered the time when her mom watched her perform in *The King and I*.

Ginsberg was especially impressed by these last, as the photograph was one that she saw every day tucked into her desk blotter, and *The King and I* was the only play that Bailey had ever had a role in.

All of this information was given without any feedback at all. After almost two hours of listening to her daughter's life being described in accurate detail, Ginsberg had yet to utter a single word. At last, Beischel gave the okay and the sitter and the medium had a real conversation.

During this period, Ginsberg mentioned that the picture of Bailey and her sister was on her office desk. Immediately, DuBois said, "Happy Valentine's Day. She says to tell you, Happy Valentine's Day." Being as February was many months away, this wish puzzled everyone. Then Ginsberg remembered that their initial contact with Schwartz had occurred on February 14th. As no other explanation came to anyone's mind, this one was accepted, but not enthusiastically. The phone call ended in the late afternoon. Ginsberg knew she had garnered an amazing amount of impressive evidence to share with her husband. The real kicker, however, did not occur until the next morning when she entered her office. There, on her desk, was the photograph of Bailey hugging her sister. Thinking that she would e-mail the photo to Beischel at the lab, Ginsberg lovingly removed it from its mount, turned it over to scan it, and there, written on the back, were the words:

Valentine's Day Dance

CSH HS[248]

Discussion

Phran had written the description on the back when she first tucked the photo into her desk blotter in February of 2001, so the link between the photo and the date must have been buried in her mind somewhere. But, it must have been buried especially deep, considering that, even though she looked at the photo almost every day and even though the phrase "Happy Valentine's Day" came to the medium just after the photo was referred to again, she could not link the phrase with the photo. Nor did the medium. If DuBois had been "reading the subconscious of someone involved" then it ought to have been apparent to her that the photo and the phrase were

---

[248] The initials standing for *"Cold Spring Harbor High School."*

part of the same package. Also, this case is unusual because, when the photo was first described, the sitter was not "involved" (that is, she was not known to, or in the presence of, the medium).

Largely inspired by this reading, and hoping to help other bereaved parents, Phran and Bob Ginsberg founded and preside over the non-profit Forever Family Foundation. All work for the foundation is voluntary and membership is free. See www.foreverfamilyfoundation.org for more information.

The Ginsbergs and the researchers have been interviewed numerous times (including personal discussions with this author) and their integrity is incontestable.

Chapter Two — Case 77
Keeping Them In the Family

Florence Pollock has the possibly unique distinction of giving birth eight times to six children.

The first six births occurred between 1940 and 1955 – four sons and, of special interest here, two daughters (Joanna, in 1946, and Jacqueline, in 1951). On the morning of May 5th, 1957, the two daughters, age 11 and 7, were murdered on the streets of Hexham, England while on their way to Sunday school.

They were walking with a friend when a woman ran the children down with her car. Investigators believed that she was depressed and incensed over the loss of her own children in a custody battle. Prior to leaving her home she had ingested a considerable quantity of pain killers and barbiturates. These were, no doubt a factor in her apparently deciding that if she couldn't have children no one else should either. She was seen to cross into the opposite lane, jump her car up onto the sidewalk, scrape along a stone wall, smash into the three kids, and continue on some ways before stopping. Joanna and Jacqueline died before help arrived; their companion died in the ambulance; their killer was committed to a mental hospital.

It goes without saying that Florence Pollock and her husband, John, were horrified at the children's demise. Florence, according to Dr. Ian Stevenson,[249] "found the loss too fraught with suffering to think about." John, on the other hand, "liked to think about the dead girls, although not necessarily to dwell on how they had died. He believed not only that the girls

---

[249] Stevenson, Ian, *Reincarnation and Biology: A Contribution to the Etiology of Birthmarks and Birth Defects Volume 2,* Praeger Publishers, 1997, p. 2045.

had survived death, but that they remained close to the family. On the very afternoon of their deaths, he had a vision of them in heaven."

Although he never could explain whether it was visions or some other psychic means, eight months later, when Florence became pregnant once more, John felt strongly that Joanna and Jacqueline were going to be born again, this time as twins. John was an ex-Catholic who believed in reincarnation. His wife, also an ex-Catholic did not. Neither did she feel that she was bearing twins; a sentiment with which her obstetrician, hearing only a single heartbeat, fully agreed.

John stuck to his intuition and, when a friend came to him at work on October 4th, 1958, and said: "I have good news for you." He replied: "Yes, I know, twins." And so Gillian and Jennifer Pollock came into the world.

Between the ages of 3, when they first began talking coherently, and 6, the twins said several things supporting their father's belief that Joanna and Jacqueline had returned.

When the twins were just a few months old, the Pollock family moved from the town of Hexham to Whitley Bay. When they were about 4 years old, the family visited Hexham for the first time since they had moved away. As they were approaching a park where Joanna and Jacqueline used to play, the twins announced that they wanted to go and play on the swings; yet the parents had not mentioned any swings and the park was over a hill and not yet in sight. A little later, as they passed their old home, they both said, "We used to live there."

At Hexham, Joanna and Jacqueline had sometimes eaten their lunch at school. In Whitley Bay, the twins always came home for lunch. One day, when they were grumbling about what their mother was serving, she told them that they could always eat at school. They responded that they had done that before. "Where?" Florence asked. "At Hexham," they answered. But the twins had neither attended school in Hexham nor eaten lunch at school in Whitley Bay.

There was one instance of recall that did not conform to the norm of forgetfulness by age 8. When she was 23, Gillian was reminiscing with her father about playing in a sandpit with her brothers in a garden by a large house. Her very detailed description perfectly matched a home and garden from which the Pollocks had moved back when Joanna was 4 years old, 8 years before Gillian was born.

Although they were identical twins – that is, one egg, one placenta, one set of DNA – Gillian (the oldest by 10 minutes) was different from Jennifer in many of the same ways that Joanna (the eldest by 5 years) had been different from Jacqueline.

Once, when John was doing some house painting, Jennifer asked, "Why are you wearing mummy's coat?" This "coat" was an old smock John had donned to protect his clothing from paint spatters. Florence used to wear it when she delivered milk, a job she stopped doing before the twins were born. Not only did Jennifer recognize it as her mother's, but she expressed annoyance when Gillian could not recall it. During the times Florence was wearing the smock, Jacqueline would have been often around her mother, whereas Joanna would not have.

Joanna's and Jacqueline's toys had been packed away in the attic after their death. The twins did not see the toys until they were 4 years old and their parents unpacked the box. Immediately, and without any prompting, Gillian said that a doll that had been Joanna's was hers, and Jennifer claimed a very different doll, one which had been Jacqueline's. Jennifer correctly recalled the names — Mary and Suzanne — previously given to the dolls. They both then announced that their dolls had come from Santa Claus — which was true.

Santa was also credited with the gift of a toy clothes wringer.[250] (Clearly English children in the early 1950s differed from today's kids in their idea of what made a fun toy.) Again, the 'older' girl, and not her

---

[250] Prior to the invention of electrically heated clothes dryers, excess water was extracted by feeding the clothing between two rollers known as wringers.

twin, was acknowledged by both twins as the owner of an item that had belonged to the older sister.

On a considerably less jolly note, although the twins never talked with their parents about the deaths of their sisters — and their parents certainly never mentioned the subject to them — their mother recalled that several times she overheard them discussing the event among themselves. What Ian Wilson refers to as "the most macabre incident of all," was witnessed by Florence when she once peeked into the twins' playroom and "found Gillian cradling Jennifer's head in her hands and saying: 'The blood's coming out of your eyes. That's where the car hit you.'"[251]

The differences between the twins carried over to physical behaviors and features. For one thing, the 'older' twin tended to mother the younger to a much greater extent than would be thought normal in siblings of the same age. This behavior could well be a carryover from past lives in which Joanna often cared for her younger sister Jacqueline. More impressively, and concretely, are the two birthmarks that Jennifer had: one of which looked and was located exactly like one that Jacqueline had on her left waist; the other which mimicked a scar that Jacqueline had received when she fell off her tricycle and hit her forehead on the edge of a metal bucket. Neither Gillian nor any other member of the Pollock family had any similar scars or birthmarks. Such differences among identical twins are extremely rare; these are totally inexplicable in light of the congruence with those of her deceased sibling. Inexplicable, that is, within any paradigm lacking the concept of reincarnation.

It seems noteworthy in this context that neither twin has any scars or birthmarks that might be attributed to the way in which their sisters had died. Very often, when children spontaneously recall another life, their bodies are marked in ways associated with the cause of death in that previous life. Many times such scars and deformities provide strong corroboration of their claims. But Gillian's and Jennifer's bodies suffered such

---

[251] Wilson, Ian, *Mind Out of Time?*, Victor Gollancz, Ltd., 1981, p. 24.

massive trauma in numerous locations that no one, apparently, bothered to precisely record or map them. To carry over such scars into a new life, therefore, would be seriously disfiguring while serving no purpose of identification.

Discussion

Some critics have suggested that this case is weakened because one of the key witnesses (John Pollock) was a believer in reincarnation and his testimony is likely biased. But the other key witness (Florence Pollock) was strongly opposed to the idea of reincarnation yet her version of the events is essentially the same. Also, as John pointed out to Dr. Stevenson, if he had not believed, he would not have made the observations and the case would never have been initiated.[252]

The unique (to my knowledge) feature of this case is the return of siblings to the same family. (The fact that they return as identical twins makes it even more special.) The separate and distinct memories and preferences — Gillian's memories were exclusively Joanna's and Jennifer's solely Jacqueline's — are definite counters to the idea that the twins picked up their memories from their mother's thoughts and dreams during their gestation. And their physical and behavioral differences in light of the equality of their DNA refutes any claim of "genetic memory" — if such were even conceivable in this case.

This is a tough case to score. It is really two cases which are inextricably entwined with one another. The ESS was not designed to determine how much one reinforces, or detracts from, the other. So, we are re-evaluating the evaluation system. No matter what the final score, though, the case, as researcher Guy Lyon Playfair has pointed out, "is as solved as any case is ever likely to be."[253]

---

[252] Stevenson, p. 2058.
[253] Playfair, Guy Lyon, *New Clothes for Old Souls*, Druze Heritage Foundation, 2006, p. 114.

Chapter Three — Case 67
Anna's Amazing Abilities

There is credible testimony for some people possessing inexplicable powers such as absorbing the contents of a book by sleeping with it under one's pillow, writing symphonic pieces as a toddler, or calculating what day of the week a particular date falls upon. As fascinating as any such transcendent talent may be, it is usually easier to assume a genetic anomaly or fortuitous accident as its cause, rather than crediting the involvement of spirits from another realm. Having two or three such talents, though, makes the spirit explanation more likely. Demonstrating a half dozen or more widely diverse and totally inexplicable abilities provides evidence for spirit involvement that cannot be reasonably refuted. This is the story of an 11-year-old girl who did just that.

Her name was Anna, and she was the daughter of the reverend Dr. Horace Westwood.[254] Westwood was a Unitarian minister who believed that tales of a spirit realm were pure fantasy. This attitude is well illustrated by the reverend's own words:

> "The summer of 1914, though I did not realize it at the time, proved itself the prelude to a series of experiences the nature of which could not possibly have been anticipated. If by chance any individual had ventured to predict them, my immediate reaction would have been, 'impossible and absurd.' If anyone had told me that, as a result of these experiences, I would come to accept as factual what I later accepted as based on indubitable evidence and that, as a consequence,

---

[254] In an effort to shield her from unwanted publicity, Westwood initially referred vaguely to the girl as a cousin, but his sons later revealed that Anna was actually their sister.

I would come to hold the views I now embrace concerning the meaning and destiny of human personality, I would at once have replied, 'If this ever comes to pass I shall regard my mental processes as seriously open to question. The entire thing is utterly foreign to the world of fact I think I know. Also, it leads to an outlook upon life which I regard as inimical to the best interest of mankind. Such a possibility is entirely beyond the range of any consideration I could entertain, even for a moment.' All of which goes to show how little we can anticipate the future and how unsafe all predictions are, particularly when they relate to our individual unfolding. For what I regarded as impossible did actually happen, and that which I had denied, by providing its own evidence, not only compelled recognition, but necessitated a revision of what, hitherto, had been fundamental to all my thinking in relation to human nature and destiny."[255]

When a prominent business executive whom he thought to be intelligent and hard headed revealed an interest in psychic phenomena, Westwood concluded that the man was either gullible, self-deceived, or "a trifle off."[256] When World War I broke out, Westwood's disillusion with the idea of heaven was exacerbated. "To be concerned with the question of individual survival beyond death when there is so much misery and suffering upon earth is the essence of selfishness," he thought. "To seek for personal consolation, in the hour of bereavement when millions are facing the perils of battle that we may live and that the blessings of democracy shall not perish, seems the height of ingratitude." Furthermore, he opined that psychical researchers were "trifling with nonsense while the world was in flames."[257]

It is difficult to imagine a man less likely to champion the cause of spiritualism. But then, that was before Anna became involved.

---

[255] Westwood, Horace, *There is a Psychic World*, Crown Publishers, 1949, pp. 3-4.
[256] _____, p. 5.
[257] _____, p. 9.

A couple who were members of Westwood's church lost their son in the war. They were, of course, both devastated and depressed. But the wife's mood quickly changed to happiness because, she told her husband, their son had begun communicating to her from beyond the grave. This caused the husband increased anxiety as he considered such delusions to indicate the onset of mental illness. So he went to his minister for advice. Westwood tried to console the distraught husband and promised to visit the wife to see what he might do to help her. Before he could schedule such a visit, however, the husband returned with a completely changed attitude. Now, he proclaimed, his wife was not delusional at all! In fact, their son had, indeed, been communicating with his mother, and now was communicating with his father also. Wouldn't the good reverend like to come and see these marvels for himself?

Westwood admits he was reticent to go, not only because he was skeptical, but he "did not wish to be placed in the position of having to tell them that they were the victims of self-deception." Finally, however, he felt he could put off their invitation no longer, so he and his wife went to the couple's home to see what there was to see. The couple had developed the practice of sitting with their daughter at a table on which sat a wood plank hand-lettered with the alphabet. One or more of the group would place their fingers on an inverted drinking glass and the movement of the glass around the board would spell out messages purporting to come from their deceased son.

As he observed this process, Westwood became convinced that the messages were the result of what he termed "sympathetic thought transference" between mother and daughter, rather than the involvement of dead people. But when Westwood gently hinted at his skepticism and asked for a more convincing demonstration, he got more than he, or his hosts, could have expected. With only the fingers of Westwood, his wife, and the couple's daughter lightly touching the top surface of the 24"x18" plank of wood, it suddenly began to race back and forth across the table so rapidly that the trio had trouble keeping their fingers in touch with it. The plank next moved off the table's edge, floated slowly downward to within an inch of the floor, and then back up again to the tabletop, where it started racing around once move.

All five (living) folks in the room were flabbergasted. None had ever seen the like before. No known principle of physics could explain how the heavy plank had risen through the air when no one was touching it at the bottom. Had it somehow been a mass hallucination? Westwood and his wife discussed the evening's events on their way home and decided the matter required futher investigation.

At first, they tried a makeshift Ouija board of stiff cardboard. When, after several hours, that failed to produce results, Westwood bought a "real" one. Still nothing happened. Then the children in the household wanted to try out this new "toy." Westwood explains: "So we let them try, one by one, and each pulled a blank, much to their chagrin, until Anna placed her little hand on the planchette. She had hardly touched it, when the indicator began to move with startling rapidity and with equally startling accuracy, spelling out words and sentences in complete and intelligent sequence." Westwood does not reveal the content of these messages, so we cannot judge their evidential value.

Turning the board around had no effect on Anna's remarkable ability, nor did blindfolding the girl. The next day Westwood drew the letters of the alphabet "higgledy-piggledy" on a large piece of paper. "Indeed," he explains, "they presented such a confused picture that if I wanted to spell out any word, and with my eyes wide open, it was an effort to find the letters." Such precautions proved pointless. When Anna was blindfolded and led to the scrambled board, the tumbler flew just as rapidly and the messages came just as intelligently as before. Furthermore, to Westwood's great surprise, "the first message to come through was to the effect that I was a fool for my pains … and that 'they' would prove they were invisible entities seeking to communicate on the physical plane."[258]

---

[258] Westwood, p. 24.

Several different entities communicated through Anna, at first via the talking board, but soon via automatic writing, and ultimately using her own vocal chords. At first, there were two spirits calling themselves Ruth and Ralph. These claimed to have been stenographers who had worked for the government in Washington, DC. These two introduced an ethereal musician named Kate. Next appeared a spirit of apparently loftier intelligence which identified itself only as "X." And finally, came the entity who was initially viewed with the most suspicion but who ultimately proved the most convincing, a Chippewa Indian named Blue Hide.

Anyone reading Westwood's account of these events, must be struck by how stubbornly he resisted accepting these entities to be what they claimed to be. In fact, he steadfastly refused to follow up when information was given that might be confirmed. It wasn't until he had experienced several other mediums that he began to admit the possibility of a spirit realm. And so, we are left with a story sincerely told by a most trustworthy source, but a story lacking in the usual confirmable information that makes the best cases so convincing. Nevertheless, as hinted at in the opening paragraph, the inexplicable skills demonstrated by this 11-year-old child, could be sufficient unto themselves to convince many readers.

Being able to rapidly pick out letters on a board, while blindfolded, when the letters are randomly scattered, is not a unique skill,[259] but it is exceedingly rare. It is also a skill which no one has ever demonstrated sans the claim of spirit involvement. Yet, Anna demonstrated a number of other astounding abilities. All of which, by the way, were accomplished while the girl was wide awake and perfectly lucid.[260] Among these other transcendent talents were:

---

[259] For other examples, see Top-40 cases #40 and #49 in the Honorable Mentions section of www.SurvivalTop40.com.

[260] Westwood insisted that Anna always be a willing and aware participant. He allowed no hypnotism and vowed to stop the experiments if Anna showed any indication of being in a trance.

- A great improvement in her ability to play chess. Under normal conditions, Anna was no match for Westwood, who had taught her the game; but when she allowed the spirit of Ralph to take control, she always challenged her father and usually beat him. She did not win every time because Westwood was pretty good and Ralph made no claim to be a master of the game. But Ralph played with equal skill and moved the pieces with equal deftness when Anna was blindfolded.
- An even greater improvement in her ability to play the piano. Although most every child of that era and social status had some training in tickling the ivories, Anna's skill was no more than average for her age. When the spirit of Kate took control, the difference was astounding ... despite Anna being blindfolded.

"As long as I live I shall never forget that night," Westwood recalls. "She began with a slow melody, the like of which I had never heard before, for it was solemn in its majesty and almost unearthly in its beauty. As I watched the child play, the bodily action and the finger technique were entirely different from Anna's own. Moreover, I had this strange reaction — a feeling that the instrument was incapable of expressing what the player wished to play. As though reading my thoughts, the alleged Kate (through Anna) took pencil and paper and began to write with rapidity. The purport of the message was to the effect that "their" scale structure was different from our own, allowing for greater variety in tonal expression, hence the inadequacy of the instrument in its power of expression."[261]

- An entirely new ability to operate a typewriter. Prior to the arrival of the spectral stenographers, Anna had never touched a typewriter. Under their influence, her small fingers flew over the keys with professional speed and accuracy. A good typist, of course, never looks at the keys; Anna didn't either — she couldn't see

---

[261] Westwood, p. 49.

through her blindfold. Neither could she see the notes that Westwood would type on the paper in the machine; notes that the spirits would answer quickly and intelligently.

Occasionally, Westwood would engage his young typist in conversation about other matters, but this had no effect on the typed responses. When she wasn't blindfolded, Anna would sometimes turn to her father and express her disagreement with the ideas that her fingers were busily putting on the paper.

- An unparalleled control of her neuro-muscular system. One evening, Westwood relates: "Ralph proposed that we take a rook and balance on the top of it a small celluloid ping-pong ball. Having done this, each of us, using a long briar tobacco pipe (the Chesterfield type) as a golf club, was instructed to hit the ball without knocking down the rook, and to try to aim the ball at a given object. We each tried and we had lots of fun. It was a task requiring the greatest delicacy in co-ordination and skill. Not once did any of us succeed. Usually, we knocked down the rook with the ball. Where we succeeded in hitting the ball without knocking down the rook, it went wild and we missed our object. Even Anna tried, with like results. (If the reader wants to know how hard it is, try it!) Evidently sure that we recognized our incompetence, Ralph wrote that if we would blindfold Anna, he would try. Through Anna, he assumed a stance, then swinging the pipe as a club, he struck. He did not miss, the rook did not fall and the ball flew with precise aim and hit the object. We set ourselves up as targets around the room, and, one by one, he caused the ball to hit us all."[262]

- The ability to read at a distance. Without seeing the title, Westwood randomly took a book from its shelf in one room and laid it open

---

[262] Westwood, p. 40.

to an unseen page on a table in another room. Anna, sitting blindfolded in an adjoining room then correctly wrote the page number and opening lines of the first paragraph on the right-hand page.

- The ability to do outlandish things. The spirit known as Blue Hide brought with him the deep and detailed knowledge of woodland lore that one might expect from a Chippewa Indian. When he was in control, Anna could converse as an equal with the most seasoned guide or hunter. She could also do things she had never before seen done, things that she would otherwise find frightening or repulsive, such as quickly and expertly skinning a woodchuck and curing its hide, or killing a rattlesnake and making a totem from its carcass.

Anna's amazing abilities began with the arrival of Ruth and Ralph and ended with the departure of Blue Hide some half-dozen years later. Although never intrusive or demanding, the spirits came and went on their own schedule. With the going of the Chippewa, all unusual phenomena ceased in the Westwood household.

An inordinate amount of psychokinetic events seem to revolve around pubescent girls, so Anna's age and gender may have been favorable to the spirits working through her. Nevertheless, the suddenly demonstrated skills at chess, piano playing, typing, seeing while blindfolded, clairvoyance, animal gutting, and "ping-pong golfing" are so far beyond typical poltergeist activity that they argue strongly for the actual involvement of spirit entities.

More Confirmation

William Stoney, M.S., a retired aerospace engineer, recently submitted written testimony that he interviewed Westwood's son in the early 1970s while the son was serving as a minister in the First Unitarian Church in Houston, Texas. The son, Horace Westwood, D.D., confirmed the accuracy of his father's book, noting that he was 8 to 10 years of age when he witnessed his sister perform the events described above. Stoney later interviewed another of Westwood's sons, also a Unitarian minister, who had been too young to remember his sister's mediumship but was well aware of all of it from having his father live with him for several years. He was so confident in its accuracy that he arranged a reprinting of *There Is a Psychic World* to make it available to his congregation.

Chapter Four — Case 76
The Spirits Seller's Spirit

Folks in southeastern USA would make it from corn and call it "white lightning," but in the island nation of Sri Lanka, they make it from the sap of coconut trees and call it "arrack." Sammy Fernando was a skilled maker of arrack. Folks all up and down the river would buy the strong spirit he distilled at his jungle hideout. Unfortunately for Sammy, he often partook rather freely of his own product and so he was drunk when he stepped from the store, where he had just bought some cheap cigars, and was run over by a speeding truck.

Sammy's funeral was exceptionally well attended, not so much by his many distraught customers, but because he was known as a generous man who gave freely to those in need.

Sammy's death by lorry (a term for truck that the Sinhalese [Sri Lankans] picked up from the British) happened in January of 1969, in the town of Gorakana. Seven months later and about 5½ miles away, in Mt. Lavinia — a suburb of Sri Lanka's capital — the family of Ulysses and Nadine Jay[263] welcomed a new addition whom they named Lucas. And only 8 months after that, Nadine noticed something she thought was most strange. At a time when Lucas was being obstinate about taking his milk, in the midst of a conversation she happened to say the word "lorry," whereupon the babe immediately began to suckle. It didn't take the mother long to discover that her new child's cooperation could be almost magically obtained by simply uttering that normally innocuous word. Clearly, but mysteriously, baby Lucas was really afraid of trucks.

---

[263] As with other case write-ups in this series, some names have been "translated" into English-sounding equivalents for ease of comprehension by Western readers.

At that time, the Jay's had no thoughts of reincarnation; but some 10 months later, Lucas started talking about a previous life. His name, he said, was "Gorakana Sammy." He clamored to be given cigarettes and arrack and to be taken to Gorakana. His parents, naturally, declined to supply booze and smokes, and resisted the trip to a town where they knew no one.

So far, the tale of Lucas and Sammy may seem typical of child-recall cases, but it has two features that make it quite special. One is that the number of confirmed facts and recognitions is exceptionally large (see the list below) as is the number of people interviewed by the research team (more than 35). The other special feature is that 16 of Lucas' statements were written down by an unimpeachable witness prior to any contact with the Fernandos. The witness was a Buddhist monk who resided at a temple near Mt. Lavinia. He not only recorded the statements but he followed up by going to Gorakana and verifying each of them, again, before anyone who knew the Fernando family had become aware of Lucas' claims.

[Note: Buddhism teaches that a soul enters its new body at the moment of conception. The overlapping dates of Sammy's death and Lucas' apparent conception did not, however, deter the monk from objectively researching the case.]

This is one of the thousands of cases carefully investigated by Dr. Ian Stevenson and company from the University of Virginia. The case is presented in great detail one of Stevenson's books.[264] Included is a table cataloging 40 separate statements and 19 recognitions made by Lucas concerning the life and family of Sammy Fernando. The more significant and telling statements/actions are given here:

[A line beneath the word "confirmation" indicates that the statement was recorded and verified by the Buddhist monk when Lucas was 18 months old.]

Lucas' Statement: His name was Sammy and he lived in Gorakana.

---

[264] Stevenson, *Sri Lanka*, pp. 235-280.

Confirmation/Fact: There had been a man named B. Selvin Fernando who lived in Gorakana since his birth in 1919. He was generally called Sammy and sometimes referred to himself as "Gorakana Sammy."

Lucas' Statement: His father was named Jamis.

Confirmation/Fact: Sammy Fernando's father was named B. Jamis Fernando. [Note: in Sri Lanka, first initials generally connote a family relationship rather than a given name.]

Lucas' Statement: When he mentioned his father, Lucas would cover his right eye.

Confirmation/Fact: Jamis' only had one functioning eye, his left.

Lucas' Statement: He used to travel by bus and train. This was indicated via sounds and motions.

Confirmation/Fact: Sammy used to take a bus to get to his job on the railroads.

Lucas' Statement: He had attended the "dilapidated school."

Confirmation/Fact: The school Sammy had attended was known literally as "the dilapidated school" as it was in serious need of repairs.

Lucas' Statement: At school, he had a teacher named Francis.

Confirmation/Fact: Sammy's widow remembered that he had had a teacher named Francis.

Lucas' Statement: He had a niece named Kusuma to whom he gave money and who would cook noodles for him.

Confirmation/Fact: Sammy's sister's daughter was named Kusuma. She told researchers that Sammy had sometimes given her money and that she used to prepare one of his favorite noodle dishes.

Lucas' Statement: Lucas asked his grandmother to give him money so that he and Kusuma could put it in the alms box at Kale Pansala.

Confirmation/Fact: There is a Buddhist temple near Gorakana where Sammy used to spend a lot of time as a child. To this day, some old-timers still call it by the name Kale Pansala, although its name officially changed about a decade before Sammy's birth.

Lucas' Statement: There were two monks at the "Kale Pansala" temple, one of whom was named Amitha.

Confirmation/Fact: True, at the time of Sammy's death.

Lucas' Statement: He had a wife named Maggie and a daughter, Susan.

Confirmation/Fact: Sammy's wife, Maggilin Awis, was usually called Maggie. Susan was his daughter.

Lucas' Statement: Lucas sometimes asked those going to the store to buy him some Four Aces cigarettes. No one in his family smoked.

Confirmation/Fact: Sammy's favorite brands of cigarettes were Three Roses and Four Aces.

Lucas' Statement: He used a boat to transport the arrack he distilled. Once the boat overturned and all the arrack was lost.

Confirmation/Fact: The boat dock was behind Sammy's house. The liquor-loss incident occurred about 8 years prior to his death.

Lucas' Statement: He had been drunk and quarreled with his wife and was following her down the road when he stopped to buy smokes. As he left the store he was hit by a lorry and died immediately. Lucas would lie down and demonstrate the position of Sammy's body on the road.

Confirmation/Fact: All true, except that Sammy was not pronounced dead until a couple of hours after he was taken to a hospital.

The discrepancy in this last item is suggestive of an NDE, in which Sammy's spirit exited his body and observed it lying on the road and then departed for other realms, leaving his physical body to struggle on for a few more hours.

Lucas' actions were in tune with his verified statements. He often asked — and sometimes demanded — to be taken to Gorakana. Once, when he was asked why he was waving at cars on the road, he said he was getting a taxi to take him there.

He would often ask for arrack or pretend to be drinking it and then stagger around as if drunk. When Lucas was visited by Sammy's friends, he seem to know which had been drinking buddies and he would suggest that they drink together. Stevenson (who was a psychiatrist) comments, "I doubt if any child has shown as vividly as [Lucas] has the several types of behavior that characterize the conduct of alcoholics." Lucas also asked to be served the hot, spicy foods that were a favorite of Sammy in particular and arrack drinkers in general. His family, which did not drink arrack, occasionally ate spicy foods but wisely refrained from giving any to a small child.

Lucas asked for a sarong and, although he was really too young, he was allowed to wear one at times. He would tie the knot with a flap protruding which, he explained, was for holding his money. No one else in his family did likewise — but Sammy Fernando did.

Chapter Five — Case 68
The Unforgotten Coin

"I confess that some of these experiences are so startling that if they had not come within my own vision and hearing, being myself fully acquainted with the details of the test conditions imposed, I should be strongly attempted to doubt them." So wrote Dr. Isaac K. Funk in the preface of his 1904 book, *The Widow's Mite and Other Psychic Phenomena*, published by his company, Funk & Wagnalls, which is known for producing *The Standard Dictionary*.

Sometime during 1894, Funk borrowed a valuable Roman coin known as the "Widow's Mite"[265] from Professor Charles E. West, the principal of a school for ladies in Brooklyn Heights, New York, to illustrate it in his dictionary. Some years earlier, Henry Ward Beecher, a mutual friend, had told Funk about the ancient coin and introduced him to professor West.

Funk gave the coin to his brother, Benjamin, the company's business manager, and asked him to return it to West after the photographic plate was made. Benjamin then gave the coin, along with another coin, both in a sealed envelope, to H. L. Raymond, head cashier of the company. Both Funk and his brother believed that Raymond had returned the coin to West as instructed.

Nearly 10 years later, Funk attended a few séances that was held weekly by an amateur, direct-voice medium. In attendance were some of her family and close friends. As a guest of the private circle, Funk did not

---

[265] "Mite" is the English term for the Greek "lepton" which means "small." The mite referred to here was a Judean coin worth two of the smallest Roman coins during the time of Jesus. According to the book of Mark, one of Jesus' parables concerned the relative value of a widow's donation of two mites as compared to the larger sums given by the rich.

feel he could impose test conditions upon the medium. "It was all 'upon honor,'" he wrote. "After considerable investigation, however, and fuller acquaintance with the family, I am morally certain that this confidence in the integrity of the medium and family … was not misplaced."[266]

On Funk's third visit to the circle, a spirit guide named George spoke up in "his usual strong masculine voice" and said: "Has any one here got anything that belonged to Mr. Beecher?" There was no reply, but Funk, having known Beecher, who had died several years earlier, asked for clarification. George bellowed: "… I am told by John Rakestraw, that Mr. Beecher, who is not present, is concerned about an ancient coin, the 'Widow's Mite.' This coin is out of its place and should be returned. It has long been away, and Mr. Beecher wishes it returned, and he looks to you, doctor, to return it."

Funk recalled borrowing the coin, but told George that it had been promptly returned. "This one has not been returned," George replied. Funk pressed for more information. "I don't know where it is," George replied. "I am simply impressed that it is in a large iron safe in a drawer under a lot of papers and has been lost sight of for years, and that you can find it, and Mr. Beecher wishes you to find it."

At his office the next day, Funk questioned his brother about the coin. Benjamin said that he was sure he had returned it to the owner some years back. Funk then questioned, Raymond, the head cashier, who also said it had been returned to the owner. Funk then directed Raymond to go to both of the company's iron safes and search for it. About 20 minutes later, Raymond returned with an envelope holding two widow's mites – one very dark and one light. He explained that it was found in a little drawer in the safe under a lot of papers.

Upon examining the two coins, Funk concluded that the lighter one was the genuine widow's mite. It was the one displayed in the dictionary.

---

[266] Dr. James H. Hyslop, a professor of logic and ethics at Columbia University accompanied Funk to one sitting with the Brooklyn medium and agreed with him that she was genuine.

On the following Wednesday, Funk attended the Brooklyn circle. Toward the end of the session, George began talking and Funk informed him that he had found the widow's mite, in fact, had found two of them. He asked George if he knew which was the genuine coin. "The black one," George replied without hesitation. Later, Funk checked with the Philadelphia mint and found that George was right and he was wrong. In fact, they had used the wrong coin in the dictionary illustration. The light one was simply a replica.

As a test, Funk then asked George if he knew from whom he had borrowed the coin. George responded that it was Mr. Beecher's friend, but he could not give a name. George reported, however, that he was being shown a picture of a college, which he identified as a lady's college in Brooklyn Heights. Funk also asked George to whom the coin should be returned. "I can not tell you; I do not know; for some reason Mr. Beecher does not tell," George said.

At a séance with another medium the following week, Funk heard from Beecher through the medium's spirit control. "I was told by the control that Mr. Beecher said that he was not concerned about the return of the coin. What he was concerned about was to give me a test that would prove the certainty of communication between the two worlds, and since that has been accomplished in my finding the coin, he cared nothing further about it."

Discussion

The strength of this case lies in the reputations of its reporter and the researchers involved and in the revelation of facts not known to anyone involved in the sittings, not consciously known by anyone living, and in contradiction to everyone's expectations. The initiator's concern with proving the communication from spirit but not caring about the actual disposition of the coin, is both fitting and inexplicable by any other reasonable scenario.

Chapter Six — Case 78
Coming Back Down Under

While under hypnosis in Sydney, Australia, Helen Pickering recalled a past life as a male doctor in Scotland during the early 19th century. She recalled having studied at the University of Aberdeen and practicing medicine in the small Scottish town of Blairgowrie.

Helen also recalled drinking in a bar in the Seaman's Mission in Aberdeen as a young man, and described the sights from the dormitories that overlooked the bay from the medical school. She recalled the layout of the medical school, as well as the town of Blairgowrie. She also recalled being an important person in civic affairs, being involved with the town council. Her/his name was Dr. James Burns.

These hypnotic sessions were part of a series of experiments by hypnotist Peter Ramster designed to explore the possibility of gaining solid evidence for reincarnation. A film about these experiments was produced, much of which can be seen in segments on YouTube. The following section is taken almost verbatim from Ramster's write up of the case, which he titled, "The Recall of Helen Pickering."[267]

Once I had an understanding of everything she recalled, Helen was taken to Scotland, to Blairgowrie.

Everything was filmed as it happened. She was blindfolded on the way there so she could gain no clues as to where she was. She was taken to a point just outside the town where the blindfold was taken off. At first she was confused. In Australia she had spoken of a grassy square in the middle of town around which the road ran on both sides. This was not

---

[267] Taken, with Ramster's permission, from the website http://www.aramai-global.org. I have made minor edits and shortened it somewhat.

visible from where we stopped. Helen walked to the end of the road and turned right into another road that led onto a bridge over a stream. This led into the town centre. She began to walk across the bridge, and as she walked, the grassy square came into sight.

It was the spark of recognition she needed. There was a sudden change in her demeanour. To that point she had been hesitant, unsure of her surroundings. Suddenly, she knew where she was and recognised what was ahead. It was exactly as she had described to me when under hypnosis in Sydney. Upon reaching the square she realised the town was just as she remembered it to be, though she had never been to Scotland before in this life. She was able to recognise the changes made since the time she recalled living there.

Dr. James Burns had been an important person of the town. He had been involved in civic affairs as well as the town council. Naturally we looked for evidence of his existence and to confirm the reality of his profession. For a start, we decided to look at the town's archived records that went back hundreds of years. The records uncovered more than we had expected.

James Burns was indeed mentioned, and he was indeed involved in civic affairs. When looking for reminders of Dr. James Burns we found them in the former minute books of the council. We even found James Burn's signature. Under hypnosis in Australia, Helen had recalled that Dr. James Burns was a Justice of the Peace. James Burn's signature written in the old books, confirmed this.

Under hypnosis Helen recalled attending medical school from the early 1830s. She recalled in detail the layout of the school as well as its other features, such as the library, lecture halls, staircases and so on, as well as the dormitories on the upper floor. She recalled the school had a U shape at the front, and at the back went out in a T shape. She recalled the chapel and other features, as well as the view from the cloisters of the old building.

We took Helen to Aberdeen to a point near the old wharves and took the blindfold off. Again we had tried to ensure that Helen gained no clues as to where she was from modern roadsigns or other modern pointers. She was left for a moment to try to get her bearings. After a short interlude, she pointed down the road to the direction she wished to go, so we again began to move forward; a few of us at the front, with the film crew filming from every vantage point. We had gained the assistance of independent witnesses: someone at the local university, and a person from a local radio station.

After walking a short distance from the place we had begun, Helen pointed out where the seaman's mission had stood. The people who were acting as witnesses had no idea as to whether it was true or not. Enquiries by our team showed it to be true. A lady from Sydney, Australia, had known something about Aberdeen that even people who lived there didn't know.

We took Helen to a place near where the old medical school once stood. Leading the way she then entered into the grounds of an old building. We all walked into the car park [parking lot]. The building stretched across in front of us but also wrapped along the sides of us as well. It came out from the front in a U shape. This was exactly as Helen had described the old medical school when under hypnosis in Sydney.

There were some differences today. The grass had gone and been replaced by bitumen. The entrance was a bit more grand. Tentatively, Helen walked towards the front of the building. It was still a part of Aberdeen university. Once past the doors and inside, the familiarity overtook Helen. She stood silent for a moment and looked upwards into the building, surveying the staircase that lay in front of her. She looked white, as if she had seen a ghost. She had been unprepared for the familiarity. Tentatively she began to ascend the stairs. She was visibly moved by what she saw. At the top of the stairs she reminded me of her words in Sydney, when she told me that you were able to look out over the first floor balcony to the entrance below. She was correct. We walked past what she recalled was the library. It was not a library at the time we were there, but it was during the time of James Burns. Helen led us along hallways and into places that she recalled. She identified where a staircase once stood, then she led us out the back of the building to confirm it went out in a T shape as she recalled. Sure enough, the T shape was there. It had been a medical school and Helen's recall was correct. Some features she recalled were very specific, and we could see once we visited the place that the important features she had recalled were there. The building did go out in a T shape at the back and had a U shape at the front. Inside the building was similar as well. Helen had also drawn a drawing of the old school as she remembered it, before we left, so one could see the similarities and some of the differences.

We found a man who had studied and written a paper on the old college of medicine as it was in the time of James Burns. He was able to confirm that Helen was correct in her memory of the details of the building, including the position of a staircase that she noticed was missing today. The building today is not as it was. Helen was able to confirm her knowledge through his expertise on the old building. He also tested her for her knowledge. There was no logical reason for Helen to have known what she knew, except for the explanation of reincarnation and a memory coming from that time. It was not the present building that Helen recalled, but the original building before it was altered, the building that stood in the early 19th century that had long since been changed.

Every piece of her findings was filmed and recorded as it happened, including the discussion with the expert. Helen's recollections initially came only with hypnosis. Her findings proved the reality of those recollections, from the details of the old medical school, to aspects of Aberdeen, to details of the town of Blairgowrie. Even the records of James Burns, a man important in Blairgowrie's civic affairs at the time, was found.

Discussion

The most evidential parts of this case are Pickering's knowledge of:
- Burn's occupation as a medical doctor

- his involvement in civic affairs
- his role as a justice of the peace
- the prior location of a seaman's mission building
- the position of a staircase in a medical-school building that had since been torn down

Any explanation other than reincarnation would require Pickering to possess unheard-of skills at clairvoyantly examining numerous old documents residing in a foreign land. And even that probably could not explain her knowledge of the mission's prior location.

Chapter Seven — Case 56
Soule Proves the Soul

Dr. James Hyslop, professor of Logic and Ethics at Columbia University, and one of the most distinguished American psychical researchers, reported the following incident.[268]

Hyslop received a letter from a woman in Germany, a stranger to him, asking for the name of a medium near her, as she wished to confirm that her recently deceased husband's spirit lived on. Hyslop responded that he was not familiar with the mediums in Germany, but if she would come to America he would arrange for sittings with someone he trusted. The widow replied that she could not make the trip, but she suggested that a sister of hers (whose name was different from her own) lived in Boston and might take her place at a sitting.

Accordingly, Hyslop arranged for the sister to have a few sittings with Minnie Soule,[269] a medium who was working with the American Society for Psychical Research. He took the safeguards of not telling the sister the name or location of the medium, not telling the medium any information about the sitter, and being sure that Soule was in trance before the sister entered the room. Because of these precautions, Hyslop was satisfied that the medium did not even know whether her visitor was a man or a woman.

Automatic writing by Soule's hand began almost immediately and indicated that a man was present who was anxious to make his existence known to his wife. Throughout the sittings (spread over a period of 36

---

[268] Barrett, *Threshold*, pp. 225 229.
[269] Then known by the pseudonym "Mrs. Chenoweth."

hours) numerous statements identifying the husband came through, including these:

- He was a philosopher.
- He was a friend of the late Professor William James of Harvard.
- He was greatly impressed by some documents which James had lent to him.
- His mother was dead.
- He had a missing tooth at a particular location.
- He was fond of fixing things, especially clocks.
- He liked to annotate his books.
- He used to carry a small bag containing his manuscripts and reading glass.
- He had taken a long railway journey shortly before his death.
- He had died with an intense pain in his head.
- He was mentally confused when he died.
- He was at home, but felt away from home when he died.

In attempting to give his name, the spirit first wrote the letter "T" then the letter "h." Later, he wrote "Taussh," "Tauch," and "Taush"; all of which are phonetically close to the actual name of the widow: "Tausch."

Hyslop tried addressing the communicator in German (a language unfamiliar to Soule) and got replies in German, among them that the visitor was his "Geschwister,"[270] which was correct.

Hyslop knew the name of the deceased husband but none of the other details. The sister would also have know the man's name, of course, and may have been acquainted with a few of the facts such as he being a philosopher and that his mother had died. Nevertheless, she claimed total ignorance of the various incidents (such as the train trip and the James papers) related by the spirit.

In response to Hyslop's written queries, Tausch's widow confirmed every statement to be accurate. Even the rather confusing final one was

---

[270] Literally: "brothers and sisters."

correct, she said, as Tausch had died in his old home in Germany and not in his preferred home in America.

Discussion

In addition to the 100 percent accuracy, three items are especially evidential. First is the reference made to documents loaned by Professor William James. Only one person alive knew about these documents. It stretches the idea of mental telepathy far beyond the breaking point for a psychic to read the mind of a sitter (whom she never even saw) well enough to link to the mind of the sitter's sister, an ocean away, and then pull out an obscure reference to that person's husband being impressed with some documents.

Secondly, it is noteworthy that the medium could not get the name quite right, even though Dr. Hyslop, who held the spelling of the name in his conscious mind, was right there in the room with her.

The most telling evidence is the conversation in German, despite the medium not knowing that language. As has been pointed out often in these case descriptions, no one has ever demonstrated the ability to acquire a skill via telepathy. And, it takes two to have a conversation. If we accept the presence of Mr. Tausch as a spirit communicator fluent in both English and German, than a conversation between he and the English- and German-speaking Hyslop is understandable. If such a spirit presence is denied, however, then we are faced with the question of how Ms. Soule could formulate a response she cannot comprehend to a question she cannot comprehend. Clearly, she would require the assistance of some other mind that is capable of reading the query (in German) from Ms. Soule's mind and then sending a proper and relevant response back to Ms. Soule. So, we would need not one, but two super-psychics, one of whom was performing as a perfect and immediate translating machine. This seems far more incredible than any theory of Survival.

As Sir William Barrett concluded in his review of the case: "The simplest and most reasonable solution is that the information was derived from the mind of the deceased person."[271]

---

[271] Barrett, *Threshold*, p. 229.

Chapter Eight — Case 72
Having a Friend[272]

When Mariana Waters[273] was young, she boarded for several years at a Catholic school in Brazil. Up until her second year of high school, she was a joyful, self-confident girl, enthusiastically committed to her studies and involved in various extracurricular activities. As often happens with the young, however, the new school year brought increased introspection, uncertainty, and an unaccountable malaise. Her feelings seemed more intense whenever she encountered Father Jonathan, the new priest at the school. This priest wasn't nearly as good looking or aristocratic as the one he replaced, but something about him stirred Mariana's soul. When he first spoke to her, asking a perfectly innocent question about their schedule, Mariana recalls, "For no reason at all, I started to tremble … My hands shook and my heart beat wildly." As time went by, Father Jonathan seemed more and more to go out of his way to speak with Mariana, although he did not seem to notice the effect his presence was having on her, at least not at first.

Now, this is not a tale of clerical wrong-doing, pubescent lust, or even unrequited romance. But over the ensuing year, the girl and the priest talked with greater frequency and confided ever more personal thoughts and feelings, forming a closer friendship than one might expect possible, given their limited free time and the constant scrutiny of the nuns. Most critically to this case, on the day that they first verbalized their friendship, Mariana told him that she would ever after refer to him as "Alexandre."

---

[272] Andrade.
[273] As with the original document, the names used here are pseudonyms to protect the privacy of the people involved and for ease of comprehension by English-speaking readers.

Mariana's senior year portended even greater intimacy, but it was not to be. The school decided to close its boarding program and Mariana's home was beyond commuting distance. Her personal contact with Father Jonathan was over, although he did write to her occasionally, the last time being in July of 1970. She did not respond to those missives.

Mariana's contact with the priest was renewed in the most extremely personal way possible. The evidence we have strongly suggests that, nearly eight years after she last saw him, she gave birth to him.

This evidence comes to us through the efforts of the Brazilian Institute for Psychobiological Research, and its president, H.G. Andrade. In 1990, the Institute received a letter from Mr. Luiz Brasil, an independent researcher, that mentioned a young boy who was claiming to have died in 1972. This sort of letter was not uncommon; the Institute receives lots of letters each year relating fantastic, unsupported, and generally dubious tales of paranormal phenomena. Typically, the follow-up questionnaires and instructions they send back do not elicit any response. (Apparently most informants don't actually wish to take the time or make the effort to perform any useful investigation.) Brasil's response was dramatically different from the norm. Its concise yet thorough account of the full details of the case prompted Andrade and company to initiate an investigation that involved numerous interviews of the parties involved.

These are the facts they discovered.

- After her boarding school, Mariana Waters continued her education through college, where she earned a degree in teaching.
- She married in 1971 and had her first child a year later. In total, she had six children, two sons and four daughters.
- On the night of May 31, 1972, she experienced a strong sense of Father Jonathan's presence and, after falling asleep, she dreamed of the priest standing on the far side of a field of lilies. They reached out to each other, but could not quite touch. The next day, Mariana's husband heard on the radio the news that Father Jonathan had just died from injuries received in a car accident.

Eight years later, after having two daughters, Mariana gave birth to her second son, whom she named Kilden Alexandre. There is no indication whether or not the boy's middle name was a conscious echo of the name she had previously bestowed upon her clerical confidant.

Although Kilden was a quiet baby who slept well, soon after his arrival the family heard inexplicable knocking and banging sounds from various rooms and objects in the house.

When, around the age of two, Kilden began to talk, he would sometimes respond to his name by shouting, "I am not Kilden, I am Alexandre!" His parents simply assumed that the toddler preferred his middle name to his first.

Then, he began to claim, "I am not Kilden, you silly! I am the priest! I am Alexandre!" To which his parents would reply, "Oh! So you want to be a priest?" and Kilden would shout, "No! I'm not going to be a priest! I am the priest!"

Despite such adamant claims, neither Mariana nor her husband considered the possibility of something as foreign to their religion as reincarnation. Not then, anyway.

Early in 1983, Mariana was dressing Kilden when she playfully asked him, "Where did mommy find this little sweetie?" This was a game she often played with her children and generally elicited a response about being fetched from the hospital. This time, however, Kilden quite seriously said: "You know! I was on a motorcycle. Then a truck came and hit the motorcycle. It fell over, and I hit my head on the ground, and I died, and went down there. And you got another me." "When did this happen?" Mariana asked. "When I was a priest!"

This event prompted Mariana to confer with some friends who were Spiritists[274] and she soon began to consider reincarnation as a real possibility. She even wondered if the soul of Father Jonathan might feel jealous of, or competitive with, her husband and cause trouble in their household.

---

[274] Spiritism is a religion akin to Spiritualism, except for its emphasis on reincarnation.

A few years later, she was moving some papers when a postcard with a picture of her old boarding school fell out of the stack and onto the floor. Kilden picked it up and, pointing to the building where the priest lived, said to his brother, "Look! This is where I lived." Then, pointing to the building where Mariana had boarded, he said, "And that's where mommy lived down there."

Mariana then asked Kilden what he used to do there. "I played soccer with all the boys, you silly! You ought to know!" Which, in fact, was a favorite pastime of Father Jonathan.

As Kilden grew older, his memories of being Father Jonathan faded, yet his personality and his likes and dislikes reflected the priest's in an impressive number of ways. These included: a habit of speaking in rhymes; a penchant for practical jokes that sometimes go too far; an almost fanatical love of soccer; and an extreme like, almost a worshiping, of the saint John Bosco.

Once, when he was twelve, Kilden made a point of how much he hated the name of a particular girl, even though he liked the girl. That name, his mother remembered, was the name of a girl in her school who was especially naughty and used to laugh at the priest.

Another time, his father brought home some fruit[275] that was native to the area of the boarding school but was not known in any area where Kilden had been raised. Nevertheless, Kilden said that he remembered eating such a fruit "a long time ago."

Of all these facts, the one that stands out as most convincing is 2-year-old Kilden's statement that, as the priest, he had been killed when a truck hit his motorcycle. This is because the radio announcement of Father Jonathan's death had clearly stated the cause as a car accident. It was not until several years later that Mariana found out that Father Jonathan was on his way to City Hall when a truck hit his motorcycle and caused his death.

---

[275] This apparently was some Eugenia (*Eugenia uniflora*) a.k.a. Brazilian cherry.

Chapter Nine — Case 30
The A.B.C. Séances[276]

Most men of integrity would be more than a bit suspicious if they received a letter asking them to adopt a false name and travel to a strange city for an unknown purpose; but for George W. Clawson of Kansas City, Missouri, such mysterious letters were intriguing signals that a new adventure was afoot. In this case, the sender of the letter was Clawson's friend, David Abbott from nearby Omaha, Nebraska. Abbott was a professional magician who had spent much of his life studying the tricks of fraudulent mediums. He and Clawson often served as investigators for the American Society of Psychical Research.

Abbott had been hearing a lot of incredible stories about a medium named Elizabeth Blake. These stories told of a woman of humble means, mother of 15 children, who had never been more than 20 miles from her Ohio farm. This farm was near Bradrick, a village so out-of-the-way that it could only be reached by a ferry that occasionally crossed the river from West Virginia. Although she was a marvel to her neighbors, Blake was hardly famous; she had been contacting the deceased for nearly 50 years before the magician caught wind of her.

In an article published in a Chicago magazine[277] in 1906, Abbott tells of his decision to "make an investigation on such lines as would entirely remove the possibility of any kind of trickery being employed." Because of this determination, Abbott went to unusual lengths to make certain that Elizabeth Blake could not obtain information by any normal means. There was no one in the area whom Abbott had met and only one person with whom he had corresponded to set up the visit. That man, Abbott says,

---

[276] Funk, pp. 158-165.
[277] *The Progressive Thinker*, September 26, 1906, Chicago, Illinois.

"merely knew my name and residence. He knew nothing of any of my relatives, nor of the towns where they resided." Nevertheless, to be doubly certain that no research could provide the medium with information, the magician asked George Clawson to accompany him.

Clawson was entirely unknown in the region, but Abbott took still more precautions. To begin with, he did not tell Clawson where they were going or whom they were going to investigate. He picked up Clawson on his way through Kansas City and did not mention Elizabeth Blake or the village of Bradrick until they had arrived at the town of Huntington, West Virginia, where the ferry crossed the Ohio River.[278] Furthermore, Clawson traveled under an assumed name and, when they reached their lodgings, Clawson registered under that name.

In short, it was extremely unlikely that anyone in the village knew any details about Abbott, and it was out-and-out impossible for anything at all to be known of Clawson.

When they arrived at the farmhouse in Bradrick, they found Blake "sitting by her window in a willow rocker with her crutches by her side." She had recently been quite ill and so hesitated to give the men sittings because of her feeble condition. But she relented and gave a total of four sessions, the first three in her home and the final one in an office in Huntington where a photograph was taken.

Blake was a "direct-voice" medium, meaning that the spirits seemed able to produce the sound of human voices without utilizing her vocal cords or tongue. Like many such mediums, she used a trumpet,[279] one end of which Abbott or Clawson would put to his ear, and the other end Blake would hold — sometimes in her hand, sometimes to her own ear. Unlike the typical direct-voice medium, however, Elizabeth Blake did not require absolute darkness to accomplish these spirited conversations. In fact, she

---

[278] Nowadays there is a bridge connecting nearby Proctorville, Ohio, with Huntington, West Virginia.
[279] A tube, generally of metal, in the approximate shape of a narrow, cheerleader's megaphone.

worked in normal room light, under the watchful eyes of both investigators.

The voices that seemed to emanate from this trumpet were neither whispers, nor mumbles, nor squeaks. They were generally clear and frequently loud enough to be heard a hundred feet away.

Abbott describes one of the séances thus:

"I took the trumpet, but as the words sounded weak, I surrendered it to Mr. Clawson. Instantly the voice began loud and strong, so that I could easily distinguish the words where I sat. Mr. Clawson said, 'Who is this?' The voice replied, 'Grandma Daily.' Mr. Clawson then said, 'How do you do, Grandma? I used to know you, didn't I?' The voice replied, 'How do you do, George? [Note that Clawson had not been using the first name "George."] I want to talk to Davie' [addressing David Abbott]. I spoke from the outside of the trumpet and said, 'I can hear you, Grandma.' I then said to Mr. Clawson, 'Keep your position. I can hear from the outside.' ... After the voice of my grandmother gave a daughter's name, it continued with these words: 'Davie, I want you to be good and pray, and meet me over here.' With the exception of the words, 'over here,' in place of the word 'heaven,' these were the identical words which my grandmother spoke to me the last time I ever heard her voice.

"Mr. Clawson now continued, 'Grandma, tell me the name of Davie's mother.' The voice replied 'Sarah.' He said, 'Yes, but she has another name. What is it?' ... The voice then said, 'Abbott.' 'This is all right,' continued Mr. Clawson, 'but I call her by another name when I speak of her. What is it?' The voice then plainly said, 'Aunt Fannie.' This was correct.

"At this instant the loud voice of a man broke into the conversation. It was low in pitch, was a vocal tone, and had a weird effect. The voice said, 'How do you do?' Mr. Clawson said, 'How do you do, sir; who are you?' The voice replied, 'Grandpa Abbott,' then repeated hurriedly a name that sounded like 'David Abbott,' and then the voice expired with a sound as of some choking or strangling and went off dimly and vanished. My grandfather's name was David Abbott.

"After this Mrs. Blake asked to rest a few moments and turned in her chair so as to use the other ear. ... When Mr. Clawson next took the trumpet the voice of a girl spoke and said, 'Daddy, I am here.' He said, 'Who are you?' The voice replied, 'Georgia,' which was correct. ... 'Where do we live, Georgia?' The voice replied, 'In Kansas City,' which was correct. The voice then continued, 'Daddy, I am so glad to talk to you, and so glad you came here to see me. I wish you could see my beautiful home. We have flowers and music every day.' Mr. Clawson then said, 'Georgia, tell me the name of the young man you were engaged to.' The name pronounced was indistinct, so he asked the voice to spell it. The letters A R C were spelled out and then pronounced 'Ark,' which was correct. The gentleman's first name was Archimedes, and he was called 'Ark.' After this the voice spelled the complete name. Mr. Clawson then said, 'Georgia, where is Ark?' The reply could not be understood. Mr. Clawson then asked, 'Is he in Denver?' A loud 'No! No!' and then the words, 'He is in New York.' I was informed afterward that this was correct.

"The voice then said, 'Daddy, I want to tell you something. Ark is going to marry another girl.' Mr. Clawson said, 'You say he is going to be married?' The voice said, 'Yes, Daddy, but it's all right. I do not care now. Besides, he does not love her as he did me.' I will mention the fact that since our return from West Virginia, Mr. Clawson has received a letter from the gentleman in question, announcing his approaching marriage.

"Mr. Clawson then asked the voice what grandmothers were there, and she replied that Grandmother Daily and Grandmother Abbott were with her. He then said, 'Are these all?' The voice said, 'Do you mean my own grandmother, my mother's mother?' Mr. Clawson replied, 'Yes.' The voice then said, 'Grandma Marcus is here.' This was correct. Mrs. Marquis had died shortly before this, and her grandchildren always pronounced her name as if it were spelled 'Marcus.'

"The reader will please to remember that Mr. Clawson's name had so far been given to no one in that section of the country. That, as no one knew he was to be there, he could not have been looked up, and as he did not himself know where he was going, trickery could absolutely play no part in the names given him. I was present at all sittings, and there was no chance of any error. Yet these names came just as readily for him, and as correctly as they did for me whose name had previously been known to one resident of Huntington.

"At this point the loud voice of a man spoke up and said, 'I am here. I want to talk to Davie.' I took the trumpet and the voice said, 'Davie, do you know me?' I said, 'No, who are you?' The voice replied, 'Grandpa Daily.' The voice then said, 'Tell your mother I talked to you, and tell your father, too.' Mr. Clawson took the trumpet quickly from me, and said, 'Hello, Grandpa, I used to know you, didn't I?' The voice replied, 'Of course you did.' Mr. Clawson (whose name had so far never been given), said, 'Tell me who I am?' The voice replied out loud, distinct, and very quickly, 'I know you well; you are George Clawson.'"

Abbott ends his report by pointing out that, in all, nineteen specific names were given by the medium, each and every one correct! Such accuracy, he asserts is "most marvelous." Regarding Blake herself, Abbott concludes that, "the information which her voices furnished is entirely beyond the possibilities of any system of trickery."

This report of the sessions involving Abbott, Blake, and Clawson (A.B.C.) is more evidential than might at first be surmised. As David Abbott points out, there is no question that the information communicated came from a paranormal source. Nevertheless, most of it, in theory, could have been obtained via a lot of marvelous reading of the sitters' minds. But not all. The fact that the man "Archimedes" (a most uncommon name, even for that time and place) was planning to be married was not in the mind of anyone present. And, since no one knew who Clawson was, there was no conceivable link (astral or otherwise) to follow from him to his deceased daughter and then on to her former fiancé. Finally, the case is strengthened by the humanity demonstrated in the statement: "It's all right. I do not care now. Besides, he does not love her as he did me."

Chapter Ten — Case 74
Guns and Rebirth[280]

When Nathan Albin[281] was 18 months old he began making statements such as:

"I am not small, I am big." and "I am fearless and strong."

Which might not be unusual for a very young boy, but then he would say:

- "I have a lot of weapons."
- "I carry two pistols. I carry four hand-grenades."
- "Don't be scared by the hand-grenades. I know how to handle them."

Then he said his name was actually Frank, that he lived in Quincy, not Bretton, and that he had young children whom he wanted to visit. Over the next few years, Nathan made numerous statements about his life and death as Frank. (See below.)

Although she accepted the possibility that Nathan had lived a previous life, his mother, Nancy, did not encourage him to speak of it because of a similar experience with one of his older sisters. "Life is not easy for such children," she noted. Nathan's father, Samuel, listened to the boy's claims but also tried to resist his persistent pleas to take him to his "home," even when Nathan threatened to walk there by himself. But, after 4 years of nagging, his parents gave in and the family drove to the village of Quincy, about 10½ miles away. Nathan had never been there before, Samuel had passed through a few times but knew no one in the town.

---

[280] Haraldsson, pp. 363–380.
[281] All names have been changed for readability reasons. See note at the end of "A Country Revival" in Volume II, Chapter 11.

When they arrived at the intersection in Quincy where six roads converge, Nathan pointed out the proper turns to reach Frank's house. As they approached the location, they were forced to stop because a man was washing his car and the runoff water made the steep road too slippery to navigate safely. While the boy and his father went forward on foot, his sisters decided to talk with the car washer. That man turned out to be Carl Carter, son of Frank Carter —a man who perfectly fit the description given by the young Nathan, a man who had died many years previously.

Carl called to his mother, Nadia Carter, who came from working in her garden just as Nathan and his father walked back down the hill. After introductions were made, Nadia tested Nathan by asking, "Who built the foundation of this gate at the entrance of this house?" Nathan correctly said that it was a man named Farkas. At that, the Albins were invited into the Carter's home, whereupon Nathan went to a cupboard, pointed to the right of it and said, "Here I used to put my pistols." Then he indicated the left and said, "Here I used to put the other weapons, where are they?" Nadia admitted that the weapons had been kept there but they had been stolen. Then Nadia asked the boy other questions and he answered each correctly.

Nathan then reminded his (Frank's) wife of several incidents in their life together. He said, "Do you remember when we were going in the car and the car stopped and twice the soldiers fixed it for us?" She did recall a trip in which soldiers had twice changed their car's battery. "One night I came home drunk," Nathan continued, "and you locked the door and I slept outside the house on a rocking sofa." This she also admitted to.

Perhaps one of the most evidential exchanges between Nadia and Nathan concerned one of "their" daughters. She asked if he remembered how their 4-year-old Felicia got seriously sick. Nathan answered: "She was poisoned from my medication and I took her to the hospital." Felicia had, in fact, found some pills in her father's jacket pocket and swallowed them.

Over time Nadia and all five of her (and Frank's) children came to accept that Nathan was the reincarnation of Frank. Not only accept, but the two families visit one another occasionally and have developed "an affectionate relationship."

Shortly after their initial meeting with Mrs. Carter and Carl, the Albin family visited Frank's younger brother Austin Carter at his home in Kendall. Described as a "senior employee of an airline," Austin responded to Nathan's claim of fraternity by asking for proof. Nathan replied that he once gave his brother a handgun as a gift. "What kind of gun?" "I gave you a Checki 16," the boy replied. "Then I hugged him," states Austin, for he was "100-percent sure" that Nathan was his brother reborn. Apparently this certainty eroded somewhat over time for, at a later date, Austin retested Nathan by showing him a different gun and asking if it were the weapon that Frank had given him. Nathan correctly denied it.

Nathan's Knowledge of Frank's Life

Stated Prior to Meeting Frank's Family:
- His name was Frank.
- Directions to reach the house Frank was living in when he died.
- Frank had lived in a villa with two stories and trees around it.
- He had a wife and young children.
- He had a friend who was a mute.
- He had owned a red car.
- He carried guns and hand grenades. [Note: Frank Carter was a manager of a religious center and parttime bodyguard for a religious leader.]
- He was killed by gunfire.

Revealed During Meetings with Frank's Wife and Son:
- The name of the person who had built the foundation of the gate in front of Frank's house.
- In what cupboard Frank had kept his weapons.
- Details of an accident in which Frank's wife had fallen and dislocated her shoulder; including the facts that she had slipped on a piece of plastic while picking pine cones, that her father-in-law

was present at the time, and that Frank had taken her to the doctor after he arrived home from work.
- How Frank's daughter had swallowed some of his medication and become seriously ill.
- How the family's car was started twice by Israeli soldiers while traveling from Beirut.
- How he came home drunk one night and had to sleep on the front porch.
- There was a barrel in the garden they used as a target when Frank was teaching his wife to shoot.

Revealed During Meetings with Frank's Brother, Austin:
- Austin was Frank's brother.
- Frank had given his brother a gift of a Checki-16 handgun.
- The location of Frank's boyhood home.
- The location of Frank's home with his first wife.
- Frank had built a wooden ladder that was still in this original house.
- The woman currently living in this house was Frank's first wife.
- The identity of each of three men in a photograph: Frank and his two brothers.
- Frank's father had been alive when Frank was killed. (But, Nathan did not know that Frank's father had since died.)

Reliability of the Source

While conducting research on claims of past lives, E. Haraldsson, Ph.D., and his interpreter were told by another family of Nathan's story, which had not yet received any public attention. Judging it a worthwhile case, Haraldsson began a most thorough investigation. Overall, his team visited the Albin's home seven times and the Carter family two times between May 2000 and March 2001. With a few exceptions the interviews were conducted in the subject's native language and notes from the interviews were later checked with the interviewees. Each of the nine witnesses to Nathan's original claims (mother, father, and seven siblings) was interviewed individually and asked to only report what he or she had personally heard or seen.

The researchers' report states: "All the major witnesses were interviewed on more than one occasion several months apart. Their testimony was on the whole consistent over time … The witnesses were cooperative. Our impression was that they were honest and open about their observations and did not try to embellish the case." [JSE, p. 365] In addition, they point out that the Carter family was significantly poorer than the Albins, so there was no financial or status motivation for the latter associating themselves with the former. Also noteworthy in this regard is the fact that the researchers had to search out the Albin family, who had made no effort to seek publicity and had not encouraged their young son to speak of a past life.

Chapter Eleven — Case 62
The Picture of Raymond Lodge[282]

In the telling of evidential stories, there is often a direct correlation between the confusing and the convincing. The more witnesses, the more percipients, the more spirits, the more events there are, the stronger the evidence but the harder the explaining. This is why some cases fail to make an impression equivalent to their value. This is why the following case — which involves two spirits, three mediums, six sessions, and an entire family of sitters — is just now being rated, even though I first read the testimony decades ago. I shall attempt to minimize any confusion by relating the pertinent events in strict chronological order.

We begin on the 8th of August, 1915, at a session with the famous trance-medium, Leonora Piper at her home in Greenfield, New Hampshire. A message came through for Sir Oliver Lodge, despite the fact that Lodge was not in attendance at the session; in fact, being at home in England, Lodge was not even on the same continent. The message purported to be relayed from the spirit of Frederic Myers: "Myers says you take the part of the poet and that he will act as Faunus."

Piper had no idea what this statement might mean, and neither did her daughter, who had been taking notes during the session. But, since Myers was one of the founders of the Society for Psychical Research and was known to have been a good friend of Sir Oliver, the message was duly sent on to England.

Lodge had no clue either, but he knew that Myers had been a scholar of Greek and Roman literature, so he inquired among those with expertise

---

[282] Lodge, *Raymond* p. 279.

in the classics. He was told that the message was a reference to a passage by Horace[283] and that it seemed to suggest that Lodge was about to suffer a terrible blow and that Myers would attempt to lighten its impact.

A little over a month after the cryptic message had been transmitted, and only two weeks after it was interpreted, Lodge's youngest son, Raymond, was killed. A Second Lieutenant in the 3rd South Lancashires, he had been in the army for just short of one year when he was struck down by a shell fragment during an assault on a German-held hill in Flanders,[284] on September 14th, 1915.

On September 25th, Sir Oliver's wife anonymously attended a session with Gladys Osborne Leonard, a new but promising medium in London. She was there merely to accompany a grief-stricken friend, but the spirit of her own son came through. He asked his mother to tell his father, "I have met some friends of his." When asked if he could name one, Raymond said, "Yes, Myers."

Lady Lodge informed her husband of this communication and, two days later, he attended a session with Leonard. As with his wife before him, he never identified himself to the medium. Nevertheless, the spirit of Raymond immediately recognized his father and once again mentioned that he was now with Myers. "I feel that I have two fathers now," said Raymond, who had been only twelve when Myers passed over.

Later on the same day, Lady Lodge attended a session with another London medium, Alfred Vout Peters. Once again she came to the medium as an unidentified stranger and, once again, Raymond came through. This time, Raymond spoke of a photograph in which he sat, holding a walking stick, among a group of other men. At the time, the Lodges knew of no such picture.

---

[283] Quintus Horatius Flaccus (65 - 27 B.C.E.), a Roman poet. Reference is from *Carmen Saeculare II*.
[284] In Belgium, near the northern border of France.

Two months later, the mother of a young soldier who had served with Raymond sent the Lodges a letter in which she mentioned a group photograph that had been taken a few weeks prior to Raymond's death. Of course, they immediately thought that this might be the photo that Raymond's spirit had mentioned, so they wrote back and asked for a copy. While waiting for a response, Lodge had another session with Gladys Osborne Leonard. He asked Raymond for more details about this picture. Raymond said that it was taken out-of-doors, and that someone behind him was leaning on him.

When the copy of the photograph arrived, it proved to be exactly as described by the spirits. Raymond is second from the right in a row of men sitting on the ground, his walking stick laid on his crossed ankles. Another row of men sit on a bench behind him with a third row standing in the rear. The officer sitting immediately behind Raymond is resting his right arm on Raymond's left shoulder — the only one to so pose.

As if this wasn't convincing enough, over the ensuing months, Raymond's parents and his siblings (Lionel, Norah, Alec, Honor, and Rosalynde) all participated in one test or another of the medium's abilities and Raymond's authenticity. Sir Oliver concluded: "The number of more or less convincing proofs which we have obtained is by this time very great. Some of them appeal more to one person, some to another; but taking them all together every possible ground of suspicion or doubt seems to the family to be now removed."

Comment

If the original communication from Myers had been a straightforward warning of Raymond's impending death, Piper (or any other reputable medium) would have been unlikely to pass it on to his father. Also, if the warning had not been couched in an arcane metaphor, nothing within it would have indicated Myers as its source.

The impact of the photograph hinges on two conditions: first, that none of the Lodge family had seen it prior to it being described by Raymond, and second, that the family could and would have an opportunity to see it in the near future. If either of these conditions were untrue, there would be no reason to even mention the picture; since both were true and the picture was discussed on two occasions through two different mediums, the involvement of a perceptive spirit with a calculating mind is strongly indicated.

This presentation of the Raymond case has been necessarily brief, but few cases have been examined and reported more extensively. Sir Oliver Lodge wrote about 200 pages on the subject in his book — *Raymond or Life and Death* — and Lodge must be ranked among the most trustworthy men who ever lived.

Chapter Twelve — Case 75
My Mother's Brother Is My Father's Son[285]

When Samuel Helender[286] was 2½ years old, he made a statement that would seem of no consequence to an uninformed stranger: "Now, Ludi has come to me." To those in the know, however, and to all who have learned the facts afterward, these few words speak volumes about the realities of life and death. The relevant facts include:

- Samuel's uncle, Peter Hastings, died 10 months before Samuel was born.
- At the age of 18 months, Samuel started claiming to be Peter Hastings. He would call his grandmother "mother" and refer to his actual mother by her first name.
- "Ludi" was what little Samuel called his great aunt Lydia.
- Lydia had purchased a tomb to be buried in.
- Peter, who was only 18 when he died, was buried in Lydia's tomb.
- Samuel said, "Now Ludi has come to me," on the day that Lydia died, before he was told of her death.

We can only speculate as to the precise event that little Samuel was attempting to convey. Did he mean that Lydia's body was joining his (that is, Peter's) body in the grave? Or, that some part of his spirit remained in heaven and met her spirit there? The former seems indicated by the uniqueness of Samuel's statement – he never said anything similar when other deaths occurred or other graves were newly occupied.

Still, this case hardly depends on a single statement for its validity. Samuel often correctly identified people in old family photographs, even

---

[285] Stevenson, *European Cases*, pp. 152-158.
[286] Somel names have been changed for readability reasons. See note at the end of "A Country Revival" in Volume II, Chapter 11.

when he had never met them and when his mother tried to mislead him. Also, Samuel was adamant that certain items in the household that had belonged to his uncle (a coat, a watch, and a guitar) belonged to him. On the other hand, he did not lay claim to any items that had not been his uncle's.

It is common for traumatic events in the life of the previous personality to be more often and more readily recalled than mundane ones. The case of Samuel Helender is reinforced, therefore, by the exceptional number of accidents and injuries crowded into Peter Hastings' brief lifetime.

Peter, when he was 3, fell into a bathtub of water and almost drowned. He almost drowned for the second time when he was 15 as he fell off a dock and broke through thin ice.

Samuel, as a child, was panic-stricken whenever his mother tried to give him a bath or a shower. Even as an adult, he refused to swim.

Peter, when he was 4, was standing near a construction project and a heavy object fell on him, breaking one leg and injuring the other. He spent 5 months in the hospital, some of the time with casts on his legs.

Samuel, when he was about 4, came across a photograph of his uncle Peter using a walker. He took the photo to his grandmother and said that the picture was of him after the plaster had come off of his legs in the hospital. Whether or not the injury to Peter's legs carried over to Samuel is impossible to say, but they did both exhibit the same habit of standing with one foot forward with hand on hip.

Peter, not long after leaving the hospital, was severely bitten by a dog.

Samuel spontaneously spoke several times about having been bitten by a dog and how much it hurt. But no such event had actually happened in Samuel's childhood.

Peter, only a few years later, injured his back and was hospitalized for a time.

Samuel, when he was barely 3 years old, talked about hurting his back and being taken in an ambulance to the hospital. Again, nothing like that had happened to him.

Peter, although he was not himself injured, once attended a social event that had to be halted due to a house fire.

Samuel once told a story of having to leave a place when a house caught fire.

As with most such childhood recollection cases, Samuel's memories of being Peter faded with time and were pretty much gone by the time he was 8 years old.

The Research

Stevenson, with the assistance of researcher Rita Castrén, interviewed the key figures in the Samuel Helender case during three trips to Helsinki, Finland, between December 1978 and October 1999.

Chapter Thirteen — Case 80
A Tale of Two Tattoos

[The following section of text was taken (with minor edits) from a book by Tricia Robertson.[287]]

Because of my jointly published research work, and interest in mediumship and other aspects of the paranormal I am often contacted by people that I do not know. In 1996, a woman contacted me and wanted to talk about the death of her daughter. I duly met her and it became obvious to me that she would have liked me to obtain a sitting with a medium for her. As she had told me that her daughter was murdered some three months earlier, I felt that it was too raw and too soon for that course of action. I asked her to tell me nothing of the events surrounding this death and I suggested that we meet again and I asked her to bring me a sealed envelope in which would be some personal possession of the girl. She agreed.

At our next meeting she handed me a sealed brown envelope. I could feel that the envelope was "bumpy" but nothing revealed if it was anything definable. At this point, I did not know which medium or mediums I would have access to for this task.

I visited a medium,[288] unannounced, and asked, as I placed the envelope on a table, "Can you get anything from this?" I told him nothing at all about the envelope, why I had it in my possession or the circumstances surrounding it. (I did not know much about the circumstances myself.)

After a blank stare the medium said, "Do I have to?" I replied, "Yes."

---

[287] *Things You Can Do When You're Dead*, White Crow Books, 2013, pp. 89-92. Used by permission of the author.
[288] This was the renowned British medium, Gordon Smith.

Reluctantly, he placed his hand on top of it and, with a surprised look on his face, he immediately said, "I have a girl here with longish dark brown hair" — he hesitated for a second then said, "She was killed!"

"She is telling me that she had two tattoos, one above her left breast, in the form of two hearts intertwined, they are done in red and blue. The other is on the back of her right arm. It is a single rose in red and green.

"She lives in a *cul-de-sac*, one up on the right. Telling me she misses her four cats." She also gave the name of her partner. I will call him Adam (pseudonym).

At this point the medium was looking at me meaningfully, possibly for some acknowledgment that he was correct but, of course, I had no idea if his statements were accurate in any sense and merely shrugged my shoulders. My apprehension grew a little with his next statement.

"She is telling me that she was in prison when she was younger." The prison's name was given.[289] I thought, well that's either right or wrong; there is no room for interpretation there. He then said that she had a terminated pregnancy when she was younger.

"She is saying, 'The newspaper reports were wrong, the description of the clothes that I was found in were [sic] all wrong. I was actually wearing a pink top, a grey skirt and ankle boots.

"'My photograph was moved from the mantelpiece to the top of the TV today by my mum.

"'Adam was the first one to know that I was killed, he phoned my mum.'"

The medium then gave a description of her attack, which I will not elaborate on, but suffice to say that all of her injuries were reported to be at her back.

---

[289] Cornton Vale prison for women, near Stirling, Scotland.

She "told" the medium that a green car (possibly a Cavalier) and a red Astra were relevant to her death. There were two men involved, a white man about five foot six inches tall and a taller and thinner Asian.

The medium also gave me a specific address in Glasgow, a top floor of a tenement building on the right hand side. With that he said "she's gone."

The total time taken for this delivery was less than 15 minutes.

I had recorded all of this information and now had to find a responsible way of speaking to the mother. I made a list of the statements and an appointment to visit the mother's home, next day, for the first time. Other meetings had been in a neutral setting.

As I entered the lounge I noticed a girl's photo on top of the TV. I said casually "Is this May? (Pseudonym) She said "Yes, I put it there yesterday; it used to be on the mantelpiece."

I then said to her that I had a list of statements made by a medium, but for all I knew they might be absolute nonsense, so I would read them out one by one and I asked her just to say if they were right or wrong. Every statement I read to the mother was absolutely correct. I did not give her the description given of the attack and did not mention the pregnancy, as she may not have known about it. I felt that she had enough to worry about without that statement. It was established later, however, that the girl's injuries were all at her back. I also did not supply her with the address given, the descriptions of the two men or the cars described in the reading.

In total there were 29 individual statements. Twenty-two out of the 29 were absolutely correct, including the descriptions of the positions, shape and colours of the tattoos. She did have four cats. The statements that were considered not correct were not able to be verified due to the fact that I did not give the mother all of the information re the pregnancy, address, description of the murder, and the description of the men. But these have been considered "wrong" for evaluation purposes.

Simply put, 78 percent of the information was correct. This was not general information that could apply to anyone, but was specific to the girl in this case. If we consider the information about the tattoos alone, regarding shape, colour, and position and remember that neither the medium nor the researcher knew anything at all about the people involved, far less the validity of the information, then this must surely give us considerable pause for thought.

The outcome of this was that it gave the mother great comfort in the thought that her daughter was 'still around' to give her this information.

Comment

To me, it seems unreasonably conservative — if not downright misleading — to count unverifiable responses as incorrect. Rather than saying that 78 percent of 29 responses was correct, it would be more accurate to ignore what cannot be known and say that 100 percent of 22 responses was correct. To do otherwise is to denigrate the medium's performance. After all, it was not his fault that Robertson thought it best not to check things out further.

In case any reader is wondering if the contents of the envelope somehow provided the medium with a clue as to what sort of response was sought, Robertson later wrote: "Only after the visit to the mother's house and after all of the statements had been read to her, by me, did she open the envelope in front of me. I found it very sad as it contained bits and pieces of items from the girl's childhood, such as a small gate from a toy. Nothing of any monetary value."[290]

The attackers, unfortunately, were never caught; the case was still open as of this writing. I have not been able to determine if the information on the men, their cars, and the apartment was ever given to the police.

Despite the name given to this case, the tattoos were not the most evidential information provided by the spirit via Gordon Smith, it was the

---

[290] Via e-mail to the author, 21 Jan. 2015

variance between the newspaper reports of the victims clothing and what she was actually wearing. The only recourse that those überskeptics — who will go to any lengths, no matter how preposterous, to deny the reality of spirit communication —have is to postulate that Gordon Smith had read all the published information on every murder in and around the city of Glasgow, and could call the needed facts to mind at a moment's notice. (Assuming, of course, that the medium could know that the session concerned a murdered girl by reading Robertson's mind, and then make a wild, but somehow correct, guess as to the identity of the victim.) But, the published information was, according to the victim's mother, not correct. The only feasible source for the right facts is the victim herself.

Chapter Fourteen — Case 81
Scotland Redux

Having a son who says he prefers his other mother is a common irritant that many stepmothers might be resigned to face; but what if there *is* no other woman and the son whom you bore claims to like his "other" mother better than you?

That was the strange situation that Norma Macauley experienced soon after her two-year-old son, Cameron, learned to talk. Over the ensuing few years, Cameron repeatedly, almost incessantly, spoke of living as a young boy on Barra, a remote island some 200 miles from his actual home in Glasgow, Scotland.

As a struggling single mother of two — Cameron had an older brother, Martin — Norma was in no position to satisfy Cameron's' strident pleas to be taken to Barra. Both his brother and his neighboring playmate grew frustrated with his talk of having another family, and when Cameron began to attend school, his teacher expressed some concern over his persistence in claiming that his "fantasies" were factual descriptions of reality. But Cameron would not yield. For four years, he persistently, almost relentlessly, asked, begged, and demanded to be taken to Barra to see his other mother, whom, he told Norma, she would like very much.

Then Norma was told of a notice in a local newspaper that sought people who felt that they had lived a previous life. In her desperation, she ignored the advice of her family and responded to the paper. The newspaper management was impressed enough with Cameron's claims that they contacted a television company called October Films. Soon thereafter, Dr. Jim Tucker became involved in investigating the case.

When Cameron was 5-years-old, the television company flew him and his family to Barra and filmed the boy as he explored the island and pointed out familiar places and things.

The sources consulted[291] spend some time presenting what I think of as in-direct evidence. This sort relies on logical "if-then" arguments, *i.e.* "If this was true, then that should be true." For example, the television show contains a scene in which Norma visits Karen Majors, an educational psychologist, specialist in children's imaginary lives. The doctor notes: "How Cameron describes his world seems to be quite different from how children with imaginary friends describe their experience. … Children who have imaginary creations feel in control of those creations; they can determine what's going to happen in that world and it feels like Cameron isn't able to direct what's going on there." Dr. Majors concludes that Cameron's experiences do not fit the expected pattern and other explanations need to be sought. The fact that Cameron is able to recall (make up?) numerous details but cannot name his family members is a good example of this characteristic. <u>If</u> he was imagining his house and neighborhood, <u>then</u> why can't he imagine his mother's name, or his siblings' names, or, at the very least, his own name?

A large amount of in-direct evidence such as this can be very convincing, but it can also be a distraction in cases where there is a solid block of more direct evidence, as does exist in Cameron's case. Why divert the viewer's attention with opinions about what ought to be true, when the revealed facts prove what is true?

Cameron described the house where he had lived on Barra as large, white, single-story, and isolated. He was currently living in a row house in the city. He could see a beach, he said, from his bedroom window. There were rock pools on the beach, some large enough for swimming, others in which he would play and "catch things." He claimed that his previous home had a telephone with a dial with holes in it. He also said that the

---

[291] Robertson, pp. 107-114; October Films; and Tucker, chapter 3.

house had three toilets, unlike his current home which had only one. He said that his previous family name was Robertson, that he had three sisters and three brothers, and that his father, who had been killed in an auto accident, was named Shane (or Sean). Furthermore, he often mentioned a black-and-white dog and that there were sheep in the yard that would come right up to the front door.

When the entourage arrived on the island of Barra, the plane landed on a beach --- much to Norma's surprise, even though Cameron had repeatedly claimed that that was how it was done. During the bus ride to the hotel, and throughout the entire next day of driving around the island, Cameron seemed happy but never claimed to recognize his home. On the second day, after being told by the local historian, Callum MacNeil, that a family named Robertson had owned a vacation home on Barra during the 1960s and '70s, they drove unfamiliar roads to the location. They were careful not to tell Cameron where they were headed or why. As they neared their destination, Cameron said that he once knew the family who lived in a house they were passing, but he could not remember their names. He also pointed to an abandoned building sitting off of the shoreline saying, "It's hard to get to that bit; because then you'd have to swim back." In fact, one could easily wade to the structure during low tide, but would have to swim to return if the tide had come in.

As they turned down the track leading to what had been the Robertson's house, Cameron pointed at it and said "That's it, that's my house there." Although it had undergone some renovations over the decades, the home matched Cameron's description in all relevant particulars. It was isolated, single-level, white, and relatively large. One could, indeed, see the beach from the window of the bedroom that Cameron claimed he had shared with a brother. The rock pools were there, some large enough for swimming. And, yes, the house sported not one, not two, but three toilets.

Later, the researchers used a genealogical company to find a living member of the Robertson family. This was Gillie (Gillian), who may have been a young girl during the time that Cameron recalled on Barra. In the film, her photo album showed the house and beach as it was then. There was a dog in one of the pictures that matched the description Cameron had given of a dog he had played with. One photo was of sheep grazing near the front door just as Cameron had described. Gillie, however, could not recall anyone named Shane in the family; this is not too bothersome, as names are traditionally the most difficult facts for spirits to recall, especially those who transitioned at a young age. Also, Gillie did not remember anyone in the family being killed by a car; again, that could have happened to someone else the boy was with, or it might be that the girl was around at the time of the incident. Then again, Jim Tucker may have brought up the true solution when he said: "He could have had memories from more than one life and they could have gotten mixed in together." The most puzzling statement Gillie made, though, was that there were no deaths of young children near the pertinent timeframe. If her memory is accurate, and assuming that she is being truthful, (neither of which are certain) we are left with a most difficult conundrum.

Perhaps Cameron's case is an unusual instance of possession? Perhaps Cameron's past life was as a friend of the Robertson's or he was related to the house's caretakers? Perhaps Seth's probable universes are the answer? Certainly further research is called for. I would be especially interested to know if there is a record of a child dying young in Glasgow or anywhere in Scotland, who had witnessed his father being killed by a car.

But, whatever the explanation, the case remains good evidence for the persistence of the human personality beyond this physical life, for the memories of planes landing on a beach, children playing in rock pools, and a house owned by the Robertson family that had three toilets and an old-fashioned telephone, those memories must have survived somewhere before being so incessantly and exclusively recalled by a 2-year-old boy some 200 miles away in Scotland.

Chapter Fifteen — Case 64
A Cameo Reappearance[292]

Olive Thomas' suicide was the act of a young Hollywood star who couldn't handle her fame, fortune, and bacchanalian lifestyle. So said the news headlines in 1920. ... She herself told quite a different story 10 years later.

Thomas' rise to movie stardom had been meteoric. Starting as a Ziegfeld girl in 1914, on the day of her death her name was spelled out in lights on the marquees of five different theaters on Broadway. Her exceptional beauty and fame helped sell many a newspaper detailing a night of debauchery leading to suicide in a Paris hotel room. The falsity of those details somehow went unnoticed in the media frenzy.

As a youth, J. Gay Stevens had a crush on Olive Thomas. He never met her, but he collected photographs of her. This was one reason her spirit gave for contacting him through the mediumship of Chester Grady.[293]

Stevens, a member of the American Society of Psychical Research, had just started a series of sittings with Grady at the ASPR headquarters in New York City, when the spirit of Thomas came through. She was most anxious to contact her mother, she said, to convince her that the newspaper stories of wild parties, immorality, and self-destruction were not true.

---

[292] This story is largely based on, and all quotes are taken from, a two-part article titled "The Girl with the Golden Hair" by J. Gay Stevens that appeared in *Fate* magazine in December of 1972 and January of 1973.

[293] Chester Michael Grady was a highly respected trance medium endorsed by the ASPR. He is known for his work with Stewart Edward White (*The Betty Book*), Frederick Bligh Bond (Glastonbury Abbey), and Gardner Murphy.

The truth, she claimed was that after visiting a few nightclubs in Montmartre with some friends, she and her husband, Jack Pickford,[294] had retired early to their hotel because he had to catch a morning flight to London. Not feeling sleepy, and not wanting to waken her husband by turning on a light, Thomas decided to take a sleeping potion. Unfortunately, the bottle she opened was not her bromides but what Stevens refers to as "a contraceptive commonly used by women in those days" … bichloride of mercury.

Immediately upon swallowing this toxic substance, Thomas dropped her glass and screamed in agony. Her husband jumped from bed in alarm. He tried having her drink soapy water as an emetic, but it did no good. He called the hotel staff for assistance. Then — the hotel kitchen being closed for the night — he rushed out to a local store in search of butter and milk. But nothing could be done. According to Stevens, by the time medical help arrived, Thomas' system "had absorbed enough poison to wipe out the population of a small town." Four days later, she died in a Parisian hospital and, despite there being nothing in the police reports to suggest any intent on her part, the newspapers reported her "suicide" to a shocked world.

Neither the medium nor the sitter had ever heard this story before, and no such version could be found in any newspaper of the time. Nevertheless, it was confirmed by the reports kindly provided by the Paris police, and by a biography of Mary Pickford that was published 24 years later.

Thomas was excited to hear of the police confirmation and urged Stevens to contact her mother with the information. She then provided her mother's name: Van Kirk — and location: Leonia, NJ. A local phone book gave Stevens the address and he paid the lady a visit in April of 1931. His reception was less than cool. Mrs. Van Kirk had been disgraced by what

---

[294] An actor, writer, and producer who was the brother of star Mary Pickford.

she considered to be a smear campaign by the newspapers and was distrustful of anyone interested in her daughter. Beyond that, she was a staunch believer that her Bible forbade any contact with spirits of the dead.

Realizing that he would have to get stronger evidence, Stevens continued to sit with Grady and the spirit of Thomas provided a plethora of intimate details about Thomas' life with her mother and her first marriage. Stevens lists over a dozen of these as highlights, and then says that altogether he compiled more than 20 pages of notes. These he delivered to Van Kirk, who promised to read them. This she did and, when Stevens next came to call, she actually smiled at him and, for the first time, invited him to come inside her home.

"In the name of common sense I should accept this," she told him, "but I can't. I have to go too far from what I deeply believe." So Stevens left the Van Kirk household, wondering if he should pursue the matter any further.

But Thomas insisted that they continue. "We've unlocked that closed door in her mind. It's opening and she's beginning to see the light. We can't leave her now. We've got to help her!" And at the next session, Thomas revealed just how her mother could be convinced. The ensuing demonstration stands as one of the most convincing ever witnessed in the annals of Survival investigations.

After her death, Thomas said, her mother had auctioned off all of her jewelry except for one piece. That piece was a cameo brooch made of lapis, flecked with gold, and surrounded by eight tiny pearls. It had been handcrafted by a famous London jeweler and was her very favorite. For a long time, said Thomas, she had been puzzled as to why her mother had not sold this cameo, then she realized that her mother did not even know where it was. After some mental searching, she located it and figured out what had happened.

She had been wearing that brooch the night she died. When her husband packed her clothes in her steamer trunk to return them to the States, he had removed the pin from her frock, placed it in its thin cloisonné case, and put it in a side pocket of the trunk. The rest of her jewelry had already been packed separately. During shipment, the jostling of the trunk caused the case to become lodged between the gathered end of the pocket and the trunk's lining; a place where it was impossible to see and difficult to feel. A place where it remained to that day, in her steamer trunk, sitting beside a small window, in her mother's attic. Also, she said, one of the pearls had become dislodged from its setting and was loose in the tissue paper wrapped around the cameo.

When told all of this her mother protested. She had looked through that trunk several times and there was no jewelry in it. Besides, her daughter had never been in her current house, let alone in its attic. But Stevens was insistent, and more to placate him than out of any belief in his words, she led the way into the attic.

The trunk was situated just as Thomas, via Grady, had described. The mother proceeded to remove all the clothing and showed Stevens the empty trunk. He asked her to examine the side pockets. She did so, but found nothing. "Dig deep into the end of each pocket," he instructed. She did so, and "suddenly recoiled — as if something had nipped her fingers." She felt something metal, but she could not pry it loose, so Stevens reached into the pocket. "It took some effort to free the object from its jammed position," he relates. "Soon, however, I was holding the cloisonné case up to the light before Mrs. Van Kirk's ashen face."

They took the case down to the kitchen table and carefully unwrapped the tissue from the brooch. The loose pearl dropped out and rolled across the table.

Discussion

Some critics, apparently searching for any reason not to believe this story, have wondered why the mother was unaware of the true facts of her daughter's death. Would not the husband have reported these to his mother-in-law? There are at least three feasible explanations for this.

- First, perhaps he did tell her and she thought he may have been lying to protect himself.
- Second, perhaps he did tell her and she believed him but was upset because the newspapers had ruined her daughter's reputation. It is true that Stevens reported Thomas' concern with getting the truth to her mother, but while Thomas could apparently tell that her mother was upset, there is nothing to indicate that she could read her mother's mind and thus know the exact cause of her torment.
- Third, perhaps the husband and mother were estranged, or he did not discuss the matter with her for some other reason of his. Pickford, known for his wild lifestyle, married two other actresses (in sequence) before dying of syphilis in 1933.

As for the bichloride of mercury, it has been pointed out that this substance was a treatment for syphilis, although Stevens refers to it as "a contraceptive commonly used by women in those days." Jack Pickford could well have had syphilis at the time. This could have provided motivation for not telling Thomas' mother the truth. The fact is, however, that both statements are true: bichloride of mercury (otherwise known as corrosive sublimate) was sometimes used to treat syphilis, but it was also commercially sold as a vaginal douche and used as an abortifacient.

Admittedly, these questions are loose ends, but loose ends only matter if they threaten to unravel the story. The key facts are solid and the unanswered questions should not greatly lessen the strength of the case.

The reception by a medium of information detailing the precise location, situation, and detailed description of a unique object with which neither the medium nor the sitter have any link and of which no living person is aware, belies any credible explanation other than Survival. The 20 pages of personal details known only to the mother, which normally would make an eye-catching case themselves, are virtually lost in the shadow of the reappearing cameo.

Chapter Sixteen — Case 79
Ex-Actor Makes Comeback

Young men and women leaving small towns in the Midwest and heading for Hollywood in search of fame and fortune are common subjects in novels and movie scripts – a few actually do become rich and famous. Marty Kolinsky seems to have found even greater fame by reversing the process and leaving Hollywood for a small town in Oklahoma ... and all he had to do was die.

In the 1930s, Kolinsky did find fortune, but not fame. He enjoyed several glamourous careers after he changed his last name to Martyn. He was a dancer on Broadway, an actor in movies, and a talent agent who hobnobbed with Glen Ford, Rita Hayworth, and other celebrities. He became wealthy enough to live in mansions with large swimming pools, be chauffeured around Beverly Hills in his custom-made Rolls Royce, and travel the world via ocean liner; but after his death, the name Marty Martyn became no more than a footnote in dusty cinema archives. No doubt it would have remained in obscurity had not a three-year-old boy in Warner, Oklahoma, begun telling his mother about a life working in the movies.

Ryan Hammons generally spoke to his mother, Cyndi, as his bedtime neared. After a while, she started taking notes of statements such as: "I liked it better when I was big." and "I just can't live in these conditions. My last home was much better." When the sight of an outdoor café prompted the child to claim that he had visited the Eiffel Tower, he responded to his mother's doubts with, "When are you going to listen to me? I have seen the world." Ryan's father, Kevin, a police officer whose upbringing was incompatible with the idea of reincarnation, counts 102 separate statements made by his son about a past life — 90 of which were ultimately verified.

Mostly, Ryan talked about living and working in Hollywood. While looking through some books on movies that his mother had gotten from the library, Ryan excitedly pointed to a picture of a man talking with actor George Raft, and said, "Hey Mama, that's George. We did a picture together. And Mama, that guy's me. I found me!"

Trouble was, "me" was unidentified in the cutline of the photograph and Ryan never recalled his previous name. It took several years and the professional assistance of an archival footage consultant to discover that the person Ryan pointed to was Marty Martyn. In the interim, the case was investigated by Jim B. Tucker, M.D., who has taken up the work of Ian Stevenson at the University of Virginia. Tucker's 31-page presentation of the case is the most thorough so far. Also, the pilot of a revival of the television show, *The UnXplained*, featured Ryan's story, as have several newspaper articles. [295]

Here are some of the more pertinent and convincing of the 90 matches between Ryan Hammons' statements made between the ages of 3 and 6, and facts unearthed about the life of Marty Martyn, as discovered in archives and interviews.

Ryan's Claims: The movie *Night After Night* (from which the picture of Martyn and Raft was taken) had a scene in which there was a closet full of guns.

Facts of Martyn's Life: There is such a scene in the 1930 movie. Ryan had never seen any black-and-white movie.

Ryan's Claims: He was friends with a cowboy who was also in *Night After Night*, and did cigarette commercials.

Facts of Martyn's Life: An actor in the movie, named Gordon Nance, also starred in westerns and was a spokesman for Viceroy cigarettes.

Ryan's Claims: He had a daughter and there were other children in his family.

Facts of Martyn's Life: When Martyn's daughter was interviewed, she confirmed that she was his only natural offspring, but that there were

---

[295] See: Tucker, pp. 88-119; Burton; and Leonard.

five step children in his family. Martyn died when his daughter was 8 years old.

Ryan's Claims: Gave his daughter a dog, but she didn't like it.

Facts of Martyn's Life: Martyn gave his daughter a Yorkshire Terrier that she did not like.

Ryan's Claims: Brought the children coloring books.

Facts of Martyn's Life: Ryan often brought elaborate coloring books to his children.

Ryan's Claims: Visited Paris and saw the Eiffel Tower.

Facts of Martyn's Life: He visited France several times.

Ryan's Claims: Visited China, also loved Chinese food and eating with chopsticks.

Facts of Martyn's Life: Trip to China unverified, but Martyn loved to eat with chopsticks in Chinatown restaurants. Ryan never saw chopsticks until he was taken to a Chinese restaurant in Hollywood. He refused flatware and his father was astounded at the dexterity he demonstrated eating with chopsticks.

Ryan's Claims: Traveled the world on ocean liners.

Facts of Martyn's Life: Went to Europe on the Queen Mary.

Ryan's Claims: Lived in a large house with a swimming pool.

Facts of Martyn's Life: Martyn's last residence was a mansion with a large outdoor pool.

Ryan's Claims: Address of his home contained "rock" or "mount."

Facts of Martyn's Life: Address was 825 N. Roxbury.

Ryan's Claims: Was involved with an agency that changed people's names.

Facts of Martyn's Life: Although his parents first thought that Ryan was fantasizing about some sort of spy organization, it turned out that Martyn operated a talent agency and would have given people stage names.

Ryan's Claims: Had been a dancer early in his career.

Facts of Martyn's Life: He danced in Broadway shows.

Ryan's Claims: Spoke of two different sisters.

Facts of Martyn's Life: Had two sisters.

Ryan's Claims: His mother had curly brown hair.

Facts of Martyn's Life: Curly brown hair confirmed.

Ryan's Claims: Was a smoker.

Facts of Martyn's Life: Smoked cigars and cigarettes.

Ryan Asked for Tru Ade.

Fact: Although popular in Martyn's time, Tru Ade soft drinks were no longer made at the time Ryan was born.

For a period of time during the investigation, it was thought that the man in the photograph with George Raft was an actor named Ralf Harolde. When young Ryan was taken to place where Harolde had resided and asked if anything looked familiar, he showed no recognition.

There are many similarities between this case and that of James Leininger [#65], and they do not all concern a previous incarnation. Both children talked of monitoring their parents prior to their birth. As Dr. Tucker tells the story: "When Ryan's parents married, they decided they would only have one child because Kevin already had two from his first marriage. Cyndi very much wanted a daughter. Ryan came over to Cyndi one night and asked why she had thought he was going to be a little girl. When she asked him who told him that, he said no one told him and that he saw it from heaven. He said, 'This doctor guy did a test and told you I was a boy. You got mad and said he was wrong. You just knew that I was going to be a girl. Mommy, it was Daddy's birthday, you went to a restaurant afterward to eat and you cried for a very long time.' Cyndi reports everything happened just as Ryan said. She had always regretted the way she acted that day."[296]

---

[296] Tucker, p. 97.

Conclusion

I trust that you have carefully considered each case herein presented and you are convinced that there is an afterlife. If not, then you do not have doubts, you are simply closed minded. Sadly, there is really nothing to be done about that. For those whose minds have been open enough to accept the truth, the question now is: So what? Or, more precisely, how does/should this knowledge affect me?

This is not the place for a sermon, so I'll just say a few words about how the certain knowledge of an afterlife has affected my current life on Earth.

Essentially, I now try harder to tune into my conscience, listen to what it tells me, and follow its advice.

Every soul comes equipped with a conscience,[297] but here in the physical realm there are many powers that compete with it. The allure of achievement, the call of duty, the drive for dominance, the need for security, the thirst for vengeance, and other such forces can diminish or virtually stifle that "still small voice" that tells us right from wrong. When someone succumbs to such forces and suppresses or ignores the urgings of their conscience, they may not suffer any ill effects --- until that is, they find themselves free of their animal bodies --- then there really can be "hell to pay." This is because the physical brain, by its nature, tends to insulate the residing soul from its conscience and, once the mind is free of the brain, it is subject to the perfect memory of its deeds and the full knowledge of its transgressions. Or, to quote Spiritualist philosopher David Gow: "The flames of a materialistic hell-fire are but a pale representation of the pangs of an outraged conscience."[298]

---

[297] For a fuller explanation, see Allen, *Realities*, chpter 19.
[298] Gow, p. 140.

Being aware of the consequences of my actions, whenever I find myself with a choice of paths to take, I seek to know which will help others the most and hurt others the least, if not at all. When so choosing, I try to keep two other points. in mind. First, I should not concern myself with things over which I have no influence. And, second, the end *never* justifies the means.

Speaking of the end, this is it.

Now that you are certain there is an afterlife, you're likely wondering what it is like. The most complete and unbiased source of that information is the book *The Realities of Heaven*. Available from Amazon.com

Appendix
References

Allen, Miles Edward, *Defending Bridey's Honor: The Reality of Reincarnation*, Momentpoint Media, 2013.

_____, *The Realities of Heaven: Fifty Spirits Describe Your Future Home*, Momentpoint Media, 2015.

Alvarado, Carlos S. Ph.D., "The Concept of Survival of Bodily Death and the Development of Parapsychology," *Journal of the Society for Psychical Research*, Volume 67.2, Number 871, April 2003.

Andrade, Hernani Guimarães, *Reborn for Love*, Roundtable Publishing, 2010. Original version in Portuguese was published as *Proceeding #7 of the Brazilian Institute for Psychobiophysical Research*, 1995.

Arcangel, Dianne, *Afterlife Encounters*, Hampton Roads Publishing, 2005, pp. 74-82.

Barrett, Sir William, *On the Threshold of the Unseen*, E.P. Dutton & Co., 1918.

_____, *Death-Bed Visions*, The Aquarian Press, 1986,

Berger, Arthur S., *Aristocracy of the Dead*, McFarland & Co., 1987.

Bernstein, Morey, *The Search for Bridey Murphy*, Doubleday & Co., 1965.

Botkin, Alan L. and R. Craig Hogan, *Induced After-Death Communication*, Hampton Roads Publishing, 2005.

Boulton, Peter, *Psychic Beam to Beyond*, DeVorss & Company, 1983.

Braude, Stephen, "Out-of-Body Experiences and Survival After Death," *International Journal of Parapsychology*, Volume 12, Number 1, 2001, pp. 83-129.

Brinkley, Dannion, *Saved by the Light*, Villard Books, 1994.

Brown, Rick, "The Reincarnation of James, The Submarine Man," *The Journal of Regression Therapy*, December, 1991, pages 62-71.

Burton, Wendy, "Show follows local child who says he lived earlier life as Hollywood actor," *The Muskogee Phoenix*, 21 May 2011.

Callanan, Maggie and Patricia Kelley, *Final Gifts*, Poseidon Press, 1992.

Carington, Whately, *Telepathy, An Outline of Its Facts, Theory and Implications*, Creative Age Press, 1946.

Carr, John Dickson, *The Life of Sir Arthur Conan Doyle*, Barnes & Noble Books, 1994.

Carter, Chris, *Science and the Near-Death Experience: How Consciousness Survives Death*, Inner Traditions, 2010.

Cerminara, Gina, *Many Mansions*, New American Library, 1950.

Cockell, Jenny, *Across Time and Death*, Simon & Schuster, 1993.
Colvin, Barrie G., "The Andover Case: A Responsive Rapping Poltergeist," *Journal of the Society for Psychical Research*, Vol. 72.1, January 2008.
_____, "The Acoustic Properties of Unexplained Rapping Sounds," *Journal of the Society for Psychical Research*, Vol. 74.2, April 2010,
Coover, John E., "Metapsychics and the Incredulity of Psychologists," in *The Case For and Against Psychical Belief*, edited by Carl Murchison, Clark University Press, 1927.
Cox-Chapman, Mally, *The Case for Heaven*, G.P. Putnam's Sons, 1995, ISBN: 1559497017.
Crenshaw, James, *Telephone Between Worlds*, DeVorss & Co., 1950.
Crookes, Sir William, *Researches into the Phenomena of Modern Spiritualism*, Austin Publishing Co., 1922.
Eadie, Betty J., and Curtis Taylor, *Embraced by the Light*, Gold Leaf Press, 1992.
Ebbern, Hayden, Sean Mulligan, and Barry Beyerstein, "Maria's Near-Death Experience: Waiting for the Other Shoe to Drop," *Skeptical Inquirer*, July/August 1996.
Ebon, Martin, *The Evidence for Life After Death*, New American Library, 1977.
Eddington Arthur, *The Nature of the Physical World*, The University of Michigan Press, 1978.
Edwards, Paul, "The Case Against Reincarnation," Parts 1-4, *Free Inquiry*, Fall 1986-Summer 1987.
Eisenbeiss, Wolfgang and Dieter Hassler, "An Assessment of Ostensible Communications with a Deceased Grandmaster as Evidence for Survival," *Journal of the Society for Psychical Research*, Vol. 70.2 No. 883, April 2006, pp. 65-97.
Estep, Sarah Wilson, *Voices of Eternity*, Ballentine Books, 1988.
Findlay, Arthur, *On the Edge of the Etheric: Or Survival After Death Scientifically Explained*, 1931.
Fodor, Nandor, *Encyclopaedia of Psychic Science*, University Books, 1966.
Ford, Arthur, and Margueritte Harmon Bro, *Nothing So Strange*, Paperback Library, 1958/1968.
_____, as told to Jerome Ellison, *The Life Beyond Death*, G.P. Putnam's Sons, 1971.
Fuller, John G., *The Ghost of 29 Megacycles*, New American Library, 1981. ISBN: 0451143051.
Funk, Isaac, *The Psychic Riddle*, 1909.
Gabbard, Glen O., and Stuart Tremlow, *With the Eyes of the Mind: An Empirical Analysis of Out-of-Body States*, Praeger Publishers Inc, 1985.

Gallup, George, *Adventures in Immortality: A Look Beyond the Threshold of Death,* Mcgraw-Hill, 1982.

Garland, Hamlin, *Forty Years of Psychic Research,* The MacMillan Co., 1937.

_____, *The Mystery of the Buried Crosses,* E.P. Dutton & Co., 1939.

Gauld, Alan, *Mediumship and Survival: A Century of Investigations,* Paladin Books, 1983.

_____, "A Series of 'Drop In' Communicators," *Proceedings of the Society for Psychical Research,* Vol. 55, July, 1971.

Gay, Kathleen, "The Case of Edgar Vandy," *Journal of the Society for Psychical Research,* Vol. 39, March 1957, pages 2-61.

Goldberg, Bruce, *Past Lives, Future Lives,* Ballentine Books, 1982.

Gow, David, "The Philosophy of Survival," in *Survival,* edited by Sir James Marchant, G.P Putnam's Sons, 1924.

Grosso, Michael, "Afterlife Research and the Shamanic Turn," *Journal of Near-Death Studies,* Fall 2001, vol. 20, p. 1.

Guggenheim, Bill and Judy Guggenheim, *Hello From Heaven,* Bantam Books, 1995.

Hannesson, Gudmundur, "Remarkable Phenomena in Iceland," *Journal of the American Society for Psychical Research,* Vol. 18, 1924.

Haraldsson, Erlendur and Majd Abu-Izzeddin, "Development of Certainty About the Correct Deceased Person in a Case of the Reincarnation Type in Lebanon: The Case of Nazih Al-Danaf," *Journal of Scientific Exploration, Vol. 16, No. 3,* 2002.

Hardinge, Emma, *Modern American Spiritualism,* 1870.

Hare, Robert, *Experimental Investigation of the Spirit Manifestations,* Partridge & Brittan, 1855.

Hodgson, Richard, "A Further Record of Observations of Certain Phenomena of Trance," *The Proceedings of the Society for Psychical Research,* 1897-8, Vol. 13, pp. 284-582.

Homewood, Harry, *Thavis Is Here,* Fawcett, 1978.

Hyslop, James, *Science and a Future Life,* G.P. Putnam's Sons, 1906.

_____, *Contact With The Other World,* The Century Co., 1919.

_____, in *Proceedings of the American Society for Psychical Research,* 1925.

Huxley, Laura, *This Timeless Moment: A Personal View of Aldous Huxley,* Celestial Arts, 1968.

Johnson, Alice, "A Case of Information Supernormally Acquired" *Proceedings of the Society for Psychical Research, Vol. 12,* 1897.

Jung, Carl Gustave, *Memories, Dreams, Reflections,* Random House/Pantheon, 1963.

Keen, Montague, "The Case of Edgar Vandy: Defending the Evidence," *Journal of the Society for Psychical Research,* Vol. 66, October 2002.

Kelway-Bamber, L., *Claude's Book*, 1919.
Knight, J.Z., *Ramtha*, Sovereignty, 1986.
Kübler-Ross, Elisabeth, *On Death and Dying*, Macmillan Publishing Co., 1969.
Leininger, Bruce and Andrea Leininger with Ken Gross, *Soul Survivor: The Reincarnation of a World War II Fighter Pilot*, Grand Central Publishing, 2009.
Leonard, John, "Reincarnation and the problem of an open mind," *Examiner.com* website, posted 5 January 2012, based on *The UneXplained* television show (which wass not available as of this writing).
Lodge, Sir Oliver, *The Survival of Man*, Methuen, 1909.
_____, *Raymond, or Life and Death*, George H. Doran Co., 1916.
_____, *Why I Believe in Personal Immortality*, Methuen, 1928.
Lombroso, Cesare, *After Death – What?*, Small, Maynard & Co., 1909.
MacKenzie, Andrew, "An 'Edgar Vandy' Proxy Sitting," *Journal of the Society for Psychical Research*, Vol. 46, September 1971, pages 166-173.
Martin, Joel and Patricia Romanowski, *Love Beyond Life*, Harper, 1997.
Mathes, J.H., and Lenora Huett, *The Amnesia Factor*, Celestial Arts, 1975.
McRae, Ron, *Mind Wars*, St. Martin's Press, 1984.
Meek, George W., *After We Die, What Then?*, Metascience Corporation, 1980, ISBN: 0935436006.
_____, "Spiricom: Electronic Communications with the 'Dearly Departed'!" *New Realities* magazine, Vol IV, No. 6, July 1982.
Mills, Antonia and Kuldop Dhiman, "Shiva Returned in the Body of Sumitra: A Posthumous Longitudinal Study of the Significance of the Shiva/Sumitra Case of the Possession Type," *Proceedings of the Society for Psychical Research*, Vol. 59, Part 233, October, 2011.
Miller, R. DeWitt, *You DO Take It With You*, The Citadel Press, 1955.
Monroe, Robert, *Journeys Out of the Body*, Doubleday & Co., 1971.
_____, *Far Journeys*, Doubleday & Co., 1985.
Montgomery, Ruth, *A Search for the Truth*, Bantam Books, 1967.
Moody, Raymond, Jr., *Life After Life*, Mockingbird Books, 1975.
_____, *Reflections on Life After Life*, Mockingbird Books, 1977.
_____, *The Light Beyond*, Bantam Books, 1988.
_____, *Coming Back*, Bantam Books, 1991.
_____, *Reunions*, Villard Books, 1993.
Morehouse, David, *Psychic Warrior*, St. Martin's Press, 1996.
Morse, Melvin, and Paul Perry, *Closer to the Light*, Ivy Books, 1990.
Moss, Thelma, *The Probability of the Impossible*, J.P. Tarcher, 1974.
Myers, F.W.H., *Human Personality and its Survival of Bodily Death*, (first published in 1903) single volume edition published in 1961, University Books.

_____, Oliver Lodge, W. Leaf, and William James, "A Record of Observations of Certain Phenomena of Trance," *The Proceedings of the Society for Psychical Research*, 1889-90, Vol. 6.

Neppe, Vernon, "A Detailed Analysis of an Important Chess Game: Revisiting 'Maróczy versus Korchnoi'," *Journal of the Society for Psychical Research*, Vol. 71.3 No. 888, July 2007.

Netherton, Morris, and Nancy Shiffrin, *Past Lives Therapy*, William Morrow & Co., 1978.

Newton, Michael, *Journey of Souls*, fifth revised edition, Llewellyn Publications, 1996. ISBN: 1567184855.

_____, *Destiny of Souls*, Llewellyn Publications, 2000, ISBN: 1567184995.

_____, "Early Visitations to Earth by Superior Beings," *Fate*, Vol. 54, No. 3, March 2001.

October Films, *The Boy Who Lived Before*, Lesley Katon producer, 2006.

Osis, Karlis and Erlendur Haraldsson, *What They Saw — At the Hour of Death*, Hastings House, 1997.

Owen, Robert, *Footfalls on the Boundary of Another World*, 1868.

Playfair, Guy Lyon and Montague Keen, "A Possibly Unique Case of Psychic Detection," *Journal of the Society for Psychical Research*, Vol. 68, no. 874, January 2004.

Pole, Wellesley Tudor, *Private Dowding: The personal story of a soldier killed in battle*, Clarke, Doble, and Brendon, Ltd., 1917.

Price, Harry, *Leaves from a Psychist's Case-Book*, Victor Gollancz, 1933.

_____, *Fifty Years of Psychical Research: A Critical Survey*, Longmans, Green & Co., 1939.

Puharich, Andrija, *Uri: A Journal of the Mystery of Uri Geller*, Bantam Books, 1974,

Radin, Dean, *The Conscious Universe: The Scientific Truth of Psychic Phenomena*, HarperCollins Publishers, 1997.

Randles, Jenny, and Peter Hough, *The Afterlife*, Berkley Books, 1993.

Richet, Charles, *Thirty Years of Psychical Research*, W. Collins Sons & Co., Ltd., 1923.

Rieder, Marge, *Mission to Millboro*, Blue Dolphin Press, 1991.

_____, *Return to Millboro*, Blue Dolphin Press, 199.

Ring, Kenneth, and Evelyn Valarino, *Lessons from the Light*, Moment Point Press, 1998.

_____, and Sharon Cooper, *Mindsight: Near-Death and Out-of-Body Experiences in the Blind*, William James Center for Consciousness Studies, 1999.

Roberts, Jane, *The Seth Material*, Prentice-Hall, 1970.

_____, *Seth Speaks*, Bantam Books, 1972,

_____, *The Unknown Reality vol. I*, Prentice Hall, 1978.
_____, *The "Unknown" Reality, vol. II,* , Prentice Hall, 1979.
Robertson, Tricia, *Things You Can Do When You're Dead*, White Crow Books, 2013.
Schmicker, Michael, *Best Evidence*, 2nd Ed., Writer's Club Press, 2002.
von Schrenck-Notzing, Albert, *Phenomena of Materialisation*, E.P. Dutton & Co., 1923.
Schwartz, Gary, with William L. Simon, *The Afterlife Experiments*, Pocket Books, 2002.
Serdahely, William J., "Pediatric Death Experiences" in the *Journal of Near Death Studies*, vol 9, no. 1, Fall 1990
Sharp, Kimberly Clark, *After the Light*, William Morrow & Co., 1995.
Smith, Alson J., *Immortality: The Scientific Evidence*, NAL/Signet, 1954.
Smith, Susy, *Life Is Forever*, toExcel Press, 1999.
Snow, Robert L., *Looking for Carroll Beckwith*, Rodale Books, 1999.
Spraggett, Allen, *The Unexplained*, Signet Mystic Books / New American Library, Inc., 1967.
_____, with William V. Rauscher, *Arthur Ford: The Man Who Talked with the Dead*, New American Library, 1973.
Steiger, Brad, *Mysteries of Time and Space*, Dell Publishing Company, 1974.
_____, "Smart People See Ghosts: Higher Education Supports Belief in the Paranormal," *Fate*, Vol. 59, No. 4, April 2006.
Stevenson, Ian, *The Evidence for Survival from Claimed Memories of Former Incarnations*, M.C. Peto, 1961.
_____, *European Cases of the Reincarnation Type*, McFarland & Co., 2003.
_____, Satwant Pasricha, and Nicolas McClean-Rice, "A Case of the Possession Type in India With Evidence of Paranormal Knowledge," *Journal of Scientific Exploration*, Vol. 3, No. I, 1989.
_____, *Cases of the Reincarnation Type, Vol II: Ten Cases in Sri Lanka*, University Press of Virginia, 1977.
Sugrue, Thomas, *There Is a River: The Story of Edgar Cayce*, Dell Publishing Co., 1942.
Talbot, Michael, *The Holographic Universe*, HarperCollins, 1991.
TenDam, Hans, *Exploring Reincarnation*, Rider Books, 2003.
Tucker, Jim B., *Return to Life: Extraordinary Cases of Children Who Remember Past Lives*, St. Martin's Press, 2013.
Tymn, Michael, "The Mystery of the Buried Crosses," *Fate*, March, 2005, pp. 12-19.
_____, "The Return of Sir William Barrett," *Fate*, October, 2005, pp. 50-55.

van Lommel, Pim, Ruud van Wees, Vincent Meyers, and Ingrid Elfferich, "Near-death experience in survivors of cardiac arrest: a prospective study in the Netherlands," *The Lancet*, vol. 358, 15 December 2001.
Wallace, Alfred Russel, *The Scientific Aspect of the Supernatural*, 1866.
_____, *Miracles and Modern Spiritualism*, George Redway, 1896.
Walsch, Neale Donald, *Conversations With God, Book. 1*, G.P. Putnam's Sons, 1995.
_____, *Conversations With God, Book. 3*, G.P. Putnam's Sons, 1998.
Wambach, Helen, *Life Before Life*, Bantam Books, 1979.
Westwood, Horace, *There is a Psychic World*, Crown Publishers, 1949.
White, Stewart Edward, *The Betty Book*, E.P. Dutton & Co., 1937.
_____, and Harwood White, *Across the Unknown*, E.P. Dutton & Co., 1939.
_____, *The Unobstructed Universe*, E.P. Dutton & Co., 1940.
Wilson, Colin, *Afterlife*, Doubleday & Company, 1985

CPSIA information can be obtained
at www.ICGtesting.com
Printed in the USA
LVHW020519250920
667092LV00017B/2046